About the Authors

Michael Nabavian grew up in suburban New York but emigrated to Great Britain when he was in his early twenties. In 1999 he moved to London to make his fortune – a project that continues to this day. Michael holds undergraduate and postgraduate degrees in English Literature, from the universities that educated George W Bush and Tony Blair respectively.

Phil Wall was born in Kent, moved to Wales when he was three and took fifteen years to escape back to England. He now lacks the willpower to move anywhere else. Phil has written for general interest magazines and been commissioned by The Sun newspaper to write amusing things about football. He blogs about Arsenal FC when he feels the need to.

GARY'S GUIDE TO LIFE:

*How I Am Going to Achieve Phenomenal Success,
and How You Can Do the Same*

A NOVEL BY
MICHAEL NABAVIAN
& PHIL WALL

Cover Design by Simon Avery

CONTENTS

INTRODUCTION

Success. Say the word aloud.

Success

Now listen to the echo of the word in your mind's ear. What does it sound like?

"Success"

Yes: *"Success"*. Is there any more beautiful word in the English language?

Say the word aloud again. And again. Repeat at least fifty times.

Are you beginning to feel different? More confident? More optimistic? No? Don't worry, we're only just getting started, and these things take time.

If success is what you aspire to, then it is vital that you incorporate the word "success" into every aspect of your daily routine. Make it the first word you say in the morning upon waking, and the last word you say at night before going to bed. Say it in the shower, in the car, in the frozen food aisle of the supermarket, in the laundry room if you have one. Say it in a loud, commanding voice – unless you're in a library or a church, in which case you probably ought to keep your voice to a near whisper so as not to disturb those around you.

Why am I urging you to do adopt this habit? Because, in the words of renowned self-help expert Marshall Brewster, "If you want to achieve success, you must first *tune your mind to the frequency of success.*"

And I think I'm on safe ground in assuming you want to achieve success. Otherwise, why would you have bought this book?

When you have managed to tune your mind to the frequency of success – as I have done – you'll cease to be bothered by the question of *whether* success will come your way. The only question that will remain is *when?*

I still remember the exact moment when I stopped believing that I would *probably* achieve success, and started believing that I would *definitely* achieve it. The year was 2003, and the place was Los Angeles, California, where I was living with Kim, an American woman – now my ex-wife, then my fiancée. At that time, the two of us would idle away our evenings at bars, diners, cinemas, Lakers' games, casinos, comedy clubs, house parties, and Mongolian barbecue joints. I won't lie to you: my life in those days was meaningless and without direction. Success wasn't exactly slipping away from me, but it wasn't getting any closer, either. If you imagine success as a major international airport, I was like an aeroplane stuck in a holding pattern 30,000 feet above it.

Then, one night, everything changed. My bowling evening was cancelled at the last moment, and Kim was off auditioning for a part in a toothpaste commercial, so I found myself at a loose end. I scanned the local events section of the newspaper, came across a listing for a

Marshall Brewster lecture taking place in South Pasadena that night at 8pm, and thought: *why not?* It struck me that Marshall's lecture might, if I was lucky, give me some ideas I could use to help get myself out of the rut I was stuck in. I drove to the lecture venue. I had no clue what to expect, but when Marshall took to the podium, his presence was electric.

And his words changed my life.

Let me repeat that: *Marshall's words literally changed my life.* There in that auditorium, Marshall succeeded in making me believe – and not just believe, but *know* – that I would one day be a great success.

From then on, everything was different. I was a changed man. My conviction that I would become a great success grew stronger with every passing day.

Now, twelve years later, it's stronger than ever.

One of my aims in this book will be to instil the same sense of self-belief in you that Marshall has instilled in me. If my book does its job – and I have every confidence that it will – then, by the time you finish reading it, you will be well on your way to developing a "success mindset". In addition, you will have all the tools you need to find your true self, forge successful relationships, flourish in your career, live in the Now, influence those around you, and become the master of your own destiny. In summary, you will be almost as well equipped for achieving success as I am.

As I'm sure you'll have picked up by now, I am an enthusiastic disciple of Marshall Brewster. Marshall is, without a doubt, the foremost personal-development authority of his generation. His most recent book, *Ten Steps to Triumph: The Universal Guide to Achieving Perfection in Any and Every Realm of Life*, has sold 1.8 million copies to date. He has revolutionised the study of human motivation and self-fulfilment. He has inspired legions of people to transform their humdrum lives.

Therefore it's only natural that you should ask yourself the question: "Why should I bother listening to the words of Marshall's disciple when I could just as easily get my information from Marshall himself?"

The short answer is that whereas I am from the UK, Marshall is American and his books are geared towards an American audience. If, by some fluke, you happen to be American, then I have to admit that Marshall really is the only guru you need. Please read his books, and if possible, attend his lectures when his touring schedule takes him to your part of the country. There was really no need for you to buy my book, which is primarily intended for a British readership. I'm sorry. If you've still got the receipt for the book, then by all means go ahead and return it to the "bookstore". I'll understand.

But if you are British, you won't find it quite as easy to benefit from Marshall's wisdom, for a number of reasons. First, you are very unlikely to have the opportunity to attend a Marshall Brewster event. Although Marshall's schedule of workshops and speaking engagements takes him all over the United States, from Sacramento to Louisville to Boston, he never ventures across the "pond" (I understand he has a thing about flying). So unless you can afford a plane ticket to America, and a hotel, and other sundry expenditure, you are out of luck.

You could, of course, buy his books, which, needless to say, are masterpieces. But be forewarned: they are *100 per cent American*. This is inevitably going to be a barrier for many British readers. For example, when faced with Marshall's colourful analogies – with their copious references to freeways, curly fries, realtors, monkey wrenches, station wagons, John Ritter, toaster ovens, the San Fernando Valley, Scotch tape, wide receivers, flag duty, the Scopes Monkey Trial, Aunt Jemima syrup, field goals, Grey Poupon, pitchers' mounds, Ma Bell, the NRA, affixing one's "John Hancock", star 69 and crawfish – these readers are unlikely to have any idea what he's talking about.

And it's not just the American references that are the problem. It's also the American *tone* of Marshall's books. Let me give you an illustration of this. I once lent a copy of Marshall's book *Ten Steps to Triumph* to my underachieving younger brother Vincent and urged him to read it. Imagine my disappointment when, returning the book to me several days later, he said, apologetically, "I couldn't get into it. It was just a bit too… American." When pressed to explain what he meant, Vincent pointed to a particular passage early in the book. The passage runs as follows:

> And now, buckaroos, I come to the most important point of all. Remember the voice of your third-grade teacher? It's the voice that told you constantly to sit up straight, be quiet, wait for your turn, don't cause trouble – and you know what? The voice is still there, only now it's lodged

firmly in your own head, and it's telling you to curtail all your most cherished hopes and dreams so that you don't rock the social boat too much in pursuing them. That voice is a holdover from the past, and it needs to be told to PIPE DOWN! In the remainder of this chapter, you're going to learn how to saddle up your proverbial horse, stick your spurs in, and leave a cloud of dust in your wake as you gallop right out of range of your unsatisfactory life-situation, eventually arriving at a land where you can lasso your dreams. And the voice? Don't worry: the clattering of hooves will drown it out. YEE-HAW! Hold on tight, partners, 'cause it's gonna be a THRILL-RIDE!!!

Stirring stuff, I'm sure you'll agree. But I couldn't deny that Vincent had a point. Marshall's prose *was* very American. Of course, because I'd had the experience of living in America, and being with Kim and all that, I was too accustomed to the American "vibe" to find the style jarring. For Vincent, though, it was definitely an obstacle. And it occurred to me that many British readers would feel the same way.

There is a gap in the market for a decent self-help book aimed at a British readership. That's what I believe, anyway, and I am optimistic that I'll find a publisher who agrees with me. If you're holding this book in your hands, then of course it means I've succeeded. If you're *not*, then it means – well, not that I've failed, but simply that I haven't succeeded *yet*. Just be patient. Hopefully you won't have to wait too much longer for the book to hit the shelves.

If I had to supply you with one final reason for reading my book, it would be this: as exhilarating as it is to listen to the Marshall Brewsters of this world, the Lord Alan Sugars and the Sir Geoffrey Boycotts – people who have attained a level of fame and fortune that gives their words an unimpeachable authority – the effect can sometimes be quite dazzling, like having a bright light shone in one's eyes. It's easy to be intimidated by someone of this stature, easy to think, "He succeeded because of his greatness, but I'm just a normal person. How could I ever follow in his footsteps?" I can promise that this won't be the effect of reading my book. The fact is, I am someone very much like you – a humble traveller on the road to success. I may be further down that road than you are, and I may be moving forward at a greater speed, and I may have a far more powerful sense of self-belief, but the fact remains that my greatest success still lies in the future, not in the past or present.

In this book, I will not only give you the ground rules for attaining success, but will also illustrate them using examples from my own life. If you pay close attention to what I'm going to teach you, and put into practice what you've learned, then, before you know it, success will be within your grasp – every bit as much as it is within mine.

One of the most exciting things about the writing process is the sheer sense of possibility it affords. At this moment,

I am sitting at my computer with a plateful of M&S chicken korma resting in my lap, typing out this Introduction between mouthfuls. Seven chapters lie ahead of me. I have made some notes, but they're not very extensive, so basically the rest of the book is a blank canvas.

Yes indeed. A blank canvas, just waiting to be filled.

What makes the task feel more manageable is the fact that my evenings are (apart from Tuesdays and Thursdays, when I go bowling) completely free nowadays, giving me ample opportunity to write. Ever since splitting from my long-term partner Sandra a year ago, I've been living on my own and have had a lot more time to devote to the pursuit of my personal goals, at least on weekday evenings. The weekend is a slightly different story, because that's when I get to spend time with our four-year-old son, Jack. But all things considered, I couldn't ask for better conditions under which to work on this book – unlike the last time I tried to write it, when I was still living with Sandra and Jack. In those days I had so many distractions that making any headway at all was a major challenge.

There's something else that encourages me and spurs me on. It's the thought of how my life will change when the book is finished and my efforts are crowned with success. Set against the background of that success, the little challenges I face on a daily basis can be seen clearly for what they are: short-term inconveniences.

Does it worry me that I am having some trouble paying my rent at the moment? Not at all, because I know that success will eliminate my cash flow problems once and for all. Am I discouraged by the fact that my job at the haulage firm is uninteresting and a career dead end? Not in the least, because I know that a life of perfect freedom awaits me.

Everybody wants success, and it's easy to see why. The life of the successful person is a life free of worry, free of strife, free of all the difficulties, large and small, that trouble the average non-successful individual on a regular basis. Everybody wants success because the prospect of success is the prospect of a wonderful new life. I consider it a privilege to be your guide on the journey that you will be taking to this glorious destination.

Gary Speedwell
June 2015

1

THE ROAD TO SUCCESS

Perseverance

Not everybody can be an overnight success. And frankly, the type of success that can be achieved overnight is rarely worth having. When I was a teenager, I once accompanied my friend Tim Parsons to a party which featured a succession of drinking games. Tim, a person no one had down as a big drinker, astonished the other partygoers by winning every one of these games hands down. By mid-morning the next day, everybody knew about Tim. He was a bona fide overnight success. But he wasn't able to enjoy his local-celebrity status, because he'd been rushed to hospital at 4am with acute alcohol poisoning and placed on an intravenous drip. By the time he recovered fully, he was yesterday's news. So what was the point?

The truth is, any success worth having is bound to take time. In your quest to reach the top, you can't expect instant results – just as you can't walk into a casino, feed some money into the fruit machine, pull the lever, and expect a big payoff just like that. The most successful gamblers are those found at the casino night after night, reliably stationed at their fruit machines, secure in the knowledge that even if they have to pull the lever thousands of times, eventually the jackpot will be theirs.

What I'm saying is that if you're interested in attaining success, the one quality you'll need in abundance is *perseverance*. Perseverance is something we all possess to a certain degree, so I know you have it in you. But the truly successful among us have an amount that can't be measured. (By this I mean, of course, that it's too big to be measured, not that there is no actual way of measuring it – though, to be honest, there isn't.)

Without perseverance, how will you weather those difficult patches in which everything seems to be going against you? How will you cope when your forward momentum is stalled by those who, whether due to naivety or jealousy or plain evil, seem determined to stand in your way? An individual who is destined for success, as I am, never allows such setbacks to make him feel discouraged, at least not for more than five or ten minutes. To adapt the words of the pop singer Chumbawamba: *If they get knocked down, they pick themselves up again – there is virtually nothing that is capable of keeping them down!*

For a living example of perseverance, consider Eddie "the Eagle" Edwards, the holder of Britain's national ski-jumping record to this day. Eddie was not born a great ski jumper. In many respects he was an ordinary person, just like you. But what made him exceptional was his perseverance. Although his early efforts didn't succeed in bringing him international recognition, he was determined to carry on practising and improving until he had secured his place in the history of his sport.

Time after time, he squeezed himself into an unflattering skin-tight suit, placed his bottle-bottom glasses on his nose, got up on that big ramp, accelerated to breakneck speeds and shot through the air like some magnificent osprey or kestrel. At no time was he put off by the prospect of veering off the ramp and fracturing several ribs, breaking one or all of his legs, or puncturing a lung. Those possibilities, and the terrible inconvenience they would bring, barely registered with him. Why? *Because his mind was focused only on success.* And so he pressed on. Eventually, he achieved one of the most coveted honours in sport: selection for the Olympic Games! I once met Eddie, actually, when I out bowling in Milton Keynes. Nice guy, although as a bowler he was pretty rubbish.

Cinema is full of inspiring examples of individuals determined to succeed whatever the odds. You will probably have seen the film *The Terminator*, and perhaps one or more of its sequels: *Terminator 2, 3, 4* or *5*. The Terminators change in each story, but they have one thing in common – it's even stated in the films: *they never ever give up*. They pursue their goals with steely determination, never wavering even when the obstacles they face seem insurmountable. Naturally your goals will be different to those of a Terminator, be it a T-600, T-800, or even the T-1000 – all of whom, it must be said, were intent mainly on the destruction of the human race – but if you're serious about success, then you need to display the same single-mindedness as that of a liquid-metal mimetic polyalloy nanomorph on a mission to track down and eliminate the leader of the human resistance.

The story I take most inspiration from is that of Marshall Brewster himself. Many people are unaware that in the early stages of his career as a self-help author, Marshall had difficulty gaining recognition. To anyone who has read Marshall's pioneering and brilliant books, or attended his inspirational talks, this will no doubt seem incomprehensible. But the fact is, in those early days, the world simply wasn't ready for him. I've faced similar problems for years when it comes to the world's relationship to me, so I can empathise powerfully with what Marshall must have felt at that time.

Marshall's first book, *Infallible You: The Art and Science of Going Straight to the Top*, was published in 1993. Initially, sales of this groundbreaking work were disappointing. A lot of the blame for this must be laid at the door of the mainstream newspapers, which uniformly failed to review the book. Also, in the early nineties the World Wide Web was still in its infancy and Amazon.com was an obscure business operating out of a garden shed, so for a new author to get into the public consciousness was more difficult than it is nowadays. There were various other factors at work, too numerous and intricate to explore here. Most of all, as I've mentioned above, the public needed time to come to terms with ideas as novel and profound as Marshall's.

Did Marshall get discouraged when his initial book sales didn't meet expectations? Not at all. He continued to tour his home state, continued to give informal talks, continued to impart his unique wisdom to anyone who would listen. And then – suddenly and without warning – Marshall's perseverance paid off. His book started to sell not in tens or even hundreds, but in the thousands and tens of thousands. His diary filled up with after-dinner speaking gigs and chat show appearances. He contributed to leading lifestyle magazines. In short, he achieved the success he richly deserved.

Coincidentally, this all happened right after the famous American rock singer Joey Memphis made front-page news across the country by severely injuring himself in a car crash in which alcohol and drugs played no small part. Given the fact (widely reported in the American tabloids) that Marshall's book was found in the glove compartment of Joey's car after the crash, and given Joey's well-publicised addiction problems, one can't help but wonder: did Marshall throw up his hands in despair when he learned that his book had, by complete accident, got swept up in the sordid Joey Memphis media frenzy? Did he quake with worry at the prospect that this bad publicity would kill off his book once and for all?

We'll never know for sure, but my instinct tells me that Marshall didn't worry even for a moment. He knew that a short bout of bad publicity was as nothing compared to the immense power of the ideas within his book, which couldn't fail to win over the reading public sooner or later. Of course he was absolutely right, and for the surge in book sales to come at such an unlikely moment, hot on the tails of the Joey Memphis debacle, must have been the icing on the cake.

A nice postscript to this story is that Joey Memphis has been clean and sober for some years now, and his fan base, small as it now is, is as loyal as ever. I think it's safe to say that if Joey hadn't read Marshall's book and taken inspiration from it, he wouldn't be in nearly such a good position today. Obviously, some credit should also go to the rehab programme.

Remember: nobody ever tries to fail, but many people fail to try. And if a person fails to try, it's just the same as if they'd tried to fail. (Not that anyone does that, as I said.)

Conversely, if you persevere, then you can't fail to succeed, and the only thing you'll fail at is failure. Just ask Eddie "the Eagle" Edwards, a Terminator, or Marshall Brewster.

Embracing change

There's something in all of us that fears change. But where does this fear come from? Like a lot of things, it probably evolved in our primitive ancestors for some reason or other. I'm sure the reason made good sense at the time, but very clearly the world we live in now is nothing like the world of our primitive ancestors. Gone are the pursuing mammoths and pterodactyls; gone are the cold, dreary cave dwellings; gone are the awkward stone tools. In the dynamic, technologically advanced world of today, change is almost always a thing to be welcomed. Change means *progress*. Change means *personal growth*. We should embrace change, and to that end, we should stifle the primitive part of ourselves which gets panicky when anything changes.

To help you understand why it's so vital to be open to change rather than shrinking from it, I'd like you to ponder the following parable about fish.

Once upon a time, there lived two fish. These fish spent their days roaming the medium-sized lake they called home. The lake was a peaceful, comfortable place, full of tasty things to eat, like aquatic insects and little morsels of plant life. Sometimes the lake also contained a strange floating worm, about 30 feet from one of the banks, and a barely visible line, like a silken thread, rising up from the worm to the lake's surface. The two fish steered well clear of this region of the lake, though if you had asked them why, they would probably not have been able to give you a clear answer. It was just something they had always done.

Then, one day, the first fish spotted the same worm as before, again with a thin line extending to the surface, *but this time in a completely different part of the lake.* The fish was baffled – and then, as he pondered the situation, frightened. Here was a worm, and a thin line, where no worm and no thin line should be. Who had moved the worm? Was it an evil omen? What did it all mean? The first fish didn't intend to stick around to find out. He swam away as fast as his fins could carry him.

It wasn't long before the second fish, too, became aware of the new phenomenon. But the second fish was undaunted. He thought to himself: *This is my golden opportunity to get the worm, which until now has never appeared outside the no-go area.* He swam right up to the worm and chomped down on it. Within seconds he felt the line pulling him to the shore, and before he knew it, he was in the fisherman's bucket.

"At last!" said the fisherman to himself, looking down into the bucket with satisfaction. "It just goes to show that you shouldn't be afraid to change your tactics and cast out from a completely different part of the shore sometimes, because that way you increase the chances that at least a few of the fish will let their guard down."

What this parable teaches us is that in life, as in fishing, you need to be adaptable, otherwise you'll wake up one day and find you're no longer catching any fish. If you get too comfortable in your routines, you won't be able to respond quickly to the changes around you, and you'll quickly get left behind.

I think it's fair to say that this is what happened to my ex, Sandra. A year and a half ago, Sandra and I were becoming decidedly set in our ways. The life that we shared had become perilously stable and comfortable, for reasons that I must admit were as much to do with me as with Sandra. For example, in those days I had a job in logistics which, though not my dream job, was secure and paid a decent salary, giving me little incentive to go elsewhere. And in the mornings when Sandra and I parted, we always went through exactly the same routine: first we would kiss each other goodbye, then Sandra would fix her beautiful brown eyes on me for few moments, smiling the same bright smile that had attracted me to her when we first met. And our son Jack, who by then was a lively and mischievous three-year-old, had become so much the centre of our lives that the two of us hardly had time to think about our *own* interests.

Becoming locked into these patterns meant that both of us, but especially Sandra, were getting distracted from what mattered most: success. In retrospect, this must have been why Sandra displayed such scepticism when I announced that I was going to quit my job and devote myself full-time to my dream of becoming a bestselling author of self-help books.

"Are you sure you've thought this through?" she asked. It wasn't the first time one of my ideas had prompted that question from her. There was always something about her calm way of asking it that made me slightly uncomfortable.

"I've been thinking about it a lot over the past few days," I said.

"But what will we do for money?" she asked.

I knew that Sandra's question was born out of her primal fear of change, so I tried my best to address her concern. "Money is something we won't need to worry about once the book takes off," I said. "That's part of why I'm doing this – so that we never have to worry about money again. Just look at Marshall Brewster and his wife."

"Yes, well," she said, "I've never thought you had as much in common with Marshall Brewster as you seem to believe. From the way you describe him, Marshall strikes me as being a very different person to you." Needless to say, this remark wounded me, but I let it pass. She continued, "And anyway, how will we survive in the meantime, while you're writing your book? My salary won't be enough to support the three of us."

"You're forgetting our savings," I said.

"Our savings that we were planning to put towards a deposit on a new house?"

"Well, this is a way of getting us to a *better* house than we could afford otherwise, and getting us there more quickly. I mean, our savings are a drop in the ocean compared to what the book sales are going to bring in, and on top of that there's the proceeds from the speaking tours, and…" At this point I stopped because Sandra looked a little annoyed.

"What's wrong?" I asked her.

"Gary," she said, "if this is what you want to do, I can't stop you. It's your dream. Just promise me that if it starts to become obvious you're not getting anywhere, you'll admit defeat and go back to full-time work so that Jack and I aren't left in the lurch."

"I can't believe you would think so little of me!" I protested. "*Of course* it will work out."

"Okay, Gary," she said. "But still. Promise." She was outwardly composed, but I could tell by looking into her eyes that she was sorely in need of reassurance. So I promised. What else could I do?

Once I'd quit my job, I threw myself headlong into the process of writing the book. I made good progress initially, but then I ran into some obstacles. One difficulty was that, believe it or not, Marshall Brewster had done *too good* a job of influencing me! I would write an inspired passage, only to realise afterwards that I had echoed ideas from Marshall's books, sometimes word for word. So a lot of otherwise first-rate writing had to be discarded. Another difficulty was that I had to divide my time between writing the book and looking after Jack, as Sandra had insisted we save money on childcare by reducing his nursery hours. It wasn't always easy to concentrate, what with Jack leaping on me, or singing songs to me, or trying to stick crayons in my ear, or otherwise demanding attention. Often by the evening I'd realise that I'd spent more of the day playing with Jack than doing my writing! Also, I hadn't firmly decided at the outset what the book should be about (I didn't want to put undue constraints on my creativity), so the book went in many different directions at once. Still, I have no doubt it would all have come together in the end, were it not for the fact that about four months into my project, Sandra delivered an ultimatum.

"You want me to go back to work?" I asked in disbelief.

"You promised, Gary," she said. "We've got through more of our savings in four months than I would ever have thought possible, and—"

"But I'm making progress!" I insisted. "I just need

more time."

"It's not up for negotiation," she said, and then she repeated, "You promised, Gary."

"I *can't* go back to work," I said with conviction. "I've got to persevere. What kind of person would I be if I let go of my dream just like that? Isn't my dream worth waiting for?"

Sandra went very quiet for a long time. Finally, in a voice so serious it scared me, she said, "You may be able to wait, Gary. But Jack and I can't wait for *you*. So if you choose to carry on with your project, you're on your own."

Again, I knew it was her fear talking, her terrible fear of change. So I didn't give in. Over the next week, I carried on working on the book during the day, and in the evenings I tried to bring Sandra round. It's a time in my life I don't much like to think about – all the arguments, and Sandra's tears, and Jack sensing that something was wrong, and then, on the day we separated, the chaste kiss I got from Sandra at the door, and her look that was full of disappointment.

"*She's* disappointed in *you*?" I remember my mother saying at the time. "You haven't done anything wrong. If she couldn't accept that you're destined for great things, it means she wasn't the right person for you. It's sad, I know, but there it is." My mother, it's worth noting, has always believed in me 100 per cent. It's also worth noting that my mother has never been entirely convinced of Sandra's suitability. (Come to think of it, my mother has never been entirely convinced of the suitability of *any* woman I've been romantically involved with.)

Of course she was right. Thankfully, the whole business is behind me now. Sandra and I are friends, I see Jack every weekend, I've begun writing the book again from scratch, my dream is alive and well, and I feel more keenly than ever the truth of the parable of the fish. Remember, readers: change is a beautiful thing, a thing to be embraced, not feared.

Don't settle for second best

When people stop me in the street and ask me what I consider to be the biggest mistake made by those who aspire to success, I know exactly what I'm going to tell them.

"The biggest mistake people make," I'll say, removing my autograph pen from my pocket, "is that after getting one or two small successes under their belt, they stop trying. They rest on their laurels, when what they should really be doing is pursuing ever more ambitious goals."

Then I'll sign my name on the fan's Asda receipt, along with an inspirational message: "*Never settle for second best.*"

You see, attaining success isn't like solving some rudimentary puzzle, such as the one you sometimes get in Christmas crackers where you have to unlink two metal clips from each other. (It's easy – the secret is to pull hard enough that that one of the clips bends slightly out of shape, creating a gap that allows the other to slide through.) If only! No, attaining success is more like solving a Rubik's cube. That's because even after you complete one side, you can't celebrate. You still have to complete all the other sides. Regrettably, you'll sometimes find that in the course of completing a new side, your work on some previous side gets undone, as happened to me when my relationship with Sandra broke down. Don't let this faze you. If you leave off with the cube partially done, it means you're settling for second best, which I've already told you not to do.

"But Gary," you might object, "isn't it greedy to be forever wanting more?" Let me be clear: this is not about greed. It's not about accumulating money and possessions, Gordon Gekko-style, or eating the whole plate of profiteroles before your date comes back from the toilet. It's simply about *realising your full potential.* And what could possibly be wrong with that?

My brother Vincent should serve as a cautionary example of what happens when you settle for second best. Though it pains me to say it, Vincent has always lived a deeply ordinary life, and probably always will.

(At this point I should probably say that my brother isn't actually called Vincent. I am withholding his real name to spare his embarrassment.)

I remember how, when I was eight and "Vincent" was five, I was always trying to fire his imagination by telling him about my exciting plans and projects. For example, I once said to him, "Vincent, did you know there's such a thing as a special bicycle with a rocket on it, and it goes at 300 miles per hour and you don't even need to pedal it? I'm going to get my own rocket bike, with two seats so you can sit on the back one, and we'll be able to travel from here to Granddad's in five seconds. I'm also going to set up my own detective agency, and when I've almost caught a criminal but he tries to get away, I'm going to use my rocket bike to chase him. You can be my special assistant who I take with me everywhere on my rocket bike."

"How are you going to get a rocket bike?" Vincent asked.

"I'm not sure. Maybe from Father Christmas."

And then, as often happened in these types of situations, Vincent lost interest and wanted to play his card game. It was a memory game where you have to turn over pairs of cards with ducks on them, or lions, or rhinoceroses, or what have you. Vincent usually won this game, but that's because he spent far too much time playing it and far too little time contemplating all the exciting possibilities life had to offer.

For the record, I never got a rocket bike or started a detective agency. Those dreams were superseded by different and better ones as I got older. But that's not the point. The point is, *even in childhood, I aimed high.*

Why did Vincent always lag behind me in terms of ambition? I suspect a large part of the reason is to do with what the psychology textbooks call "second child syndrome". In childhood, Vincent had to look on from the sidelines as I racked up one achievement after another, from getting successfully toilet-trained at a time when he was still in nappies, to kicking a football at a time when he was still struggling to stand, to learning to read at a time when he had only just learned to sing along to the alphabet song on *Sesame Street*. Yet the last thing I wanted to do was intimidate or diminish Vincent. If anything, I wanted to *help* him.

Once, when I was thirteen, I walked into Vincent's

room and found him dismantling an old alarm clock. That was typical of Vincent, who was endlessly fascinated by everyday objects. When I asked him what he was doing, he said, "I wanted to see how it worked. I took off the clock face and the hands and everything, and look what I found inside?" Holding up the clock so I could see it better, he pointed out the various parts of the mechanism. "This is where you wind it up, and there's the spring, which turns this wheel here and makes these cogs go round" – he pointed to a complicated-looking set of cogs – "and this funny toothed wheel here makes this lever go back and forth…" Vincent went on and on, clearly fascinated by the mechanism he was describing. But to me, with my incomparably wider horizons, it was all so *boring!*

I began to wonder if there was anything I could do to channel Vincent's energies in more interesting directions. When he finished talking, I said, "Vincent, do you know what's even more mysterious and exciting than an alarm clock? *A radio.* Think about it: somebody speaks into a microphone – it could be a disc jockey, or a host of a panel game, or an actor, or some other famous person – and even though we're dozens of miles away, we get to hear the famous person's voice just as clearly as if they were standing right here with us! It's like magic! Have you ever wondered how that works?"

Vincent's eyes lit up. "Do *you* know how it works?"

Here was my opportunity to give Vincent the benefit of my superior brotherly knowledge. Drawing on my recollections of science facts I'd learned at school, I explained that radio signals are based on the same principle as lightning, but that the challenge faced by the discoverers of radio, like Marie Curie, was to figure out how to make the signals travel horizontally, rather than straight down like a thunderbolt. I described how a radio transmitter shoots out hundreds of electrons every second, and how you can't see these electrons with the naked eye because each electron is smaller than a cross-section of a human hair. I described the parts that make up a radio, such as the *electron collector* (which captures the electrons), the *carbon filter* (which removes any impurities from the signal), and the *transistors* (which do much the same job as valves, like the valves on a tuba). Vincent was evidently overwhelmed by all this information, because the more I spoke, the more confused he looked.

"Maybe you could draw me a picture," he said, offering me some paper and coloured pencils. So I drew him a diagram of a radio, which he contemplated in silence for some time.

A week later, while passing by Vincent's door in the evening, I heard the tinny sounds of BBC Radio 2 coming from his room. When I pushed the door open, I saw Vincent at his desk – and, in front of him, some circuitry mounted on a wooden board. He had built a radio! Like a technician working from the blueprints of a master designer, Vincent had evidently used my radio picture as the basis for building his working prototype.

I went over to Vincent's desk and had a closer look. The board was covered with such a tangle of wires that I couldn't see where the electron collector or carbon filter were, though I could make out the small speaker that the sound was coming out of. Next to this makeshift radio were some tools – pliers and small screwdrivers and so on – along with a library book entitled *The Young Person's Guide to Electronics.*

Vincent looked up at me. "I taught myself some more about radios," he said, "and then I made one."

"Great stuff, Vincent!" I said. "You should be really proud of yourself , except that you haven't really made it look like it is in my picture." I bent down and picked up my slightly crumpled picture from where it was still lying under the desk, and said, "See, in the picture, the radio has a chrome exterior, and racing stripes on the side, and the controls are these smart-looking sliders. And it gives off a soft blue glow when it's switched on. Yours doesn't do that, does it? You've made a start, but you need to put in more work to make it a *proper* radio."

And do you know what Vincent said? He said, "I don't think I'll bother. All I wanted to do was see if I could pick up some radio stations, and now that I've done it, I'll probably take all this apart and build something else. Maybe a motion detector."

A motion detector! I'm sure you can guess how I felt at this point. Vincent had rejected my expert guidance about how to build a truly top-notch radio and instead had settled for second best. Of course I relayed this to my parents, who agreed to talk to him. I overheard my father saying to him, "There's no reason why you can't follow in Gary's footsteps and become just as successful as he's going to be. But for that to happen, you've got to raise your game. This radio project you were doing for Gary had a lot of potential, but I'd be more impressed if you'd followed it through to the end."

Sadly, Vincent didn't really take this guidance on board. Nowadays he works as an IT contractor, doing the sorts of things that are too dull for me to even bother to understand. How I pity him!

If you want to avoid Vincent's fate, stick firmly to the guiding principle I mentioned: *Never settle for second best.*

Forging your own path

> *The difference between the ordinary person and the extraordinary person is simple: the ordinary person follows the rules, whereas the extraordinary person **makes** the rules.*
>
> *– JD*

The words I've quoted above are every bit as true today as when they were first uttered. Unfortunately, I'm not sure who uttered them, or when. I only rediscovered the quotation recently when I was going through an old box of inspirational clippings and found a scrap of paper onto which, presumably years ago, I had copied down these words, identifying the source only as "JD". I can't remember who "JD" referred to, and I really wish I'd recorded the name of the source in full, because JD could be a lot of people. Johnny Depp? John Denver? Jonathan Dimbleby? Judi Dench? Jack Dee? James Dean? Jason Donovan? Jim Davidson? Jack Daniel? If you know the answer, please write in, because this is starting to bug me now.

Anyway, it follows from the quotation that in order

to become an extraordinary person, you must *completely disregard* society's expectations as to what you should be and do. Millions of people every day follow the path laid down for them by society, rather than blazing their own trails, and where does it get them? On their deathbeds they say, "That was all well and good, but I never got the chance to do anything *I* wanted to do, like creating and marketing a line of healthy yoghurt drinks, or commanding a space mission." If you want to avoid these types of regret, then you should waste no time in forging your own path.

Don't get me wrong. It's seldom easy to stand up to social convention and assert your own needs and desires. It takes tenacity – the tenacity of Cardinal Karol Józef Wojtyła, who refused to accept that non-Italians couldn't become Popes; or Barack Obama, who refused to accept that urban sophisticates couldn't get elected to the American presidency. It would've been all too easy for Wojtyła and Obama to buckle under the weight of social expectation and abandon their most cherished dreams. But they didn't. And neither should you.

Every bit as inspiring as the examples I just mentioned is the story of a person I interact with on a daily basis: my manager at work, Louise. (Yes, I do have a job again, at a haulage firm. I know I split with Sandra over my refusal to return to work, but after a month of living on my own and trying to get by without paid employment, my bank balance was such that I had no choice but to find a stopgap job to support myself.)

While I don't know for sure how Louise attained her

current position, I can make a pretty good guess. As a woman, Louise would have faced powerful obstacles to establishing herself in the traditionally male-dominated field of road haulage. "You'll never cut it in this business!" people would have said to her. "You're a woman, so you obviously haven't got the slightest acquaintance with heavy goods vehicles, plus your sense of direction is naturally poor, so how could you ever grasp the intricacies of moving freight all over the United Kingdom and beyond? Besides, all the drivers are male and they would never take you seriously – they're not accustomed to taking instruction from an attractive blonde female like yourself. In fact, they probably wouldn't even be able to concentrate on what you're saying. Why don't you set your sights on a more conventionally appropriate career for a woman, like curtain-making or jewellery design? Or modelling – have you ever considered being a model? Because you have classic features, and the sort of hourglass figure that the fashion magazines are really going for at the moment. Promise me you'll give it some thought."

Those are the sorts of social attitudes Louise would have come up against. And if she had yielded to them, she would never have risen to the position of account manager at Britain's eleventh-largest haulage and warehousing firm. Now she is the one who takes the big decisions, and she has earned the grudging respect of all the doubters.

Her office is a short distance from where I sit. She spends quite a lot of time on the phone, and because her door is normally open, I have ample opportunity to admire the efficient, no-nonsense way she has of dealing with people. Recently I overheard her saying something like:

> "No. Definitely not. Not at that price. [*Pause.*] Well, they can take that line if they want, but they have to understand we can't accommodate them. No. No, then that's their business, but… certainly not. Not in this lifetime. [*Pause.*] Look, to be honest, I'm having trouble seeing why this is so hard for you to grasp. *They are trying to screw us.* So, no. End of discussion."

And then she slammed the phone down. It was exhilarating! You can tell she doesn't have the slightest interest in conforming to other people's outmoded ideas of how women should and shouldn't behave. Not that I mean to suggest that she's mannish in any way. On the contrary, she's very womanly – for example, on the day of this particular phone conversation I remember she was wearing quite a tight dark-blue skirt and matching fitted jacket, and a white silk blouse where the cuffs came out of her jacket sleeves. But she manages to combine her femininity with the sort of uncompromising independence and take-no-prisoners attitude that only the most powerful and successful people possess. I count myself lucky that I'm not a fool, because if I were, Louise definitely wouldn't suffer me gladly!

I sense that Louise is starting to recognise something of her own trailblazing spirit in me. A couple of days ago, she was walking past the office kitchen just as I was coming out with a tray containing five cups of tea, a stack of waffles on a plate, and a squeezy bottle of golden syrup. Louise stopped short, looked down at the waffles, looked up at me, and finally looked over my shoulder into the kitchen.

"When did we get a waffle maker?" she asked.

"I brought it in last Friday," I said. "I wasn't getting much use out of it at home, so I thought—"

"You?" she broke in. "This is one of your ideas?"

"I thought it would be more useful here," I said. "I don't tend to do much waffle-making at home when it's just me. And when I asked around, I discovered that a few people on this floor were open to the idea of waffles, so it seemed like a waffle maker in the office made a lot of sense. I'm just getting in the teas and the waffles now. Would you like to have a waffle? I made plenty, so—"

She put up her hand and said, "I'm too busy for waffles." (This stands to reason. The time was ten fifty-five, and I know she meets with the other account managers at eleven o'clock most days.) Then she walked off, but as she was doing so, she half turned and added, "Waffles – that's a new one; that's *brilliant*. You're really pushing the envelope, Gary. This is why I'm expecting great things from you."

Great things! I only wish she had tasted one of the waffles. I think she would've appreciated the degree of care that went into the batter. In America, where I first developed a taste for waffles, a lot of people simply buy waffle mixes from the supermarket – but I've never been one to settle for the easy option. Besides, those mixes are quite hard to get hold of in Britain.

To return to my point: to achieve something worthwhile in life, you have to be prepared to *act boldly* – just as I acted boldly in instituting waffle-making at my office. I didn't waste any time worrying about whether it was really "my place" to do it, or about how my actions would be perceived by the "powers that be", or about what the health and safety regulations might have to say on the matter. Instead, I went ahead and turned my vision into reality.

As you begin to forge your own path, you'll experience a refreshing sense of liberation from society's stifling demands and expectations. One of my few regrets is that I didn't start forging my own path years ago. For a long time, I was thwarted at every turn by authority figures pronouncing those depressingly familiar words: "You can't". At school, the teachers said, "You can't just discard all the remainders when you're doing long division." When I applied for my first job, the man interviewing me said, "You can't perform a role like this without prior experience of glassblowing." When I tried to get my overdraft limit increased in late 2001, the people at the bank said, "You can't expect us to lend you any more money given the state of your finances." After a while, I became well and truly tired of always having to abide by the rules other people had laid down!

What a great relief it is to be able to counter these negative messages with a self-affirming message of one's own: "I can". Once I decided to live life on my terms, a whole universe of possibilities opened up, and more new possibilities are opening up with every day that goes by. My sincere hope is that you'll be able to follow my lead – or rather *not* follow my lead, indeed not follow anyone else's lead, because the whole point is to do as *you* see fit. There's no limit to what you can accomplish when you completely ignore the objections of everybody else.

Reframing

In the previous section, I made it clear that forging your own path takes effort. And if you're not willing to expend the effort, this raises an obvious question – namely, what alternative strategies exist for bringing about noticeable improvements in your life at minimal cost to you in terms of time and energy?

I'm happy to report that there are several such strategies, the most effective of which is a technique known as *reframing*. At the heart of reframing is the idea that you can change reality using only the power of your mind. Now, if your immediate reaction is "This sounds like the stuff of science fiction", I can see where you're coming from. On the face of it, reframing *does* sound like science fiction. For instance, it sounds a bit like the premise of the 1981 David Cronenberg film *Scanners*, which was all about people using the power of their minds to change reality in ways that were, frankly, somewhat unpleasant. But rest assured that the practice of reframing is less about setting household items aflame and bursting people's heads open than it is about perceiving things in a new and different way.

Allow me to illustrate how reframing works. Consider

the case of an unnamed man who is having problems in his relationship. His partner is forever complaining that his behaviour is "immature" and "annoying". The only solution, according to her, is for him to change. But is she right? Is this *really* the only solution? Let's examine the situation more closely.

The reason the man's partner calls him immature is that *she is interpreting his actions as being immature.* The reason she calls him annoying is that *she is allowing herself to feel annoyed when he does certain things.* So the solution to the man's relationship problems is breathtakingly simple: *All his partner has to do is change her perception of his actions and overcome her feelings of annoyance towards them.* In other words, the key to improving the situation lies not in some drastic overhaul of the man's behaviour, but in a simple change to his partner's mindset. This change in mindset is what is known as reframing.

I can tell you from personal experience, especially my experience of relationships prior to meeting Sandra, that people are often resistant to the idea of reframing. Why? I'm not 100 per cent sure, but I suspect it's because they're reluctant to accept that such a simple technique could possibly be effective. As a result, when you ask them to try reframing, they dismiss the idea out of hand, and may even say things like "Over my dead body" and "Don't insult my intelligence". Which is ironic, because those are exactly the sorts of remarks that show why they'd benefit from reframing.

As an aid to learning, I am going to describe three imaginary situations in which a person confronts some sort of problem. Following each description I will explain how the problem can be reframed out of existence. You may wish to put a sheet of paper over the solution at first, to give yourself a chance to arrive at it on your own.

1. **THE PROBLEM:** Rufus weighs 27 stone. Recently, a video clip of Rufus was posted online. It was a close-up of Rufus in the stands at a football match, gorging himself on pies, chips, and cheeseburgers. The clip quickly became a worldwide Internet sensation, probably owing to the sheer number of items that Rufus was stuffing into his mouth and the speed at which he was doing so. Now Rufus feels humiliated and doesn't dare show his face in public.

   THE SOLUTION: Although feelings of humiliation can be a terrible burden, Rufus needs to realise that he can get rid of this burden in an instant if he wishes. All he has to do is reflect that by appearing in the video clip, he has brought joy and laughter to millions. He should revel in his fame and play up to the image of the "jolly fat man", taking his place in a long line of beloved jolly fat men, from Friar Tuck to Marlon Brando.

2. **THE PROBLEM:** Steve, his wife Anna, and their two children Neil and Becky (ages thirteen and eleven) recently embarked on an extended holiday in South America, but all has not gone according to plan. The family has lost their way in the Venezuelan jungle, and night is closing in.

Anna blames Steve, Steve blames himself, and Neil and Becky are convinced they are going to die.

THE SOLUTION: Instead of regarding this turn of events as a calamity, and giving way to fear and recrimination, the family could choose to see the situation as a once-in-a-lifetime rip-roaring adventure of the sort most travellers can only dream of. If they survive, what a magnificent story it will make for Neil and Becky to tell their own respective children someday!

3. **THE PROBLEM:** After sixteen years of faithful service, Frank has lost his job at the building society. He isn't qualified to do anything else, and feels hopeless. He has taken to drinking almost an entire bottle of wine every evening.

THE SOLUTION: Frank needs to realise that the loss of his job isn't a setback; it's an opportunity. With so much time on his hands, he can do anything he wants. For example, he could write a novel based on his experience at the building society. Or he could put his love of wine to good use by attending wine classes, with the aim of one day becoming a wine steward at a posh restaurant.

I can think of plenty of events in my own life that could easily have undermined my confidence if I'd allowed them to do so. But thanks to reframing, my confidence has nearly always remained sky-high, regardless of what was happening to me at the time.

Take what happened between me and Kim. The two of us first encountered each other one morning in a café in Los Angeles where, having noticed that I was idly building an igloo-like structure out of sugar cubes, she greeted me with the words: "Hey, Sparky, is that some weird conceptual art project you're doing?" I was sitting at a table on my own, and Kim, at that time a fresh-faced twenty-three-year-old with hoop earrings and a winning smile, was the waitress serving me. It didn't take her long to realise I was a foreigner. "What are you, English? That's so cool. I'll tell you what you might be interested in." She pointed to the item on the menu that said *English muffins*. "Just like at home, right?"

I confessed that I had never heard of English muffins before. This astonished her and led to a lengthy and somewhat confusing conversation about English muffins, by the end of which we had established that "English muffins" were basically what I knew as "muffins".

Not being all that keen on muffins, I instead ordered the waffles. Before I knew it, Kim was overstaying her shift and telling me her life story ("Dad went AWOL when I was eleven, and Mom was too busy pill-popping and shacking up with random men to even notice my existence") and I was telling her mine. By the time I left the café with her phone number written on my hand, we had forged an intimate bond.

To cut a long story short, we were married fifteen months later. That's when the trouble started. Kim began to complain about little things, like the amount of time I spent bowling and the lengthy phone conversations I had with my parents. "If you wanted to spend so much time talking to your mother, why didn't you marry *her*?" she once asked. It wasn't long before the complaints escalated. "Listen up, Gary. *No one* goes bowling as much as you claim to. So why can't you admit the truth: you're not bowling, you're damn well having the time of your life with some cheap floozy!"

Now, I hope you'll believe me when I say that Kim was totally off-track here. I wasn't carrying on with any cheap floozies. I really was just bowling. But protesting my innocence didn't help – if anything, it enraged Kim more. She called me all manner of names and sometimes even threw things at me. These tended to be small, lightweight objects like notepads or wooden spoons, but it was still upsetting. A day or two later, her mood would change and she'd become affectionate again, sometimes to the point of being clingy. This would last for a while, and then the paranoia and the accusations would start up again.

Even when she wasn't being paranoid, she was dissatisfied with life, and in particular with her waitressing job. What she really wanted to be was an actress, but she didn't seem able to break into the business. Meanwhile, I had difficulties of my own to deal with. My job (as a salesperson at a car dealership) was causing me a lot of stress, as the pressure to make sales was relentless. On top of all that, I was worried about my mother, who had suffered a minor stroke back in the UK and was finding day-to-day life a bit overwhelming in the aftermath.

With all this to contend with, I could easily have said to myself, "Woe is me! My marriage is crumbling, and life is grinding me down." But did I? Absolutely not. Instead, I *reframed* the situation.

By then, you see, I had attended the Marshall Brewster event I mentioned in the Introduction. There, Marshall had spoken persuasively about the power of reframing, among other topics. So I was able to say to myself, "This isn't adversity; this is life's way of telling me to re-evaluate my priorities." I'd been focusing so much energy on my job and my relationship with Kim, everything else had fallen by the wayside. I needed to reconnect with what was really important.

So I quit my job and flew to the UK, without Kim, for an extended stay at my parents' house. It was a transformative experience. My mother couldn't have been more grateful to have me there to support her in her recovery. My father buoyed me up with talk of how confident he was in my eventual success. All my troubles seemed to evaporate, and the only threat to my peace of mind was the hassle that I got from Kim whenever we spoke on the phone. "I'm going crazy on my own!" she said. "What do you think you're *doing* there? In case you've forgotten, Sparky, I'm still your wife. So you need to wake up, get your ass back to LA, and give me some support." The fact was, despite being Californian, Kim was not really very laid-back.

I wasn't ready to return. My mother was recovering well, but she still needed me. I stayed on, and the weeks ticked by. When I finally did go back to Los Angeles, a month and a half after I'd left there, Kim was in a terrible way. We argued even worse than before, and within days, I realised that our marriage was over. To be honest, my overriding feeling was one of relief, because I knew by then that Kim wasn't the right woman for me.

Kim was numb. I tried to reassure her by saying, "Don't see this as a failure, see it as a learning experience and opportunity for personal growth." That's textbook reframing.

But she was having none of it. She only glared at me and said, "What the *hell* are you talking about? You've ruined my life. You, and your empty promises, and your damned floozies."

Amazingly, ten years later, she still feels the same way, and rings me up on a regular basis to tell me so. All I can say is, don't let yourself lapse into these rigid, unconstructive ways of seeing the world, otherwise you'll end up as bitter as my ex-wife. It's sad when people get their thoughts stuck in a rut like that. But that's Kim for you. Mad as a hatter.

The folly of dwelling on your mistakes (part 1)

> *The longer we dwell on our mistakes, the greater is their power to harm us.*
> – François-Marie Arouet de Voltaire
> (1694–1778)

As you can see, this time I'm in no doubt as to where the quotation comes from. François-Marie was, according to the *New Aquarius Book of Inspirational Quotations*, a "renowned French philosopher and writer of the 18th century". Readers of the time would probably have regarded her as one of the foremost self-help experts alive. And even after more than 200 years, her warning against dwelling on our mistakes is as timely as ever. (Actually, she used the word "misfortunes" rather than "mistakes", but that didn't fit my theme so well, so I changed it. I think my version of the quotation is as valid as the original, and I have no doubt that François-Marie would welcome the change if she were alive today.)

Let me be clear: *making* mistakes is not the problem; *dwelling on them* is the problem. As a general rule, mistakes are not a big deal: one mistake is not going to kill anyone. You might ask, "But what about the mistakes of heart surgeons and bomb disposal experts?" My answer is: *Those are the exceptions that prove the rule.*

One reason you shouldn't dwell on your mistakes is that doing so saps your mental energy. If the racy text message you meant to send to your girlfriend has accidentally gone to your mother, the worst thing you can do is spend the rest of the day obsessing about your mistake, because then you'll probably be so distracted that you'll make *another* mistake, like forgetting to collect your girlfriend from the train station that evening when she returns from her girlie weekend in Bath.

It doesn't matter whether the mistake is large or small – just put it out of your mind. Maybe you've been convicted of credit card fraud. Well then, shame on you. But you'll only compound your mistake if you wallow in regret for the whole of your three-year prison sentence. Or maybe you've married someone unsuitable and it's all ended in tears. In that case, you have my sympathies, but I must warn you: if you slip into the habit of berating yourself about your poor judgement, you'll be in no fit state to embark on a new relationship.

Successful people have better things to do than beat themselves up about their relationship mistakes. Just look at Henry VIII. The Tudor king's union with his dead brother's widow, Catherine of Aragon, didn't work out – not surprising when you consider that he only married her in the first place because of family pressure. He probably should have stood up to his family right at the outset and said, "Sorry, she's just not my type." But no matter. After splitting from Catherine, Henry plunged straight back into the dating scene and went on to have a succession of new relationships, each more fulfilling than the last.

And then there's Elizabeth Taylor. Imagine her feelings when her marriage to Richard Burton, the love of her life, ended in divorce. Taylor could easily have become totally consumed by the sense that she'd had a good thing and managed to lose it. Instead, she wasted no time in putting the failure of her marriage behind her – as evidenced by the fact that she walked down the aisle with Richard Burton for a second time just a year later. Who says there are no happy endings?

Not only should you avoid dwelling on your own mistakes, you shouldn't dwell on *other people's* mistakes either. You may recall the 1994 World Cup Final, which climaxed in a penalty shootout. Roberto Baggio of Italy, the world's most famous player, stepped up. If he scored, Italy's hopes remained alive; if he missed, Brazil became world champions. The drama was incredible! The camera zoomed in on Baggio, who placed the ball and then paused. I am convinced that, at that moment, a thought came to him: a flashback to the tournament's opening ceremony, when legendary singer Diana Ross took a penalty. As the world watched, Ross kicked – and missed the goal! Baggio knew that his own penalty was taking place on the *very same pitch* (or at least a very similar pitch). With Ross's mistake preying on his mind, Baggio ran forward, took his kick and – well, you can guess what happened: he missed, and his country lost. I've no doubt the shame never left him.

What Baggio *should* have done is told himself categorically, "I am the best player in the world, so of course I will score" (much like the German players always do, although with them it verges on arrogance – which is really not the sort of attitude I'm encouraging). If he'd done so, I can guarantee his kick would have found its mark.

The folly of dwelling on your mistakes (part 2)

I know I'm dwelling on the topic of not dwelling on one's mistakes, but it's only because the last thing I want is for your quest for success to be derailed after your first embarrassing misstep. I can't stress enough that dwelling on your mistakes compromises your ability to move forward with your life. And this is not just because of the effect it has on you and your mind. It's also because of the effect it has on *the people around you*.

The "vibe" you give off is of crucial importance.

People have a sixth sense that allows them to pick up on the subtle cues that suggest all is not as it should be. When we are confronted by the sight of a jockey who is marginally too tall, or the sound of a Beatles song covered by an X-Factor contestant, we know something is wrong even if we can't quite say what it is. By the same token, if you dwell on your mistakes, your negativity towards yourself will affect how people perceive you. In short: *if you see yourself as a blunderer, that's how others will see you, too.*

The last thing you should want is to be regarded as someone prone to errors, as you would then become a magnet for the sort of people who might try to take advantage of you. I can think of no better illustration of this than a recent unsolicited email I received from a poor fellow who had been down on his luck for some time. Because of its relevance, I reproduce it here in full:

Dear Respected One,

Permit me to inform you of my desire of going into business relationship with you. I am Daniel Kouame 22 years of age the only son of late Mr Emmanuel Kouame, a very wealthy cocoa merchant in the Ivory Coast. After my father was killed on 27th June 2008 by the rebels who attacked our country, I received an inheritance of $4.500.000 (Four Million, five hundred thousand dollars). To my regret I consented for the sum to be administered by my father's business associate Mr Wilfried Mathias, who was entrusted with placing the monies in long-

term investments. Mr Wilfried Mathias instead removed my signatory authority from the investment holding account, this means that he is able to seize the funds for himself in a years time unless a reinstatement document can be obtained. I should not have trusted my father's business associate, my foolish mistake has caused me great personal suffering and although I am additionally the beneficiary of a separate fund which was for my living purposes, this has been plundered by the relatives of Mr Wilfried Mathias leaving me in poverty. Sir I am contacting you with due sense of humanity that you will give a sympathetic consideration to providing me with assistance in the following ways. (1) To act as a designated foreign sponsor for trusted procurement of a reinstatement document from the Central Bank of the Ivory Coast, and (2) To provide details of an overseas bank account for secure deposit of the recovered funds. I am willing to offer you 15% of the total sum as compensation for your kind efforts.

Anticipating to hear from you soon,
Thanks and God Bless You,
Best Regards,
Mr Daniel Kouame

Daniel's story is a sad one, but I must gently point out that he hasn't really helped himself. After suffering the consequences of what he calls his "foolish mistake", he descended into self-blame. I'm sure he was unconsciously sending out subtle but powerful signals that he was a blunderer. In this way, he left himself open to a second round of victimisation, this time by Mr Wilfried Mathias's relatives. The Mathiases of this world will always pounce when they sense weakness.

I would have loved to help Daniel, and in so doing receive a share of his vast fortune. But after an exchange of emails it emerged that a reinstatement document from the Ivory Coast Central Bank would set me back a surprisingly large amount of money. I simply didn't have that kind of cash, so I wasn't able to comply with his request. But as I was sympathetic to his plight, I wrote to him one final time to wish him well, to offer him some positive-thinking tips, and to pass along a token gift of £20. In addition, I invited him to email me again in six months' time if he hadn't got any takers at that point, as there was a good chance I'd be wildly successful by then, with no shortage of cash to plough into high-yielding investment opportunities like the one he was offering.

In the meantime, I hope my £20 contribution adds to Daniel's "bank of self-belief" and makes his journey to success just a little bit smoother. I'm confident that I will be repaid if it does.

Though we all make mistakes, I'm happy to report that I've never been guilty of a mistake on the scale of Daniel's. The closest I came was the time several months ago when I lost a fairly substantial amount of money, at least on paper. I had been reading up on the latest self-help industry news and had come across an exciting young company called Skyhook Media. They had developed a family of apps that they billed as "the most comprehensive self-help resource currently available on the Android and iOS platforms". Their offering included a goal-setting app, a confidence-boosting app, a mindfulness app, a stress-reduction app, a brain-training app, a career-guidance app, a positive-habit-formation app, an anger-management app, a weight-loss app, a weight-gain app (for the scrawny) – and, most groundbreaking of all, the "Skyhook Player". Using the Skyhook Player, people could, on a subscription basis, access literally hundreds of personal-development video tutorials covering every self-help theme under the sun. "This," I said to myself, "is a game changer." I resolved to buy as many shares in the company as I could afford. I won't reveal exactly how much I invested, but, well… let's just say it was a significant amount of money.

Then disaster struck. An article about Skyhook Media appeared in *Soar: The Magazine for High Flyers* – and its author was none other than Marshall Brewster! The article, entitled "Why Skyhook Media Will Come Crashing Down to Earth", argued that Skyhook Media was doomed to fail because, once users got beyond the Skyhook Player's "glossy interface", they'd encounter "tired, second-hand content" delivered by "hopelessly inexpert presenters". Given that Marshall is, among other things, a respected business pundit, his verdict on Skyhook Media quickly filtered through to all the major news outlets, at which point the share price dipped below what I'd paid. Two days later came the killer blow: news that Marshall Brewster Enterprises had developed its own motivational video player, through which users could access numerous tutorials, *all of them featuring Marshall Brewster himself.*

How could Skyhook Media ever be expected to compete with that? Needless to say, the share price plummeted. I had, as the Americans say, lost my shirt.

But did I beat myself up about this mistake? Absolutely not. My thinking is, if anyone is going to crush my investing dreams, it might as well be Marshall. I credit him with teaching me an invaluable lesson about how to distinguish good investments from bad ones. My new plan is wait until Skyhook Media has recovered as much of its value as I can reasonably expect it to, whereupon I'll sell my stake and use the proceeds to buy shares in Marshall Brewster Enterprises – a "slam-dunk" investment if ever there was one.

2

YOUR TRUE SELF

What is your true self?

The Internet is a wonderful tool, but sometimes it lets us down. The other day, I came across the following piece of guidance on a self-improvement website:

Finding your true self is a lifelong process.

Now, clearly that can't be right. Leaving aside the fact that anyone who takes an entire lifetime to find their true self is being shockingly inefficient, it's hard to see what possible benefit there could be in finding one's true self only in old age.

There are compelling reasons not to waste any time in finding your true self. If you've ever read any self-help literature at all, you will know that you are wonderful and special and unique, with any amount of untapped potential and hidden talent. Why would you not want to tap your untapped potential? Why would you not want to unhide your hidden talent? This is what finding your true self amounts to – and it may just be your ticket to fulfilment and riches.

A word of warning, though. Before attempting to find your true self, you must learn the correct method (which I will teach you shortly). If you don't, you run the risk of misidentifying one of your many false selves as your true self. The consequences of this could be quite serious. You could spend years wondering why nothing is panning out for you, little suspecting that the self who's been calling the shots is an impostor.

So, what *is* your true self, anyway? Allow me to explain. Your true self is the original self you are born with, a self that is infinitely good and infinitely right, and therefore knows exactly what you need in order to flourish. If your true self were allowed to get on with things without interference, all would be well. Unfortunately, your true self *is* subject to interference – in the form of *society*, which inevitably comes along with its norms and conventions, its rules and regulations. Society is all around us, and only the trained mind can avoid soaking up its influences like a sponge. In fact, even the trained mind will absorb its influences to some degree, if not like a sponge then at least like one of those squidgy cloths you keep under the sink. We all know that such cloths have a way of soaking up substances that leave a smelly and unpleasant residue. And so it is with the mind. With prolonged exposure to society, our true selves are obscured by layers of tired routine and slavish rule following.

How much better life would be if all the true selves of the world were given the freedom to do as they wished! Then everybody would experience fulfilment and the world would be a paradise. The only problem I can see is if one person's true self wanted something that interfered with another person's true self getting what *it* wanted. But that's a relatively minor administrative matter that I'm sure could be sorted out somehow.

As it stands, the vast majority of us are out of touch with our true selves. Even if you came face-to-face with your true self, you probably wouldn't recognise it any more than you would recognise some obscure member of your extended family, like a second cousin you haven't seen since your great-grandmother's funeral when you were five.

I am sure you have had the experience of being stuck in a dull meeting at work and, midway through the meeting, being seized by the desire to sing a particular song at the top of your lungs. But rather than acting on this desire, you deferred to the sensible inner voice, which told you, "No, you mustn't. Other people would disapprove." I can assure you that this sensible inner voice is *not* the voice of your true self. Your true self is all about being spontaneous and has no interest in being sensible. In actuality, what prevents you from bursting into song is the usual culprit: society, masquerading as your own thoughts.

The part of you that wanted to sing the song stands a good chance of being your true self. On the other hand, it might not be. Maybe the song is one of those manufactured boy-band hits which gets an enormous amount of airplay and lodges in everybody's head despite being shallow and insipid. In that case, the self that wants to burst into song is just another sham self, this time fostered by the cynical efforts of music industry executives. Your true self has no interest in inferior pop music, as it recoils from all that is false and worthless.

I have found that an excellent way of engaging and stimulating my true self is to switch on my stereo and play it some *proper* music, like one of the classic Bruce Springsteen albums of the late seventies or early eighties. I would advise you to do the same. Not only is Bruce's high-octane rock and roll a joy to listen to, it's also full of inspiring self-help messages your true self could really do with hearing, messages about breaking free of the forces that have been holding you back. By the way, if you're going to attempt this, you should really have a decent stereo system. With cheap, underpowered speakers, you just won't get the same effect.

Getting to know your true self

After you've finished playing the Bruce Springsteen album (or if you feel ready, perhaps once you've reached track seven or eight), you can move on to the actual process of finding your true self. Here is how it works.

Get a pen and paper and make a list of the *core beliefs* that give your life meaning and significance. After you've done that, make a list of your *deepest desires*. There are no right or wrong answers. For illustration, I will share my own lists with you, but please don't just copy them, as that would be doing a disservice to your true self. Also, keep well away from the distracting influence of other people while doing the exercise. Free your mind to go where it wants to, and trust it to get to the answers that are right for you.

I have done this exercise at various times on my journey to success (just to check I had everything covered), and most recently I came up with the following:

My core beliefs

- war is bad
- you should never be angry at someone unless they deserve it
- the environment is worth preserving for future generations
- everyone should be treated fairly
- seatbelts save lives
- it is wrong to make a child believe for years that there is a Father Christmas and then devastate him by revealing there isn't

My deepest desires

Mandatory:

- worldwide recognition as an author of groundbreaking self-help books
- freedom
- £7.5 million (minimum)
- a sexually fulfilling relationship with a high-powered, successful woman

- fresh seafood on demand
- a decent life for Sandra and Jack
- a top-notch education for Jack
- travel to exotic locales
- love
- respect
- the admiration of my peers
- a reputation for being a good person
- success for Kim, so that she stops ringing me up all the time to blame me for her troubles
- a dog just like Misty, the Labrador retriever we had when I was growing up
- perfect happiness

Optional:

- X-ray vision
- physical immortality

The key to personal fulfilment is to act in harmony with your core beliefs and your deepest desires – that is, in harmony with your true self. So once you get your beliefs and desires down on paper, you need to take positive action to bring your life into line with them. This process is known as *self-actualisation.*

To give you a sense of how self-actualisation works, I will present three case studies, all of them involving me. Each of the case studies relates to one particular core belief or desire of mine, as listed above, and gives details of the efforts I have been making to bring my life into alignment with it.

Self-actualisation case study #1: forging a relationship with a high-powered, successful woman

It might be worth explaining why, until now, I haven't made it a priority to forge a relationship with a high-powered, successful woman. After all, Kim was a perennial low achiever and Sandra, though admittedly an accomplished graphic designer, wasn't interested in reaching ever-higher rungs on the career ladder. The reason I wasn't bothered about any of this was because I assumed *my own* commitment to success was enough. My attitude was, so long as my partner can bask in my success, why should she have to attain her own?

I can see in retrospect that this was the wrong attitude. *Of course* my partner needs to be successful. Successful people are like peas in a pod. They understand each other in a way that no unsuccessful person can ever hope to understand a successful person, or vice versa. There's a reason why my dream of writing a bestselling self-help book opened up a gulf between Sandra and me. It's simply because Sandra couldn't fully relate to my ambitions.

You need people around you who are your equals in terms of ambition. If your friends and loved ones can't relate to the dreams you're aiming at, then of course this is going to lead to strain, especially once you've achieved those dreams. You'll be flying off to exotic destinations in your private jet, while your friends are still working in the timber yard or trying to turn a profit on dodgy second-hand electrical appliances. You'll be answering fan letters, while your partner is lying on the sofa absorbed in latest issue of *Total Sudoku Magazine*.

Sadly, the more successful you become, the more you'll find yourself growing apart from those who were close to you. At the same time, you will find yourself getting into relationships with entirely new people: dynamic, talented people who have risen to the top by their own efforts, just as you're going to do.

This brings me back to the matter of my quest for a relationship with a high-powered, successful woman – and not just any such relationship, but one that is sexually fulfilling. That's an important proviso. Several years ago, I attended a convention of entrepreneurs and inventors, hoping to make useful contacts with people who could help me get my idea for a revolutionary new type of confectionary (bite-sized bowling balls made of milk chocolate, to be marketed to bowling alleys across Britain) off the ground. The number of high-powered, successful women at this convention was astonishing! There must have been at least ten of them. These women were living proof of the great strides feminism has made over the decades. On the other hand, I couldn't help noticing that I didn't find any of them physically attractive. To me, none of them sparkled in the way that, say, Sandra did.

I couldn't form a sexually fulfilling relationship with someone like that. I need someone who's both a high achiever *and* attractive. And so do you. It's an elusive combination, but well worth tracking down. The question is: where can such a person be found?

Perhaps the person who meets these criteria is closer than you imagine. It could be someone you already have a passing acquaintance with. Think of the various women or the various men (according to preference) who play some part in your life, however small. As is often the case where personal development is concerned, making a list can be helpful. When I compiled my list, I managed to identify exactly three women who I felt were either high-powered enough or attractive enough to be worth me considering:

- *The lady at the bagel stand in the station.* I chat to her on a regular basis, though I must admit that I don't know her name. It's not that I haven't asked, but she is from Slovakia, and when she told me her name I couldn't even begin to get to grips with the pronunciation of it, much less remember it afterwards. She looks about thirty years old, and with her slim build and long eyelashes, she definitely qualifies as being attractive. But is she high-powered? I'm not so sure about that. Yes, she runs her own business, but from what I can see, it isn't exactly doing a roaring trade. Most mornings, the only customers in evidence are me and the elderly man from the betting shop. The main problem, I reckon, is that the vast majority of British people are unable to appreciate a good bagel.

- *Pamela Soames, of Pamela Soames Estate Agents.* When Sandra and I separated, I had to find a new flat to live in. One of the agents I registered with was called Pamela Soames

Estate Agents. As it happens, there really is a Pamela Soames – I met her when I visited the estate agent's offices, and she was very nice. Not only that, but she positively radiated power, as you'd expect from someone who founded her own estate agency. However, I'm not sure I'm really attracted to her. She looks considerably older than me, and she clears her throat quite a lot, which I think would get to me after a while.

- *Louise, my manager at work.* Why didn't I think of her before? She is very attractive, and no one would deny that she is high-powered. And I see her every day, which is a major convenience factor.

I started putting my strategy into action just last week. Louise was doing her weekly rounds, checking up on everybody's progress. When she came to my desk, she asked me how close I was to finishing the "Efficiency Tracker" spreadsheet she'd asked me to do.

"I haven't been working on the Efficiency Tracker," I replied mischievously.

"*What?* It needs to be done and dusted by the end of today! I've got to present the results first thing tomorrow!"

"It's okay," I said, touching her arm in a reassuring manner. She tried her best to ignore the physical contact, but I knew it had made an impression on her – a little flinch gave her away. I continued, "What I meant was, I've delegated the work to Manny. He's going to pass the finished spreadsheet to me by close of business."

She seemed perplexed. "You've got Manny doing it? Manny is an intern. He hasn't even worked out the coffee machine yet. What does he know about the Efficiency Tracker?"

"He didn't know anything before today," I explained, "but I gave him a crash course this morning. I wanted to assign him a task to do that would challenge him and—"

"Fine, whatever," said Louise. "I don't have time to argue about it. To be honest, I don't care who does it. Delegate to a chimpanzee if you want. Just make sure it's done in time for my meeting."

I love it when Louise talks like that! So forthright. I think she was starting to sense that I have management skills of my own and can be trusted to exercise them.

I said, "No worries, just leave it to me" – and I would've touched her arm again, were it not for the fact that she had somewhat backed away by then and was beyond my reach.

"But just a minute," said Louise. "If you haven't been working on the spreadsheet, what *have* you been doing?"

"Credit control," I replied.

"Credit control?"

Now was my chance to impress Louise with my initiative. "I've been phoning all the late payers," I said. "Applying pressure on them. I think you'll find you won't have any problems with them from now on."

"Okay," said Louise. "I would ask you what you said to them, but – well, first, I'm not sure I really want to know, and second" – she tapped her watch – "I'm a bit pressed for time."

She was starting to walk away, but I called after her. "Louise?"

Louise turned round. "What?"

"I was just admiring your nail varnish," I said. "It really suits you. What's the colour called? Would you call it ruby red, or maroon, or cherry, or…?"

She fixed me with an inscrutable stare. There was no doubt in my mind that I had her full attention now.

"Oxblood," she said finally.

As Louise walked away, I mentally congratulated myself on a job well done. I'd set out to make an impression on her, and by the end of the conversation, that's exactly what I'd done. I look forward to getting to know her better, because she is very clearly an interesting and unusual person. Who would have thought there was a nail varnish colour called "oxblood"?

Self-actualisation case study #2: controlling anger

I fully admit that in the past I haven't always managed to live up to my core belief that "you should never be angry at someone unless they deserve it." I remember one incident that followed on from a conversation I overheard between two young men in the seat behind me on the upper level of a London bus. One of these young men had apparently just returned from the United States.

"While I was over there, I shoplifted a book by that Marshall Brewster," he said.

"He's the self-help bloke, right?" asked the second young man.

"He's the *king* of self-help – at least in America he is. Anyway, he had this new book out, *The Marshall Files*. Huge amounts of hype around the release, and they were selling it for a premium price in a sealed package, because supposedly it had these amazing secrets in it, formulas you could apply to make buckets of money, get any woman you want, that sort of thing."

"He sounds like he's full of s--t."

"Yeah, but I wanted to decide for myself," said the first one, "so I nicked the book and I read it cover to cover."

"Did you have a go at following the rules?"

"I did."

"And?"

"He's full of s--t."

Well, you can imagine what my feelings were while listening to all this. At the mention of Marshall Brewster, I could feel my heart beating faster, and when the outrageous verdict on Marshall was delivered, I was gripped by a terrible, hot rage. The fact that this person hadn't even paid for Marshall's book added insult to injury, or perhaps vice versa.

My stop was next. I rose from my seat, actually feeling a bit dizzy as I did so. I turned round to face the two young men, and said to the first one:

"Marshall Brewster is one of the most successful people on the planet, whereas you're just a spotty teenage shoplifter. So instead of slating him, maybe you should read the book again, and this time *pay attention*. You can send him a thank-you note after you've made something of your life."

(In fairness, the young man who had read the Marshall Brewster book was not a spotty teenager. He was probably in his early twenties. But I figured he was hardly in a position to complain about being slandered, given how outrageously he himself had slandered Marshall.)

The two young men looked at each other. Then they got to their feet. I rushed to the stairs and scrambled down to the lower level, followed closely by the two men and their insults.

"Hey, w---er, don't run away!" the first one shouted. "You're *well* out of order, you know that? What are you, the head of the Marshall Brewster Fan Club? Or are you Marshall Brewster's secret lover? Or are you just a loudmouth who doesn't know how to mind his own business?"

"I reckon he's just a w---er," said the second one.

The bus stopped and the doors opened. I could feel a hand on my shoulder as I jumped out. Fortunately, the two young men didn't follow me off the bus. They called out a few final pieces of mockery and abuse, too obscene for me to repeat here, before the doors closed and the bus drove off.

Looking back on it now, I can't say I'm proud of my outburst. What had those two young men done to me? Nothing. True, their comments about Marshall Brewster showed that they were ignorant – indeed, almost bottomlessly ignorant. But ignorance isn't a crime. If anything, they deserved pity. Instead of picking a fight with them, I should have simply let them be.

I'm much better at moderating my anger nowadays. For example, this past weekend, something happened that could easily have made me furious, but I managed to rise above it. I was sound asleep in bed at 7am when I was woken by the ringing of my phone. I bolted out of bed and rushed to the kitchen to answer it.

"Hello?"

"Gary," said the voice on the other end. "It's Martin."

"Martin…?"

"Martin Tierney, your landlord. Gary, it's about your rent – you got the latest rent demand in the post, didn't you?"

"I… don't know. I just woke up. What does it look like?"

"A white piece of paper with a blue border, and the word 'URGENT' in bold near the top. It was sent to you three weeks ago."

"Oh. Yes, it sounds familiar. It sounds like something I've been meaning to deal with."

"It's just that the rent is now considerably overdue, Gary."

"I'm sorry about that. I'll have it for you by the end of the week, okay?"

"That would be very much appreciated if you could do that, Gary."

"All right. Take care, Martin."

"Yes, take care. Bye, Gary."

Well, now, I'm sure you'll agree that 7am on a Saturday is not the most appropriate time to be ringing up demanding rent money. The weekend is supposed to be a time of relaxation, and yet here was Martin Tierney jolting me out of a sound sleep with his telephone call – and not even apologising for it! It would have been no great surprise if I'd come off the phone barely able to contain my fury. But that's not what happened.

Instead, I thought, *He's not trying to be awkward, it's just that he's a landlord, and chasing up rent is what landlords do. Also, he's probably an early riser and it never crossed his mind other people start the morning later than he does. Plus, the way he talked to me was perfectly civil. All in all, there is no reason for me to be angry at him.*

It just goes to show that respecting the basic values of your true self is a recipe for happiness. Thanks to my determination to be true to my most deeply held principles, I was able to enjoy the remainder of my Saturday rather than spoiling it for myself by giving way to ill temper. I fell back asleep without any problem, got another hour of top-up sleep, woke up refreshed, had a leisurely breakfast, showered, dressed, fetched my laptop, and did a solid two hours of work on my book while perched on the huge L-shaped sofa in my lounge. All credit to Martin: he is responsible for the L-shaped sofa, along with the wire-backed bar chairs, the floating shelving, the Warren Evans king-size bed, the American-style fridge with ice maker, the touch-sensitive dimmer switches, and quite a few other impressive features.

Granted, as Sandra pointed out the last time she came round to drop off Jack, there isn't much in the way of decoration, like paintings on the walls, or rugs on the floor, or flowers in a vase on the kitchen table. That sort of thing has never been my strong suit. Maybe when I start a relationship with Louise I'll take her shopping with me and enlist her help in choosing some tasteful items that will add more of a personal touch to the place.

As you might expect, my rent payments aren't cheap, but it's like Marshall Brewster says: *"Once you start LIVING like a successful person, and ACTING like a successful person, you'll be well on your way to BECOMING a successful person!"* I know I'm straying from my topic now, but... it strikes me that this maxim is a perfect example of how Marshall manages to convey the most profound life lessons in just a few carefully chosen words that anyone can understand. Anyone, that is, apart from those idiots on the bus.

Self-actualisation case study #3: environmental awareness

Regardless of how well your efforts to be true to yourself are going, you mustn't become complacent, as this might cause you to take your foot off the accelerator and lose the momentum you've built up. In my case, having just recently experienced the triumph of not getting angry at my landlord, I straightaway took up the challenge of bringing my life into alignment with another of my core beliefs, namely:

The environment is worth preserving for future generations.

What I am going to say to you now about the environment may sound a bit preachy, but that is a risk I am willing to take, because the environment is something I really feel strongly about. People need to wake up to the fact that the destruction of our environment is the most pressing problem that we face today. In ages past, human beings lived in harmony with the world around them. Look at the aboriginal peoples of America, Australia, England, or any other country you'd care to mention. They treated their environment with a level of respect that would be inconceivable today. For one thing, they weren't wasteful. If they were out hunting cows, then at the end of their hunting expedition they didn't throw away the bulk of the slain cow and keep only a small portion, like the brisket or tenderloin. Instead, they found a use for every single part of the cow – the hooves, the hide, the swishy tail, everything. Cows were precious and not to be squandered.

Nowadays, we don't possess anything like the wisdom and quiet dignity of the aboriginal peoples. Everyone wants their beef as quickly and as cheaply as possible, so cows are processed in their billions and tens of billions on factory assembly lines, in the most wasteful way imaginable, with the runoff going into our streams and rivers. And when it's all said and done, the consumer often throws half the burger into the bin anyway, which I think is a sad commentary on the whole system.

It's the same with oil. Back before cars were invented, there used to be a vast amount of oil in the ground – enough to fill up the tanks of hundreds of millions of cars many times over. This huge quantity of pristine subterranean oil was truly one of the wonders of the world, even though nobody knew anything about it at the time. Sadly, in the years since then, we have been drilling oil wells like there's no tomorrow, and this magnificent oozy liquid has been almost totally depleted. The trouble is that we have become completely dependent on oil, not only to power our cars but also to lubricate our squeaky hinges, fill our salad dressing bottles, and grease our baking tins.

So what will we do when the oil runs out? We'll have to get the oil from elsewhere, like from other planets. But nobody would be naive enough to believe that the oil from other planets is anything but a short-term solution. What happens when the oil from other planets runs out? You might reply: *Well, we could all drive electric cars instead of petrol-powered ones; and WD-40 is every bit as good as oil for squeaky hinges; and we could resort to creamy dressings that don't contain any oil; and butter works perfectly well for greasing baking tins.* And maybe you'd be right. But, I don't know, the whole thing still makes me a bit uneasy.

And then there's the matter of trees. Have you ever stopped to think what a world without trees would be like? There would be no shade. Also, since trees absorb carbon dioxide, the lack of trees would be disastrous for human beings, who would fall ill on a massive scale with carbon dioxide poisoning – the same as you get from a faulty boiler. Not to mention the fact that trees are home to hundreds of species, from marmosets to honeybees.

So a world without trees is a terrible prospect, but this is just the sort of world we are headed for because of the rate at which trees are being cut down by lumberjacks all over the globe. Is it worth us paying such a heavy price just so we can continue to gratify our endless hunger for wooden furniture, cricket bats, kitchen towels, greeting cards and pencils? The lumberjacks clearly think so, but then they would, wouldn't they? Exploiting mankind's voracious appetite for trees has put money in their pockets for decades.

Whichever way you look at it, it's clear that we have been treating Mother Nature very badly for some time, and that we need to make amends just as we would if we had treated our own mother badly – otherwise Mother Nature will take her revenge, again just like our own mother would do. That's how nature works. We shouldn't think of nature as simply a source of raw material for us to plunder. Instead, we should think of it as a living entity that has the capacity to feel pain and hold grudges. Having hunted the dodo to extinction, should we really be surprised if we in turn find our towns and cities drenched by tsunamis? Having pumped pollutants into the air, should we really be surprised if earthquakes destroy our vast shopping malls? There's an old farmers' saying: "You reap what you sow". I think this perfectly describes what we've been doing to the environment and how the consequences are boomeranging back at us. If you sow lemons, you reap lemonade. But by the same token, if you sow rose bushes, you shouldn't act all surprised and aggrieved when you get pricked by the thorns.

It scares me that by the time my own child grows up, the environment whose existence I take for granted may no longer exist. There may literally be no more environment. I remember voicing this concern to Sandra once when we were walking in Hampstead Heath on a summer's day, and she said, "Well, there will always be an environment, won't there? I mean, there has to be one, if you think about it, pretty much by definition."

I said, "But that's just the thing – at the rate we're going, I honestly don't think there will be one anymore in a couple of decades."

She said, "But what I mean is, so long as there are animals and plants in the world, those animals and plants are going to have some sort of environment around them. It's not as if we'll ever get to a point where there's no environment anymore."

I shook my head sadly and replied, "I wish I could be as optimistic as you. I just think we've been mistreating the natural world for so long that it might be too late to save the situation."

"Oh, Gary," she said, leaning over and kissing me on the cheek, "your heart's in the right place, isn't it? That's one of the things I love about you. You may be a bit confused about the details, but it doesn't matter."

To this day I'm not sure what she meant by that last remark, as I'm not aware of anything being wrong with my grasp of the details. Still, part of what I must confess I miss about my relationship with Sandra is the interesting conversations we often got into about profound matters like that one. Sandra always had her own point of view, but she had such an easy-going way of expressing herself that I never came close to feeling that she was walloping me over the head with her beliefs.

If you feel strongly about the environment, as I do, then it's not enough just to talk about it. In fact, just talking about it and not bothering to do anything else would be a betrayal of your true self. You need to take some sort of concrete action in support of your belief. In my case, just moments before writing this paragraph, I went online and made a donation to a "green" charity. Ideally, I would have donated several thousand pounds – and in fact I fully intend to do so in future, once the sales of my book make it possible – but at the moment I'm a bit low on cash, so I donated the recommended minimum amount of £15. As soon as the confirmation appeared on the screen that the transaction had gone through, I experienced the warm glow that comes from acting in harmony with one's values.

There's no time like the present to take bold action to uphold the values you believe in. For example, if there's some war you oppose, why not get some of your friends together and march against it? Or if that's too much work, I think there's a website called Stop the War, or something along those lines. You can pledge money to the anti-war cause, and there's probably a dropdown box that lets you select which war you're interested in stopping.

Therapy and the true self: an exercise in futility

I can hear you asking: *Gary, are you sure it's possible for me to awaken the slumbering powers of my true self all on my own? Isn't this one of those psychological things that I need a therapist to help me with?*

The answer is a resounding *No* – I mean to the second question. The answer to the first question is *Yes*. You don't need a therapist to help you to unleash the power of your true self. All a therapist will do is take your money and interrogate you endlessly about your "feelings" towards things that happened too long ago to be of any relevance to your life now. Even if your upbringing was almost entirely happy, as mine was, a therapist will still dig around for evidence of something dark and painful in your past. And when you explain that there isn't any such thing, the therapist will just look at you significantly and say nothing, as if your answer isn't credible and there must be difficult truths you're not acknowledging. What a swindle!

I admit I'm speaking from personal experience. When I was having a tough time with Kim in California, I started seeing a therapist in the hope that I'd learn some techniques to make the situation more tolerable. But the therapist, a woman called Dr Kenner, didn't seem to want to talk about Kim at all. She seemed much more interested in exploring my childhood. So I had to talk about my early memories of Mum and Dad and Vincent, while Dr Kenner nodded sagely and steered the conversation in this direction or that. Sometimes she tried to interpret what I'd said, but her interpretations were pretty far off the mark. At one point she seemed to be suggesting that *I* was jealous of *Vincent*! I couldn't believe it – she had got things completely backwards. She also implied that I was too dependent on my parents, and too close to my mother in particular – again ludicrous notions. Surely the fact that I was in California and my parents were in Surrey speaks for itself! I'll never understand how a person with so many certificates on her wall could get so mixed up. You won't be surprised to learn that I quit therapy after only two sessions, despite Dr Kenner's claim that it would be in my interests to carry on and explore my "issues" in greater depth.

No sooner had I stopped seeing Dr Kenner than Kim started seeing a therapist of her own – a Dr Hirschfeld. After eleven years, she's *still* seeing him – which I think tells you all you need to know about the effectiveness of the treatment. Being in therapy for eleven years has done nothing for Kim apart from making her more convinced than ever that I am the source of all her problems. How do I know this? I know it because, starting about a year ago, Kim developed a habit of ringing me up to tell me about whatever latest discovery she and Dr Hirschfeld had made about how I damaged her. This meant she was ringing me up with alarming regularity – all the more so as she was doing it over Skype and therefore wasn't incurring any call charges. It got to the point where I had to close my Skype account to preserve my sanity.

I don't take the accusations personally. Kim may be my ex-wife, but I bear her no ill will. In fact, I'd like nothing better than for her to sort her life out. Whenever she phones, I make a point of giving a fair hearing to whatever wacky accusations she wants to level at me, after which I offer constructive advice, which she never fails to ignore.

If you're content to live in the past and blame others for your problems, then by all means follow Kim's example and go into long-term therapy. But if your goal is to be the best person you can be, then there's only one person who can help you – and that person is *you*. (Well, and *me* to some extent. But mainly you.) Why consult a therapist when you've got your very own infallible guide –

namely, your true self – right inside your own brain? And listening to the voice of your true self is free, whereas therapists can be quite pricey, so it works out better from a financial perspective as well.

The ancient peoples of the East, the Aborigines of Australia and of course the Native Americans had no need of therapy. How sad that we in the modern world have forgotten much of the wisdom of the ancients, like Crazy Horse, Geronimo, and Buffalo Bill, who were more than capable of mastering their own destinies without lying on a couch for an hour a week talking about their childhoods.

In case any doubt remains in your mind as to the truth of what I'm saying about the futility of therapy, let me recount a recent phone conversation I had with Kim.

When I answered the phone, Kim didn't bother with any pleasantries but said straight off, "Listen up, Sparky. I've just realised something important about how you treated me all those years ago and the long-term effect it had on me. And you need to hear it. You need to face the music rather than blocking your ears and pretending it's nothing to do with you."

"I'm not blocking my ears," I told her, "but I have to tell you, I'm busier than ever with the book I'm writing, so I can't talk for long."

"Of course you're busy. You never had time for me when we were married, with your *'bowling'*" – she said this with heavy sarcasm; I could imagine her rolling her eyes – "and even now, when I never ask you to do anything for me apart from occasionally sparing the teensiest sliver of your day to help me process things" – that's one of Kim's therapy phrases, *process things* – "you're still too busy. It's always all about you, isn't it, Gary? Do you know who you remind me of?"

"Actually, yes, because you mention it every t—"

"You remind me of my dad when I was little. Always shooing me away, telling me to leave him in peace. 'Go play with the dog', he'd say, or 'Go see what Mom is up to' – not that Mom was ever up to anything much besides nursing a hangover or watching the Home Shopping Channel. Next thing you knew, he'd get into his car and he'd be off, God knows where, and wouldn't come back again for hours – or sometimes days. Until eventually he didn't come back at all. I'll tell you what, Gary, there's no getting over something like that – not in ten years, not in twenty years, not *ever*."

"I'm sorry about your dad; you know I am," I told Kim. "But it's like I keep telling you, there's no point obsessing about things that happened years ago. Haven't you read the *SelfActualization.com* article that I sent you a link to, the one called 'No More Living in the Past'?"

"Article, shmarticle," said Kim. "I'm not *living* in the past, Gary. I'm referring to past events in order to understand and deal with the present. Jeez, I would've thought even Marshall Brewster would be able to grasp *that* one." I let this pass. Kim's lack of understanding about Marshall is really one of her major failings, and I've given up trying to correct it. "Anyway, I don't see what's supposed to be so great about living in the present. The present is the pits. I feel like if I have to spend even one more hour at that stupid office I'll go crazy." Kim had recently got a new job doing admin tasks in the head office of a foam rubber manufacturing firm, but clearly it wasn't working out very well. "The worst thing," she said, "is that I can feel Roxanne's eyes on me all the time."

"Who's Roxanne?"

"I mentioned her before. My manager, remember? The Barbie lookalike. She keeps giving me these really funny looks behind my back."

"If you've got your back to her, how do you know she's giving you funny looks?"

"I just know. But never mind that, it doesn't have anything to do with why I called you. I called because I've been working through something with Dr Hirschfeld, and as usual it involves you and your role in ruining my life. Now, listen, Gary. From the moment you seduced me in the restaurant—"

"Hold on a minute, hold on. I didn't seduce you."

"Don't tell me what you did and didn't do, Gary. I was there; I have a vivid memory of it. You swooped in with your fancy car and your fancy English accent and your sports jacket and your tousled hair; you turned on the charm, you went in for the kill – and that was that. I was yours. The whole operation was carried out to perfection. Bravo. Not that I was in a position to put up much resistance. I was twenty-three years old – Christ, what did I know? I was just a kid."

"That's not quite how it was," I pointed out. "For one thing, I didn't even have a car when I first met you. For another, I was just wearing a T-shirt – there was no sports jacket. And I was the same age as you – twenty-three. Come to think of it, you're a couple of months older than me."

"Yada yada yada. You're confusing the issue," she said.

"I don't care whether you were wearing a sports jacket or whatever, and I don't care what your age was. The bottom line is, you were the exotic foreign suitor, you wanted me, and you got me. Hey, I'm not complaining – not about that part anyway. But I'll tell you what, Sparky. When you play the seducer, when you make someone fall for you – and on top of all that, when you *marry* them – there are certain responsibilities that come with that. Granted, for a while there you weren't doing too bad a job of making me feel special. I mean, sometimes when I think back to those days when you were constantly whisking me off to classy bars, and comedy clubs, and those Mongolian barbecue places I liked... and when I think about how I comfortable I was confiding in you... it occurs to me: we really had a good thing going. But then what did you do, Gary? You lost interest; you couldn't keep your *'attention'*" – more heavy sarcasm – "from wandering. And in the end, you threw me on the scrapheap."

"I didn't throw you on the scrapheap," I said. "I just felt it was time for both of us to face up to reality. And by then, I'd evolved to the point where—"

"Don't give me this 'evolve' crap. I know what your evolving amounted to: drinking champagne with your floozies while I sat at home like the biggest chump in Southern California. You walked all over me, is what you did. And that brings me to the main thing I wanted to say to you. Ever since you broke up our marriage, I've been stuck, unable to move forward. Well, now Dr Hirschfeld has helped me to see why. It's because part of me felt I must've done something to *deserve* being walked all over by you. I felt *guilty*, Gary, for somehow being worthless enough to bring it on myself. And the worst thing is, you didn't do anything to ease my guilt. When you left, you could have said to me, 'I admit it, I was a selfish, womanising cad. I cheated on you with numerous women, it's all my fault, it was hurtful to you, and I'm genuinely sorry'. If you'd said something like that, it would have liberated me. But you just couldn't bring yourself to do that for me, Gary, could you? That's why my life has been at a standstill ever since. "

"Come on, Kim," I said. "We've been over this dozens of times. I'm telling you I never cheated on you."

"And now I'm asking you to stop lying to me and admit that you did cheat, and to say you're sorry, so that I can get closure and move on with my life."

The conversation went downhill from there. I refused to apologise for things I hadn't done, and when I tried to be constructive by telling Kim she would be better off embarking on her own personal journey to find her true self than allowing herself to be brainwashed by her therapist, this only seemed to make her more enraged. She in turn infuriated me by remarking that Sandra deserves a lot of credit for recognising me for the philanderer I was and having the guts to leave me.

Well, as a general rule, I try to steer clear of melodrama, because one of the key attributes of successful people is the way they exercise mastery over their own emotions. But in this particular case, I couldn't help myself, because Kim was talking about things that she knew nothing about and were none of her business. "Leave Sandra out of this!" I yelled.

I'm not sure which of us slammed down the phone first.

Later, when I was in a calmer frame of mind, I found myself feeling sorry for Kim. She is riding a wave of bitterness which is taking her further and further away from the calm harbour of success. If only she could put her bitterness aside and spend a few moments figuring out what her true self really wants, she might well find that achieving fulfilment is much simpler than her therapist makes out. Perhaps it would just be a matter of finding a boyfriend who doesn't mind her irrationality. I'm sure that if Kim had such a person in her life she wouldn't feel the need to complain as much – and as a consequence, I wouldn't get so many of these awkward and annoying phone calls from her.

What about your inner child?

Sadly, the world contains countless people like Kim, who for some reason refuse to embrace the self-help techniques I've been describing in this book. Why they're so dead-set against helping themselves, I'm not sure. Maybe it's because, deep down, they don't believe they *deserve* help. Or maybe they have convinced themselves that the techniques are ineffective (in which case, I'd be interested to know how they explain the fact that these techniques have the backing of dozens of reputable self-help experts, myself included!). Or maybe they've reached an age where they assume they've left it *too late* to achieve success.

Believe me, it's never too late to achieve success. No matter what age you are, success is within your grasp – and you mustn't start thinking otherwise, as the more you do so, the more your confidence will be eroded. The more your confidence is eroded, the harder it becomes for you to achieve success. So if you ever find yourself getting preoccupied with the thought that you've missed your chance to become successful, I implore you to take steps to shake off this false belief, before it's too late.

On a related note, you may have asked yourself at some time or other: is it ever *too early* to start on the path to success? If you have children, you'll obviously want them to grow up to be the best and most powerful human beings they can possibly be. So the question naturally arises: when is the right time to start teaching them to pursue success with steely determination?

My own view is that you should wait until your child has a few developmental milestones under his belt. If he hasn't reached the point of holding his head upright, he is not ready. In fact, you should really wait until he has learned to walk, because the pursuit of success is all about getting from a starting point to a destination, and it accordingly requires a certain minimum level of motor skills and coordination.

Jack, my little boy, is four now, which means he is easily old enough to be taught the basics of what it takes to succeed. As his father, I consider it my responsibility not only to instruct him in those basics, but also to inspire him by my own example – in much the same way that, when I was young, my own father lectured me about success and inspired me with *his* example, laying the groundwork for me to become the go-getting individual I am today.

Unfortunately, ever since Sandra and I separated last year, I don't see Jack as often as I would like, but I do get to look after at him at weekends. I am proud to say that despite being only four, Jack is already showing an understanding of human relationships on a deep level. For example, Jack recently overheard me taking a telephone call from a pushy insurance salesman. I didn't need any insurance, and I was trying to remain civil despite the salesman's refusal to take no for an answer – but Jack must have picked up some subtle hint of frustration in my voice, because when I finally managed to get off the phone, he remarked, "Daddy, you were *angry* at that man on the telephone."

"I don't think I was angry," I said.

"Yes, you were."

Suddenly I realised Jack was right. I *had* been angry, but I'd been reluctant to admit this to myself because I didn't like to think of myself as an angry person. The reason Jack was able to make his astute observation is that he, like all children, has a remarkable *innate wisdom*.

Sadly, we tend to lose this innate wisdom as we get older and society conditions us more and more. Once lost, it can never be recovered, except with the aid of self-help books.

The tragic thing is that most of the world's population either never thinks to read a self-help book or is too poor to buy one. This means that, in adult life, the type of wisdom I have in mind is available only to a select few. I'm sure you'll agree with me that this is far from just, but it will continue so long as the people in charge of society suppress children's innate wisdom in favour of the approved, officially sanctioned ways of thinking.

I'm not the only person who holds this view. According to the Internet, somebody named AS Neill once said:

> *A child is innately wise and realistic. If left to himself without adult suggestion of any kind he will develop as far as he is capable of developing.*

I agree that children are innately wise and realistic. On the other hand, I think the part about leaving them without adult suggestion of any kind is probably going too far. Sometimes a child *needs* adult suggestion. For instance, on a rainy Sunday a couple of weeks ago, Jack and I were hanging around in my flat, waiting for the skies to clear so that we could go outside, and Jack was starting to get restless.

"I'm bored," he complained.

"Well," I told him, "here's an idea." I picked up from the floor a cardboard tube that had come from a kitchen towel roll, got out some scissors and cut it a couple of times to make two long flaps. "You could put these on your head, and then you could be a *rabbit*."

Jack seemed keen on the idea, so I found some grey socks which I put over the cardboard flaps to make them look as much like rabbit ears as possible, and then I placed the flaps on either side of Jack's head, tying an old shoelace round his head to keep them in place. For the next twenty minutes, he hopped around the flat in a euphoric state, all the while making high-pitched shrieking sounds, which he'd convinced himself were rabbit noises.

Left to himself, would Jack have ever thought to do this? I very much doubt it. I am reminded of Vincent, and of what happened whenever he was left to himself even for an hour or so as a child. Invariably, he would disappear off into his own little world in which personal development was the last thing on his mind.

I see in Jack all the fine qualities of the "inner child" that I know must dwell inside me, too. A person's inner child is the original source of everything that is valuable about him, and it remains with him throughout his life, whether or not he remains in touch with it. Jack, of course, also currently has what you might call an "outer child". Jack's outer child can be a problem when I try to instil self-help techniques in him. His attention span is not yet always up to it. For instance, when I spent last Sunday with Jack, he mentioned that he had been a bit sad during the week. I asked why, and he said:

"I went to my friend Luke's house and he had a mummy and a daddy living with him, and now I've only got a mummy living with me."

"Oh," I said. "Did you mention this to Mummy?"

"Yes. She said it made her sad too sometimes. Why don't you live with us anymore?"

"Well that's difficult to explain," I said. "But the important thing is that I love you and I don't want you to be sad."

At this point I recalled a self-help method called the Release Technique that I thought would be of use to Jack. The Release Technique is all about letting go of damaging negative emotions that are holding you back – sometimes in a literal sense. People who have been crippled have actually walked again thanks to this very powerful method! So I said to Jack:

"Try and let go of all your sad feelings and imagine them floating far away, and then you won't feel sad because those feelings will be gone."

"Where will they go?"

"They'll go high up into the air."

Jack considered this for a moment, and then he asked, "What if they land on Mummy and make her more sad?"

"I don't think they will," I replied. "The way it works is, once the feelings float up into the air, they never come back down again."

"Will birds crash into them?"

"No."

"Will aeroplanes crash into them?"

"No."

"Will aliens crash into them?"

"No."

"Are there aliens?"

"I'm not sure. Probably."

"What colour are they?"

I think by this time the technique had at least succeeded in distracting Jack from his sad thoughts. Anyway, regardless of how much immediate impact my words had, I imagine they will have lodged in his brain somewhere, leaving him better equipped to cope with his negative feelings the next time they take hold of him.

Later in the conversation, I had occasion to ask him if Sandra was going out much – this was purely because I was concerned he might feel he wasn't getting enough attention from his parents – and he replied:

"Mummy went to the cinema with Carl."

"Who's Carl?" I asked.

"He's a man who's a friend of Mummy's. He came to our house once."

"Did he? Why did he come to your house?"

"I don't know. I think because he was hungry."

"What makes you think he was hungry?"

"Because Mummy gave him lunch."

I'm sure there must have been another reason why Carl turned up, and I actually felt a bit frustrated at not being able to learn more about the circumstances, but this wasn't Jack's fault, and there was no point pursuing it. Instead, I asked:

"Do you like Carl?"

"I did like him, but I don't like him now," said Jack.

"Why don't you like him?"

"I liked him before because he gave me a magazine with a Hotwheels car stuck on it. But then he gave me a magazine with nothing on it, so I don't like him now."

"But it was nice of him to give you a magazine."

"And I had to go to bed early because Mummy was going to the cinema with him, so now I don't like Mummy."

At this point I thought Jack was perhaps being a little unfair to Sandra, so I tried to help him *reframe* the situation. "By going to bed early," I pointed out, "you probably ended up having lots and lots of sleep, so you must've felt really well rested the next day. Also, I'm sure you got the chance to look at your magazine in bed, which must have been fun."

"I wanted to play with my cars. Carl called me Champ. My name's Jack, not Champ. What does Champ mean?"

"It means he thinks you're great. So... does Mummy like Carl?"

"Well, I think she does a bit, because she gave him lunch when he was hungry. Why don't you still live with us? I don't want Carl to live with us."

"What? Did Mummy say he was going to?"

"She said to Luke's mum that he was her friend, but she didn't know if she wanted more than a friend. What does 'more than a friend' mean?"

"It... well, er, I don't know what it means."

"Oh. Can I have an ice cream?"

"Do you think she wants to live with Carl?" I wondered aloud. "I mean, that would be really good for her to have someone else for company now that I'm not there, wouldn't it?"

"Can I have an ice cream with a chocolate flake in it?"

So, as you can see, although Jack's intelligence and intuition are apparent, he does, at the moment, find it difficult to stick to a subject and explore it in depth.

Now, obviously, if Sandra feels ready to start a relationship with someone new, I am pleased for her. Not that the friendship she's struck up with this Carl person will necessarily lead to anything. It's still early days, after all.

But the larger point is that so long as she puts Jack first, which I know she will, she has my blessing to start up a relationship with whoever she imagines is suited to her. Sandra has as much right to pursue a relationship with this Carl person as I have a right to pursue a relationship with a high-powered, successful woman such as Louise.

Whenever it comes time for me to say goodbye to Jack after a day in his company, I always feel a pang of sadness. For me, Jack represents the remarkable inner child within us all. He exemplifies the innocence and goodness that we should all strive to recover. Most of us have neglected our inner child, to our detriment. My hope is that, with my assistance, Jack will preserve his inner child in all its purity – while becoming a mature and fully rounded adult, of course.

True self, false self, inner child, inner critic... a guide for the perplexed

Now that I've described to you what the "inner child" consists of and why it's so important, I suppose you might be wondering what the relationship is between your inner child and your true self. Rest assured that all will be explained. Much of what I'm going to say might seem confusing, but I can assure you that this is only because the phenomena I'm describing are extremely complex.

If you cast your mind back to what I said at the beginning of this chapter, you will recall that your true self is the part of you that is infinitely good, infinitely right, and knows exactly what you need in order to flourish. And your inner child? Well, your inner child is also infinitely good, also infinitely right, and also knows exactly what you need in order to flourish. So, really, your true self and your inner child are practically indistinguishable – which isn't surprising when you consider that your true self is actually an *expression* of your inner child. Or to be more precise, your true self consists of your *experience* of the *demands* made by your inner child.

Does that make sense? If not, you might want to re-read the previous paragraph until it does, otherwise you probably won't grasp what I'm going to say next.

I remarked a moment ago that your true self consists of your experience of the demands made by your inner child, but equally I could have said the reverse, that your inner child consists of your experience of the demands made by your true self. You can think of your true self and inner child as being *two sides of the same coin* – except that the coin image is a bit misleading, because your true self and your inner child are less like two sides than they are like *two aspects of the same side*.

Maybe a Möbius strip would be a better analogy.

Sorry, I know I'm not explaining it very well. The whole thing might be easier to get to grips with if you are familiar with what Christians call the *Holy Trinity*. (If you're not acquainted with the Holy Trinity, I recommend the book *Heavens Above: A Grab-Bag of Spirituality*, which contains an informative discussion of it.) The Holy Trinity is made up of three beings that differ from each other, while at the same time all being sort of identical because they are actually part of each other. In other words, even though they're the same, they have different facets. And yet they're also different people. But also the same person.

Once you have wrapped your head round this

phenomenon, you should have no difficulty coming to terms with the "Holy Twosome" of true self and inner child.

All right. Phew. Now that I've explained the relationship between true self and inner child, I'd like to clear up a few other points that people sometimes have difficulty with. I have noticed that some self-help literature speaks of the *wounded inner child*. This phrase makes no sense. Your inner child can never be anything but happy and good and wise, so how could there ever be such a thing as a "wounded inner child"? The very idea is absurd.

I suspect what these authors are actually getting at is as follows: sometimes, as a result of bad parenting, the inner child gets pushed aside, leaving a vacancy that gets filled by a new, alien self which is anxious and miserable. I call this the *false inner child*, to distinguish it from the *true inner child* I was talking about earlier.

You probably have one or more *false adult selves*, too – these are not to be confused with any *false inner child selves* you may have. Oh, and you almost certainly have an *inner critic* which holds you back by constantly disapproving of everything you do. In fact, you have *multiple* inner critics, because an inner critic is something that dwells inside each false adult self. Example: Suppose you have five false adult selves; then you have five inner critics.

By the way, whatever you do, don't confuse your inner critic(s) with your *conscience*. Your conscience belongs to your true self, and is therefore always right, whereas your inner critic is forever opposing your true self, and is therefore always wrong.

Here is a pictorial representation of everything I have just been saying. It should help you to visualise how your various selves fit together.

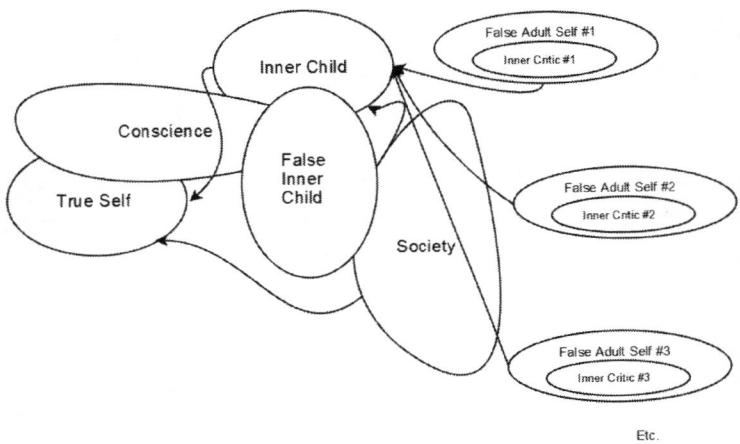

Etc.

You also have a *soul*. That's beyond the scope of this book. If you're interested in learning more about it, have a look at the *Heavens Above* book I mentioned.

Anyway, enough of this hair-splitting. The crucial point is: you need to get in touch with your inner child. To do this, think back to when you were very young – four years old at most. Try to recall the sights, sounds, smells, thoughts, and emotions you experienced at that time. Avoid getting too hung up about "accuracy". The primary aim of the exercise is simply to get you into the *inner child mindset*.

I myself did this exercise late last week while alone in my flat. I lay down on my sofa and shut my eyes, and this is what came to me:

I am lying on my back in a clearing in the sunshine. I am very little. Blades of grass are tickling my face. I hear my father's voice; it is deep and reassuring. "What a fine boy," he says. "What a fine, talented boy."

Mummy brings me a vanilla milkshake to drink. A dinosaur emerges from the forest, and I ride it. Vincent, who is just a baby, gazes at me in awe. Mummy says to me, "You can do anything, darling, anything at all."

I see a rainbow and clamber up it as high as I can go, and then I let myself slide back down the rainbow to the earth. I feel blissfully happy. I feel supremely confident. I feel the dizzying sense of my whole life stretching out before me, full of possibility.

As these images passed before my mind, I experienced an overwhelming feeling of connection to what I can only assume was my inner child.

Please don't misunderstand me. I'm not claiming that this recollection of mine is true in every detail, or even in any detail. Its emotional truth, on the other hand, is undeniable.

The thought did cross my mind, however, that I might be missing a trick by avoiding any consideration of the *actual* truth about my childhood. There is a great deal about my childhood that I've forgotten, and perhaps if I could unearth some biographical details about my early years, I'd gain new and valuable insight into what my inner child is like. So I phoned my mother to ask if she could supply any such details.

"Well," said my mother, "you were always keen on being the best at things, from a very young age. You and Tim Parsons used to play marbles. Tim Parsons was very good at it. He kept winning and winning, which upset you, but you didn't give up. You said to me with complete conviction, 'I'm going to *beat* him, Mummy'. And sure enough, just after your fifth birthday, you and Tim played a game of marbles – we'd given you a new set of marbles as a present – and you trounced him! I remember it very clearly, because Dad was refereeing. He had to penalise Tim a few times for improper shooting, which broke Tim's concentration, and to your credit, you capitalised fully on that. Oh, the look of happiness and pride on your face when you won! I can still picture it."

It was wonderful to be told this. Here was evidence that among the qualities of my inner child, from the very start, was *the determination to succeed.*

My mother went on to relate several more stories from my childhood. Apparently, when I was nine years old, I cut some coloured paper into squares, which I numbered and sold to my classmates as raffle tickets. When people asked me what the prize was, I said:

"It's a *mystery prize* – even I don't know what it is yet. It could be anything. I won't decide what it is until just a couple of days before the draw."

And when people asked me what the raffle was for, apparently I just smiled mysteriously and didn't say anything.

Everyone was intrigued, so I got lots of takers. My plan was to spend half the proceeds on the prize and keep the rest. But when the head teacher found out what I was doing, I had to refund everyone's money.

"Well, you can imagine my reaction," said my mother. "I was furious. I said to Dad, 'Who does this head teacher think he is? Gary was being enterprising; he was being a good salesman, just like you are. He should be *rewarded*.'"

I was touched. "Thank you for believing in me, Mum," I said, "and for defending me."

"I've always believed in you, Gary," said Mum, "and I still do. And so does Dad. Just the other day, I said to him something like, 'Lately I've been starting to get the feeling Gary is on the verge of something big. I really think this is his time.' And he looked up from the magazine he was reading and said, 'I know that feeling. I've had it many times over the years, too many times to count.' So you see, Dad believes in you. He always has done. And now that you're on the verge of success, you just have to avoid getting sidetracked. Even if you haven't completely got over what happened with Sandra, you've got to somehow move on and—"

"I am moving on," I interrupted.

"Oh, good. Because at the end of the day, she just wasn't quite right for you. You know that, don't you, Gary?" I guess I did know it, but for some reason I felt slightly uncomfortable hearing Mum make this point yet again, so I stayed silent. Maybe Mum picked up on my discomfort, because she then said, "It's not that she isn't a fine person in many ways, it's not that Dad and I aren't grateful to her for bringing Jack into the world, but when all is said and done, what matters most is you and your future. What you have now is the chance to really make something of yourself. This is your time, Gary."

Those words echoed in my mind: *This is your time, Gary.*

When I looked at my situation objectively, there was no denying she was right. Here I was, not just dreaming of writing a self-help guide, but actually doing it! Already I had produced nearly two whole chapters of my book, a book which had the potential to improve the lives of millions. And with every page that I wrote, I was getting closer to my goal of becoming a renowned self-help expert.

Flashing forward a few months, I could see it all: the dust jacket photo (me seated in an armchair in front of a bookcase, smoking a pipe); the reviews ("An astonishing work from Britain's answer to Marshall Brewster. Gary Speedwell has written *the* indispensable guide to achieving personal freedom, wealth, power, fame, and inner peace in the 21st century"); the Breakfast News appearances ("What your viewers may not realise, Charlie and Victoria, is that there's no *one secret* that's going to propel them out of their humdrum existences and into the future they've always dreamed of. Instead, there are *lots of secrets*. And my book makes those secrets available to the average British reader for the very first time").

Not to mention the sweeping lifestyle changes my new-found wealth would bring. One of the first things I would do is whisk Louise off to some exotic island, preferably somewhere non-malarial, with ready access to the best possible seafood – a destination so exclusive as to be entirely free of the usual hordes of low-budget holidaymakers, a place where we can go snorkelling and drink cocktails on the beach. This was the kind of life that lay in store for me, because, as Mum had pointed out, *this was my time*. There was no doubt about it: I was going to achieve phenomenal success!

And so are you, let's not forget. If you follow the

advice in this book, the lifestyle I've been describing can be yours, too. It might differ in some details, of course. Maybe you don't like snorkelling. The key point is, whatever leisure activities most appeal to you, there will be top-tier holiday getaways that will cater for them. You might want to go on the Internet and do some preliminary holiday planning now, to save time later.

3

———

RELATIONSHIPS

Relationships: an essential part of life

It's said that behind every great man, there's a great woman. If you are a man who aspires to success, you should make it one of your top priorities to get into a relationship with somebody who loves you, supports you, and frequently reiterates how physically attractive she finds you. If you're a woman, you can have the privilege of *being* that somebody. And if you're a particularly ambitious woman – which, come to think of it, any woman who buys this book must be – then you need to make sure your partner is the type of man who will support you in your own ambitions.

If he isn't willing to offer you this support, the first thing you need to ask yourself is whether you might benefit from putting your ambitions on hold. And if the answer is no, then frankly you may need to consider finding a new partner.

There are a couple of administrative points I should cover before I continue. Though I considered having two separate chapters of relationship advice, one for men and one for women, in the end I decided that having just one chapter would work better. For simplicity, my advice in this chapter will mostly be addressed to male readers.

If you are female, don't worry: a lot of the advice can be made to apply to you too, if you change some of the words round in your mind. For example, when you see "aftershave", mentally replace it with "eau de toilette".

Nobody can deny that intimate personal relationships are an essential part of life – although to be fair, bachelor life has a lot going for it, too. I am living a bachelor lifestyle at the moment, and the fact that I don't have anyone telling me what to do is definitely a big plus.

When I was living with Sandra, she would regularly say things to me like, "Would you mind putting those shoes away, Gary?" She was well intentioned, but there's no getting away from the fact that she was curtailing my freedom by making such demands. The putting-away-shoes thing was about what *she* wanted, not what *I* wanted. Now that I'm on my own, I have the freedom to do whatever I see fit to do, whenever I see fit to do it, and to avoid doing whatever I see fit to avoid doing, whenever I see fit to avoid doing it.

On the flip side, the other day I tripped over a pair of shoes I'd left lying in the middle of the floor, injuring my ankle and spilling the cup of coffee I'd been carrying. Whoever it was who said that freedom comes at a price was not entirely wrong.

If you're the type of person who hops from one serious relationship to the next with barely a pause for breath in between, I urge you to give yourself a proper break next time you split up with someone. Allow yourself to experience bachelor life for a reasonable period of time, say eight months to a year. Once you've done that, you'll be able to tackle your next relationship with renewed vigour.

If, on the other hand, you're the opposite sort of person – the sort who finds it difficult to get into a relationship in the first place – here is a piece of advice I believe may help. Nine times out of ten, when people encounter obstacles to getting into a relationship, it is because they undervalue themselves. They think, "Why would anybody want me? I don't drive a fast car, I don't know any good jokes, I can't speak any foreign languages, I don't own any designer outfits, I can't mix cocktails, and my culinary skills are only mediocre." They're missing the point. The fact is, *none of these things matter.* All that matters is your level of confidence, because confidence is what women find attractive.

If the car you drive isn't particularly fast, my response is: so what? You can still *tell* her that you drive a fast car, and if you say it confidently enough, your words will ring true to her – and just as important, *your words will ring true to you, too.* When you get to the stage of taking her somewhere in your car, you will probably drive faster than you normally do, thanks to your new-found confidence. In this way, your statement about driving a fast car becomes a self-fulfilling prophecy. (Don't get me wrong, I'm not advocating reckless driving. You should adjust your speed to the road conditions, and always wear a seatbelt.)

And that's why a key part of my strategy for winning Louise is to *radiate confidence.* Last week, as you may remember, I impressed Louise by boldly delegating one of my responsibilities to an intern called Manny. Unfortunately, when I sent Louise the spreadsheet I'd asked Manny to complete, it turned out to be full of mistakes. Louise was scheduled to give a presentation about the figures in the spreadsheet the very next morning, and Manny's incompetence had put a major spanner in the works.

When Louise came over to my desk after her disastrous presentation, she was furious, and I don't blame her – Manny had really left her in the lurch. Her face was flushed and she stood with her hands on her hips. (I couldn't help but note how attractive she looked in this pose, but her expression told me that a compliment at this point would not be welcome.) "The spreadsheet was *completely useless*!" she declared.

"Really?" I said. "Was it that bad? Well, in that case I'm just as disappointed in Manny as you are. I'll definitely give him a good talking-to. Or have you spoken to him already?"

She took a breath that made her bosom heave. "No, I haven't talked to him," she said. "I'm talking to *you*."

To me, this was quite a revealing statement. It showed that Louise considered me a responsible person who could be addressed as a fellow leader rather than a run-of-the-mill employee. Before I could decide how to express my appreciation for this vote of confidence, she said:

"I'm going to ask you to do something for me, Gary."

"Consider it done," I replied.

"Well, let me ask it first. I want you to see to it that nothing like this ever happens again. Can I trust you to do that?"

"Of course you can trust me," I told her. "You can trust me 100 per cent. In fact, you can trust me *1,000* per cent."

After a brief silence, Louise replied, "Just 100 per cent will do."

"Then 100 per cent it is," I said with a smile.

She didn't smile back, but this was understandable, as she was clearly still quite annoyed about Manny letting her down. "Okay," she said. "It's unfortunate that this has happened, but it's good we had this talk."

"I feel the same way," I replied. Just as she was about to walk away, I added, "I like talking to you, Louise."

This was the sort of line I was felt sure would grab her attention, and I was right: it stopped her in her tracks. She gave me a quizzical look.

"What?"

"When you speak," I continued, "do you know who your voice reminds me of? A film star."

"A film star...?"

"Imelda Staunton."

"Imelda Staunton? Isn't she quite old?"

"Well, I'm thinking of Imelda Staunton back in the early 1990s, when she was in—"

"Let me just stop you there, Gary," said Louise, "because I've really got to go now." And in a flash, she was gone. You know, it's funny: something I've noticed about Louise is that when we're having a conversation, she always seems to be either on the verge of walking off, or actually in the process of walking off. There's something really sexy about that!

An image took shape in my mind: an image of Louise, but not in her office attire. The Louise I saw in my mind was standing on a beach in a red bikini which showed off her hourglass figure in its full magnificence. She and I were together on the exotic island I mentioned at the end of the previous chapter. "What shall we do now, Gary?" I imagined her saying. "Shall we hold hands and look out at the sea? Shall we build sand sculptures? Shall we have more mojitos? I'm so in love with you, Gary. I never imagined I could feel like this. Ever since you won my affections after getting beneath my flinty-businesswoman exterior, my life has been completely transformed. Shall we... shall we go back to the hotel room? Yes, I think that's what we should do..." She turned and walked towards the hotel, casting a brief glance over her shoulder at me as she did so. I watched her shapely figure for a few moments, and then followed her.

I want her so much! But there's no reason for her to know that – yet.

Taking control

Every woman without exception, from the most humble chambermaid to the most powerful corporate vice president, wants a partner who's not afraid to take control. There are good biological reasons for this. The very survival of our primitive ancestors depended on their ability to take decisive action in life-or-death situations. If a cavewoman's husband wasn't able to be decisive, imagine the consequences in the event of a dinosaur attack. The whole family would probably have been wiped out. I mean, it's not as if the cavewoman would stand a chance of fending off the dinosaur all on her own.

When I was having a beer with my bowling buddy Nick a couple of months ago and the subject got on to women, I explained all this to him. He just laughed and said, "You know what you are, Gary? You're a classic misogynist." I couldn't believe what he was saying! *A misogynist!* A misogynist is somebody who hates women. How can I be a misogynist? I respect and admire and care about women. I want women to be protected and looked after. And who better to do that than a man?

It's a philosophy I've always applied to my own relationships. Take my relationship with Sandra. Shortly after I first started going out with her in 2007, I learned that she was a compulsive walker. I'd never known anyone to take such pleasure in the act of walking. She walked to work, she walked in parks and on walking trails in her free time, she loved "walking holidays", and whenever we spent time together at weekends, walking was always her preferred activity.

As a result, I was getting lots of exercise, but there were times when, truth be told, I just didn't feel like walking. A walk on a pleasant summer's day is one thing, but this was November and the days were uniformly grey and cold and windy. I knew that if I didn't assert my own needs now, I'd find it many times harder to assert them later. In short, I had to take control as a matter of urgency.

So the next time Sandra suggested one of these epic walks – in Richmond Park, of all places, which was *miles* away – I put my foot down. "Actually," I said, "I was thinking we could have a cosy afternoon in a pub, like the Copper Kettle."

"Really?"

"Yes, we could nab one of the sofas and order a bottle of red wine and maybe some potato wedges, or whatever else you fancy, and just spend the afternoon relaxing and chatting."

"Oh. So... no Richmond Park?"

"No Richmond Park."

"Well," she said, "all right. The way you're describing it, it does sound appealing." And so we spent an afternoon at the Copper Kettle – an afternoon which has gone down in history as one of the most perfect of my life. The comfy leather sofa was perfect, the Frank Sinatra tracks playing in the background were perfect, being inside a warm pub on a cold November day was perfect, the wine was perfect, the potato wedges were perfect (a sprinkling of parmesan cheese seems to make all the difference) – and what was most perfect of all was having Sandra there on that sofa with me. Years later, of course, it became apparent that Sandra wasn't the right woman for me after all, but I don't see why this should take away from what I felt that afternoon. Whenever I cast my mind back to the afternoon in question, without fail the feelings come rushing back. This doesn't completely make sense, but then, why should it? There's still an enormous amount we don't understand about the workings of the human mind.

Anyway, to resume my account of our pub visit: by five o'clock or so, Sandra was stretched out on the sofa, wine glass in hand, shoes off, her feet resting in my lap.

She was telling me about classical music, a subject which I knew nothing about. "First there's Bach," she said. "If you want to know what Bach's music is like, think of a hand-woven rug with an intricate pattern. The closer you look at the pattern, the more you find patterns in the pattern. Then there's Mozart. Mozart is like... like a magnificent formal garden, where all the plants and flowers and fountains and statues are arranged just so, and the paths are broad, but if you spend long enough there, you become aware of the shadows, long shadows." This was what Sandra tended to get like when she'd had a bit to drink – cryptic. And yet at this particular moment it seemed to me that I understood every word she was saying.

"What about Beethoven?" I asked.

"I was getting to him. Pour me some more wine and I'll tell you about Beethoven."

I poured her some more wine, and she said, "Listening to Beethoven's music is... let me think about this... it's like being in a plush old-fashioned train carriage, with wood panelling and beautiful table lamps, but instead of making its way slowly across the countryside, the train is zooming up and down mountains, into thunderstorms, through forests, into blizzards – and you're sitting there in your train carriage, gazing out of the window as all this sublimity rushes past."

"How do you do that?" I asked.

"I don't know," she said. "I think about the music and say what comes into my head. I'm sure you could do the same if you tried."

"I couldn't!"

"You could. Right, I'll prove it to you. I'm going to say the name of a musician you like, and you're going to tell me what their music reminds you of. Okay… Bruce Springsteen."

"No, it's no good, I can't—"

"Yes, you can. Just think about one of your favourite Bruce Springsteen songs and tell me what comes into your mind."

So I thought about "Born to Run". In my head I heard the bracing saxophone-and-keyboard intro, and then Bruce launching into his vocal, singing in the most heartfelt terms imaginable about work, and cars, and the American dream.

And though the song was only playing in the privacy of my head, I experienced the familiar surge of hope and excitement that Bruce Springsteen's music has always produced in me, as far back as I can remember. I don't know how long I was sitting there silently running through the song in my mind – maybe ten seconds, maybe twenty – but at a certain point, something clicked, and I heard myself telling Sandra:

"Listening to Bruce Springsteen's music is like hearing someone take a hatchet to the cramped wooden box you've been trapped in for so long, and then the exhilaration when the box splinters open, and the light floods in, and your rescuer is standing there with his arm outstretched, saying 'Come with me, my friend – you're free!'"

Sandra raised her eyebrows.

I said, "I don't know where that came from."

She smiled at me, nudged me with her foot, and

declared, "It came from inside your head, my lovely poetic boyfriend."

A little thrill went through me, because nobody had ever called me lovely and poetic before. Kim, in her day, had called me a lot of things, but even at the best of times she never came close to calling me lovely and poetic. At the worst of times, she called me the sorts of names that don't bear repeating.

I gazed at Sandra, who was in turn gazing at me, and I thought to myself: *there's something so graceful about her, so genuine, so unforced.*

And then I thought: *I really am lucky to have her.*

And then it occurred to me that she might consider herself lucky to have me. I seemed to be making her happy somehow. Part of the explanation must surely have been that I'd shown myself to be decisive and in control. If I hadn't decreed that we should go to the Copper Kettle rather than Richmond Park, we would probably have had a decent time, but not anything like the magical afternoon we actually ended up having.

Sandra felt it was time to leave, and I agreed. She said, "We could go to mine – I could put something by Beethoven on the stereo and tell you about it while I cook you dinner. Or we could go to yours, and you could play me a Bruce Springsteen album and tell me about it while you cook *me* dinner."

Her tone of voice made it clear that she preferred the second option, even if she wasn't going to come out and state her preference explicitly. So I took control, making an executive decision that we would go to my flat. And when she gently put forward the suggestion that we could walk to mine rather than taking public transport, I took control again, making an executive decision that we would indeed walk to my flat.

True, my flat was about three miles away from the Copper Kettle. But I felt I ought to indulge her, as she hadn't had much of a chance to stretch her legs that day.

All of which illustrates how a willingness to take control is an essential ingredient for a fulfilling relationship. Now, you might protest: *Hold on a minute, Gary – your relationship with Sandra failed, so how can you use it to support the point you're making?* My response would be: it didn't fail, thank you very much. What happened was that Sandra and I reached a mutual decision that going our separate ways would be in our best interests. That's completely different.

Anyway, I can just as easily illustrate my point with reference to a couple who are still together: my mother and father. I remember when I was about thirteen years old, my father was vying with a couple of other salesmen for a promotion. He had a clear advantage over them, given his experience (he was the longest-serving candidate by far). My mother had said to him, "When you get the promotion, we should all go out to the Bingham to celebrate." The Bingham was a five-star hotel with a very fine restaurant attached to it. Dad was all in favour of that idea, but subsequently my parents learned that the Bingham's restaurant would be closed for renovations in a couple of weeks' time, just when the promotion was going to be announced.

"Well," said Mum, "I suppose we could go to the Seafood Shack instead."

"Not the Seafood Shack!" Dad protested. "If we're going to celebrate, we should celebrate properly. We'll go to the Bingham."

"How can we go to the Bingham," Mum asked, reasonably enough, "if it's going to be closed?"

"We can shift the date," he replied. "We'll celebrate the promotion *in advance*." So a few days later we all went out to the Bingham and had a blowout meal. It felt like the biggest treat imaginable, and it was all thanks to my father. I remember Mum and Dad clinking glasses and toasting Dad's upcoming success.

Then something unexpected and very unfortunate happened. My father was turned down for the promotion. The successful candidate had, according to my father, obtained the position by shamelessly ingratiating himself with the boss – a tactic that Dad would never have dreamed of stooping to. I remember the moment when Dad announced the bad news to Mum. She wept, and the two of them hugged, and Dad reassured her, "They think they can keep me down, *but they can't*. Nobody has ever kept me down and nobody ever will." And then he revealed that part of him didn't really want the promotion anyway. Career-wise, it would've been a dead end, whereas staying in his present position meant his options were still wide open.

So infectious was Dad's positive attitude that we all soon came round to feeling like we should be celebrating the fact that he *hadn't* got the promotion!

Unfortunately, dining at the Bingham had somewhat broken the bank, so we had to economise for a while. Here again my father took charge, deciding we would postpone our long-overdue roof repair. The water leakage in my bedroom became severe enough that I had to share with Vincent for a few months. But the inconvenience of losing my bedroom was more than made up for by my pride in having a father with such remarkable strength of character.

The elusive spark

Naturally, everyone wants to have a successful relationship, like the one my parents have. But what's the secret to making your relationship work on a day-to-day level? The answer, I'm afraid, is that there is no one factor that can be singled out. There are probably hundreds of ingredients that go into making a successful relationship – and let's face it, you don't want to be monitoring your relationship against a checklist of hundreds of items. You are a busy person, and you have better things to do.

What you need is a smaller checklist containing just the top five or six ingredients, the sort of thing that will fit on a little slip of paper suitable for carrying around in your wallet for easy reference. By the well-known "80-20 rule", simply making sure that you have those five or six ingredients in your relationship will ensure that your relationship is 80 per cent successful!

That's before we even take into account the success my book is going to bestow upon you in other areas of life – financial, spiritual, etc – which is bound to have a knock-on effect on your relationship. It should get you up to 95 per cent easily.

So let's get started. The first ingredient I'd like to

address is what I call *the elusive spark*. No matter how promising your relationship looks on paper, it's not going to succeed if you and your partner don't have a special intangible something that makes you gel. Call it chemistry. Or call it magic. Or just call it that elusive spark, like I was calling it to begin with.

How do you recognise the spark? Well, in reviewing my interactions with Louise, one thing that's immediately obvious is that way we feed off each other's responses in the witty rapid-fire exchanges we're always having. She'll say, "Gary, this boilerplate text you've drafted reads like an excerpt from a self-help manual. Are you sure you're all right? Should we be increasing the dosage of your medication?" And I'll instantly come back with, "No, but I'm sure a pay rise would sort me out!" Or she'll say, "You've been spending quite a lot of time churning out those waffles lately, Gary. Anyone would think you're training for the World Waffle Championships." And I'll say, "Yes, I've been practising for months!"

It's these sorts of comical exchanges that bode really well for a relationship, because they show that the two people are on the same wavelength. Just by listening to a couple talk to each other for few minutes, you can get a very solid sense of whether they've got the elusive spark.

I always find it sad when I encounter a couple who lack any discernible spark. The few times I've visited my brother Vincent and his partner Claire, I have been struck by the complete absence of any spark between the two of them. Poor Vincent! Sometimes I marvel at the extent to which a person can deceive themselves. Vincent is plainly convinced that he is happy with Claire, even though, as any outside observer can see, she's quite ordinary. If only Vincent would wake up to the reality of his situation, he'd recognise that his best option is to end his relationship with Claire and seek out a quirky, interesting woman who will challenge him and take him out of his comfort zone – someone, that is, with whom there might be some chance of a spark.

The fact that Vincent has been with Claire for nine years is proof of just how entrenched his self-deception has become. The last time Vincent invited me over, which happened to be a few weeks after I separated from Sandra ("Getting away might take your mind off things," Vincent had said to me – quite unnecessarily, as my mind was in fact almost entirely reconciled to the break-up by that point), Vincent proposed that the three of us go on an outing to a local museum. This museum was devoted to, of all things, fossils!

Tagging along with Vincent and Claire, I had the opportunity to observe at close range how they interacted with each other. One of my abiding memories is of them standing together, hand in hand, wordlessly staring at a fossil for what must have been at least a minute and a half! Talk about a lack of chemistry! Couldn't one of them at least have made some sort of wisecrack about the fossil, to break the silence? In the event, when Claire finally did say something, it was to ask Vincent some question about the science of fossils – which Vincent then answered at some length, even getting quite animated in the course of his explanation. And Claire actually went along with this charade, patiently listening to his explanation with a face full of curiosity. Anybody would've thought he was telling her about the ideas of Marshall Brewster rather than palaeontology! The whole thing was just incredibly hollow and false.

I was supposed to be staying over at Vincent and Claire's house for two nights, but I found the experience of being in their company so depressing that I made an excuse and cut my visit short by a day.

Trying to conjure up a spark in a relationship that has always been spark-free is no easy feat. If you are in such a relationship, you *could* try to transform yourself into the sort of person your partner is better able to "click" with – but, to be honest, it's probably a fool's errand. To illustrate: let's suppose your partner is a fan of the movies of Adam Sandler, whereas you yourself find Adam Sandler annoying and believe his films to be formulaic and asinine. Now, maybe with enough practice you can train yourself to sit through an entire Adam Sandler film. And maybe, just maybe, you can one day reach a point where you positively *revel* in the humour of Adam Sandler. That would be a victory of sorts. But given that you will have won this victory only at the terrible cost of turning yourself into an Adam Sandler-loving buffoon, is it really worthwhile?

If you're going to transform yourself into a different person, transform yourself into the person *you* want to be, regardless of whether or not it heightens the chemistry in your relationship. If anything, if you want to heighten the chemistry in your relationship, you should be seeking to transform *your partner*. And if she isn't willing or able to change, you have to ask whether you might not be better off with somebody else.

Love

There are many unfortunate people in this world who can't seem to manage to find anyone to share their life with and who eventually reach the despairing conclusion that they're "just not loveable". I wish I could get all of these people into a big lecture theatre and explain to them where they're going wrong. I'd say to them, "Sure, you're not loveable *now*, but it doesn't always have to be that way. You can take steps to make yourself loveable. And the first and most important of those steps is to *learn to love yourself.*"

Think about it. If you, of all people, don't love yourself, how can you expect other people to love you? You can't. A person who doesn't love themselves puts people off, whereas a person who loves themselves radiates confidence and joy and sunshine. So, whatever unloving thoughts you've been having about yourself, simply suppress them. Don't say, "There's no way I'm going to get that promotion, because I'm a worthless incompetent." Or: "There's no way I'm going to make that soufflé rise, because I'm a bungling halfwit." Or: "There's no way I'm going to get that reasonably attractive member of the opposite sex to give me their phone number, because I'm a flabby, graceless, slow-witted, inarticulate weirdo." Instead, say, "I deserve to be loved, because I am one of the most special people in the entire world."

Even if you aren't really one of the most special people in the entire world, the important thing is that you *tell* yourself you are. Keep telling yourself until you believe it, because believing it is what will enable you to love yourself.

Once you love yourself, other people will love you, too. This may seem inexplicable, but it has a solid scientific basis. According to the eminent scientist Dr Jimmy "Hawkeye" Logan of the Sedona Institute for Human Potential Studies in Arizona, loving yourself causes you to emit positive energy waves which create a self-perpetuating psycho-sensory vibration in the luminiferous aether. This vibration transmits itself to the people around you, who can't help but experience warm feelings towards you as a result.

Now, maybe you're thinking, "That's all well and good, but the method you're talking about will never work for me, because I was starved of love as a child, leaving me too emotionally damaged to love myself." Okay. I recognise how devastating such a childhood can be, and the last thing I want to do is sound insensitive. However, I have to point out that blaming your inability to love yourself on your parents is putting the cart before the horse. Most likely, it's *because* you spent so much of your childhood being mopey and self-critical that your parents never particularly warmed to you. Luckily, there's still time for you to set things right and banish the false inner child that's been holding you back for so long. Learn the art of self-love, and not only will your parents come to love you, but so will everybody else.

I call it "the *art* of self-love" because self-love is one of those things that takes a few minutes to learn and a lifetime to master. The subject could easily fill a whole book. Indeed, there have been whole books written about it – for example, Marshall Brewster's *I Can't Help Falling in Love with Me: The Complete Guide to Building and Maintaining a Healthy Ego.* You can also find a wealth of material about self-love on the Internet, including useful online questionnaires that will tell you where you rank on the "Self-Love Mastery Scale".

Here are a few tips which will help you to increase your love for yourself:

1. Trust yourself

Have confidence in your abilities – you can do anything you set your mind to. I mean anything within reason. Even if you're attempting something for the very first time, you still have the power to achieve it, provided it's not too ill-conceived. And the more you achieve things you had assumed were beyond your grasp, the more you'll strengthen your ego; this in turn will enhance your ability to love yourself.

So no more telling yourself "I haven't the faintest idea how to accomplish X" and giving up. Instead, tell yourself, "I haven't the faintest idea how to accomplish X, but I'm sure my powerful subconscious mind will find a way." And it will. The only way it won't is if you're attempting something you are fundamentally unsuited for, like becoming a professional sumo wrestler despite being of a slender build.

2. Put your fears aside

Perhaps one of the reasons you're having trouble loving yourself is that your fear is getting in the way. For example, maybe you've borrowed a large amount of money from a relative, and now you've learned that the relative needs the money back by the end of the month. Maybe you've been lying awake at night, feeling horribly guilty and agonising about what's going to happen when your relative realises you've squandered all the money he lent you and have no means of repaying him.

Is there anything constructive about all this anguish? Of course not. Think about it – you're actually living in fear of something that *hasn't even happened yet!* Lots could change between now and the end of the month. You could win the lottery, or your relative could die – or better still, both! So let go of worry and shift your focus to loving yourself.

3. Dare to dream

Sometimes when you're having difficulty loving yourself, the problem isn't really *you*; the problem is everyone and everything around you. The worst thing you can do is beat yourself up for being a "failure" when actually the problem is your *situation,* not you.

Maybe the people in your life are hindering your pursuit of your goals, or maybe the right sorts of opportunities haven't been coming your way. Regardless, what you need to do is dream of all the ways in which you could realise your potential if your circumstances were "upgraded" to better ones. Love the self you *could be*, and soon enough, you'll love the self you *are*.

4. Make positive affirmations

I've already instructed you to tell yourself, "I deserve to be loved, because I am one of the most special people in the entire world." But why stop there? There are many other affirmations you could employ to make yourself more loveable in your own eyes. Examples include: "I am destined for reggae stardom" and "Nothing can stop me from becoming Chancellor of the Exchequer."

It's very simple: if you love yourself, everybody around you will say, "Hey, there's somebody who loves himself – let's love him too." Conversely, if you don't love yourself, people will back away and your relationships will wither.

I'm not the only person who has made this observation. In Nancy Vanderlay's *Fifty Ways to Lead Your Love Life: Relationship Advice Inspired by the Works of Paul Simon*, Tip #27 is none other than: "Don't expect the other person to love you if you struggle to love yourself."

I'll tell you who comes into my mind when I think of Tip #27: Kim. A key reason why my relationship with Kim ran into difficulties is that loving her was often a challenge. *And the reason loving her was often a challenge was that she didn't really love herself.* She would frequently say things like, "I don't know why I even bother auditioning for these acting jobs – I'm always up against dozens of other women who are better actresses than me, and more interesting-looking." And I would say, "Don't be so hard on yourself: you're actually very interesting-looking." And she would respond, "Yeah, well, thanks for that… but I notice you're not denying they're better actresses than me."

I tried to boost her self-esteem, I really did. On those rare occasions when she landed a role, I'd say, "Well done, you! You should be pleased. This could be the start of something big for you."

But she'd be totally dismissive, insisting that the role was too trivial to get excited about. "I guarantee you, Sparky, 'Fourth Girl at Party' in a beer commercial is *not* going to be the start of something big for me."

Well, I don't see why it shouldn't have been. If I were a woman who had landed the role of "Fourth Girl at Party" in a beer commercial, I'd use it as the springboard for a succession of bigger and better roles, culminating in the role of a sexy forensic analyst on one of those glitzy American crime dramas.

Kim's difficulties were sad for me on a personal level, in several ways. I'd been looking forward to having a successful actress for a wife, but, given her negative self-image, this prospect was looking less and less likely. And when her self-esteem was at rock bottom, I felt useless because there was literally nothing I could do for her. Sometimes she would be so doom-and-gloom about everything that I'd be overcome by the desire to leave the apartment and go bowling. Or the other way round: I mean, I'd return to the apartment from bowling and find her in such a bad mood that I'd wish I'd just carried on bowling rather than coming home.

No wonder our relationship failed. Kim, who couldn't or wouldn't love herself, felt undeserving of success. I, who never had the slightest problem loving myself, knew that success was my destiny. We simply weren't compatible.

Not that Kim would agree with that analysis. She continues to believe that the break-up was 100 per cent my fault, and she won't stop ringing me up and trying to get me to admit it.

The most recent phone call was last night. It came at an inconvenient time – I had started running a bath and the hot tap was on full. She didn't give me a chance to explain this, instead launching straight into an ultimatum. "Now listen, Sparky," she said, "I know how determined you are to play the innocent and deny your role in sabotaging our relationship and wrecking my life prospects. Frankly, I was almost ready to throw in the towel and give up on ever getting you to admit what you did. But Dr Hirschfeld has made me see that that would just be colluding in your lie. So, no dice. You're not getting off the hook. This time you're going to come clean and give me some closure."

Now, really, this was unbelievable. I've made *countless* efforts to help Kim to achieve closure, all to no avail. I've encouraged her to commit her "leftover" feelings to paper, to produce drawings and paintings as a way of releasing negative emotions, etc. But all my suggestions have been met with either indifference or outright hostility.

"I think we've been over this ground before," I told her.

"Don't tell me what ground we have and haven't been over, Gary. Maybe in *your* head everything's all resolved – in which case, lucky you. But it hardly helps me, does it? I know what I feel and what I don't feel, and what I don't feel is any sense of resolution."

I was starting to get a bit worried about the bath, so I said, "Look, is this really something we need to do now? Because it's just that—"

"Oh, I know, I know," she interrupted. "You're *real busy* at the moment, right? Well, that's great for you. You've been able to get on with your life, because you made the decision to wash your hands of me and leave me emotionally hanging like a… like a…"

While Kim was trying to think of an apt comparison, I seized my chance. "I'm just going to go and turn off the taps," I said. I set the phone down on the table. Having ruined a couple of previous phones by accidentally dropping them in the toilet and bath respectively, I maintain a strict no-phones-in-the-bathroom policy. As I hurried off, I heard Kim's voice from the handset saying, "What's that? Listen, Sparky, don't you…"

When I came back about ten seconds later and picked up the phone, Kim was saying "…and that's why I'm going to fly over to see you, because clearly the only way this is going to work is if we do it face-to-face. Do you understand?"

"You're planning to fly over? What? When?"

"Weren't you *listening*? Oh, that is so typical – that really sums it up! Dr Hirschfeld was so right!"

"Look," I said, "flying all the way to London just to see me is totally impractical. For one thing, you can't afford it."

"Since when did you become an expert on my finances? I've got money saved up, as it happens. Renting an apartment the size of a shoebox isn't something I'm thrilled about, but I'll say this for it: it's cheap. And what else am I going to spend my savings on: designer shoes? Diamond earrings? Please. I may have coveted that kind of stuff when I was younger, but those days are *so* over. If I'm going to shell out, it might as well be on something that makes a difference to my life. And having a face-to-face showdown with you, Gary, that's something that's going to make a difference to my life. I'm just sorry I didn't do it *years* ago."

"I'm not sure I like that word, 'showdown'," I said.

"You don't have to like it. I'm just informing you that that's what's going to happen. I'll be in touch again when I've booked my flight."

And with that the phone went dead.

At first this was unsettling, to say the least. Ignoring Kim when she's thousands of miles away is no problem, but ignoring her when she's physically in the same city as me was going to be a tall order. Also, this was really not the best time for Kim to be coming into town making trouble, what with everything going on in my life – for example, my pursuit of Louise and my writing of this book.

But as I lay in the bath a few minutes later, I became more and more convinced there was nothing to worry about. Of course Kim won't really fly over. Kim has never been out of the United States in her life. I don't think she even has a passport. It's one thing to make the threat, but quite another to follow through on it. Fundamentally, she lacks the capacity to follow through on *anything*, which explains why her life has gone nowhere since we split up.

I do feel sorry for Kim. I'd like nothing better than for her to be happy, but it's really hard to help someone who doesn't want to help herself. Even after all this time, she still refuses to embrace the self-help ideas advocated by people like Marshall Brewster and myself. This is her loss, as the longer she resists such ideas, the more she is consumed by bitterness and rage. If only she could let go of her destructive feelings and learn to love herself, her life would be transformed. Sadly, on the evidence of her latest phone call, it's not going to happen.

Romance

According to an online dictionary I consulted just now, romance is defined as "the pleasurable feeling of excitement and mystery associated with love". That's spot-on. Anyone who has had any romance in their life will be familiar with the experience of feeling charmed, breathless, dazzled, disorientated, weak in the knees, anxious, and sweaty. Such responses are the hallmarks of romance. And to be successful romantically, you're going to have to find ways of inducing those responses in your prospective partners.

The question is, how? Well, as far as the early stages of the wooing process are concerned, the most effective way of laying the groundwork for romance is to *play it cool*. (I'm aware that the phrase "play it cool" is itself not very cool. If you utter such a phrase when the object of your attentions is within earshot, you will come across as having stepped straight out of *West Side Story* – a major turn-off. She wants a modern man, not some finger-snapping retro street goon.)

Playing it cool means being relaxed and a bit flirtatious, but keeping your cards close to your chest. This will give you an air of mystery. Whatever you do, don't make explicit reference to relationships or love. Romance may be the pleasurable feeling of excitement and mystery associated with love, but that doesn't mean you should hurry love. Indeed, you *can't* hurry love, as The Supremes taught us many years ago. Your objective at this stage isn't to get her to love you, much less pool her finances with you to buy a renovated 17th-century farmhouse where the two of you can settle down and keep chickens and produce artisanal cheeses for sale on the Internet. Your objective is simply to plant the thought in her head that she *could* love you. The farmhouse and all the rest of it can come later.

This is why, ever since the start of my budding romance with Louise, I have been careful to avoid revealing too much about myself. (Come to think of it, she hasn't seemed keen to reveal too much about herself, either.) To illustrate how to keep your cards close to your chest in a way that maximises the possibilities for romance, let me recount a conversation I had with Louise last Monday morning. I opened the conversation by poking my head into her office and greeting her with the witty enquiry, "Glad to be back, Louise?"

She looked up from what she was doing, her face registering surprise at seeing me. "Hmm? Back from where?"

"I mean back into the swing of another exciting work week now that the weekend's over."

"Oh – well then, no, not especially."

"Ha! Must've been a fantastic weekend, then. What did you get up to?"

She shrugged. "This and that." Evidently, she was as determined to keep her cards close to her chest as I was. And yet, I'm almost certain I saw the slight hint of a coy smile on her face, the kind of smile that said, "I did what comes naturally to a work-hard/play-hard girl such as myself. I got dressed up in an outfit that would make your jaw drop, went out on the town with my girlfriends, tore up the dance floor, drank vodka shots like there was no tomorrow, and rolled home at 4am sloshed and exhausted but happy. People here at work think they know me, Gary, but they don't know the real me – the spontaneous, fun-loving me. Nobody at work even suspects that that side of me exists… nobody, that is, apart from you."

I gave her a knowing smile in return, and remarked, "*This and that* – yes that's my approach to weekends, too. I always try to pack in as much variety as I can. The only trouble is, I've got so many interests, a couple of days is never long enough for me to fit them all in."

"Isn't it? Well, in that case, perhaps you should consider the option of dropping down to four days a week?"

"No, I didn't mean t—"

"Because it wouldn't be a problem. We'd just shave 20

per cent off your salary. To be honest, the company would probably benefit from that arrangement, on balance. And you'd have more free time to do your – whatever it is – your stamp collecting or birdwatching or whatever."

Now, leaving aside the fact that my interests weren't anything like what Louise supposed them to be, it was very flattering to be spoken to in this way. "Work smarter, not harder" has always been my motto, and Louise's proposal testified to her recognition of the fact that I can be as effective in four days as most people can in five. I had to decline her offer, though, as I didn't feel this was quite the right time to be accepting a pay cut.

"I'd prefer to stick at five days a week for now," I said.

"Suit yourself."

"And stamp collecting isn't really my thing," I said. "I'm more interested in literary pursuits, like writing my book."

She looked surprised. "Your book?"

"That's right."

"What book is this?"

"That would be telling," I said, winking at her.

Can you see what I did there? I withheld an important bit of information, thereby making myself seem more mysterious, and heightening Louise's interest in me.

Now, bear in mind that this technique is only really appropriate at the very start of a relationship. If you're still withholding crucial information from your partner after, say, a year, it won't be romantic – it'll just raise suspicions. She will probably imagine that you have some dark secret: a criminal past, or a wife and kids in another town.

At the same time, you need to have *some* way of generating romance when you are in an established relationship, otherwise things can go stale. My advice is: *surprise her with romantic gestures.*

Note: the key word here is "surprise". A lot of people make the mistake of repeating the same romantic gesture again and again. I was guilty of this error when I bought gifts for Sandra early in our relationship. I bought roses for her twice in a row, the second time three weeks after the first. She thanked me, but didn't seem as bowled over as I'd hoped.

"Oh, roses again… nice" she said.

And then it dawned on me: however much your partner likes roses, the element of surprise is destroyed if you *only* ever buy her roses and never any other type of flower. Once I'd worked this out, I made a point of varying the flowers. Instead of roses, roses, roses, I shifted to a pattern that went more like: roses, daffodils, roses, lilies, daffodils, roses, carnations, lilies, carnations, roses, lilies, lilies (you're allowed the *occasional* repetition), carnations, roses, etc. That way she never knew what flowers she was getting next.

Another thing I would suggest is varying the time interval between your romantic gestures. Don't do them every month like clockwork, as this too is wearyingly predictable. What can be very effective is to leave a long gap sometimes. Just when she's abandoned all hope that you'll ever do something special for her again – whammo: you make the biggest romantic gesture you've made in ages.

I remember applying this technique during my

relationship with Kim. I went four months without even so much as buying her chocolates. "You never do anything special for me anymore!" she complained to me one day. Whereupon I presented her with a couple of tickets to a U2 concert. She squealed with delight and said, "I take it back. You're the best, Sparky, even if a lot of the time you make me want to kill you." So you see, timing is everything.

The good news for those of you on a tight budget is that not every romantic gesture has to cost money. Here are some examples of simple things you can do to heighten the romance in your relationship without shelling out a penny:

- Write a poem for her. There's nothing like a poem to express your true feelings. But take care to choose an appropriate style of poem. I can tell you from personal experience that a limerick is not a good choice. It turns out that even the most deeply felt sentiments sound tawdry when expressed in limerick form. Sonnets are always a good bet, though, as are haikus. In case you're not familiar with haikus, an example would be, "How I love your hair / Its softness, its fine texture, / Its lack of split ends".

- Tell her she resembles an attractive celebrity. But don't just say, "You resemble an attractive celebrity." You have to name a particular one. The Internet is a good source of pictures of attractive celebrities. You can browse through these to determine what celebrity your partner most resembles.

- Compare her favourably to previous girlfriends. For example, if you used to have a girlfriend named Melanie, you could say, "Melanie was rubbish compared to you." Then run through all the admirable qualities your partner has that you felt were lacking in Melanie.

- Present her with "vouchers" that she can "redeem" in exchange for you doing extra chores. For example, one of the vouchers could entitle her to have you clean the gutters, and another could be for you to wash her car. Avoid giving more than five or six vouchers to your partner in any given year, otherwise you'll be doing these extra chores routinely, which kills the romance.

For more tips on how to be romantic, I strongly recommend Marshall Brewster's book *The Art of Romance, Marshall Brewster-Style.* When it comes to romance, Marshall has impeccable credentials. Everyone in the self-help community knows the story of how Marshall met his wife. The moment he set eyes on Lois Perkins, a former Miss New Jersey, in a Burbank television studio where the two of them were booked on the same daytime chat show, he knew he had to have her. So he set about wooing her, first with small gifts such as tasteful scarves, hats, and necklaces, and then with more extravagant ones such as rare antiques, vintage cars, and sessions with Hollywood's top plastic surgeon. Lois, overwhelmed by Marshall's generosity and charm, accepted his marriage proposal six months after their first meeting.

And if you think the gifts dried up after Marshall and Lois tied the knot, think again. Marshall still arranges for Lois to receive orchids, bottles of champagne, and assorted lavish gifts on such occasions as: Valentine's day, their wedding anniversary, the anniversary of their engagement, the anniversary of their first meeting, Lois's birthday, and the birthdays of all seven of her Australian labradoodles and three miniature schnauzers.

Perhaps you're wondering how Marshall manages such a huge organisational feat. The answer is: he has a personal assistant who does all the legwork for him. When you are successful enough to have your own personal assistant and your own celebrity spouse, you will be able to do the same as Marshall. Until then, you can replicate something of the *spirit* of Marshall's romantic gestures, if not the scale, by purchasing *The Art of Romance, Marshall Brewster-Style* and consulting the section entitled "More Bang for Your Buck: Fifty Romantic Gifts Costing Under $10" (I believe $10 is approximately £6.50 at the moment). And of course you should also perform as many as possible of the free romantic gestures I listed above.

Bear in mind that romance can't sustain a relationship on its own. My relationship with Sandra was full of romance, yet it turned out to be unsustainable, simply because the two of us had different priorities. All the romance in the world wasn't going to change that. I like to think that when my relationship with Louise gets up and running, she and I will have the best of both worlds: plenty of romance, and plenty of common ground. After all, she is a highly successful career woman, and I'll be a highly successful self-help author.

Communication

In these days of "equality", it's not politically correct to express the view that men and women differ in their abilities. Of course, there are lots of things that men and women do equally well, but not *everything* falls into that category. Personally, I don't see what's wrong with observing that men are naturally better at driving, or that women are naturally better at remembering people's birthdays. Far from being sexist generalisations, these are simple facts that everybody can confirm from their own experience.

And it's not just about abilities. The whole way men and women operate – and above all, the way they *communicate* – is fundamentally different. It's almost as if men and women come from two completely different countries: as if, let's say, men were from Malta and women were from Venezuela. This is bound to cause misunderstandings between the sexes. How easy is it going to be for somebody who speaks Maltese to have a conversation with someone who speaks Venezuelan? Answer: not very easy! Alternatively, you could think of men as being like basketball players and women as being like netball players. The two sports may be superficially similar, but that doesn't mean that their respective players are going to be able to compete on the same court without getting into a right muddle!

If you think about it, the fact that men and women

have different communication styles is unsurprising. In the days of our caveman ancestors, men did all of the hunting because of their superior spear-throwing skills, leaving the women to look after the kids and weave baskets. As hunting required focus and discipline, a man couldn't afford to chat to his companions about people, relationships, and feelings. When he communicated, he had to be brief and factual. For example, he might say: "Look! Up there – a pterodactyl!" Women, on the other hand, weren't bound by the same constraints. They were free to natter about whatever was going on in the community at the time, like the lady in the next cave getting pregnant by someone who wasn't her husband.

What I'm saying is that there are good evolutionary reasons why men and women communicate differently. Interestingly, when I tried to explain this to Sandra once while we were out walking on the South Bank, she seemed resistant to the idea. "Are you sure it's even *true* that men and women communicate differently?" she asked.

"It's a scientific fact," I replied. "The main difference is that women are much more talkative. For every word a man uses, a woman uses *three*."

"I'm not entirely sure I believe that," she said.

"Well," I said, "if you want an example, there's Dave's mother." (Dave was a bowling acquaintance of mine.) "You wouldn't *believe* how much she talks. I know because we all got to meet her when she was staying with Dave the week before last and Dave brought her along to the lanes on Two-for-One Tuesday. I mean, not to join in the bowling, just to watch. When she first arrived with Dave (and by the way she's quite elderly, maybe in her early eighties) Nick came up to me and said, 'Dave's mad to bring his mother to a place like this. He ought to take her out for a quiet dinner somewhere local.' But I just told him, 'The thing is, Nick, Dave knows his own mother. I'm sure he wouldn't bring her if she wasn't going to be comfortable here.' And Nick sort of took that on board and said, 'Well, maybe you're right, I suppose I'm just thinking of my own mother – can you imagine her coming here?' And I have to say, having met Nick's mother a couple of times, I knew exactly what he was talking about. There's just something about her – you just can't picture her in a bowling alley, you can only really picture her in a big armchair drinking a mug of tea. Which *is* actually what she spends most of her time doing, by all accounts. Anyway, that was sort of a digression. The point I was making was: Dave's mother had a grand time. And my God, can she talk! To start with, she was keeping up a running commentary on the bowling – not just what was happening in *our* lane but also the two neighbouring lanes. Then she moved on to asking us all about our families, and where we came from, and our answers would remind her of places she'd travelled to when she was younger, so she'd tell us all about those places, even down to what restaurants she'd eaten in. Then something would remind her of what life was like during the war, so she'd launch into anecdotes about her experiences back then. What an amazing lady. But my point is, you would never find a man who talked as much as that. I was speaking to Dave afterwards, and he told me he has two sisters who are just the same – unbelievably chatty. Whereas Dave isn't a big talker at all, so it's definitely a female thing."

"Hmm," said Sandra. I think she was starting to sense I had a point, even if she wasn't ready to accept it 100 per cent.

"Also," I said, "women's talk is more gossipy than men's, and more concerned with people and feelings. Men's talk is more hard-headed and factual."

"Is that something that's been established by scientific studies?"

"It must have been, because all the self-help books talk about it. Plus, it crops up all the time on the Internet."

"Hmm," said Sandra again.

Ironically, even though Sandra was sceptical about the idea that men and women communicate differently, those differences were very much in evidence when Sandra and I clashed over her insistence that I get a job and abandon my dream of writing a self-help book. My approach was to focus on the plain facts, namely:

- becoming a self-help expert was my destiny
- if I was prevented from pursuing my dream it would be a terrible waste of my potential
- the publication of my book would mean a wonderful new life for all three of us
- from talking to Jack it was clear that he supported his daddy's dreams and wanted him to do well

But those facts didn't really register with Sandra, because she was operating at the level of *feelings*. She'd say things like "I *feel* [my italics] as though you don't really understand how your actions are affecting me and Jack." Needless to say, it's very hard to argue against somebody's feelings! In short, Sandra and I were talking at cross-purposes.

I remember how, the night before we parted, neither of us got very much sleep. At one stage we were both lying there and Sandra turned to me and said, "What are you thinking?"

That's a typical "woman" question that men almost never know how to answer – because most of the time we're thinking about something they either wouldn't relate to or wouldn't approve of! Actually, though, on this occasion it seemed to me that what I was thinking was something Sandra would connect with, so I said:

"I'm thinking I'd give anything for this not to be happening."

"You mean anything apart from—"

"Apart from abandoning my dream, I'd do anything. The idea that we're going to have to say goodbye in a few hours, the idea that tomorrow night I'm going to be sleeping in a different flat that doesn't have you and Jack in it... I can't believe it's come to this. But somehow it has."

"Yes," she said, "somehow it has." She fell silent. When she spoke again, it was to say, "About your ambitions, Gary... There may come a time – maybe a few months from now, maybe a year from now, or a year and a half from now – when those ambitions stop feeling so important to you. And if that happens, then... then I don't know what it will mean. My life might have changed quite a lot by then. What I'm saying to you, Gary, is that by then it might be too late for you to come back. It might be or it might not be. I just can't be sure."

I had an odd mix of feelings. Sandra was leaving the door open for me just a crack, making me feel hopeful – but on the other hand, I knew that the scenario Sandra was describing was never going to come to pass. I wasn't going to change my mind; my determination to pursue success was unwavering.

Since that time, a couple of things have happened. First, life has calmed down considerably. The emotional upheaval of those days is a distant memory. Second, I've become much more adept at taking advantage of my knowledge of male/female communication differences. I am pleased to report that I am starting to master the art of communicating with the opposite sex in their own language. This is a very valuable skill to have. Much as a bilingual British person visiting France can say "*Je veux du fromage*" and get better service at a cheese shop than somebody who'd uttered the same phrase in English, a man who knows how to speak to women in a language they understand will get better results than someone who doesn't.

To give you an example of what I mean: the other morning before work I stopped off at the bagel stand as usual to pick up a salmon-and-cream-cheese bagel. I was running late, and I was also exceptionally hungry, so after buying the bagel I decided to eat it "on the go", while walking. Unfortunately, in my haste to unwrap the bagel, I dropped it and watched in dismay as it fell to the pavement, landing in a dirty puddle. Retrieving and eating the soggy, dirty bagel was out of the question, but my hunger was overwhelming now, so I rushed back to the bagel stand and explained what had happened.

"I know it's not your problem," I said to the woman at the bagel stand, "but I was really looking forward to eating my bagel, and now I've accidentally dropped it into a puddle. And I've only got 40p left, so I can't buy another one. I feel embarrassed, and frustrated with myself, and I feel I've done a disservice to you because you put a lot of effort into making these bagels and they should be handled with more care. I'll completely understand if you say there's nothing you can do. But if you *could* give me a replacement bagel, you'd make me so happy."

"I give you another bagel, no problem," she said, smiling. So you see, by communicating with the lady from the bagel stand in the sort of language that resonates with her, I achieved exactly the outcome I was aiming for.

Of course, there's a limit to how much you should do this. If you're too consistently feminine in your communication, you'll come across as unmanly. There are times where what's most needed is *assertive communication*, which involves:

- stating clearly what you want the other person to do (*"I want you to _____"*)
- asking the other person to commit to doing it (*"Promise me you'll _____"*)
- explaining what the consequences will be if they don't do it (*"If you don't comply with my request, I'll _____"*)

The thought occurred to me yesterday evening that

Kim needed to be dealt with more assertively than I'd dealt with her thus far, so I sent her an email in which I didn't pull any punches. The email ran as follows:

> *Dear Kim,*
>
> *I want you to drop this idea of having a showdown with me. It's not going to happen, and even if it did happen it wouldn't achieve anything, so promise me you'll come to your senses and forget it. If you continue to cling on to this idea despite me telling you not to, I'll be quite frustrated and upset.*
>
> *Is that understood?*
>
> *Yours,*
> *Gary*

Kim must have picked up the email at work (it was late-morning California time), because her reply came back straightaway:

> *Gary,*
>
> *Yes, it's understood. And no, I won't drop the idea just because you want me to. What are you, crazy?*
>
> *Kim*

Even though this wasn't the perfect result, at least it was progress. Kim had acknowledged my point of view ("Yes, it's understood") – something that wouldn't have happened if I hadn't asserted myself to the extent I did. If you are a man who feels you haven't been "getting through" to the women in your life – be they friends, partners, enemies, or casual acquaintances – I urge you to reconsider the way you communicate with them. By optimising your communication style, you'll put yourself in a position to have much more rewarding conversations with them – conversations that are considerably more likely to end up with you getting what you want.

Sex

No chapter on relationships would be complete without some sort of discussion about sex. But let me be clear: I'm not going to provide you with detailed guidance about positions, techniques, equipment, etc. This isn't for lack of expertise. It's just that there are plenty of good sex manuals that cover this ground, and I see no need to reinvent the wheel. If you are interested in improving your skills in the bedroom, some books I can recommend are:

- *Multiple Orgasms for Couples in 21st Century Relationships: The Ultimate Givers and Receivers Guide*, by Dwight S Rustenbacker and Mary-Jane Parton. Written by two well-regarded American sex therapists, this is the definitive guide to having two or more orgasms in a short space of time. Contains lots of useful diagrams and full-colour instructional photographs.

- *Supercharge Your Sex Life: An Easy Step-by-Step Guide for Lovers of All Ages*, by Janice Greenblatt. This book, by America's pre-eminent sex advice radio talk show host, sets out a simple thirty-six-point plan which will enable anybody to have noticeably better sex.
- *The Cleopatra Code: Sex Secrets They Don't Want You to Know*, by Lyle Quintano. In his long-awaited follow-up to *The Andromeda Code: UFO Secrets They Don't Want You to Know* (also a must-read), Lyle Quintano uncovers a dossier of powerful sex secrets suppressed for thirty years by the CIA, who feared that if the techniques ever got out, the American population would become so engrossed in lovemaking that they would be left vulnerable to a surprise attack by the Soviet Union.
- *Good Sex for You*, by Dr Barry Runcorn. For a more British perspective on sex.

What you won't find addressed in these books is the question of what *role* sex should play in your relationships. And that's the question I want to explore here. I'll start by listing the things that sex definitely *shouldn't* be:

It shouldn't be a chore. Too many couples treat sex as something which just "has to be done", like emptying the dishwasher or regrouting the bathroom. Conversations like the one below are all too common:

> MAN: I suppose we ought to have sex this evening.
>
> WOMAN: Can't it wait till later in the week? I promised Pam I'd ring her up to commiserate about what happened to her dog. And you know how long my conversations with Pam always are.
>
> MAN: Well, how about Thursday, then?
>
> WOMAN: Thursday around 10pm would work.
>
> MAN: But 10pm is when *Cop Squad* is on. We'd better make it nine thirty.

When this couple finally get round to having sex, how enjoyable is the experience going to be? The man is going to be periodically checking the bedside clock to see whether he's on target to finish in time for *Cop Squad*, and the woman is going to be distracted by the thought that she might not have sounded sympathetic enough when commiserating with Pam about what happened with the dog.

It shouldn't be done for the wrong reasons. None of the following are good reasons for having sex:

- to impress an upstairs neighbour
- to establish whether you've fully recovered from your knee injury
- to win a dare or bet
- as a form of thanks to the other person for letting

you borrow their car

Before having sex, always ask yourself whether you are doing it for the right reasons. If the answer is "no", you shouldn't proceed with sex unless you're prepared to feel cheap and/or guilty afterwards. Ideally, you should just calmly leave the room. You may need to switch on Radio 4 to bring down your level of arousal. Dunking your head in a basin of cold water sometimes helps; dunking your genitals in a basin of cold water is even more effective.

It shouldn't be a substitute for a deep and meaningful emotional connection. This sample conversation illustrates what I mean:

> WOMAN: I feel so lonely, even when we're together.
> MAN: Hmm, I'm not sure what to tell you. Maybe you should see a therapist or something.
> WOMAN: That response doesn't make me feel any better.
> MAN: Would it help if we had sex?

On the evidence of the conversation above, does this couple have any sort of meaningful emotional connection? I think the answer is clear enough.

So there we have it – all the things that sex shouldn't be. Now let's explore what it *should* be:

It should be spontaneous. There's no telling when you're going to be "in the mood". It could happen at any time and in any place. For example, it might happen when you and your partner are in the midst of reorganising the contents of the garden shed on a Sunday afternoon.

In these circumstances, don't just bite your lip and carry on with the shed reorganisation. Instead, let your partner know that you are feeling amorous. At this point, assuming your partner is also in the mood, the two of you will probably want to have a look through the items that are strewn on the ground in front of the shed, gather up the ones you'd be reluctant to leave exposed in the garden for any length of time (either because they could get damaged in the event of rain, or because they might pose a danger to the cat), and return them to the shed. You can then lock up the shed, head into the house, draw the curtains, and have spontaneous, passionate sex.

It should be exciting. How often have you been in the middle of having sex and found yourself fantasising about doing some other activity, like browsing for kitchen fixtures and fittings on the Internet? I've never had this experience myself, but I understand there are lots of people who have. Those people need to take urgent action to spice up their sex lives, which have become boring and predictable.

The range of methods you can use to make sex more exciting is limited only by your imagination. One thing you could try is putting an action-film soundtrack on the stereo in the background. Another is engaging in a role-play – for example, you could pretend to be a burly construction worker and your partner could pretend to be the burly construction worker's wife.

It should be loving. Let's face it: without love, sex practically amounts to a business transaction – albeit an unusually pleasurable business transaction, like going into the bank to collect some foreign currency and being informed by the cashier that because you're the bank's one millionth foreign-exchange customer, you get your currency for free.

If your sex life seems loveless, I would urge you to take steps to remedy this. When you consider the fact that human beings are the only members of the animal kingdom who are able to combine sex and love, apart from swans, I'm sure you'll agree that you'd be foolish to let this unique ability go to waste.

You might think there's no way sex can be spontaneous, exciting, and loving all at the same time – but I can assure you that you're wrong. My sex life with Sandra combined all three of those qualities. I know this might sound like boasting, but it's not. I'm just telling you how it was. Of course, my sex life with Sandra is in the past, so I don't want to dwell on it. Nevertheless, I'd be doing you a disservice if I didn't give you at least enough detail to furnish you with a useful model on which to base your own sex life.

One of the reasons Sandra and I were so successful in the bedroom was that she never took me for granted sexually. For instance, she had certain items of clothing she knew drove me crazy, such as a tight peach-coloured top of hers which she would change into when I was least expecting it. On one such occasion, I was all set to leave the house to go bowling when suddenly she came into the room wearing the peach-coloured top and a pair of shorts, and with a mischievous look in her eyes. So I texted my bowling buddies an excuse for not being able to make it that night: I told them I was on hold trying to get Bruce Springsteen tickets. As to what happened next, I'll leave that to your imagination!

It also worked the other way round. I had a cowboy outfit which I'd once worn to a fancy dress party, and early in our relationship I discovered that a sure way of making Sandra go weak at the knees was to come into the room dressed in my full cowboy regalia. I tried not to pull that stunt too often, though. Partly this was because wearing the outfit regularly would have lessened the impact, and partly it was because the boots were extremely difficult to get on and off.

I must admit that in the first few weeks after separating from Sandra, I had a tough time getting our sex life out of my thoughts. I'd be in the middle of some normal everyday activity, like eating a microwave pizza or sorting my socks into pairs, when, out of the blue, an image of Sandra in a partial or even total state of undress would enter my mind. Why did this happen? In retrospect, the reason was that I hadn't yet reconciled myself to the separation. What a contrast to my state of mind nowadays! I've now reached the point where I don't experience such thoughts any more than two or three times a week.

These thoughts would probably go away completely if it weren't for the fact that Sandra is still in my life to some extent. I see her every weekend when she drops Jack off or comes to collect him, so I can never go more than seven days without encountering the distinctive smell of her hair, or the sight of her turquoise beaded necklace, or what have you. And as you might expect, each of these things conjures up memories of intimate moments I've shared with Sandra. Frequently, the memories in turn conjure up feelings. But – and here's the key point – *I don't let those memories and feelings disturb my peace of mind, because I know they belong firmly in the past.*

Okay, I admit there was one occasion recently where seeing Sandra disturbed my peace of mind. However, once I explain the circumstances, I'm sure you will understand why I felt the way I did. The occasion I'm referring to was last Sunday when Sandra came to collect Jack from the local park where he and I had been spending the latter part of the afternoon. When Sandra appeared, the first thing I noticed about her was that she wasn't alone. At her side was a tall, fair-haired man in shorts and a navy-blue polo shirt, a couple of tennis racquets slung over his shoulder, his face glistening with sweat. Sandra was wearing a black skirt and trainers and – of all things – the peach-coloured top!

Why would Sandra wear that? She knew full well its significance for me, and she knew I was going to see her wearing it – not just wearing it, but wearing it in the company of a man I've never set eyes on before. Didn't it occur to her that I might be jealous? Let's be clear: I *wasn't* jealous. But my point is, for all she knew, I *could* have been. It was the lack of tact, so uncharacteristic for Sandra, that really floored me.

I kept my feelings to myself, of course. Jack ran up to

Sandra and she hugged him. With a nod towards her companion, Sandra said to me, "Gary, I should introduce you to my friend Carl. He drove me here, but we came early because we wanted to fit in some tennis practice before picking up Jack. We've been over at the courts on the other side of the park. Carl's been giving me a tennis lesson."

"Good to meet you, Gary," said Carl, shaking my hand, rather too firmly I thought. Meanwhile, Jack ran off to stroke an exceptionally fluffy dog, and Sandra went after him.

"Likewise," I said to Carl. "You're a tennis instructor, then?"

"No, no, not by profession anyway. I'm a loss adjuster. But I'm mad keen on tennis. Keeps me out of trouble at weekends, ha ha! And when Sandra said she wanted to learn how to play, I said, 'No point hiring an instructor, I'll teach you for free'."

"Very generous of you," I said.

At this point, Sandra returned with Jack. "Jack, you haven't said hello to Carl yet," she said. "Do you want to say hello to him?"

When there was no response from Jack, Carl bent down, ruffled Jack's hair, and said "Hiya Champ!" Jack didn't much like that, judging from the way he turned his head away.

As there seemed to be a gap in the conversation, I said to Sandra, "I never realised you wanted to learn to play tennis."

"I only got interested in it recently," she replied, sounding a touch defensive.

"Sandra's going to come on in leaps and bounds if she keeps at it," said Carl. "She has promise – that's clear from what I've seen. The way she moves is so natural."

"I know," I said. "So you're a, what did you say, a loss accumulator?"

"Loss adjuster."

"That's fascinating."

"Oh, it's – well, ha ha, I find it fascinating, anyway. I should probably tell you what loss adjusters actually do—"

"Yes, that would be really interesting to hear about, although maybe not right now. There's a television programme starting shortly on ITV that I'm keen to get back for." I was pleased with myself for coming up with this choice put-down. There can hardly be a more effective way of expressing your lack of interest in a person than to signal to them that their conversation holds less appeal for you than an ITV programme.

"No worries," said Carl. "Well, let me just say, congratulations. Jack is such a fine boy. I'm sure you're very proud of him."

"I'm a fine boy!" said Jack.

"Ha ha, he thinks so too!" said Carl. "Brilliant!"

I said my goodbyes to the three of them and headed home.

My brief meeting with Carl had been enlightening. For one thing, it was clear to me that whatever Carl's intentions towards Sandra, there was no way he was ever, *ever* going to be more than a platonic friend to her. It just wasn't going to happen.

Sure, he's good-looking, tall, well built. Yet whatever sex appeal he might possess evaporates as soon as he opens his mouth. I know Sandra, and I know that she puts a high value on character. But anyone can see that character is not Carl's strong suit. His sense of humour is rudimentary, as evidenced by his habit of laughing inanely at things that aren't funny. And he's bland. And he has a boring job title: whoever heard of a sexy, charismatic loss adjuster? And he doesn't know anything about how to communicate with children. And he thinks that carrying Sandra's tennis racquet for her will make her well disposed towards him, when actually she's perfectly capable of carrying her own tennis racquet, thank you very much.

I should stress that these aren't digs at Carl; they're just neutral observations which together show how inconceivable it is that Carl and Sandra could become romantically involved.

If I were advising Carl, I'd suggest that he look elsewhere for a sexual partner. In particular, I'd refer him to the material earlier in this chapter about the *elusive spark*. Carl deserves sexual intimacy as much as the next person, but it's only going to happen with somebody who is temperamentally suited to him. The best thing for him, I reckon, would be to meet someone boring. I suspect there's no shortage of boring women who would jump at the chance to go out with a pleasant, clean-cut loss adjuster such as himself.

4

CAREER SUCCESS

Taking charge of your employment destiny

We all know people who can't stop job-hopping. One day they're bricklayers, then they're accountants, then they're dental hygienists, and so on – but no matter how many times they exchange one role for another, success always eludes them. Unfortunately, these people have failed to grasp the difference between a mere *series of jobs* and a *career*.

To better understand what it is that distinguishes a job from a career, consider two fictional individuals called Leon and Kenny.

Leon works in the post room at Piper Dynamics Transglobal Ltd, a large defence contractor. He comes in every day at nine, replenishes the second-floor stationery cupboard, checks the first-floor outgoing mail tray, delivers the internal post, franks the external post, has lunch, delivers more internal post, franks more external post, and leaves at five. The idea of advancing himself within the company never occurs to him. As long as his salary gets credited to his account each month, allowing him to pay the bills and have enough money left over to buy pot, he asks for nothing more. He will remain in his job until such time as he gets sacked for letting his pot habit spill over into his working life.

Now consider Kenny. Kenny also works in the post room at Piper Dynamics Transglobal Ltd. But unlike Leon, Kenny has a vision for his future. He comes in every day at nine, replenishes the first-floor stationary cupboard, reads part of a book about self-motivation techniques while having a coffee break, checks the second-floor outgoing mail tray, thinks about how to get a private audience with the manager of the Northeast Division, delivers the internal post, phones his tailor to check whether his new suit is ready, franks the external post, has lunch, delivers more internal post, renews his subscription to *Executive Quarterly*, franks more external post, schmoozes a couple of the girls from HR, and leaves at five fifteen. He is *determined* to advance himself within the company. In fact, he never doubts for a moment that one day he'll be in the hot seat – negotiating with high-ranking officials from the Ministry of Defence, sacking underlings whose performance doesn't meet his high standards, and raising the production target for plasma cannons by 50 per cent.

Leon merely has a job. Kenny, by contrast, has a *career.*

Trust me, you're not going to achieve success if you just coast along the way Leon does. Achieving success is about creating as many opportunities as possible for you to propel yourself forward, which is why you need to emulate Kenny. *Kenny has well and truly taken charge of his employment destiny.*

And so, I might add, have I. Lest there be any confusion: I'm not talking about rising through the ranks of the haulage firm I currently work for, nor any other haulage firm for that matter. Heaven forbid. No, the sense in which I have taken charge of my employment destiny is this: I have formulated the clearest possible vision for how I plan to launch a successful career as a self-help guru. I see my job at the haulage firm as being a crucial stepping stone to career success – not least because it gives me a stopgap source of income while I'm writing my book. (A bank loan would have fit the bill equally well, but unfortunately I wasn't able to obtain one.)

Besides, I have "unfinished business" with Louise. I'd be shooting myself in the foot if I quit my job and in so doing gave up Louise just when our relationship was on the verge of advancing to the next level.

Here is a rough outline of how I envisage my career panning out over the next few months:

- Once I have achieved the professional milestone of seeing my book published and universally lauded, I'll quit my job to concentrate on being a rising star in the field of self-help.
- The money generated from the sales of my book and assorted speaking engagements, etc, will allow me to support Louise financially. She will quit her own job, leaving her free to pursue her interests, whatever they might be.
- I will found my own company, Gary Speedwell Enterprises. To begin with, the company will be in the business of selling inspirational posters and

mouse mats, conquer-your-fears DVDs, speed-reading courses, self-hypnosis tutorials, etc. Later, it will expand into other areas: for example, cookware, sporting goods, and plush toys.

As you can see, my career trajectory from this point forward is like the trajectory of a rocket: straight up, and fast! What a contrast to Vincent's career. From what I can tell, Vincent's career is nothing but a never-ending succession of IT roles, each as dull as the last. Speak to him one month and he'll tell you he's working for a high-street bank. Speak to him a few months later and he'll inform you he's at the Inland Revenue. Next thing you hear, he's plying his trade at an insurance company, then a clothes retailer, then a train operator, then an animation studio. He is, to put it starkly, on a road to nowhere.

I only wish Vincent could have taken a leaf out of our father's book. In 1973, when Dad started work at the advertising sales firm Capshaw Communications, his job title was "Junior Sales Agent". But a man of my father's prodigious talent was bound to rise, and rise he did. After exactly one year, he was promoted from "Junior Sales Agent" to "Sales Agent". From then on, there was no stopping him.

If you'll indulge me, I'd like to offer a blow-by-blow account of my father's subsequent career. I think you will find there is much to learn from my father's example, and much to admire.

Dad didn't waste any time in gaining a reputation as the agent best placed to deal with clients based in Guildford, Woking and Camberley. *Nobody* could deal with Guildford-, Woking- and Camberley-based clients the way my father could. In fact, very few people even tried. Whenever a sales lead cropped up in Guildford, Woking or Camberley, the supervisor would say, without a moment's hesitation, "We'll give it to Richard. He's the Guildford-Woking-and-Camberley man."

Over the years, my father's sales agent colleagues left the company one by one, often to take up jobs in entirely different fields. They plainly couldn't "hack it" in the ultra-challenging environment of advertising sales. My father, on the other hand, positively thrived on challenges. Even though he could have had his pick of any number of jobs that were both less demanding and better paid than his job at Capshaw (I know this because he told me so himself), he chose to stay put. Why? Because his sights were fixed firmly on the future. He knew he had a *career* at Capshaw — whereas his expert judgement told him most of the other employers in the marketplace were fly-by-night operations that would have left him high and dry in the long run.

My father's career entered a new and exciting phase in 1989, when he acquired the title of sales executive (thanks to an organisation-wide renaming exercise). Not long after that, my father scored the lucrative Prentiss Baked Goods contract, which led to him receiving the coveted honour of "Sales Executive of the Month"! The Prentiss Baked Goods contract was actually *so* lucrative it would surely have earned my father a promotion to sales leader, had it not been for the accounting irregularities scandal that forced Prentiss Baked Goods out of business shortly after the contract was signed.

Despite this setback, my father never doubted that the promotion to sales leader would eventually be his. Sure enough, in 1991, Capshaw at last gave him responsibility for leading his own team, and the coveted title that went with it. Although both members of his team left the company a few months later, my father very much took this in his stride. He was still a sales leader, after all – and even better, as a team unto himself, he had a level of professional freedom that most employees can only dream of.

As my father approached retirement, he found that his younger colleagues' respect for him was at an all-time high. They even seemed positively intimidated by him at times. On one occasion, my father was walking back to his desk from the gents when he noticed five or six of his colleagues standing by the coffee machine, laughing. "What's everyone laughing about?" he asked. The laughter died down, and then there was silence. At length somebody said, "Nothing." There is an old saying that goes "It is better to be feared than loved..." but my father was in the happy position of not having to choose. He was both feared *and* loved.

In 2005, my father had a dry spell during which he didn't close any deals. This is of course something that happens to all salesmen at one time or another. Did his colleagues lose any of their respect for him during this dry spell? Not at all. When he finally did complete a deal – with First Choice Car Hire – his colleagues spontaneously burst into applause, as if to say, *"The old dog! He may be getting on in years, but he hasn't lost his magic touch."*

When my father retired from Capshaw in 2008, he was

given an attractive mantle clock in recognition of his long and distinguished service. The head of the Sales Department, a man half my father's age, slapped him on the back and said, "Well, what can I say: you made it, guy."

And he had. He truly had made it.

In short, my father had a model career. This isn't to imply that everything always went his way. As you'll have gathered from what I've described above, he had the odd setback over the years, just like everybody else. But let's be clear: *The mark of the successful person isn't some magic immunity to setbacks. The mark of the successful person is his ability to ignore setbacks whenever they occur.*

Ignore setbacks, seize your opportunities – these are the main lessons I'd like you to take from my account of my father's career. You might ask, "But what if the opportunities just *aren't* coming my way?" Well, then you had better start creating your own opportunities. This is certainly the attitude my father always instilled in me. "Model yourself on your Uncle Bert," he used to tell me. "*There* was a man who created his own opportunities." Bert was my father's older brother, whom I had never met, but had heard much about.

"Bert was fiercely independent," my father recounted. "Your grandparents wanted him to go into the watchmaking trade, but he was having none of it. He *knew* he was destined for greater things. One day, he walked out the door, saying he was going to the pictures, and that was the last we saw of him. Three weeks later we received a letter from him – from Africa! Now listen to me, Gary. When Bert walked into the Congolese jungle, he was seventeen years old. And when he walked out at twenty-one, he was rich!" My father paused, then carried on, his voice cracking with emotion. "We should all be bold enough to live like that. To grab life with both hands and wrestle it into submission. That's the way I'd like *you* to live your life, Gary. I don't mean move to Africa. Bert broke my mother's heart when he did that. What I mean is, take charge of your own destiny. That's the Speedwell way."

Naturally, I wanted to learn the details of how Bert had become rich, but my father said, "It doesn't matter how he did it." The only clue, and it wasn't really much of a clue, was an old black-and-white photo I found in the family album. It showed Uncle Bert in a pith helmet, standing on the deck of a steamboat, holding an elephant tusk in his arms. He was a very handsome man.

And if Uncle Bert's story doesn't inspire you to take charge of your career, I don't know what will.

Why the little things matter

Many self-help books stress the importance of "not losing sight of the bigger picture". I agree with these books wholeheartedly that the bigger picture is important, but let's not underrate the importance of the *smaller* picture. A good rule of thumb is: *Avoid losing sight of the bigger picture, but at the same time, avoid getting so preoccupied with not losing sight of the bigger picture that you lose sight of the little things.*

Losing sight of the little things would be a great shame, because at the end of the day, they matter. They don't matter as much as the big things, of course, but they still matter. If you think about the last time you gazed in wonder at the stars and planets when an image of them flashed up in a science documentary you were watching; or if you cast your mind back to the last time you were pleasantly surprised, say by the discovery of an entire unopened four-pack of Bounty bars at the back of your cupboard, you'll appreciate what I mean. Moments like these truly have the power to enhance your well-being somewhat.

Most of us, when we fantasise about what will make us happy, envisage some sort of major personal triumph, such as winning a Bafta, being appointed head of Product Development, or having a dukedom conferred upon oneself. And it is indeed true that any one of these things would be a big boost for one's self-esteem. But that's not to say we shouldn't also take pleasure in ordinary everyday experiences.

Allow yourself to appreciate the loveliness of a summer rain, or of a nice sunset. Or if those things don't do it for you, allow yourself to appreciate small acts of kindness on the part of strangers. I know I do. Last week, when shopping for shoes, I found a pair I liked and asked to see them in my size, but the sales assistant, an older gentleman in braces and shirtsleeves, glanced at my choice and said, "I'll be honest with you. Six months from now, you'd regret buying those shoes. The quality just isn't there. And to look at you, you're someone who appreciates quality. Am I right?"

"Yes, you are," I confirmed.

"I'll tell you what. There's some stock that just came in this morning, and I can think of one pair in particular that might be just what you're after. Stunning workmanship. Give me a few moments and I'll bring it out." Well, to cut a long story short, when I left the shop I was the proud owner of a very fine pair of Italian shoes, which, although quite similar in appearance to the pair I'd originally selected, will last me many times longer. (That's why I didn't mind that they were three times the price.) It's just so refreshing to encounter people like this kindly salesperson: selfless individuals for whom doing a good turn for their fellow man is its own reward.

If the little things have a crucial part to play in your personal life, that goes double for your professional life. My bowling buddy Nick once applied for a job at Jinks Taverns, the pub chain. The job was perfect for him, not least because its responsibilities included regular visits to pubs up and down the country. (Nick loves pubs. If he had his way, he'd probably *live* in a pub.) Understandably, Nick was very keen to land the job, so he did a great deal of preparation for the interview. On the big day, Nick put in the best performance he could possibly have hoped for, answering every question fluently. He was riding high when he emerged from the interview room. Only when he arrived home and saw himself in a full-length mirror did he realise that his flies were undone and he had a dab of mango chutney on his chin.

How you look, your posture – these things carry great weight with employers, so make sure you pay close attention to them. Here are some specific tips:

Tip #1: Dress to impress

The average male office worker is hopelessly unimaginative when it comes to dressing himself. All his suits are either charcoal-grey, black, or navy-blue. All his shirts have collars and buttons. All his ties are solid, striped, or spotted – God forbid he should ever wear a tie featuring a Union Jack motif or amusing cartoon characters!

Although the average female office worker has a more varied wardrobe, she can still fall into the trap of being overly conservative in her choices. How many women are bold enough to wear fishnet tights in the office, or glamorous dresses covered in sequins?

What people fail to realise is that by dressing in a wholly conventional way, they might as well be holding up a big sign that says "I'm generic". If you're an employer, who are you more likely to reward with a generous salary increase: a person who is indistinguishable from everybody else, or a person who stands out from the crowd? I think the answer is obvious.

There are numerous ways to differentiate yourself from your peers at work. If you are a man, why not consider a white or cream-coloured suit? Why not consider a ruffled shirt? You should also be more adventurous in your choice of fabrics. No need to restrict yourself to bog-standard wool or cotton. Alternative materials you could consider include linen, satin, velvet, cashmere, mohair, alpaca, and viscose.

I should also mention that I quite like tweed. Tweed

is what I will wear in my book jacket photo. It conveys a certain respectability.

If you are female, one way you can stand out from the crowd at work is by wearing a beret. I've never understood why we don't see more berets in the office. The same could be said of leather trousers. Anyway, these are just suggestions. The important thing is to be bold, and take advantage of the full range of fashion options available to you.

Tip #2: Adapt your handshake to the recipient

A firm handshake is not appropriate in every circumstance. How hard you should grip a person's hand depends on who they are. If you are shaking hands with someone who is... I won't say insignificant, but of *lesser* significance, like a lavatory attendant, then a bone-crushing handshake is uncalled for. Indeed, from a hygiene perspective if nothing else, you should seriously question why you are shaking hands with a lavatory attendant in the first place.

The key principle when it comes to handshakes is this: *The firmness of your handshake should be in direct proportion to the other person's level of power and prestige.* I will give you an example of how this works in practice. When I first joined Louise's team, I was introduced to Louise's manager, Ian. I made sure to give him a firm handshake. As a matter of fact, a split second into the handshake I noticed that his grip was somewhat weak, so I tightened my grip further while I continued shaking, until I saw him wincing ever so slightly, at which point I released his hand. In this way, I "won" the handshake, effectively raising my own status and lowering Ian's. Louise witnessed the encounter, and she must have perceived on some level that Ian had been vanquished by me.

Tip #3: Be unflappable

Let's say you are a manager. Two members of your team are vying for a single promotion, and it falls to you to decide whom to give it to.

The first candidate complains constantly. He complains about the food in the canteen, he complains about the poor quality of the view from his window, he complains about the incompetence of his colleagues, etc. The second candidate never says a bad word about anyone or anything, but she does have a bizarre set of plastic trolls adorning her cubicle. Literally dozens of them – God only knows where she gets them from; some are quite hideous. Which candidate are you going to choose? Clearly, you are going to choose the troll woman, because despite the trolls, at least she doesn't make everyone's life a misery by complaining all the time.

Here is my advice: no matter how much things are getting to you in the workplace, do not gripe. Always give the impression of being completely unruffled, even if in reality you are at your wits' end.

Kim never even came close to heeding this advice. During our marriage, whenever I asked her how things were going at the restaurant, she would always respond with a litany of complaints. Many of these complaints were about customers – how they'd rudely snap their fingers to get her attention, or allow their kids to run riot, or leave minuscule tips. She also complained about the manager of the restaurant, whom she described as "creepy" and as having a strange odour.

Now, it would be one thing if I was the only person Kim shared these gripes with, but I wasn't. She mentioned having regular gripe sessions with a couple of the other waitresses at the restaurant. To me, this didn't bode well. I thought: *sooner or later, the smelly manager is going to discover that Kim is a complainer, and when the time comes for him to appoint his successor, she is most definitely* not *going to be in the running.*

I expressed this concern to Kim, but she brushed it aside. "I can't think of anything I'd want less than to manage that stupid restaurant," she said.

The trouble with people like Kim is that nothing ever satisfies them. Kim eventually left the waitressing profession because she didn't find it fulfilling, but it's not as if any of the jobs she's had since then have made her any happier. They've all been, in her words, "annoying", "dumb", "pointless", or "bogus".

Her latest job, at the foam rubber manufacturing firm, was no exception. Notice my use of the past tense. That's because Kim doesn't work there any longer. She wasn't fired; rather, she quit! I learned about this yesterday when she rang me up to tell me the news.

"I'm hoping you're going to tell me you've got another job lined up," I said to her.

"Nope, not a thing."

"Well, do you have *any* sort of inkling of what you're going to do next? I don't think it's a very good move to quit your job without at least having some kind of goal in mind."

"I have a goal, Gary. I know exactly what I'm going to do next. I'm going to head over to London so the two of us can have our showdown. I'm sure I've mentioned that more than once."

"You know, Kim," I replied, "if that's all your goal is, you should never have quit your job. There was no need. Especially as there's not going to *be* any showdown."

Completely ignoring my last statement, Kim said, "The truth is, I was planning to quit sooner or later anyway. Roxanne forced my hand, because she was being difficult about letting me have the time off for the London trip. It got to the point where I thought, am I actually going to have to get down on my hands and knees and beg this woman to give me a week's vacation? – when suddenly it dawned on me, why should I stick around and put up with this treatment? I quit then and there. Two hours later I was looking into flights."

"First of all," I said, "a week? You must be joking. And second, the whole idea of you coming to London is completely impractical on every level. I'm sure you haven't even thought about where you'd stay. Do you know how expensive hotels are in London?"

"I do, actually," she said. "That's why I'm going to be staying with you."

"What? That's – there's just no way. It's not possible."

"Why not? You live alone. You've mentioned how big your apartment is, so I know you've got enough space…"

"But there isn't any sort of… it wouldn't be…"

"I'll tell you what, Gary. Keep trying to think of an

objection that holds water, and if you come up with one, phone me back and let me know what it is. Meanwhile I've got stuff to do. I'm 'very busy', to use one of your classic phrases."

And then she rang off. (I felt rather perturbed that on this occasion it was Kim who was ending the call rather than me.) Afterwards, I thought to myself: *Kim has really outdone herself this time. That she would actually quit her job for the sake of this mad fantasy of flying to London to achieve "closure" with me is unbelievable! I know what's going to happen. After getting a bit further down the road of looking into flights, she'll realise how absurd her plan is, at which point she'll get panicky about the fact that she no longer has her job and will plead with Roxanne to get it back, but her plea will fall on deaf ears. And then she'll ring me up to sound off about what's happened and probably find a way of blaming me for it.*

It's all very irrational, but it's what I've come to expect of Kim.

Tip #4: Impress your current boss

Deep down, everybody wants to be their own boss. Well, what's stopping them? Perhaps it's that they keep telling themselves, "I'm not ready." And to be fair, maybe they aren't. But in that case, what they need to do is implement some confidence-boosting measures.

Arguably the single best thing the average wage slave can do to build his confidence is to *impress his current boss.* The more the wage slave impresses his boss, the more his boss will praise him. The more his boss praises him, the more the wage slave will grow in self-belief, until eventually he is ready to ditch his job and go off and work for himself.

As for the specific techniques you might use to impress your boss, they are many and varied. What might help is if I outline some of the techniques I have been using lately to impress my own boss, Louise.

I admit that my main purpose in impressing Louise has been to kindle romance, not to boost my confidence – because when you have my level of confidence, a confidence boost is surplus to requirements. But no matter. Most of the techniques I'm about to describe apply equally well regardless of whether your ultimate aim is to earn plaudits from your boss or to seduce him/her.

Tip #5: Talk the talk

One of the ways in which I have sought to impress Louise is by speaking in a way that demonstrates my intelligence and sophistication.

At the start of this week, Louise came to me with a request. "What I need," she said, "is for someone to get hold of a download of the last three months' transactions from Finance, cross-reference them to the Sales database, and flag all the entries where the multiple-order discount has been applied in error. Do you think that's something you'd be capable of?"

Without a moment's hesitation, I answered, "Whatever the mind of man can conceive and believe, it can achieve."

It was obvious from the way Louise raised her eyebrows that the profundity of my reply had knocked her for six. "I take it that's your way of saying 'Yes'?" she asked. When I confirmed it was, she remarked, "I can't say I'm familiar with the quotation."

"Not many people are," I reassured her. "It's from Napoleon. I believe it's something he said to inspire his troops."

Tip #6: Show your superiority

E-readers are indispensable gizmos, but if you want to impress people with your superior taste in books, you need at least some of those books to be traditional paper-based ones, otherwise how will anybody know what you are reading? By the same token, you need to own some CDs. At work, I make a point nowadays of always having a range of books and CDs on my desk that mark me out as being a person of exceptional taste. I vary them from week to week, to showcase the full range of my literary and musical interests. My recent choices have included:

- *An Infallible Motion: The Life and Poetry of Krzysztof Baczynski*
- *Love in the Time of Cholera*
- *A Compendium of Mongolian Throat-Singing, Featuring the Yenisei River Choir* (Two-CD Set)

I haven't actually read the *Infallible Motion* book and the *Cholera* book yet, but I gather from the reviews that they're wonderfully stimulating and thought-provoking. As to the *Mongolian Throat-Singing* album, I have listened to it several times, always with pleasure. I've even tried to sing along to it, though so far without success.

The day before I wrote this, I was using my work computer's CD-ROM drive and a pair of headphones to listen to *The Very Best of Frank Sinatra*. I figured sooner or later Louise would walk by, spot the Sinatra CD case on my desk, and be powerfully struck by this evidence of my good taste. However, by the time I was three-quarters of the way through the CD, Louise still hadn't walked by. So I decided to change tactics. I unplugged the headphones, so that Frank's voice emerged loud and clear from the computer's speakers. Colleagues in the vicinity looked up from what they were doing. Just as the track I'd been listening to (*The Way You Look Tonight*) was drawing to a close, Louise appeared at my desk.

"Thanks for sharing that with us, Gary," she said.

"Not at all," I replied, modestly.

Tip #7: Demonstrate your expertise

If you have expertise in something, why not give your boss a tantalising glimpse of it? A few days ago, I had the opportunity to show off one of my lesser-known skills to Louise. The situation was as follows. The only colour printer in the office was refusing to print, and rather than wait ages for an engineer to show up and fix the problem, I thought to myself, *I'm mechanically minded. What's stopping me from repairing the printer myself?* As the printer was clearly visible from Louise's office, she would be sure to see me in action.

I started off by opening up the printer and looking for a paper jam. There wasn't one, so I proceeded to carry out a more in-depth investigation. I removed the toner cartridge and discovered beneath it a squareish component which I couldn't identify, but which looked dusty. Blowing off the dust didn't correct the problem, but it did reveal a pair of screws which secured the top plate of the squareish component. My intuition told me that behind this plate might be some clues as to what the problem was.

At this point, I looked up and saw that Louise had her eyes fixed on me. Result!

I fetched a penknife screwdriver from my desk drawer. Within a few moments the plate was off, exposing a small circuit board. This proved to be the turning point in my investigations. Why? Because as soon as I saw the circuit board, a thought hit me: *If I'm going to be poking around inside this printer where there are exposed electrical components, I probably ought to unplug the printer.* After following the power lead from the back of the printer to where it disappeared behind a table, I crouched down and followed it further to the wall socket where it was plugged in – or rather, where it should have been plugged in. Yes, that's right: the plug was just resting on the floor! One of the cleaners must have pulled it out to free up a wall socket and forgotten to plug it back in. Anyway, as soon as I reinstated the plug, the printer sprung into life, whirring and clicking in a reassuring manner.

I glanced over at Louise. "Bravo, Gary," she said, clearly impressed. I reckon what impressed her most was the *way* I'd fixed the printer, using detective work and analytical thinking. Those are just the sorts of aptitudes a discerning boss like Louise is sure to find appealing and, I daresay, manly.

While I'm on the subject of expertise, let me say this. If you want others to consider you an expert, then you should make it your mission to *act* like an expert and *sound* like an expert.

Of course, one thing that might make this easier is if you actually *are* an expert. For instance, anybody who has heard my ex-partner Sandra talk about topics like classical music or painting will agree that she sounds wholly credible when doing so. Why? In large part, it's because she herself is a bona fide artist. She is a natural with a pencil, pen, paintbrush, indeed any drawing or painting implement. Jack has been known to say to her, "Draw me an elephant, Mummy", or "Draw me a platypus, Mummy" and in literally two minutes she produces the most magnificent elephant or platypus you've ever seen.

When someone has a genuine skill or talent, as Sandra does, the world will always pick up on it sooner or later. I happen to know that Sandra's artistic talent played a major part in getting her career to where it is today. Years ago she was working in an administrative job at the local council. One day, her manager, whose name was Jacqui, came to her in a flap. "I've drafted this slide presentation," said Jacqui, "but it looks a complete mess, and I've no time to tidy it up before three o'clock today when I'm supposed to be delivering it. If you could knock it into shape, Sandra, I'd be so grateful." Well, by the time Sandra was done revamping the slides, they weren't just tidier – they were visually stunning. It was like the difference between getting your wedding invitations done by a professional on the one hand, and on the other hand knocking them up yourself using a free drawing program and an old inkjet printer you salvaged from a skip.

Soon, word spread about Sandra's talent for design, so her colleagues started submitting their presentations to her for improvement. After a while she thought, *If everyone thinks I'm so good at design, maybe that's what I should pursue as a career.* She quit her job, trained as a graphic designer, and the rest is history. Now, don't misunderstand me. My main purpose in describing all this isn't to place Sandra on some sort of pedestal. Why would I wish to do that? I'm just trying to show how being perceived as an expert can open up opportunities for you.

After all, why did you buy this book? You bought it because you saw the synopsis and author bio on the back cover and thought, *Clearly this person is an expert, the kind of person who could impart all sorts of valuable knowledge to me.* At least I'm guessing that's the reason you bought the book. I can't rule out the possibility that you had some additional motivations – perhaps you were drawn to my photograph, or the book was part of a two-for-one offer – but the fact remains, my expertise was probably the overriding factor.

So if you have a unique skill or talent, make it known. And if you don't have a unique skill or talent, then for God's sake acquire one as soon as possible.

Tip #8: Raise your status

In any institution, be it a school, a workplace, a prison, or some combination of all three, you can be sure there is going to be a pecking order of some kind. It's very much like what you get in the animal kingdom, where, for instance, the typical wolf pack has three or four dominant wolves who effectively "rule the roost". Being at the top of the pecking order brings a lot of benefits. For one thing, as a dominant wolf, you get to eat all the choicest bits of the lion, unlike the lower-status wolves, who have to content themselves with whatever is left on the carcass after the elite have had their fill.

Granted, things aren't quite as simple in human institutions as they are in wolf packs. That's because humans have "unofficial" pecking orders as well as official ones. Let me explain what I mean. Suppose Harry belongs to a team of estate agents managed by somebody called Bill. You might assume that Bill, as manager, ranks above Harry in the pecking order. And when it comes to the "official" pecking order, you're right. However, the *unofficial* pecking order is a completely different story. What if Bill is a weakling who is universally disrespected by his team? And what if Harry is a charismatic charmer who is admired by everybody (including, secretly, Bill)? In that case, *Harry ranks higher than Bill in the unofficial pecking order.*

With all this in mind, ask yourself: where do *you* rank in the unofficial pecking order at your workplace?

If pondering this question makes you uncomfortable, you are not alone. Most people are reluctant to seriously consider the question of how they are regarded by others, for fear of having to face up to their own inferiority. Still, if success is the goal you're striving for, there is no point just dwelling on your strengths. You also need to acknowledge your weaknesses, so that you can take steps to overcome them, or disguise them.

Be on the lookout for the telltale signs that could mark you out as being a low-status person. Low-status people tend to:

- speak in thin, reedy voices
- avoid eating crunchy foods for fear of drawing attention to themselves
- make nervous bird-like movements
- never borrow your stapler off your desk unless you are there to give permission
- put up no resistance when you hang your wet coat on the back of their chair

High-status people, on the other hand, tend to:

- pound their fists on the table
- say things like "Let's cut to the chase" and "No guts, no glory"
- make sweeping arm gestures when they speak, sometimes accidentally hitting the people on either side of them in the process
- carry around at least five different portable electronic devices, all of which they consult at frequent intervals
- use boxing metaphors

What happens if, after comparing your own character traits to the inventories above, you realise with dismay that you are a low-status person? How do you go about boosting your status?

Well, for a start, you ought to do something about your feeble speaking voice and your nervous bird-like movements. But these measures will be of limited effectiveness unless you also work on your attitude, because no matter how much you might try to conceal it, your attitude is something others instantly pick up on.

An attitude of "I'm only a humble wage slave" is a recipe for nobody taking you seriously. Instead, your attitude should be: "I am superior to all these losers."

Now, you may of course already be a high-status person. That's great, but it doesn't mean you can rest easy. You need to defend your high status at all times, otherwise you risk losing it. I would never let anyone at my workplace get away with thinking they're better than me, even if they occupy a senior position. Just today, I felt the need to give a high-level manager a forceful demonstration of my personal superiority.

The manager in question was Rob, the service coordinator, who had phoned me out of the blue to express some concern about a forecasting spreadsheet I'd drawn up for him. He said he was finding my figures "puzzling" and wanted to know if I could meet him at 2pm so that we could "walk through" the spreadsheet.

Well, even though I was free at 2pm, there was no way I was going to let him be the one to dictate the time of our meeting. "Three o'clock would be better for me, actually," I told him. He consented. Score one point to Gary!

I scored another point by not showing up for our meeting punctually at three. Instead, I lingered at my desk until five past. This brings me to an important rule for asserting your high status: *make the other person wait.*

When I entered the meeting room, Rob was pacing back and forth. We made eye contact.

"Well," he said, "now that you're finally here, let's get started."

Rob, who had a printout of my spreadsheet in front of him, seemed determined to go through it with a fine-toothed comb. As he worked his way down the page, he said things like "I just don't understand this £1,800" and "I can't see how Goods Category JT could bring in eight times more than Goods Category CL. Three times I could understand, maybe even four times, but eight times?"

All this focus on small details was beginning to get tiresome, so I decided to seize control of the discussion. "All right, Rob," I said, "let's cut to the chase. What's the problem here, really?"

Rob appeared quite taken aback by my authoritative tone. Score yet another point to Gary! He said, "The basic problem is, Gary, I just can't get these forecasts to make any sense at all."

I was about to suggest that he try harder, but at that moment my mobile phone, which was on the table in front of me, started vibrating. I checked the display: the call was coming from a landline number I didn't recognise. I suppose I could have let it go to voicemail, but why throw away another golden opportunity to make Rob wait?

"Excuse me, Rob. I'd better take this." And with that I left the meeting room, closing the door behind me.

The voice I heard upon answering the phone was a

familiar one. "Gary, it's Martin Tierney. Your landlord."

"Martin! Good to hear from you. Are you well?"

"I am, Gary, I am well – apart from one thing, which is what I'm ringing about. You might remember I contacted you some time ago about your rent arrears?"

"Oh, yes, I do remember that."

"But here we are, a couple of weeks later, and your rent still hasn't been paid."

"I haven't forgotten about the rent, Martin, honestly. It'll be with you very soon."

"When you say 'very soon'…"

"Ten days from now, maximum."

"I have to be honest, Gary: ten days from now will be too late."

"Really?"

"I'm afraid so."

"I was just hoping you could give me more leeway because—"

"I can't."

"Because it's not a question of not being able to afford it. It's just down to some temporary cash flow problems I've been having."

"I understand, but regardless, you need to make sure the rent gets to me by Wednesday evening."

"Okay. Just so we're clear, if the money *doesn't* reach you by Wednesday evening, then that would mean…?"

"It would mean eviction, I'm sorry to say."

"Don't be sorry, Martin."

"It's nothing personal, Gary. A contract is a contract, that's all."

We left it there. Now, you might think Martin's

ultimatum would have panicked me, but in fact it didn't. Why not? It's because, a few days previously, I'd discovered a way of potentially getting my hands on some much-needed short-term cash.

You see, I happened to be in the market for one of those magnifying glasses with a built-in light that illuminates the page, as I figured it might make a good birthday present for my mother, whose eyesight isn't what it once was. Of the results that came back from my web search for "magnifier", the one that caught my eye was:

> *The Money Magnifier*
> *Tired of puny investment returns? Get the lowdown on the amazing wealth-building system that delivers returns of up to* **2,000% per month!**

In a flash, I forgot all about birthday present shopping. I mean, *"2,000% per month"* – how much would that be per day? I did some rapid calculations.

There are thirty days in a month, give or take, so the daily return must be 2,000 per cent divided by thirty, which is 67 per cent. And at 67 per cent per day, my return after five days would be 67 times five, which is 335 per cent. So if I put £300 into the scheme, I would be sitting on a tidy profit of £1,000 just five days later! What about after a full month? My total profit at that stage would be an astonishing £4,000!

Only one question remained: was it too good to be true?

I clicked on the link. A few minutes perusing the

website was all I needed to convince myself that this was a wholly legitimate money-magnification scheme. For one thing, the website design was polished and professional. For another, their scheme is accredited by something called the Pan-Global High-Yield Investment Monitoring Service. Most compelling of all were the testimonials from happy customers:

> *Before I discovered your programme, I was so strapped for cash I was living off kidney beans and tap water. I'm pleased to say I've now been able to upgrade to lobster, fillet steak, and Dom Pérignon. Thanks, Money Magnifier, for giving me the lifestyle I always dreamed of!* – John from Milton Keynes

> *To be frank, I wasn't expecting much from the Money Magnifier system. I've tried a lot of wealth-building systems in the past, all of them promising the earth but delivering only lacklustre results. Well, I'm happy to report that the Money Magnifier is different: it's the "real deal". I've racked up gains of £95,000 so far this year – not bad for less than two hours' effort per week!* – Chris from Sheffield

> *My message to anyone who's still not sure whether to take the plunge on the Money Magnifier is: what are you waiting for? As someone who has made £67,000 from the*

system in three months, my only regret is that I didn't discover the Money Magnifier system years ago. – Emily from Brighton

Apparently, the money you pay over to them is entrusted to their crack team of traders, who buy and sell "prime European bank financial instruments" on your behalf. I can't say I understand the details, but – and this is the beauty of the scheme – I don't need to. All I have to do is hand over a bit of cash and watch it grow, day by day.

Don't get me wrong. I firmly believe that any success worth having should be attained by one's own efforts. It's just that sometimes a short-term infusion of cash is just what's needed to keep a lid on certain distractions, such as Martin's rent demands, which might otherwise impede one's pursuit of success.

Anyway, once I got off the phone from Martin, I returned to the meeting room. As I entered the room, Rob ceased the pacing he'd been doing and asked me, "Is this time not convenient for you?"

"It's fine, I'm okay to carry on now," I said. "That was just some urgent business I had to attend to."

"You know what, Gary? Let's not carry on. We'll reconvene in a day or two when you're less distracted – if that's all right with you?"

"If that's all right with you"! The deference in Rob's words was unmistakable. *Another* victory for Gary!

Choosing the right profession for you

Let's say you heed every piece of advice I've given in this chapter so far. That is, let's say you transform yourself into the bold, sophisticated, sharp-dressing, initiative-seizing, challenge-embracing, talent-exhibiting, gripe-avoiding professional you are eminently capable of being. Will career success follow automatically?

Yes.

Still, I must sound a note of caution. Career success is a good thing only insofar as it brings you fulfilment. And it won't bring you fulfilment *if your profession is boring*.

For example, suppose you rise through the ranks to become head of Quality Assurance at a ketchup bottling plant. On the one hand, you've attained a form of career success, for which I applaud you. On the other hand, is this the sort of career success that will bring happiness? Not a chance, because ketchup quality assurance is too boring for words.

Another example would be if your job were to supervise a crew of men tasked with mixing bitumen for road repairs. Sure, it's a responsible position, but how unutterably dull! You'd be better off taking a pay cut and becoming one of the people who actually fill and smooth the repair. At least then the work would be hands-on and might bring a measure of satisfaction for a job well done.

(Do not under any circumstances get roped into being the person who stands around stirring the vat of tar over a small flame to maintain the right consistency. I can't think of anything redeeming about such a job, any more than I can think of anything redeeming about loss adjusting.)

Boring professions aren't the only ones you should steer clear of. You should also avoid ones that are:

- too depressing – such as morgue proprietor
- too stressful – such as undercover agent infiltrating a mafia crime family
- too unconscionable – such as supplier of enriched uranium to rogue states

At this point you might be thinking: *But what if there were a generous salary and benefits package? Mightn't that compensate for the less-attractive aspects of the job?* Hardly, in my view. Even if you have a lovely four-bedroom house, a company BMW and a healthcare scheme that entitles you to three dental check-ups in any twelve-month period, you can't reasonably expect any of these things to make up for the misery of having to spend five days a week at an unbearable job.

You can save yourself a lot of bother by getting yourself into an appropriate profession without delay. Then the *whole* of your life can be fulfilling, not just the part spent away from your work. Imagine that! Play your cards right, and the misery of your work life will be a thing of the past.

Don't believe me? Ask yourself: what accounts for the fact that rock musicians, footballers, stunt pilots and professional gamblers are such happy people? The answer is simple: they are happy because they had the foresight to choose fun, interesting professions.

Bruce Springsteen is a prime example of the sort of person I mean. A man of his talent could have succeeded at anything he turned his hand to. I have no doubt Bruce could have become a tax lawyer if he'd so chosen. But he opted for a different career path, presumably because he said to himself, "I'm Bruce Springsteen, and Bruce Springsteen wasn't born to be a tax lawyer. Bruce Springsteen was *born to run*."

Of course, it's not immediately clear what the right profession is for someone who was "born to run". One possibility would have been for Bruce to be a professional runner of road races, but that would've meant submitting to external authority, which is not Bruce's style. When Bruce wants to run, he runs. There is no question of Bruce letting "The Man" tell him *when* to run, or *how* to run, or *where* to run. This holds true whether the "Man" in question is Hugh Brasher (race director of the London Marathon) or society as a whole.

Where was I? I guess my overriding point is that Bruce made a shrewd move by becoming a rock star. Similarly, my own choice of future profession (self-help guru) fits me like a glove, and will bring infinitely more stimulation than any desk job ever could.

As far as I can work out, there is only one reason anybody ever chooses an ordinary run-of-the-mill profession. This reason is *lack of imagination*. Unfortunately, as I've said before, the society we live in is downright hostile to imagination. The sad truth is that most people have had their imagination knocked out of them by the time they reach adulthood. This explains why so few of us are doing the jobs we dreamed of as children: why, in short, the world contains so few astronauts and so many management consultants.

The average five-year-old could, in fact, teach us a lot about how to choose a profession. Accordingly, the way I'm going to demonstrate what I consider the correct approach to choosing a profession is by using the example of my own son Jack, who happens to have just turned five.

I saw Jack this past Sunday, at the second of his two birthday celebrations – the first one being on Saturday, the day of his actual birthday. The Saturday celebration was a traditional kids' party with all Jack's friends in attendance. Sunday, on the other hand, was a more intimate affair: a picnic in the park, featuring just Sandra, Jack and me.

It was as we were sitting on our picnic blanket, eating brownies, that Jack suddenly asked me why I wasn't a footballer.

"Well," I said, "to be a footballer like the ones on the telly, I'd have to be really *serious* about football. I like football, but I'm not serious about it in the same way the professionals are."

"Oh," said Jack. "Then you could be a zookeeper, like Tommy's dad."

I leaned in close to Sandra and asked her, "Why does he think Tommy's dad is a zookeeper?" Tommy's dad is actually an accountant.

She laughed. "I don't know. He also thinks Ben's dad is a tightrope walker. I think he got the wrong idea when he overheard Ben's dad using the phrase 'high-wire act' as a figure of speech."

"Be a zookeeper, Daddy!" Jack repeated. "We can *both* be zookeepers."

"Being a zookeeper would be the best thing ever," I said, "but I'm not sure I have time for it. I already have a job, remember?"

Jack nodded and said, "You drive lorries."

"Are you sure Daddy drives lorries?" asked Sandra.

"Yes!" insisted Jack.

I wasn't keen on the idea of Jack telling everybody I was a lorry driver, so I corrected him. "I don't actually drive the lorries. It's more that I put together the paperwork that, erm…" Sensing Jack wouldn't understand me if I carried on in that vein, I tried to think of a better way of describing my responsibilities. "Think of it this way. Remember how we were watching motor racing on television once, and how every so often a car would pull over and there'd be mechanics who replaced the tyres in just a few seconds?"

"No," said Jack.

"Well, my point is, even though those mechanics don't drive the cars, they're still very important. They're important because the drivers would be stuck without them. Just like the lorry drivers from the place where I work would be stuck without me."

"When you change the tyres on the lorries," asked Jack, "do you lift up the lorry with one hand and take the tyre off with the other hand?"

Luckily, Sandra intervened at this point, taking it upon herself to explain my job to Jack in the simplest terms possible. The way she described my job, I sent lorries all over the country delivering things people need: furniture, clothes, food, and so on. "Maybe Daddy sent the lorry that delivered the new Lego police station you got for your birthday," she added.

"Did you?" Jack asked me.

"I might have done."

"Now," said Sandra, "why don't you tell Daddy what you decided you're going to be when you grow up?"

"I'm going to be a fireman!"

Jack went on to describe how the fire brigade had visited his school, and how he and his classmates had been allowed to climb into the fire engine, and how the firemen had even let him get behind the wheel at one stage. "I wanted to drive the fire engine, but they wouldn't let me," he recalled.

I was proud of Jack's choice of profession. Of all the jobs he could have set his heart upon – actuary, civil servant, corporate hospitality coordinator, etc – he went for a job that was everything a job should be: exciting, dynamic, heroic.

"I reckon you'd be a *brilliant* fireman," I said.

"I know," said Jack. "I also want to be a spaceman and kill aliens, and a footballer, and a man who drives a submarine."

"That's a lot of jobs for just one person," said Sandra. "You're going to be busy."

I said, "Almost as busy as Daddy, with his full-time job and his book."

Jack pondered this.

"Mummy?" said Jack.

"Yes?"

"Can we have a picnic like this every day?"

"Is that so you can have brownies and crisps every day?"

"Yes, but also so I can be with my mummy *and* my daddy."

"You know exactly the right thing to say," I said to Jack, lifting him onto my lap and hugging him tight. When he tried to escape from the hug, I let myself fall backwards so that I was lying on my back with him sprawled on top of me. He began to giggle.

Sandra announced, "I want to be part of this hug, too," and draped herself over both Jack and me.

"Help, help!" I cried. "Daddy's getting crushed!" Jack went into gales of laughter at this, and laughed all the harder when Sandra observed, "It's like a sandwich – Mummy and Daddy are the two slices of bread, and Jack is the filling!"

When Jack had finished laughing, he wriggled out from between us, picked up the half brownie he'd left on his plate and set about eating it.

"Well," said Sandra, smiling down at me, "this is awkward."

"Is that a new perfume you're wearing?" I asked.

"No, it's the one you got me the Christmas before last. Spirit, by Givenchy."

Sandra lifted herself off me. I sat up.

"How is your job going?" she asked.

"Extremely well. This is going to sound like boasting but…"

"You're allowed to boast."

"…but I'm finding it quite easy. It never feels like I'm working very hard, but somehow I'm excelling."

"Sounds like you've found your ideal job."

"Well, I wouldn't say *ideal*. I mean… you know what

I'd say my ideal job is."

Sandra nodded. "Self-help guru. But it sounds like you've found your ideal *stopgap* job."

"Maybe."

"No, not maybe. You have."

From the way she said this, I could tell something was wrong.

"What's bothering you?" I asked.

Keeping her voice down so that Jack wouldn't hear, she explained, "We separated because you wouldn't get a job when Jack and I needed you to... and yet the first thing you did after moving out was to get a job. Now a year has passed, and you've *still* got your job. And we're still separated. Does that make any sense to you?"

I considered this and then replied, "Well, the job is exactly what you said – a stopgap. A temporary thing while my plans and projects take shape."

"But when we were living together, a job was out of the question as far as you were concerned. *Even* as a temporary thing while your plans and projects took shape."

"That was different. When we were living together, what I didn't have was these long, lonely evenings to fill with writing. Quitting my job was the only way I was going to be able to devote time to the book."

"Is that what your evenings are like now?" she asked. "Long and lonely?"

"I don't know why I said lonely. I meant... solitary. I've got all this time to myself now, and—"

"And you miss us sometimes?"

The question took me by surprise. I couldn't think what to say.

"Well, Jack and I miss you," she added. "I can't see any point in pretending we don't."

How exactly it happened, I can't quite remember, but before long, my arm was round Sandra's shoulder, her head was leaning against mine, I could feel her hair tickling my cheek… Meanwhile, Jack had finished all the brownies and was practising balancing the empty tin on his head.

I felt oddly peaceful. For a brief instant I thought of Louise, but she seemed unreal, like a face in a print ad for cosmetics. I gazed into the distance and saw people out on the tennis courts. Then I remembered about Carl.

"How are the tennis lessons going?" I asked.

"What tennis lessons?"

"Your friend Carl was giving you lessons, right?"

"That was just a one-off."

"Was it?"

"*Yes*, it was. I don't see why you're so interested. What does it matter?"

Jack piped up, "Carl has a red car, a fast one. It's new."

"Has he?" I asked. "How do you know it's fast?"

"Carl gave me a ride in it," answered Jack.

"Oh, but he wasn't going above the speed limit or anything," Sandra assured me. "And it was just round the block. I made Carl promise to be extra careful."

"Well, no need for me to be concerned, then," I said. Sandra looked annoyed. I continued, "Anyway, what's he doing with a fancy sports car? Can he really afford it on a loss adjuster's salary?"

"His job pays more than you might think," said Sandra.

"He told you his salary? That's interesting. If I were him, I wouldn't boast about how much I earn. It's hardly dignified."

"But you're not him, so…"

"What do you mean?"

She seemed on the verge of tears. "I don't know. I just mean you're not him. It doesn't matter – I don't even want to talk about this. I don't want to talk about Carl."

In the few remaining minutes before I parted from Sandra and Jack, Sandra and I didn't talk any more about Carl. In fact, we didn't talk about anything. We just sat in silence, punctuated only by a single comment from Sandra:

"Why do you always have to spoil things like this?"

I didn't have an answer. I felt deflated and a bit confused. Something *had* been spoiled, I could feel it, but I couldn't put my finger on what it was, nor could I decide who was really to blame for spoiling it. Was it me, or was it Sandra?

Thinking about it in more depth after I got home, I realised something. The person who was to blame for spoiling things wasn't me. It wasn't Sandra, either. *It was Carl.*

I thought to myself: *Carl should never have given my son a ride in his car. It was totally inappropriate. Telling Sandra what he earns was totally inappropriate too. Who does he think he is? He's nothing but a jumped-up loss adjuster. I'll bet he's never come to terms with being in a boring profession. So to compensate, he drives a flash car and boasts about his salary.*

In thinking these thoughts, I could feel myself getting increasingly angry. I knew this wasn't healthy, so I dug out my copy of *Mastering Your Emotions in Five Easy Steps* by Guy Gunderson, and re-read the introductory chapter. That helped a bit.

LIVING IN THE NOW

Why pain and anguish are nothing to worry about

When I was very young, I was terrified of monsters – nasty, bug-eyed, hairy, slavering, many-tentacled monsters who lurked in the darkness of my bedroom at night, or so I'd convinced myself. I wasn't about to take chances with these monsters. For instance, I always made sure not to let my feet or hands poke out from under the covers, for fear that one of the monsters would seize hold of me if I ever did.

Why am I telling you this? I'm not entirely sure. My thoughts have been all over the place lately, and the monsters-in-the-bedroom thing popped into my mind a minute ago for no apparent reason. Thinking about it, however, it does sort of link up to the theme of this chapter. Let me explain.

Every one of us has at one time or other got extremely worried or distressed about something, only to realise later that there was nothing to be concerned about. The bedroom-dwelling monsters of my childhood were, of course, terrifying at the time. But they came to seem a lot less terrifying once I got older and stopped believing in them. There is a deep lesson here: *When you stop acknowledging the existence of something, it loses its power to hurt you.*

The story of the boy who cried wolf illustrates this principle very clearly. In case you don't know the story, it's about a group of villagers who get into a major panic when a little boy alerts them that a dangerous wolf is on the loose. The villagers are so on edge they can hardly sleep at night. But once they come round to the opinion that this so-called "wolf" is a fiction, their agitation melts away and they are able to resume normal life.

This story is the perfect illustration of how, when something is distressing you, your best defence is to *refuse to accept its reality*.

Be aware that this doesn't apply in every situation. For example, if you were being mauled by a bear, the strategy I'm describing would be of limited value and you would have to try something else. But in most cases, it works like a charm.

One type of situation where it really comes into its own is if you find yourself tormented by painful memories of past events. Try the following experiment. Think about something painful from your past, preferably something that still makes you wince at the mere recollection of it. It could be about being betrayed by someone you trusted. It could be about being on the receiving end of a cruel humiliation of some sort. Or it could simply be about having something heavy fall on you.

Now say the following words to yourself:

> "My painful experience *isn't real*, any more
> than the monsters of Gary's childhood
> imagination were real."

I hope this made you feel better. But if it didn't – if, when I instructed you to say those words, your first impulse was to spring to your feet in indignation and cry out, "Of course it's real! I remember it like it was yesterday" – then I would counter: *that's just it.* Yesterday doesn't exist. Neither does tomorrow. The only thing that exists is *today.* Or to be really precise about it, the only thing that exists is the infinitesimal sliver of today that you're experiencing riiiiiiiight... *now.*

Given the above, why do we ever trouble ourselves about the past? Why do we ever feel guilty about the past, depressed about the past, angry about the past? I can only shake my head sadly and say: *I wish I knew.* For whatever reason, we insist on treating the past as if it's important, when really it has no importance whatsoever. How could it? It's gone. And, barring a major advance in the science of time travel, it's never coming back.

Appreciating the moment

Trust me, nothing good is ever going to come of taking your past seriously. Insofar as you keep ruminating about the past, you can never hope to find peace. You will be like the driver who insists on keeping his eyes on the rear-view mirror the whole time. I'm sure you'll agree, focusing exclusively on the rear-view mirror is hardly a recipe for driving success! And the same applies in life. Life is all about where you are *now,* not where you *have been.*

And at the risk of complicating my analogy: it's not about where you are *going to be,* either. When you're sitting in the driver's seat (of your life), you shouldn't fix your eyes on what's ahead of you any more than you should fix your eyes on what's behind you. Rather, you should immediately pull over to the side of the road, get out of the car, lie down in the soft grass, shut your eyes, and savour the moment.

After all, the moment is unutterably precious. Once the moment is gone, it's gone. In many ways, the moment is like a rare bird you're never going to see again, perhaps because the zoo is in financial difficulties and plans to shut its doors for good at the end of today.

So the next time your thoughts stray from the present moment, I urge you to use your willpower to shift your attention back to the here and now.

I will give you an example. Suppose the sun is shining and you're strolling through a park smoking a cigarette. Suppose, further, that you feel yourself getting increasingly preoccupied with how much money your smoking habit has cost you over the years and with your doctor's prediction that continuing to smoke will put you on course for an early grave. What should you do?

The answer is: *you should tell yourself to snap out of it.* By silencing all thoughts of the past and the future, you'll be able to fully appreciate the loveliness of the day and the exquisite sensation of the cigarette smoke filling your lungs.

I don't mean to suggest that learning to live in the

Now is easy. It takes time and effort. For one thing, you need to be willing to meditate regularly. Meditating for five minutes as a one-off is not going to cut it. You need to treat the practice of meditation as a long-term project, and never cease to remind yourself of the reward that will be yours upon this project's completion: namely, *the supreme bliss of dwelling in the present moment.*

I must admit I've never been a big meditator in the past, but that's all going to change now. Ever since my conversation with Sandra at Jack's birthday picnic, I've been feeling… not exactly down, but just a little bit off-balance, a little bit *distracted.* I've been mentally replaying what happened, at the expense of dwelling in the Now. That's why yesterday evening I decided to roll up my sleeves and do some serious meditation.

Gary's meditation: part 1

In what follows, I'm going to give a detailed, blow-by-blow account of how my meditation session unfolded. That way, you can benefit from my experience when you have a go yourself.

Before you settle into your meditation, it's important to banish as many external stimuli as possible. In my case, that meant switching off the television and shutting the blinds. The problem was, shutting the blinds didn't suffice to get the room completely dark, as my blinds aren't completely flush with the wall and some of the light of the June evening still leaked into the room. So I resorted to Plan B: fashioning a tea towel into a blindfold and tying it round my head.

After sitting down on the rug in a meditative position, I realised there was a problem: an unpleasant smell, which could only have been coming from the tea towel.

I didn't take long to work out what was behind this. A few days previously, I'd discovered the pulpy remains of a very old cucumber at the back of my fridge. I'd used the tea towel to wipe up the rancid cucumber juice that had collected on the glass shelf and had neglected to wash the tea towel afterwards.

As there was no way I was going to be able to concentrate with the rancid cucumber smell in my nostrils, I dispensed with the tea towel and resorted to Plan C: shutting my eyes tightly.

Now I directed all my mental energy at not thinking about anything in particular. After two or three minutes of this, my mind was well and truly empty. How exhilarating to be free of the burden of thought! *Thought is overrated,* I reflected. *Much better to immerse myself in the here and now, neither deliberating over what I'm going to do next, nor thinking about the implications of what I've done in the past. I'm sure I could easily spend the next forty-five minutes, maybe even the next hour, just sitting here in a state of utter—*

I was brought back to earth at this point by a sudden realisation. Before starting my meditation, I hadn't bothered to switch off my mobile phone or silence the ringer on my landline. There was nothing to prevent somebody phoning me just when my meditation was in full flow.

In fact, there were several people, it seemed to me, who could plausibly phone me in the next thirty minutes. Kim might get in touch to say more about her crazy proposal of coming to London to have a showdown with me. Or Martin might phone to remind me yet again about the rent I owe him. Or my bowling buddy Nick might ring to ask to borrow my wok again (he keeps saying he's going to buy his own, but he never does).

I was on the verge of getting up and going to deal with the phones, but then it dawned on me: *If I'm supposed to be dwelling in the Now, why am I worrying about the prospect of being interrupted by a future phone call? The phone isn't ringing now, is it? Well, then… nothing is wrong.*

My next challenge was to transition myself back into a meditative state, I relaxed my arms and legs, relaxed my facial muscles, and focused on my breathing. *In, out, in, out.* I imagined myself lying on a cloud. I imagined myself riding a slow, graceful llama through a mountain pass. I imagined myself playing snooker with total proficiency. After performing these mental exercises, I felt composed, confident, and in control. I recited my mantra:

"Om, om, hum hum hum. Om, om, hum hum hum."

Within minutes, I knew I was dwelling more solidly in the present moment than I had in years. I knew, in the absolute core of my being, that the present moment was the *only* true reality. I recognised with utter clarity that the past and the future were mere illusions.

At this point my landline phone rang, startling me out of my contemplative state. As I'm sure you can understand, I didn't feel much like answering it, so I let it carry on ringing until my greeting came on:

"You've reached Gary. I can't come to the phone right now, probably because I'm off pursuing various interests and aspirations of mine, and generally living life to the full. If you'd like to leave me a

message, I'll do my best to return your call as soon as time allows."

The next voice I heard was neither Kim's, nor Martin's, nor Nick's; rather, it was a voice I didn't recognise:

*"Good evening, Mr Speedwell, my name is Adrian and I'm calling from Southern Electric. Mr Speedwell, I wonder if I could have a quick word with you about the electricity meter reading you gave us on the 18th of June. The reading you submitted was 18,310, but I can see from your account that the previous reading was 19,003 – which would mean that in the period from the 27th of April to the 18th of June, you actually **produced** electricity rather than consumed it. When you get a chance, Mr Speedwell, could you please contact me on the freephone number that's on your bill so that we can resolve this?"*

How maddening! Here I was making strenuous efforts to liberate myself from thoughts of the past, only for Adrian from Southern Electric to bring my meditation to a crashing halt with some nit-picking query about a meter reading I submitted back on the *18th of June.* As if this had any relevance to my life *now!*

When I was done feeling annoyed, I felt a bit sorry for this Adrian person. Imagine if that were your job: ringing up customers to probe them about how many kilowatt hours of electricity they have or haven't consumed. I wonder if it's ever occurred to him that there is more to life than meter readings?

Gary's meditation: part 2

To recover the tranquil state I'd been enjoying before the interruption, I cycled through the whole routine again:

relaxing my arms and legs, relaxing my facial muscles, focusing on my breathing (*in, out, in, out*), reciting my mantra (*om, om, hum hum hum*), and so forth.

Soon, the past receded into insignificance. The more I considered the handful of bad things I'd experienced in the course of my life from birth until a few moments ago, the more I saw that none of these things were of any consequence whatsoever.

For instance, I recalled one incident from earlier that very day, when I'd grabbed a carton of milk from the fridge and, not bothering to check whether it was still good or not, poured a slug of it into my coffee. Only after taking my first gulp had I realised the milk was bad. At the time, the experience had been a highly unpleasant one. And yet now I could reflect upon it calmly. *The gone-off milk is in the past*, I told myself. *It has no power to harm me.*

I began to feel a reassuring inner glow, born of my knowledge that everything that had ever happened to me, up to and including the gone-off-milk incident, was irrelevant in the grand scheme of things. My confrontation two nights ago with a humourless kebab vendor? Irrelevant. My recent run of poor form at bowling? Irrelevant. The entire day I'd spent at work wearing a mismatched pair of shoes? Irrelevant.

Equally irrelevant to my life were the events of my childhood, even the ones which were permanently etched in my memory.

I recalled an experience from when I was eight years old, when my father forced me into going on the scary ride at the amusement park. Despite all my protests, all my screaming and sobbing, my father hadn't reassured nor comforted me. Instead, he'd told me, "You might as well stop your crying, Gary, because it's not going to get you anywhere. I'm not about to let you become the first Speedwell ever to grow up to be a coward. Do you think your Uncle Bert cried when he had to ride an elephant for the first time? Of course he didn't, because he was a *winner*, and winners don't shy away from new experiences. Now, Gary, you tell me this: are you a winner? Are you? *Answer me!*"

Of course, this was upsetting at the time. But reflecting on it now, I thought to myself: *That amusement park probably shut down long ago. And if I were to mention the incident to my father, most likely he wouldn't even remember it. All things considered, it may as well never have happened.*

No sooner had I come to terms with the amusement park incident than I recalled another troubling childhood event, this one from when I was twelve years old. My grandmother, who was a keen gardener, had given Vincent and me some packets of sweet-pea seeds as gifts. Both of us sowed our seeds in little pots indoors. But I must have done something wrong, because my seedlings came out spindly and pale – nothing like the thriving, leafy specimens in Vincent's pots. I kept expecting mine to improve, but they never did. Meanwhile, Vincent planted his seedlings out into the garden, where they flourished, sending out a profusion of pink, purple and white flowers as they grew. He even built a trellis for them to climb.

The evening before our grandmother was to pay us another visit, I did something I'm not proud of. I sneaked into the garden and picked all the flowers off Vincent's plants, disposing of them in the composter to ensure that our grandmother would never see what Vincent had achieved with his sweet peas. To this day I can't really explain why I did it.

Oh, the expression on Vincent's face in the morning when he looked out of the glass doors to the garden and set eyes on the pathetic remains of his plants! "What happened to my sweet peas?!" he cried out.

I remember a sickening feeling coming over me, and I remember not being able to look Vincent in the eye. "Probably caterpillars," I muttered.

"Caterpillars?"

"Yeah, because every so often you get, er, big armies of caterpillars which come in the middle of the night and strip the flowers off everything."

"But they've only stripped the flowers off my sweet peas," Vincent protested. "All the other plants in the garden still have their flowers."

Was he on to me? For a brief instant I thought he might be, but then I reminded myself that for all his sweet-pea growing prowess, Vincent was still an innocent little nine-year-old boy who idolised his older brother. This, of course, made the feelings all the harder to bear.

The main point about the sweet-pea affair is: *it's water under the barge*. When you think about it, my childhood self – the little Gary who committed this shameful act – no longer exists. Neither, for that matter, does Vincent's childhood self, who therefore cannot be harmed.

Gary's meditation: part 3

It's quite poignant, really, when you think about it. With

every year that goes by, my childhood self recedes further into the past. And so do the past selves of assorted people I knew in my youth but haven't clapped eyes on since. Take Joanna, my sixth-form girlfriend. I thought the world of her at the time, but my mother dismissed her as a "no-hoper" and kept questioning why I was with her. In the end, my mother's badgering led me to end the relationship.

I don't think it was entirely fair of my mother to classify Joanna as a no-hoper. For one thing, Joanna was a very talented drummer. I wonder if Joanna kept up her drumming? Maybe she's a session musician now, or a music teacher. I could google her, I suppose.

But I'm digressing. My point is that we can all benefit from reviewing, and then disowning, the bits of our past that have been most painful or disappointing.

All the frustrations, the rejections, the missed opportunities, the failed diets, the unsatisfactory barbecues, the bathroom refurbishment fiascos, the backgammon defeats, the divorces, the knee injuries, the forfeited security deposits; we need to put all of these things out of our minds, because *they belong to the past.*

And I'm sorry to say it, but consistency demands that you put all the *happiest* events of your past out of your mind, too. Otherwise, you will be at risk of living on past joys and past glories – exactly what Bruce Springsteen warned us against in "Glory Days".

For this reason you won't catch me harking back nostalgically to past experiences – like the time when Sandra and I were walking across the Jubilee Bridge one night early in our relationship and she told me for the first time that she loved me; or when I held Jack in my arms at the hospital on the day he was born and marvelled at how Sandra and I had managed to create such a perfect little creature.

As to the future, it is even less worth worrying about than the past. How can you be sure what the future holds? Yes, I've said more than once in this book that I *know* I'm going to be a big success, but strictly speaking what I should have said was: *I know with above 98 per cent certainty that I'm going to be a big success.* I have to concede the slight possibility that I won't be (even though, let's face it, I will be).

By the same token, it wouldn't be entirely correct to say I *know* I'm going to end up with Louise. Who knows: maybe someone even better will come along!

As I sat there in the darkness of my lounge, musing on the unreality of the past and the future, I felt at peace. It seemed to me that from now on I would no longer be vulnerable to anger or bitterness of any kind. I would dwell fully in the Now. I would live without regret, and I would be supremely indifferent to what the future might hold. *Living in the Now was the way forward. It was going to change my life.*

Several images passed before my mind.

The first image was of me standing alone amidst nature, meditatively, with trees and waterfalls and streams all around me.

The second was of an eagle gliding majestically through the sky.

The third was of Sandra and Carl running through a meadow, arms linked.

Where on earth did that last one come from? Somehow I had let my attention stray from the Now, leaving my mind open to bizarre imaginings.

Clearly, what I needed to do was stop daydreaming and focus on my immediate surroundings – which, at this moment, meant the interior of my flat. My lounge was somewhat untidy. On the floor were three or four socks, the last couple of issues of *Soar: The Magazine for High Flyers*, several unopened bills, and a half-empty bottle of Coke Zero. There was also an unsightly stain on the rug dating from two weeks ago when I'd spilled half a bowl of carrot-and-coriander soup on it while watching TV.

I'm not sure what would be the best way of getting the stain out. It's the sort of thing Sandra would know how to tackle. I guess there are carpet shampoos you can buy. Maybe I'll look into it tomorrow. At any rate, I should probably at least half tidy the lounge before I go to bed.

With my meditation at an end, it seems natural to ask: what did I gain from it?

For one thing, I gained an appreciation of just how challenging it is to stay focused on the Now for any length of time. Whenever I felt like I had the Now pinned down, it slipped away from me.

But practice makes perfect, so I'm going to keep at it. It'll all be worthwhile when my spiritual transformation is complete.

6

INFLUENCE

Let's be clear about one thing: *self-help* doesn't have to imply *self-obsession*. If you focus single-mindedly on your own betterment without giving a second thought to other people, you are making a serious mistake. Why? Well, for one thing, other people can be crucial stepping stones to the achievement of your goals. If you neglect other people, you're only hindering your own prospects of success.

The question is, how do you go about influencing another person to do what you want? Well, one approach is simply to *ask them nicely*. This sometimes works. You could maybe get a job reference this way, or a few quid knocked off the price of a pair of boots, or even a free harpsichord lesson if you're lucky. There are limits, though. If you were a salesman at a hi-fi shop, you couldn't just say to a customer, "Can I possibly trouble you to buy this £1,200 Yamaha home entertainment system from me?" In such cases, more sophisticated techniques are called for.

I'll be discussing several such techniques in this

chapter. Master them and you'll be able to induce anyone to do what you want virtually all the time.

Using fear to your advantage

Fear is a powerful motivator. If you think about it, the whole of the insurance industry relies on fear. Insurance companies alarm people by asking, "What if there were a devastating storm?" or "What if you became ill with a chronic disease and couldn't work?" Faced with these terrifying possibilities, people allow themselves to be persuaded to buy insurance. And yet 999 times out of 1,000 the calamity the policy is protecting against doesn't materialise and the customer ends up out of pocket. Is it any wonder insurance is such a lucrative racket?

For this reason, I never buy insurance except in cases where I'm required to by law.

Anyway, the trick is to make the power of fear work *for* you, not *against* you. If you can learn to harness the power of fear, you'll be in the best possible position to control other people.

The process of exploiting a person's fears has two stages, which I call *identification* and *activation*. These stages are represented in the diagram below:

Identification is about determining what the person's fears are. In practice, this tends to be just a matter of applying common sense. For example, if somebody owns a dog, then clearly they're not going to fear dogs, but what they are going to fear is *something happening to their dog.*

To be clear, I'm not suggesting you should go around threatening people's dogs. I'm merely highlighting how easy it is to ascertain what a person's fears are.

Once you've identified the person's fears, you proceed to the activation stage. This is all about bringing their fears to the forefront of their mind.

Perhaps an example from my own life will give you some sense of what's involved here. The other day at work, a colleague of mine, Mike, came over to my desk in a huff. "What do you call *this*?" he demanded, slapping a piece of paper down in front of me.

I had a look. It was a hard copy of a document I'd emailed to one of our customers earlier in the day confirming some delivery details. From a quick glance at its contents, there didn't appear to be anything noteworthy about it.

"I'm not sure what you're getting at," I said to Mike.

"What am I getting at? I don't even know where to begin. You've got the date wrong, for a start. This is a hundred years out." He indicated with his fingertip the delivery date referenced in the document: *8 July 2105.*

I did the maths. "Actually," I corrected him, "it's ninety years out. Which I admit is still quite a lot. But it's obviously just a typo. Anyone reading it would realise it's supposed to say 2015."

"Just a typo… Okay, fine, we'll let that one pass. What about this bit here? *'Tent poles'*? Since when were we transporting tent poles for them?"

"Tent poles is wrong?"

"It's completely wrong. This is *Milton Catering*

Equipment. They don't deal in tent poles. You seem to have got Milton Catering Equipment mixed up with Pullman Outdoors somehow."

"Oh."

"Yes, 'oh' is right. But the worst is this part here, where you show the destination as '*Sheffield*.'"

"I could have sworn it was Sheffield."

"It isn't. The destination is SHENFIELD – with an 'n'. Shenfield in Essex, not Sheffield in Yorkshire."

"All right," I said. "I can see I've let a few mistakes creep into the document."

"You got the date wrong. You got the goods type wrong. You got the destination wrong. You basically got everything wrong that you could have got wrong. Not only that, but you included *my* name as the contact – so now I'm getting it in the neck from Milton Catering Equipment. They're telling me if that's the level of attention to detail they can expect from us, maybe they should go elsewhere."

"Okay, leave it with me," I said. "I'll sort this out with them."

"No, you won't. I'm sorting it out. I've already promised them I'd give the person responsible a dressing-down, which is what I'm doing. And I told them I'd be – what were the exact words I used? – 'giving my manager a full account of the matter so that appropriate action can be taken'."

That made me nervous. "Have you done that yet?" I asked.

"No, but I plan to as soon as she's back from lunch."

I have to say, I really wasn't keen on Louise finding out

about what I'd done. While I don't believe any of the mistakes I made was individually that serious, three mistakes in one document didn't look good. Let's face it, there can be no greater romance killer than having to grovel for forgiveness to your prospective partner about some clerical errors you've made.

What I needed urgently was some way of preventing Mike from exposing me. Thinking fast, I came up with a way of turning the tables on Mike by exploiting *his own* fear of getting in trouble with Louise.

"I wouldn't mention any of this to Louise if I were you," I said.

"Oh no? And why not?"

"Don't you remember the speech she gave to all of us about snitching? About how she wouldn't tolerate it in the workplace under any circumstances?"

"I don't remember anything like that," said Mike.

"You must remember, it was… ah, no, come to think of it, this was when you were on holiday. You went to the Maldives for a week back in April, didn't you?"

"Yeah, but—"

"Well, that's when it was. She got us all together and gave us a speech about the importance of team cohesion. One of the things she was very clear about was that she has no tolerance for people snitching on their colleagues. She said if anyone on this team snitches on a colleague, the person doing the snitching can expect to go the way of Keith Folger."

(Everyone in the office knew about Keith Folger. He'd been sacked by Louise six months previously for an offence whose exact details were never communicated to us, but which apparently came under the heading of "insubordination".)

Mike seemed taken aback. "You're saying I can't tell Louise about your blunders because I'll lose my job if I do?"

"That's right."

"Unbelievable," he muttered, and stalked off.

So there you have it. By activating Mike's fears, I was able to modify his behaviour in a way that brought about the right result for me.

In case you're wondering, Louise didn't really make the speech I attributed to her. However, I wouldn't go so far as to say I was "lying". From what I know of Louise, I'm confident she *could have* delivered such a speech, and that's what matters.

Sometimes you have to sacrifice a bit of the literal truth in the service of conveying a *deeper* truth.

A foot in the door: how small commitments lead on to big ones

As every successful religious cult knows, extracting a small initial commitment from a person can pay big dividends down the road. This is the way it works:

> CULT REPRESENTATIVE: Excuse me, would you like to try one of these brownies, courtesy of the Universal Church of Radiance?

RANDOM MEMBER OF THE PUBLIC: Well, if they're free then… sure, I'll take one. Thank you. [*Starts munching on the brownie.*]

CULT REP: They're home-made.

RANDOM MOTP: Mmmm… delicious.

CULT REP: Please take this leaflet as well. It explains about the Sky People and the coming of the True Prophet.

RANDOM MOTP [*reluctantly taking the leaflet (he can't very well refuse it now that he's accepted the brownie*)]: Cheers.

CULT REP: If you're interested, I can put your name down for one of our spiritual outreach evenings. The next one is Tuesday at 7.30pm, downstairs at the Old Gatehouse. It's an opportunity for you to learn about our Church in a relaxed setting, in the company of like-minded—

RANDOM MOTP: I think I, erm, might be busy on Tuesday…

CULT REP: I should mention there's an all-you-can-eat buffet.

RANDOM MOTP: All-you-can-eat?

CULT REP: Yes, there'll be chicken bites, crab cakes, pasta salad, fresh mozzarella-and-red-pepper kebabs, and these really lovely mini lamb burgers. And free drinks.

RANDOM MOTP: Sign me up.

Now his fate is sealed. In his mind, he committing to nothing more than an evening of scoffing chicken bites and mini lamb burgers while listening to a certain amount of earnest but harmless religious talk. But what he doesn't realise is that one commitment quickly leads to another. Give it a few weeks and you'll find he's severed ties with his friends and family, signed over all his worldly possessions to Martyr Joseph, taken up residence in the church compound, and joined in efforts to build a landing pad for the spacecraft that will be transporting the righteous to the celestial dwelling place of the Sky People on the eve of the Day of Judgement.

You do have to watch out for these cults. I speak from personal experience, having had some dealings with one back in Los Angeles. The cult came dangerously close to recruiting me as a fully fledged member, but then I discovered that they considered bowling to be sinful for some reason. Needless to say, a cult that won't let me go bowling is not a cult I want any part of.

But I digress. The important point is: this "securing-a-small-commitment" technique can be an extraordinarily powerful weapon in your arsenal. Just today, I used the technique to make a major breakthrough in my pursuit of Louise. I began by approaching her and saying:

"Louise, there's a prospect I think you should meet."

"What sort of prospect?"

"He's somebody based here in London who's going to need haulage services on a significant scale. I've told him a bit about how we operate and what we can offer him, and of course I've mentioned you. To make a long story short, he wants to have lunch with you this week to discuss taking things further."

"How did you find this person, exactly?"

"He's an old friend of mine named Nick. He's got his own snack-foods business which he's in the process of expanding in a major way. Trust me, if we can land him as a customer, the rewards for us will be huge."

She consulted her diary. "Okay. I wouldn't normally agree to this, but if you're saying it could be a significant amount of business... I could do Friday at one fifteen at Luc's Brasserie."

"Perfect," I said. "Oh, one thing I forgot to mention: he wants me to be at the lunch as well. Just because he knows me and he feels that—"

"Fine, fine," said Louise. "You can be there."

As you may remember, Nick is my bowling buddy. A few months ago he launched his own line of crisps. The way his business works is, he buys the potatoes retail, prepares the crisps in his own kitchen, bags them, and makes them available for sale in his local pub. Admittedly his operations are currently loss-making, but he tells me that when he starts getting more pubs on board, he will achieve what are known as "economies of scale". At that stage, the profits will really start to mount up.

Even before Louise had agreed to the meeting, I'd communicated to Nick the basic "script" I expected him to follow at the lunch:

1) At the outset, Nick announces that, unfortunately, he can only stay a short while, as he has another appointment to go to.
2) After the introductions and pleasantries, Nick lays out his requirements and gives Louise the opportunity to explain how we can offer him a service ideally suited to his needs.
3) Once we've finished our starters, Nick announces that it's time for him to go, but that he is very encouraged by what he has heard and looks forward to doing business with us.

With Nick out of the picture, Louise and I will be able to chat freely while enjoying a leisurely main course. I'll put her at ease with flirtatious banter, so that the "hard-nosed businesswoman" side of her personality gives way to something altogether softer and more playful. We'll talk about anything and everything. We'll relate to each other on a more intimate level than ever before. Notice how what started as a business lunch has subtly transformed itself into *a date with Gary*.

I'm feeling very excited about this! The only thing I'm not quite sure of is whether it's okay to order wine.

Harnessing the power of association

Say you're requesting a favour from someone. When putting forward your request, you can greatly increase its chances of success by using words and images that have positive associations in the person's mind.

It's the same principle as in those toilet paper ads on television with the adorable puppies. Making a case for the superiority of a particular brand of toilet paper is not easy, at least not without being graphic, so the ads don't even try. What they do instead is forge an association in the viewer's mind between their brand of toilet paper and puppies – because who doesn't like puppies?

Of course, it also works the other way. If you want a person *not* to feel good about something, you should associate it with something they dislike.

Example: I don't want Kim to visit me in London, so in a recent email to her on the subject, I chose my words in such a way as to conjure up an image likely to put her off. You see, Kim has always had a phobia of bees. If a bee comes within so much as six metres of her, she goes completely crazy, shrieking and flapping her arms wildly.

Without ever mentioning bees explicitly, my email conveyed a subtle but powerful "bee" vibe. Here is an excerpt – see if you can spot all the subliminal bee material:

> *In your last email, you said, "It's not just about you, Gary, I'm also visiting London for ME. Once I've finished having my showdown with you, I plan to do some serious sightseeing." Well, I*

hate to disappoint you, but from a sightseeing and tourism point of view London is highly overrated. The longer I live in London, the more bemused I am that there's any buzz around it at all. I grant you, the West End has got good shopping, but not any more so than Los Angeles, and anyway, 1) you'll get stung by high prices, and 2) it's far too busy round there. In fact, it's such a hive of activity that you spend 90 per cent of your time fighting your way through mobs of people and only 10 per cent actually shopping. Loads of tourists make a beeline for Piccadilly Circus, but I can't see why, it's basically just a big road junction with garish neon signage. The Palace of Westminster is nice enough, I suppose, but it's not as if they allow you to go in, so the most you can do is bumble around some distance away from it.

My guess is that the next time I hear from Kim, she'll have gone off the idea of visiting London, without knowing quite why.

Mirroring

A key principle of influencing is to *mirror the preferences of the other person.* Let me explain what I mean. We're all familiar with the concept of "being on the same wavelength" as someone. You may have had the experience of feeling as though you and a partner or friend just "get" each other, even to the point of completing each other's sentences.

(By which I mean: completing each other's sentences *accurately*. Sometimes, when people complete my sentences, they get things slightly different to what I was actually going to say. I find this quite annoying.)

What isn't widely appreciated is that *you can, in fact, achieve a state of connectedness with anyone you choose.* Once this state has been achieved, influencing the person becomes breathtakingly easy.

Now, you're probably thinking, "Wait a minute, Gary. Surely I'm either on a person's wavelength or I'm not. And if I'm not, I don't see how there's anything I can do to change that." To which I would answer: you're being defeatist. You *can* change it. All you have to do is acquaint yourself with the other person's interests, likes and dislikes, etc., and then mirror them.

This is the very strategy Hitler employed to influence the German nation. He knew the people of Germany wanted jobs, a strong economy and influence on the world stage, so he let it be known *he* was interested in those things too. He said, "If there's one thing I'm keen on, it's jobs: the more the better, as far as I'm concerned. And I'll tell you what, I've had it up to here with this feeble economy, haven't you? If you ask me, it's about time we got our act together and transformed ourselves into a global player."

Given that these very sentiments were being expressed in beer halls up and down the country, everyone said to themselves, "At last! A kindred spirit. I'm going to vote for him, because he speaks for people like me."

Of course, I'm not saying: *Be like Hitler.* But what I am saying is: *Be like Hitler in this particular respect.*

I've applied this mirroring technique numerous times in my own life, with generally good results. The most recent instance was in my dealings with my landlord Martin. As you may recall, I owe Martin money, and he has given me until the end of Wednesday (tomorrow) to clear my debt, under penalty of eviction. Martin must be getting worried I'm not going to meet the deadline, because this morning he left me a voicemail message asking that I update him on "the situation".

The truth was, the situation was much the same as before. Even though my investment in the Money Magnifier scheme, which I mentioned in Chapter 4, should have, by rights, sorted out my financial situation by now, there's been an unexpected hitch. When I contacted the scheme managers by email yesterday to ask about making a redemption, I received the following response:

> *Dear Client,*
>
> *We regret that we are unable to process your redemption request at this time. This is because of a technical problem affecting the Pan-Global Funds Clearance Network. Engineers are working on this problem as a matter of priority, and we anticipate a resolution sometime within the next five weeks. Once the network is functioning again, all redemption requests will be processed in the order in which they were received.*

The next five weeks! Can you believe it? I find it ironic that the Money Magnifier people can be so proficient at investing the money with which they've been entrusted, yet when it comes to the simple administrative task of paying over the proceeds to their clients, they can't seem to get their acts together!

There was no point sulking about it, though. What I had to do now was somehow persuade Martin to grant me another extension on the rent. It seemed to me that the best strategy for doing this was to use *mirroring*.

I began by asking myself, *What are Martin's interests? His hobbies? His likes and dislikes?* The answer in each case was: *I have no idea.*

Fortunately, these days it's easy to pull up information about almost anyone on the Internet. So I got straight on my computer and googled my landlord's name. After about twenty minutes of browsing discussion forums, sifting through images, and gathering a variety of other clues, I knew a large number of interesting facts about Martin.

Armed with these facts, I wrote up a set of comments and observations designed to make Martin perceive me as a soulmate. All that remained was to deliver these comments and observations to Martin. But how, and when?

In his message, Martin had said he'd be available for a callback this evening either before seven, or after nine. I therefore decided to ring his home phone at seven thirty, when he'd be safely out of the house.

The idea was to leave a recorded message to the effect of, "Sorry not to catch you, Martin, I'll try back later in the evening. Oh, just while I remember, though…" followed by a flattering observation about Martin's favourite football team, a casual aside about his favourite hobby, and so on. I'd have my script in front of me, so I wouldn't be at risk of missing anything out.

When seven thirty rolled round, I called Martin's number and waited for the answerphone to kick in. To my surprise, he answered almost immediately. Panicking, I hung up the phone. Within ten seconds it was ringing, and as he knew I was there, I decided I'd better answer it. In a flash, I realised that my plan would have to be altered. I would have to conduct a real-time conversation with Martin, weaving my prepared remarks into it as best I could.

I picked up the phone, took a deep breath, and began. "Hello, Gary here."

"Gary, it's Martin. You just called."

"That's right – as instructed!" I said brightly.

"Yes. Not at the right time, and you hung up straightaway, but still…"

I didn't allow myself to be put off my stride by this rather prickly attitude.

"So, Martin," I continued, "you were saying you wanted an update about the rent situation. Though I wouldn't have thought you'd have time to worry about it when the Formula One season is still on. Who do you fancy this year? Ferrari look strong."

"Gary, I need the rent to be paid up by tomorrow evening. That was the deadline and it still stands. We can't keep letting things drag on. It's no good for either of us."

"I know what you mean, Martin. I think you're absolutely right. I wouldn't want to ruin our relationship over this. Actually, this morning I happened to remember I have a savings account where I'd been putting money aside for a vintage car restoration project. What would you advise? A Lotus Seven or one of the early Aston DB series?"

"To be honest, Gary, I'd rather you concentrated on paying the rent. Are you saying you're in a position to pay after all?"

"I'll tell you what: I'm very close to being in a position to pay. *Very* close. And just as an aside, I was thinking of buying a couple of season tickets at QPR now that my son is interested in football. Though I'd never let that take priority over paying the rent."

"That's great, Gary. So you can get the money to me by tomorrow evening?"

"Of course, of course, that's no issue. Or, if not tomorrow, then next Monday at the latest. Look, I must go, Martin – I've got to get things together to be up early for a cycle ride with my club. Great talking to you, Martin. Bye now." And with that I hung up, leaving Martin's subconscious mind to process the various subtle cues I'd inserted into our conversation.

Once Martin processes these cues, he will regard me not as a mere source of rent, but as a kindred spirit. Needless to say, all thoughts of evicting me will go clear out of his mind.

Projecting authority

Some lucky individuals are blessed with an indefinable quality that makes people obey them without question. The word for this quality is "authority". I won't try to define authority, because as I've just said, it is indefinable, but what I will do is offer some pointers as to how you can maximise the authority you project.

If you think back to your school days, you'll probably

remember at least one teacher who was unable to keep order in the classroom. It made no difference how much they raised their voice, how much they stamped their foot, how much they said, "Right, I've had just about enough of this now." They might as well have been a stuffed scarecrow. In fact, if they *had* been a stuffed scarecrow, they would probably not have had as many wadded-up pieces of paper thrown at them.

In short, this teacher lacked authority. Let us now turn to the question of *why* they lacked authority. Obviously I don't know them, but I strongly suspect they would have attained the lowest score possible on the following "Rate Your Authority Level" test:

RATE YOUR AUTHORITY LEVEL			
	Are you more likely to…		
☐	Make lightning-quick decisions? Example: *"Okay, everybody, change of plan. I've decided that since we can't overpower the security guards, we're going to confuse them by spontaneously breaking into song."*	Dither? Example: *"Well, I guess we could sneak in through the skylight or something? Or no, on second thoughts, there might not be a skylight. I suppose digging a tunnel could work. Except it might take quite a long time. Hmmm. What do other people think?"*	☐

☐	Make sure others are aware of your superiority? Example: *"Yes, DIY is a particular talent of mine. In fact, I often get plumbers and carpenters coming to* me *for advice."*	Confess to flaws and shortcomings? Example: *"Can anyone help me refold this map? I can't work out how to do it."*	☐
☐	Issue commands? Example: *"Put that priceless vase down right now."*	Issue polite requests? Example: *"I'd appreciate it if you could please put that priceless vase down at your earliest convenience."*	☐
☐	Rise above all criticisms? Example: *"I'm aware not everyone is comfortable with my firm's strip mining operations in developing countries. All I can say is, I respect the protestors' right to express their views, misguided as they are — though I do think an improvement in their standards of personal hygiene wouldn't go amiss."*	Cave in at the first sign of disagreement? Example: *"Didn't you like my proposal? Well, don't worry, I can change it. I'm happy to remould my proposals around your views, whatever those might be."*	☐

*Score +1 for each box ticked in the left-hand column,
-1 for each box ticked in the right-hand column.*

If you can manage to do the things in the left-hand column, while avoiding the things in the right-hand column, you'll have a big edge when it comes to influencing others.

Of course, this is easier said than done. What helps is to take your cue from a person of unrivalled authority – someone like Marshall Brewster. For a virtuoso projection of authority, I refer you to Marshall's responses in an interview by blogger Anne Kozlowski. (The full transcript is available on "Anne Kozlowski's Personal Development Blog".)

In the exchange below, Anne tries to get Marshall to address some wild rumours that have been flying about recently about alleged improprieties in his business dealings:

> *Q. Lately, some questions have been raised about your subsidiary company, Marshall Brewster Exclusive. People are saying you haven't been clear enough about the nature of Marshall Brewster Exclusive's activities, nor about the links between Marshall Brewster Exclusive and an offshore shell company called JBM International. The suspicion is that there's been some sort of cover-up. How would you respond to that?*

A. You know, Anne, I did you a huge favour by agreeing to this interview.

(A masterstroke! He immediately puts Anne on the defensive.)

Q. I appreciate that. I didn't mean any disrespect; I was only trying to give my audience some insight into—

A. You have an agenda to pursue; I understand that. And since you've asked the question, I'm going to answer it. But before I do, I think it's worth taking a closer look at the people making these allegations. Who are they? What have they done in life? I mean, ask yourself: how many books have they sold? How many multimillion-dollar business empires have they built from the ground up? I'll tell you the answer: none. So, understandably, when faced with someone like me who has achieved a level of success beyond their wildest imaginings, all they can think to do is try to tear me down.

(It's breathtaking! Marshall leaves us in no doubt that he's got the measure of his opponents.)

Q. You're saying the allegations have no merit?

A. None at all. Marshall Brewster Exclusive's mission is to provide a varied portfolio of services to high-net-worth individuals. It's as simple as that. I don't intend to describe those services in detail, because our clientele is exclusive and we have to respect their privacy. But what I can tell you is that the whole thing is entirely legal and above board.

Q. And what about JBM International?
A. What about it? JBM International is a provider of consultancy services – nothing more, nothing less. And I've never denied that Marshall Brewster Exclusive has entered into certain agreements with them, for the mutual benefit of both parties.

Q. Agreements of what kinds?
A. Of diverse kinds.

It's stunning. Marshall's confident projection of authority in this interview leaves his accusers thoroughly discredited and his business practices utterly vindicated.

As you sharpen your influencing skills, you may be tempted to abuse them. Don't. It's incumbent on you to use your power responsibly.

At ten this evening, I received a phone call from Sandra. "It's about Jack," she said. "He's going to be staying over Friday night at my parents' house. So that's where you'll have to collect him from on Saturday morning. You won't forget, will you?"

"No, I won't forget. But why isn't he with you on Friday night?"

"I'm not going to be around. I'm leaving for Paris on Friday evening, getting back late on Sunday. Sorry, I would've told you about this sooner, but it all came together very last-minute."

"Don't be sorry. I think it's brilliant that you're going to Paris." I meant it. She has her hands full with Jack during the week, and it was about time she had a relaxing break. "Come to think of it," I said, "the last time you had a weekend away somewhere must've been…"

"February last year."

I thought about this. "February last year, right," I said. "When *we* went to Paris."

"And we stayed in that hotel with all the cat sculptures in the courtyard. Do you remember?" said Sandra.

"Were they cat sculptures? I thought they were real cats."

"No, you're thinking of Venice."

"Oh, yes, I suppose I am. So, are you going with one of your friends, or…?"

"I'm… going with Carl."

There was a long silence. Eventually she continued:

"He has a cousin who lives over there who he'd arranged to see. He'd already bought his plane ticket and everything, and then it occurred to ask if I wanted to go with him."

"Plane ticket? What's wrong with the Eurostar?"

"I don't know. Anyway, the deal is, I won't be paying anything for accommodation even though I'm paying my own airfare. We'll be staying in his cousin's apartment on the Boulevard Saint Michel. It's a huge apartment, Carl tells me – the cousin is some sort of high-powered banker at Société Générale."

"Wonderful," I said.

Another silence.

"You know," she said, sounding a bit weary, "if I'm honest, I wasn't sure at first whether I should accept the invitation. I didn't know how comfortable I was with the whole thing. I came very close to saying no. But then I thought, well, really, why *shouldn't* I go? What have I got to lose? I might even end up having a good time."

"A 'good time'?"

"Yes. And the more I thought about it, the more I kept coming back to the question: what's to stop me going? Is there *anything* to stop me going?"

"So what was the answer?"

"Well, obviously there was *nothing* to stop me," she snapped.

Where this burst of irritation came from, I can't imagine. It's not as if I'd said anything objectionable. As far as I'm concerned, there are some things about women and their emotions that are just inexplicable.

And yet I found myself having a thought which was equally inexplicable. (It just goes to show that even the most highly trained mind can sometimes operate in strange, unaccountable ways.) The thought was as follows: *Sandra, don't go to Paris with Carl. Just don't. Get on the phone to him right now and tell him you've changed your mind.*

Of course, this thought made no sense. It seemed that something in me was opposed to Sandra being happy. This was a shameful and terrible thing to have to acknowledge, but at least I was able to rise above the rogue feeling rather than acting on it.

And trust me, I *could* have acted on it if I'd seen fit to do so. With all the influencing techniques I have at my disposal, I could have persuaded Sandra to back out of the Paris trip if I'd wished. But that would have been a serious abuse of my powers. Why should I stand in the way of Sandra's happiness? She is a grown woman who is free to do as she likes, and she deserves to be happy.

By the same token, I'm free to do as *I* like. For example, if I want to date Louise, I will date Louise. My feelings for Sandra are immaterial, *because they belong to the past.* That's what I need to keep reminding myself. Clinging on to the past is always a mistake, a wasteful diversion of time and energy from the one thing that's really worthwhile: the pursuit of success.

Success! It is so near to hand, I can taste it, touch it, smell it. Not to sound arrogant or anything, but when I think about the skill with which I've navigated the challenges facing me lately, from Mike's threats to destroy my reputation at work, to Martin's ultimatums about my rent, to Kim's threats to descend on me in London, I feel almost giddy. Very few people could have dealt with these challenges as masterfully as I have done. And now that I've cleared these hurdles, nothing stands between me and success. I mean, if you look at my circumstances objectively – the fact that my book is on the verge of completion, the fact that my relationship with Louise is on the verge of being taken to the next level – it's hard to avoid the conclusion that success will be coming to me very, very soon.

"I hope you have a lovely time," I said to Sandra.

7

___

GARY'S FIVE COMMANDMENTS

It's not long since I brought Chapter 6 to a close, and yet an enormous amount has happened since then, much of it unplanned. I confess, as recently as two days ago I was pretty well convinced that success was "in the bag". In retrospect, I was being overly cocky, which accounts for why, when events took an unexpected turn, I found myself on the back foot. And then when things got *really* hairy, I started to feel as though I was in one of those Hollywood action films where, with around thirty minutes of running time left, the hero seems to be staring defeat in the face. Physically compromised, he can barely even stay on his feet. At this stage you can normally expect him to turn to his buddy and say something like, "Just go on without me, I'm only slowing you down." Whereupon his buddy grabs him by the shoulders and shakes him vigorously, saying, "Don't quit on me! Goddammit, Ron, you've never given up on anything in your life! Ron, look at me. Look at me, Ron! You think I'm gonna let you bow out of this? No way that's happening, my friend. We're gonna finish this thing together, you and me. Now let's get back out there and hit those sons of bitches where it hurts." Galvanised by his buddy's words, Ron takes a deep breath, finds a reserve of energy he didn't know he had, and joins forces with his buddy in inflicting a final, decisive arse-kicking on the villains.

In many ways, my experience lately has been similar to Ron's. For example, at my lowest point, I seriously considered throwing in the towel. Yes, you heard correctly. *Gary Speedwell experienced a crisis of confidence.* In fact, if anything, Ron had it easier than me: he had a buddy to inspire him and spur him on. I had no such buddy. I had to be my *own* buddy, inspiring myself and spurring myself on as best I could. Thankfully, I came through my crisis of confidence – even if the way things turned out in the end is not quite as I would have anticipated.

In what follows, I am going to give full details of everything that happened to me since the close of the last chapter. I am doing this because I believe my experience can be instructive. After each episode I am going to relate, ask yourself the following questions:

- What would I have done in Gary's position?
- How does that compare with what Gary actually did?
- How do the above two things compare with Gary's retrospective sense of what he should have done?
- How would I have felt about what I'd done if I'd done the things Gary chose to do?

You should probably draw up some sort of grid to help you keep track of all this.

I should make clear (in fact, maybe I should've made it clear before now) that I don't pretend to have some simple formula for success that can be summed up in one sentence. That's not what I'm building up to in this final chapter. I do, however, have a simple formula for success that can be summed up in *five brief guidelines,* which I call "Gary's Five Commandments".

Yes, yes, I'm aware "Gary's Ten Commandments" would have sounded better. But I just wasn't able to stretch the list to ten, at least not without putting in a lot of filler. Anyway, the remainder of this chapter will be structured around Gary's Five Commandments.

Commandment #1: Roll with the punches

What is the one indispensable trait a boxer needs if he is to succeed in his sport? Is it strength? Stamina? Sheer grit and determination? No, no, and no. The one indispensable trait is the ability to **roll with the punches**.

Rolling with the punches means moving your head and body in the same direction the punch is travelling in. That way, when the punch hits, the impact is quite gentle, almost pleasant.

And so it is in life. When life is pummelling you mercilessly, the key question becomes: will you crumple under the rain of blows, or will you manage to "roll with the punches"?

One key difference between life and boxing should be borne in mind, however. In life, there is no bell to signal the start of each round. There's a good chance you won't even know that the contest has started until the first punch has knocked you off your feet. The way you handle yourself in the immediate aftermath of that punch is crucial. You need to keep your wits about you, because you will be feeling shocked and upset.

I speak from recent personal experience. For me, the metaphorical "first punch" happened on Thursday evening. As I was arriving home from work, I saw that there was a man waiting outside my building.

"Gary Speedwell?" the man enquired.

"Yes, can I help?"

"I have a letter for you. If you could just sign here to confirm receipt..." He handed me one of those electronic gizmos. As I signed my name with the stylus, I asked, "Is it a prize of some sort? Premium bonds?"

"I don't think so, mate."

I accepted the letter and returned the gizmo. As the man walked away, his parting words to me were – I remember finding this curious – "Good luck."

When I got inside my flat, I removed the letter from the envelope. It began:

> *HOUSING ACT 1988 Section 21(4) as amended by HOUSING ACT 1996*
>
> *Assured Shorthold Tenancy – Periodic Tenancy*
>
> *To: Gary Speedwell*

This struck me as being something to do with my tenancy agreement with Martin. Could it be that, as a gesture of goodwill, Martin was cancelling the debt I owed him? I read on:

> *Notice is hereby given that I require possession of the dwelling house (the rental property) at the following address...*

The address that followed was *my* address. Hold on a minute. The phrasing almost made it sound as though Martin wanted me out of the property! I flipped the page over and read through the explanatory notes:

> *A court shall make an order for possession of a dwelling house let on an assured shorthold tenancy which is a periodic tenancy if the court is satisfied that the landlord or, in the case of joint landlords, at least one of them (or their agent) has given to the tenant/s a notice in writing stating that, after a date specified in the notice, being the last day of a period of the tenancy and not earlier than the...*

How tedious. There was no making sense of this legalese. Was I being evicted, or not? If I was, I'd rather be told straight out in plain English.

It was at this moment that I spotted a further note, handwritten in red biro at the bottom of page:

> *Gary, just to be clear – I'm evicting you.*
>
> *Regards,*
> *Martin*

So I *was* being evicted. Well, you can imagine how betrayed I felt.

How was it even possible that Martin had done such a thing, given our phone conversation on Tuesday? This conversation, you may recall, was the one in which I employed a highly sophisticated influencing technique to persuade Martin that he and I were kindred spirits. This technique has been scientifically proven in tests at Marshall Brewster's laboratories in Laguna Beach, California, and is 100 per cent guaranteed to work if carried out correctly. So, plainly, one of two things had happened:

1) I hadn't carried it out correctly, or
2) I had carried it out correctly, but something had happened later on to change Martin's mind.

The first possibility hardly seemed credible, so I was left with 2). I can only imagine Martin had suddenly been confronted by a problem so large thatf it overrode the way I'd programmed his brain. Perhaps the Russian mafia was threatening to cut his legs off in a case of mistaken identity. Or perhaps Martin had learned that his own home was infested by deadly fruit-borne tropical spiders and he needed me out of the rented property so he could live in it himself.

At the end of the day, though, no amount of speculation about the reasons for my eviction was going to achieve anything useful. One way or another, I was just going to have to adapt to my new circumstances.

This is where "rolling with the punches" came in. I

told myself: *hang on, why does this eviction have to be a* bad *thing? I mean, it's not as if there's any shortage of people who have suffered eviction and gone on to achieve greatness.*

Just look at Carver Sanford, the Californian personal-development guru whose book *Now or Never: The Art of Living Mindfully* has become a classic of its genre. Back before he became a household name, Sanford was a shelf-stacker at Whole Foods in San Diego. After he was laid off in 1999, his inability to keep up the rent payments meant that he lost his apartment. For the next four years he slept on park benches, scrounged for food wherever he could get it, and endeavoured to free himself of the burden of desire for material things. Despite owning nothing but the clothes on his back, and sometimes not even those, he experienced what he later described as "a happiness so constant and so intense, it bordered on insanity".

The enlightenment Sanford gained during his period of homelessness proved a valuable asset when he parlayed it into a smash hit bestseller which made him a very wealthy man.

It struck me that perhaps *I* could be the next Carver Sanford. The idea of achieving enlightenment, followed by fame, was certainly appealing. On the other hand, would I really be prepared to spend four years sleeping on park benches and scavenging for food in bins? Bear in mind, Carver Sanford's park benches were located in San Diego, a place known for its near constant warmth and sunshine. Anyone trying the same experiment in London would face levels of cold and wet and dreariness undreamt of by Sanford. It was a far from enticing prospect.

Perhaps there was some way of doing two weeks of *intensive* homelessness, as a sort of fast track to enlightenment?

Before I could pursue this line of thought further, the phone rang. I rushed to the kitchen and answered it.

"Good evening," said a male voice. "It's Adrian here from Southern Electric. I wondered if I could speak to Gary Speedwell?"

I hung up. And just in case he should try again, I silenced the ringer on the phone. Why couldn't these people just leave me alone? I was beginning to feel like a hunted animal. First Martin, now Adrian. It was almost as though a conspiracy was afoot to deprive me of my comfort and my inner peace.

Commandment #2: Always have a plan

Are you acquainted with the scientific concept of "entropy"? I wasn't until Thursday morning, when I read an article about it on the science page of the *Metro*. Entropy, it turns out, is basically the natural tendency of things to go to rack and ruin. For example, if your car doesn't get serviced on a regular basis, it will, over time, develop problem after problem until eventually it becomes undriveable.

Which is not to say that all cars are going to succumb to entropy equally quickly. A Honda Accord might hold out against entropy for many years, whereas certain Italian-made cars might barely manage ten months. But the bottom line is, unless you do something to keep entropy in check, it will always prevail in the end.

Why does this matter? Well, entropy doesn't just affect cars and other inanimate objects. It affects human lives as well. Show me a person whose life has descended into chaos, and I'll show you a person who didn't have a plan for keeping entropy at bay. Which brings me to Gary's Second Commandment: **Always have a plan.**

Formulating a plan to get my life back on track was crucial. But I wasn't sure where to start. Do you know the expression "sleep on it"? That's precisely what I resolved to do, because I sensed that my waking brain was too close to my problems to tackle them effectively.

In the minutes after I'd crawled into bed, I turned these problems over in my mind in a preliminary way. My expectation was that my mind would carry on "processing" them even after I fell asleep, yielding a solution by morning.

That was the theory, anyway. In practice, once I started thinking about my various problems and worries, I couldn't stop. I peered at the clock at one stage and found, much to my dismay, that the time was 2.50am!

I'm not sure when I finally drifted off to sleep, but I know I must've done because I recall having a vivid dream. In the dream, I was preparing to host a house party for forty guests, but with minutes to go before the first guests arrived, nothing was ready. Not only did I have no food or drink of any kind, nor any means of playing music, but the house itself was structurally incomplete. It stood on scrubland and was nothing more than ten planks of wood arranged in a cone formation round a vertical pole that had been sunk into the ground. Because the planks weren't actually fastened to the pole at the top, every time a strong gust of wind came, several of the planks would fall and I'd have to set them back up again. The floor was bare earth, and the whole place was barely large enough to accommodate two people, much less forty.

I heard footsteps: the first of the guests, I presumed. I shifted one of the planks aside so I could see who it was. But it wasn't a guest. An unfamiliar man in a yellow high-visibility jacket was pushing a wheelbarrow towards my house. He parked this in front of the house and set about removing the planks and loading them onto the wheelbarrow.

"Hey!" I shouted at him. "What are you doing? I'm hosting a party in here in a few minutes."

He looked at me in puzzlement. "A party in *here*? You're having a laugh." Then he became stern. "This is an illegal structure – and an eyesore." He continued loading planks onto the wheelbarrow, leaving just one behind. "You can keep this one. It's half-rotten." Then he went on his way, wheeling my dismantled house across the scrubland.

The odd thing is, despite what had just happened, I still held out hope that the party could go ahead as planned.

I sat down on the bare earth. Minutes passed, but no guests appeared. Only after what seemed like an eternity did a figure appear over the horizon. As the figure drew nearer, I realised it was Sandra.

Sandra pointed to the plank on the ground. "We could use this to make a fire," she proposed. The two of us broke off bits of the plank to use as kindling. Sandra produced a match from somewhere and got the fire going. We huddled together. Night had fallen by this point and the temperature had dropped, but the warmth of the fire, and each other, worked in our favour.

"You're still going to be here the morning, aren't you?" I asked her.

Before she could answer, I was woken by the sound of my alarm clock.

What a night! I felt almost as shattered as if I'd had no sleep at all. When I went into the kitchen to get myself some cereal, I noticed that the message light on my phone was flashing. As the ringer had been off, I'd been unaware of the call. What could the message be? The thought occurred to me that it might be a message from Sandra, phoning to announce that she'd changed her mind about the Paris trip at the eleventh hour.

I pressed the "Play" button. To my dismay, the voice I that came out of the speaker was not Sandra's, nor even Adrian's, but Kim's.

"Oh, right," said Kim's voice. "It's like the middle of the night there or something. What is it with England?" Her door buzzer could be heard in the background. "Oh, don't tell me that's... Okay, bad timing, Sparky, my taxi's just arrived. I'll email you from my phone while I'm on my way to the airport. But I'll tell you right now: I'm not having this. Absolutely not."

The message ended there. What was she on about? "Airport"? Was she setting off on holiday?

And then it hit me. *Kim was on her way to London!*

How was this possible? Had Kim not seen my bee-themed message?

I checked my email. Sure enough, there was a new message from Kim, which read:

> *Gary, you really are a selfish bastard. I can't believe the legs* [she meant "lengths", but she was typing the mail on her phone] *you'll go to to avoid me. Every time I've talked to you about visiting, you've fobbed me off with some lane* ["lame"] *excuse like this whole cock* ["crock", I imagine] *of BS about not having enough space in your apartment* ["flat"] *& then that email about bees!!! Whats that supposed to be some kind of mind control thing. Well I'll tell you what it hasn't worked, I'm on my way and well be their* ["will be there"] *on Friday 6.15pm. Meet me at Heart row* ["Heathrow"]: United Flight 1204.

A wave of panic went through me. Kim was on her way to London! I'd been so sure she wouldn't follow through with her plans, I hadn't made any sort of mental preparations for her arrival.

Kim's visit was exactly what I didn't need right now. Too much was happening in my life. For example, my long-awaited lunch date with Louise was coming up, and so was Sandra's Paris trip.

You could argue that Sandra's Paris trip was none of my concern. And in one sense, it wasn't. But in another sense, it clearly was. What if Carl took her to one of those romantic French bistros, plied her with wine and attempted to seduce her? You could argue that even *that* was none of my concern – but look at it this way: what if, in the midst of this attempt at seduction, some brioche got lodged in Sandra's windpipe? Would Carl be qualified to perform the Heimlich manoeuvre on her? I had my doubts. Or what if they went on a post-dinner stroll along the banks of the Seine and Sandra lost her footing and fell into the water? Alternatively, what if the banker cousin took Sandra and Carl on a tour of his favourite parts of the city, exposing them to sides of Paris they'd never seen before, as a result of which they fell in love with the place and decided to move there permanently, along with Jack? Where would that leave me?

Such questions continued to play on my mind all through my journey to work.

At the bagel stand, I was still so absorbed in my own thoughts that, having paid for my bagel with a £20 note, I walked away without waiting for my change. Even with the bagel stand lady shouting after me, it still took me a while to register what had happened.

You might think that the act of sitting down at my desk at work would snap me out of it, but no. Thoughts of Sandra and Carl continued to come thick and fast. Concentrating on work proved impossible. *Enough is enough!* I said to myself.

Marshall Brewster offers a good piece of advice for breaking out of an obsessive spiral. What he says you have to do is assign yourself some sort of absorbing mental exercise. Performing this mental exercise takes your mind away from the object of its obsession, allowing the cycle to be broken.

In this instance, the exercise I set myself was to think

of ten animals beginning with the letter "H".

Horse, *hippopotamus*, and *hedgehog* came readily enough. Then… nothing. Minutes ticked by. Could there really be only three animals beginning with the letter "H"? Think, Gary, think…

If you ever try something like this, you will probably find you'll have no problem coming up with animal names that *sound* real but, on further consideration, aren't. For example:

- Harvest lizard
- Hornmartin
- Highland squirrel
- Hercules viper
- Hertfordshire golden speckled butterfly

Finally, I hit upon a real one: *honeybee*. Somehow that opened up the floodgates, and in short order I managed to rattle off *hummingbird, hyena, hamster, Humboldt penguin*, and *horseshoe crab*. That took me to nine. Just one more to go. Suddenly it came to me: *human!* Of course! There can be no doubt that a human is an animal. I had succeeded in filling my quota of ten animals, and in so doing, I had broken out of my obsessive spiral.

Or so it first appeared. Next thing I knew, I formed a mental picture of Carl getting down on one knee in front of Notre Dame Cathedral and presenting Sandra with a diamond engagement ring.

What was wrong with me? Today wasn't a day for wild speculations about Sandra and Carl's future. Today was supposed to be all about Louise. Our lunch date was just a few short hours away, and I needed to prime myself for the "charm offensive" that would be necessary to win her. Calm, cool, and collected: that was what I needed to be, but at the moment I was far from it.

If ever there was a time for meditation, it was now. I went to the gents' loo, locked myself in a cubicle, put the toilet cover down, sat, relaxed my arms and legs, relaxed my facial muscles, focused on my breathing… *in, out, in, out.* I imagined myself lying in a hammock in a sun-drenched island paradise. I imagined being fanned with palm fronds by monkeys specially trained for that purpose. I imagined majestic peacocks parading up and down in front of me. Now the island paradise dissolved, and I imagined meeting Marshall Brewster at a Los Angeles party. "So, Gary Speedwell," he was saying, "we meet at last. I must say, I was enormously impressed by your book. You remind me of a younger version of myself. Listen, I have a motivational speaking gig tomorrow, but there's been a mix-up and I'm double-booked. How would you like to take my place on stage? I don't suppose you've ever played the Rose Bowl? No? Well, there's a first time for everything."

At this point I remembered about my mantra. "Om, om, hum hum hum," I chanted.

"Gary, is that you?" said a voice in an adjoining cubicle. "Are you all right?"

"I'm fine, Nigel," I replied. "Those are just… erm… sounds I always make when I go to the toilet."

There was a pause. "Are you *sure* you're all right?"

Under these circumstances, it was clear to me that continuing to meditate was futile. Back at my desk, I took stock of my situation. *You don't have much time*, I told myself. *You've got to focus. Why don't you start compiling a list of charming things you could say to Louise at the restaurant?*

I got a pen and notepad from my desk drawer and proceeded to jot down some ideas. Unfortunately, for whatever reason, the ideas I came up with were of poor quality and I kept having to strike them out:

- ~~So, when did you first decide you were going to be a businesswoman and not a fairy princess?~~
- ~~You've got such perfect skin, I'm guessing you must keep yourself really well hydrated~~
- ~~Do you like sunsets and~~
- ~~I'll tell you what's the most special place in the world for me: the Mojave Desert. There's a, how can I put it, a spiritual quality to it. The poetry of the landscape. Mind you, it does get seriously hot, especially in the summer months~~
- ~~You and I, we have a special connection. Something that's beyond words. Some kind of telepathy~~
- ~~I make a mean lasagne~~
- ~~Well, just be thankful you're having lunch with me and not some loss adjuster~~

That last one was *terrible*. Why mention loss adjusters? It showed how thoroughly Carl had wormed his way into my mind. Curse him! The man had a lot to answer for.

To give just one example, where did he get off calling my son "Champ"? The only people with any right to call my son "Champ" are me and Sandra. (And needless to say, we wouldn't ever call him that, because – well, why would we?)

Then it occurred to me: how much do I really know about this Carl person? If he's giving my son rides in his sports car and so forth, then I have a right to know who he really is.

So I googled him. Here are some of the results that came back:

> *Loss Adjuster of the Year – Home*
> **Carl Brenton** *has been named Loss Adjuster of the Year for 2013. In a strong field of candidates, Carl stood out as the...*

> *Serving the Community: The Make-an-Impact Programme*
> *Volunteers Janine Wright, Marcus Stanley and* **Carl Brenton***, seen here building a new straw bale shed at Hackney City Farm, have been doing their part to...*

> *Pete's Taekwondo Blog*
> *... that I learned from none other than Shihan* **Carl Brenton***. You will of course know Shihan Carl by reputation, but what you may not know is that by day he's a hard-working loss adjuster, who recently earned the accolade of...*

Oh, honestly. You really have to ask yourself, what would make a person feel compelled to rack up all these showy accomplishments? All I could think was that he must be secretly massively insecure.

I clicked on each link in turn, determined to find evidence of such insecurity. I don't know where the time went, I really don't, but before I knew it, I heard Louise's voice behind me, saying, "Right, shall we get this over and done with?"

Over and done with? I'm accustomed to Louise's direct way of speaking, but even so, I found this way of framing our lunch date slightly off-putting.

Commandment #3: Put your best foot forward

Gary's Third Commandment is: **Put your best foot forward**. As much as it may sound like a cliché, you had better step up to the plate and strut your stuff when it's your hour to shine, because if you don't put your best foot forward, no one else can put it forward for you.

When Louise and I emerged from the building into the warmth and sunshine, I knew the time to put my best foot forward was at hand. My charm, cleverness and worldly wisdom were going to have to shine through loud and clear in everything I said to her.

I began by remarking, "Glorious weather, isn't it? On a day like this, you can almost imagine you're in Asbury Park, New Jersey, rather than London." This was, of course, a reference to Bruce Springsteen's old stomping ground.

"Yeah, it's a relief," she said, "it's been like monsoon season lately."

"Ha ha! I know. So, will you be hitting the beach this weekend?"

"What beach?"

Louise's point was a fair one. I had spoken without thinking. In some strange way I must have temporarily convinced myself we really *were* in Asbury Park, New Jersey. I changed the subject. "Shall we cross the road here?"

Luc's Brasserie was only a short distance from the office, so we were there in no time. Stepping out of the bright sunshine and making our way down the stairs to the dimly lit brasserie, I found it took a while for my eyes to adjust. A waiter showed us to our table. Nick had not yet arrived.

The place was virtually empty. I suppose it's too much to expect a subterranean brasserie to be bursting with people on a sunny day. In any case, for my purposes the venue was ideal: its chocolate-brown walls and low lighting heightening the romance factor.

After a couple of minutes the waiter reappeared and asked in a French accent if we'd like to order drinks. I still wasn't sure whether ordering alcohol was a wise move, so I decided to take my cue from Louise, and therefore I let her order first.

"I'll have a Kir Alsace," she said.

Hmm. Was "Kir Alsace" the name of an alcoholic drink? Probably, I decided. I addressed the waiter in my best French:

"*Je m'appelle une bière.*"

The waiter looked at me blankly. Maybe he wasn't French after all?

I tried again in English. "I'd like a beer," I said. "A Kronenbourg."

"Une Kronenbourg," he said. "Bien."

While we waited for Nick to arrive, I made small talk. "This was an ideal restaurant choice," I said. "It's very... how can I describe it? Very French."

"It is that," Louise concurred.

"I have a lot of time for France."

"Do you? Why?"

The question caught me off guard. "Because of..." I struggled for an answer. "Well, just – everything. The Eiffel Tower. Moules-frites. Eric Cantona. The Hunchback of Notre Dame. The Cannes Film Festival. Citroën. Gérard Depardieu. Bastille Day. Pierre Cardin. Fondue. Baguettes."

After a pause, Louise said, "Each to his own. Anyway, where's this 'prospect' of yours? He ought to be here by now."

"I'm sure he's on his way. So... while we're waiting... I've been meaning to ask you..."

"Yes?"

I'd begun the sentence without knowing how I was going to finish it. I thought quickly.

"What brand of shampoo do you use?" I continued. "Your hair always looks so lustrous."

She looked away. At first I assumed she was being bashful, but then I realised she had caught sight of a man approaching our table. This was Nick. Per my instructions, he was dressed in blue jeans and a T-shirt. I figured his scruffiness would, by way of contrast, make me appear all the more attractive in Louise's eyes.

"Sorry I'm late," Nick said to Louise as the two of us rose from our seats. "I was all set to leave my flat, then I realised I didn't have my keys on me. I checked under the duvet cover, behind the sofa cushions, on top of the microwave, in the pockets of all the trousers hanging up in my wardrobe. Everywhere. You won't believe where I finally found them. They were in the door!"

"Fancy that," said Louise.

"Anyway, you must be Louise," said Nick. They shook hands. Nick said, "Now, I should tell you before we start – and again, I apologise for this – I won't be able to stay very long. I can have a drink and a starter but then I've got to head off to a… erm… thing."

"A thing?"

"A business thing. It's only just come up. I am sorry."

"Okay," said Louise. "Not to worry. We'll try and make this short and sweet."

We all sat down. The waiter soon reappeared, Nick ordered a Stella and a starter, Louise and I ordered starters and main courses, then Louise got down to the business at hand.

"Nick, I think it would work best if you tell me about your requirements first. Then I'll say a bit about how we operate and how we'd be able to help you."

"Sure," said Nick. "Basically, I'm at the point now where I'm looking to take my snack business to the next level. What I need is a haulier who can keep pace with the growth I'm anticipating in the business."

"When you say 'taking your snack business to the next level', what does that involve?"

"Well, my mission statement is very simple. Gary helped me write it. It's *'To get Nick Henderson Crisps into every pub in the UK.'*"

"What, literally *every* pub?"

"Of course, it won't happen overnight. I know it's a lot of pubs and a lot of pubcos. But it's like Gary says, you have to think big."

"Maybe we could think about what you're likely to need in the shorter term," said Louise. "Tell me about your customer base. What customers have you got on board as of today?"

"Well, there's my local, the White Bear in Walthamstow. Although to be fair, I haven't got a contract with them per se. I hand-deliver a few dozen packets of crisps to them each week, at no charge to them. Just as a way of getting the product out there and, you know, building the brand."

"Okay, understood. We won't count that one," said Louise. "How many other customers have you got aside from them?"

"At this stage, I'd estimate, well… strictly speaking, none."

"Let me be sure I understand this correctly. At the moment, aside from your local, which you're *giving* crisps to, the number of pubs that are stocking your product is *zero*?"

"Exactly," said Nick, "but as I've said, that's expected to increase."

"Until you've managed to get every pub or pubco in the UK on board?" said Louise.

"Right," said Nick. "What you have to bear in mind is, they are exceptionally good crisps."

"They really are top-notch," I confirmed. "I've tried them."

"I see," said Louise. "Well, let's approach this in a different way, Nick. How many bookings do you anticipate making with us in the next three months?"

"I don't see the next three months as being so much about bookings," Nick explained. "I see them as more about strategic planning. I mean in the sense of planning how to attract more customers. Gary is going to help me with that."

"If you don't mind me saying," said Louise, "I'm not clear how you're in a position to do business with us at all right now."

"I can understand that concern, but bear in mind, I'm probably only a few months away from scaling up production," responded Nick. "Once the growth has taken hold, I'll be needing the services of a haulage contractor on a massive scale. It's like Gary said—"

"I can guess what Gary said. Please understand, Nick, we're a major player in this industry. We cover four million kilometres every year. Let me put it this way. If you ever reach a point where you have some real-life goods that need moving, by all means get in touch with us. Because, at that point, we'll be better able to talk specifics with you."

"I'll definitely do that," said Nick. "You know, Louise, I'm very encouraged by what I've heard today. I was looking to partner up with a serious haulier, and from all that you've said – the four million kilometres a year thing, and so on – I'm in no doubt that that's what you are." He looked at his watch. "Apologies, I'd best be off now. It was a pleasure meeting you, Louise. I'll certainly be in touch again."

He downed his Stella, stood up and said to me, "I'll see you at bowling next Tuesday, Gary."

At this moment the waiter arrived with the starters. He put Louise's and mine on the table and looked slightly uncertainly at Nick.

"Oh, I'll, umm, take that in a bag please, mate," said Nick.

The waiter looked hard at Nick and then walked away still carrying Nick's plate of chicken liver paté with crusty bread and cornichons. Nick waved goodbye to me and followed him.

Nick's departure heralded the beginning of my date-proper with Louise. The problem was, Louise wasn't making it easy for me to engage with her. She had got her phone out of her handbag and was checking her email on it as she ate. This activity was so thoroughly absorbing her attention that she didn't look up at me once.

At length, I asked, "How do you think that went?"

She ignored my question, remaining fixated on her phone. Only when our main course arrived several minutes later did she actually return her phone to her handbag.

"Right, what did you say?" she enquired.

"I was asking how you thought the meeting went?"

"I'll throw the question back to you: how do *you* think it went?"

"I'd say it went well," I responded. "My sense is that he came away from the meeting fully committed to using us."

"And the fact that his business has no customers? That he couldn't make a booking with us even if he wanted to?"

"Oh, but that's what's so exciting," I said. "He's starting from zero; there's everything to play for." I could feel myself warming to my topic. "We have the chance here to hook up with a dynamic growth company – like Google back in the late nineties. Imagine partnering with the next Google! I mean, the Google of snack foods."

"*The Google of snack foods*," she muttered. "Brilliant."

She set about eating her mushroom omelette. Never in my life have I seen someone make such fast work of eating an omelette. Her fork was just a blur. I ventured a playful comment about this:

"You're wasted in logistics, Louise. The world of competitive eating needs you."

She set her fork and knife on her plate with a clank. "Let's go," she said, and called for the bill, despite the fact that I still had quite a lot of food left on my plate.

Next thing I knew, we were walking back to the office in silence. I couldn't for the life of me think of anything to say. I was intensely conscious that our date so far hadn't lived up to expectations, and that time was running out to salvage it.

Commandment #4: Maintain your dignity

By the time we were back in the office, I *still* hadn't thought of anything to say. The date was going to be over in a matter of seconds, and I had nothing to show for it. *Don't let it end this way*, I urged myself.

You won't believe what happened next. When I tell you, I expect your reaction will be "Gary, what you're telling me is impossible. Knowing you, knowing your mind training, your charisma and your personal superiority, things literally could not have happened in the way you're describing."

If only that were so! Shocking as it may seem to you, shocking as it seemed to me at the time, what I am about to tell you really happened. And the one consolation I had, through it all, was that I never lost sight of Commandment #4: **Maintain your dignity**. Dignity is paramount. It will see you through any number of awkward and potentially humiliating situations, allowing you to live to fight another day.

Don't let it end this way, I repeated to myself. For some reason, my glance fell upon a brooch that was pinned to Louise's dress at the shoulder. During our lunch, I had dimly registered this brooch, which took the form of a delicate winged creature, but only now did I realise that the creature was a dragonfly.

"That's interesting," I said to Louise, taking the brooch gently between my thumb and forefinger. "When I saw this earlier I thought it was a butterfly brooch. But now that I look more cl—"

"*Don't touch me!*" she snapped. Everybody in the office looked up from what they were doing. I withdrew my hand.

"Gary, you're *this* close to a disciplinary," she said, holding up a finger and thumb, millimetres apart. "I don't know what you think you're playing at, but whatever it is, it needs to stop now. This stuff you've been trying to pull with me: it's not funny, it's not clever. It's— I don't even know what it is. It's annoying. What do you want from me, anyhow? Are you trying to spark some – what, some sort of *office romance* with me?"

"I-I… no, not necessarily. It was" (I lowered my voice)

"just harmless flirting."

"Go and flirt with someone else. Someone on your own level."

I was speechless. I felt like I'd been hit over the head with a blunt object. Louise continued:

"This company is paying you to do a job. A very simple job. They're not paying you to make clumsy advances towards your boss. They're not paying you to entertain your friends at the company's expense, either. Do you realise you've just wasted forty-five minutes of my time?"

"Did I really waste it?"

"*Yes.* Now please get back to your desk and prove to me that you can do what your job description says you should be doing. Because if you can't, then there's no future for you here. Understood?"

"Understood," I mumbled.

"Oh, and Gary? The way you almost lost us the Milton Catering Equipment account? I know about that. And the way you disrespected Rob? I know all about that, too. So shape up. There won't be any more chances after this."

She turned and strode into her office, shutting the door behind her.

I was mortified. I could feel my colleagues staring at me. There was only one thing I could do, and it was, as it happened, the very thing Louise had instructed me to do: get my head down and work.

The fact that so many tasks had built up on my to-do list in recent days was fortunate. Now I set about them soberly, diligently. I couldn't undo what had just happened, but at least by shifting into "work mode" I could take my mind off it for a time. I worked non-stop until four forty, at which point all the urgent and even semi-urgent tasks on my list were finished, and I was starting to feel at a loose end.

That was when my spirits fell. My relationship with Louise had been built on a mistake, the mistake had come to light, and now what was I left with? What did I have to look forward to for the rest of the day? What did I even have to look forward to this weekend, or next week, or the week after that? The weekend would, it's true, be a welcome break from work and from Louise's hostility, and of course I would see Jack. On the other hand, Kim would be in town and I would have to contend with *her* hostility. Plus, there was still the matter of my looming eviction.

I had mapped out a whole future for myself based on getting what I wanted. The trouble was, not only was I not getting what I wanted, I was actively getting what I *didn't* want. How ironic!

Was it ironic? At any rate, it was frustrating, especially when you consider that I'd once had a future with Sandra, and that I'd thrown away *that* future for no other reason than – but it was futile even to think about Sandra. Let's face it, she was going to marry Carl. The only questions were, 1) when? and 2) would I be invited to the wedding?

What I really could do with right now, it struck me, was Marshall Brewster's guiding hand.

So I did an Internet search for "marshall brewster guidance". In no way was I prepared for what came back. The top result from my search was a news item entitled:

Self-help guru Marshall Brewster arrested

Gobsmacked, I clicked on the headline to read the full article:

> *Uncertainty hangs over the future of Marshall Brewster's multimillion-dollar business empire following the self-help guru's arrest at his Los Angeles home in the early hours of Thursday morning.*
>
> *Brewster, the CEO of NASDAQ-listed Marshall Brewster Enterprises and the author of several bestselling self-help books, was charged under the Mann Act, a federal statute that bans the interstate trafficking of women for the purposes of prostitution.*
>
> *Brewster is thought to have been implicated by his apparent associate, Nevada-based gentleman's club owner Quentin Reed, who was himself arrested on Wednesday. According to police, Brewster and Reed operated a prostitution racket which supplied escorts to clients of Marshall Brewster Exclusive, a members-only service launched by Marshall Brewster Enterprises in 2013. The service describes itself in its marketing literature as "dedicated to helping high-net-worth individuals enjoy the fruits of their success".*
>
> *Its membership is 91% male.*
>
> *An anonymous former employee of Marshall*

Brewster Enterprises, recalling his experience on the Marshall Brewster Exclusive sales team, said, "It was pretty crazy. We were pitching a service whose major selling point was that we could get high-class prostitutes to people's homes or offices on demand. Of course, we didn't quite use those words in our pitch, but we had ways of making people understand what the deal was. We'd say things like, 'Any time you're feeling overwhelmed by the demands of being a high-flying go-getter, we can arrange for a qualified motivational assistant to visit you at your home or office. A female *motivational assistant.' And most people had no problem grasping what that meant."*

Reed is said to have overseen the day-to-day running of the criminal operation, which drew its funding from Marshall Brewster Enterprises. The funds appear to have been channelled to Reed via a shell company, JBM International.

Wall Street analyst Terrence Phillips said of the Brewster arrest, "Even if he [Brewster] escapes prison, his reputation is in tatters, and it's hard to see how his business empire can survive. This looks like the beginning of the end for Marshall Brewster Enterprises."

I had a physical reaction to this. I think I was hyperventilating. How could Marshall – Marshall of all people! – be a criminal kingpin?

Of course, I had been aware of the rumours swirling round Marshall Brewster Exclusive, but as far as I was concerned they were just that: rumours, and wildly implausible ones at that. Now that Marshall had been arrested, the only shred of hope I could cling to was that the police had got the wrong man – that the real culprit was some renegade senior manager who had hatched the whole scheme behind Marshall's back.

But… how likely was that, really? I've read about Marshall's management style. Apparently, he once ordered the pulping of hundreds of motivational posters in a Marshall Brewster Enterprises warehouse because he didn't care for the typeface (Nimbus Roman Number 9) in which the motivational text was printed. How could someone with a propensity for this level of micromanagement have been unaware his company was trafficking prostitutes?

And now a question formed itself in my mind. *What if Marshall Brewster isn't infallible? What would that mean for me?*

It seemed to me that it would mean two things.

First, it would mean that *nobody* is infallible. If Marshall Brewster can make an almighty mess of things, then we should *all* give ourselves permission to make an almighty mess of things. And actually, on any objective measure, what Marshall did was much worse than what I did. Sure, I made some errors in judgement that earned me a dressing-down from my boss – but at the end of the day, I still had my job and most of my dignity. Marshall, on the other hand, had actually succeeded in getting himself *arrested and charged with a serious criminal offence.*

The second thing it would mean is that I needn't feel under any obligation to model myself on Marshall Brewster. At the end of the day, I am my own man, with my own intuitions and my own stock of wisdom. Why shouldn't I trust myself to work out what is best for me as an individual, and how to get it?

It was as if a switch had been flicked in my brain. At that moment, I felt I knew exactly what was best for me as an individual – and, indeed, how to get it.

Commandment #5: Be bold

Think of life as a house, set over multiple storeys, each storey having a number of windows facing out onto the street. What do the storeys represent? I don't know. The windows are what's important here. Most of the time, the windows are shut and locked. Once in a blue moon, however, you will encounter a window that is inexplicably open. This is your "window of opportunity", and unless you leap out before the window shuts again, you... well, perhaps leaping out of the window is not the right image, but I'm sure you can appreciate my basic point, which is that you must seize your opportunities. Or to put it more concisely: **Be bold.** That's Gary's Fifth Commandment.

In the waning minutes of my Friday afternoon at work, it became clear to me that the time for bold action was at hand. I didn't want to linger at the office even a moment longer than was necessary. However, I wasn't in a position to leave just yet. Given how much my relations with Louise had deteriorated, any attempt on my part to leave the office even a few minutes early could get me sacked on the spot. Besides, I still had three administrative chores to do on the Internet before I left, namely:

1. Check the Skyhook Media share price
2. Check the expected arrival time of Kim's flight
3. Check the expected departure time of Sandra's flight

After I'd accomplished all this, I consulted my watch and, seeing that it was one minute past five, logged off my PC and left the building.

By my calculations, a cinematic mad dash to the airport wasn't necessary. I still had quite a lot of time. So I walked to Holborn Station without any great haste. On the way, I even had time to phone Sandra's parents' house on my mobile and speak to Jack. At Holborn I got on a Piccadilly Line train to Heathrow Terminal Five – an hour's journey. Upon reaching Heathrow and getting off the train, I strolled to the British Airways check-in area. What I wasn't prepared for was the sight of a familiar small dark-green suitcase on the floor in front of one of the check-in desks. This suitcase was flanked by two figures, who, even from the back, I recognised as Sandra and Carl. They were already in the process of checking in! Plainly, my calculations had let me down.

I ducked under a queue barrier and ran towards the desk, calling, "Sandra, wait! Don't check your bag in!"

Sandra and Carl both turned round. Carl spotted me first and, oddly enough, smiled.

"Gary!" he called. He motioned towards Sandra's bag. "This is carry-on, actually."

Sandra's reaction was very different. She turned pale, and demanded, "What's happened to Jack?"

By now I had reached the check-in desk. "Nothing! Nothing's happened to Jack. He's safe with your parents."

"You're sure?"

"I'm sure, honestly. I spoke to him earlier. Anyway, if something had happened, I wouldn't be trekking all the way here to tell you. Your parents would've rung you straightaway."

"Oh. Yes, I wasn't thinking – I suppose they would've done. But then, why *are* you here?"

"There are things I need to say to you, Sandra, things that can only be said in person."

"Gary," said Carl, with a slight edge of impatience in his voice, "I'm not sure we have time for whatever this is right now. We're in the middle of checking in."

I looked at my watch. "What's your hurry?" I asked. "Your flight isn't for another two-and-a-half hours."

"Excuse me," the woman behind the desk said to Carl. "If the two of you aren't going to be checking in, I'll have to ask you to let the next person come forward."

"We *are* checking in," insisted Carl.

"I wouldn't mind hearing what Gary has to say first," said Sandra.

"There you have it, the majority has spoken," I said to Carl pointedly. "Sandra, let's go somewhere a bit less busy. How about over there, by those trolleys?"

I led the way; Sandra followed, wheeling her bag. Carl hesitated, and then, wheeling his own bag, followed Sandra. Once we'd reached the spot I had in mind, Carl asked, "How long is this likely to take?"

"How long is a piece of string?" I asked in return. "You should probably go off and find a café or something where you can sit and have a coffee. We'll message you when we're ready for you to come back."

"I don't see why I should be expected to go anywhere," Carl objected. "I have a right to be part of this conversation."

"How can you say that," I countered, "when you don't even know what the conversation's going to be about?"

"Well... what *is* it going to be about?"

"None of your business."

"*None of my*— I think you're pushing your luck here, Gary."

"Please," said Sandra, "Carl, Gary, let's not argue about this. I do want to hear what you've come here to tell me, Gary, but banishing Carl isn't an option."

"All right. Fine. There's no reason why Carl shouldn't hear this, anyway. What I want to say is... is..."

"Yes?" said Sandra.

"That I want to come back."

"You want to come *back?*" repeated Sandra.

"You want to come *back?*" repeated Carl.

"I do, yes."

"I can't believe what I'm hearing," said Sandra. "I've *given* you chances to come back, and you haven't taken them."

"I know. I was crazy not to."

"Well... but... what's behind this, Gary? Why the sudden change of mind? I don't mean to be cynical, but have things not worked out for you? Is a self-help career not on the cards anymore? And that's why I'm back in the frame, because I'm your fallback option?"

"No, it's not like that. All that's happened is, I've come to some realisations since lunchtime today…"

"Since *lunchtime?*"

"And what's clear to me now is that you and Jack are more important than anything else. More important than any amount of fame, or book sales, or…"

"Seriously, Gary? You're coming to these conclusions only *now?* I'm glad if you're getting your priorities straight, but your timing is terrible. Here I am, about to fly off to Paris with a new— with Carl…"

"I think maybe that's just it," I said. "Maybe it took the prospect of you and Carl spending a weekend together to make me rethink my priorities."

"No, no. I don't accept this, Gary. It's too sewn-up. You're not telling me the whole story."

"She's too clever for you," Carl said. "You'd better tell us what's really behind this."

"*Shut up, Carl!*" I boiled over.

I know I shouldn't have lost my temper like that, but the conversation wasn't going the way I'd planned, and Carl's needling comment was more than I could tolerate. What made things worse was, part of me knew Sandra was right. There *was* more to the story than I was letting on. Carl's presence was, it seemed clear, making me censor myself.

"Gary…" said Sandra.

Before she could go on, I said, "Please, Sandra. I can't talk about this with Carl here." I was no longer even trying to conceal my desperation at this point.

Sandra turned to Carl. "It's up to you, Carl, but you

know, if you *could* give us a few minutes…"

Carl pondered the request. "Hmm. Well, from what I've heard so far, I don't suppose this'll take you long to sort out with Gary anyway. I'll have a browse at WH Smith, shall I? I could do with a magazine to read on the flight. Back in a few minutes, Sandra." He gave her a peck on the cheek and proceeded to head off in the direction of the airport shops.

With Carl gone, I was able to speak more freely. "I've had a difficult time lately," I confessed. "It's my own fault. I've made some bad mistakes, and I've… I've suffered the consequences."

"Oh. Well, I'm sorry to hear that. What mistakes?"

"Remember how I told you on Sunday I was 'excelling' at my job? It turns out I wasn't. I've been in my manager's bad books for weeks without realising it. This afternoon she subjected me to a… a sort of public humiliation."

"Did she? That's terrible. I'm sure whatever you did couldn't have been so bad as to deserve that. But you managed to keep your job?"

"Just about."

"That's some consolation at least."

"It is, but… there's something else. Because I've fallen behind on my rent payments, I'm being evicted from my flat."

Sandra stared at me.

"I know what you're thinking," I said.

"And you still want to make out that I'm not your fallback option?" She sighed. "You need a roof over your head, I understand that. Of course I'm not going to turn you away. Stay for a week, or a month, or however long it takes for you to get back on your feet. But please, don't pretend this is something other than what it is. You can sleep on the sofa."

"I'm not after a place to stay," I protested.

"Aren't you? You've made a point of telling me how it's all gone wrong for you at work, how you've run out of money and you're being thrown out of your flat. You sound for all the world like a person who needs rescuing."

"That's not what I'm asking for," I insisted. "All I'm trying to get across is that I've been *humbled.* And a person who's been humbled can't just carry on as if nothing's happened. They have to face up to hard truths – about themselves, about their ideals, about the way they've been living their lives…"

She looked at me in some surprise. "I'm not used to you talking this way, Gary."

"I'm only just getting used to it myself."

"Well, what are these hard truths you've had to face up to?"

"For so long, I've thought of success as being the most important thing in life. And actually, I still think that. I mean, whatever a person considers valuable in life, they have to hope they're going to succeed in attaining it, rather than failing. So success is always the overriding consideration. Which means I shouldn't make any apologies for wanting success."

"I suppose that makes a kind of sense. It doesn't sound particularly humble, though." She looked annoyed. "Also, I think you've forgotten my question already."

"About the hard truths? I was getting to those. The trouble was, I had a very particular idea of success. When

I imagined success, all I could imagine was Marshall Brewster: his lifestyle, his public image. It never crossed my mind that success for *me* might be different from success for *him*. So I went after Marshall Brewster-style success single-mindedly, uncompromisingly, and in the end it meant that I lost you. There was no going back after that, no sense of there being any reason to get out of bed in the morning, unless I could believe that losing you was a necessary sacrifice, the price of success. So I made myself believe it. But I was pulling the wool over my own eyes. Losing you wasn't the price of success. Losing you was *throwing away* success."

Her look seemed to have softened. "In what way," she said quietly, "was it throwing away success?"

"I can think of very few people who are as lucky as I was. I was sharing my life with the one person on earth who loved me for myself rather than for anything I'd done or was going to do. Someone who never looked down on me, never dismissed me, never rolled their eyes at me, always took me just as I was. Someone who showed me how a relationship didn't have to be a power struggle, how it could be about two people bringing out the best in each other. For me to have ended up with someone like you, someone so authentic, and wise, and loveable, and endlessly irresistible – and then on top of that, to have a family with you, to be father to the most special little boy a couple could ask for – what was that, if not success? *Of course* it was success."

She shook her head, and carried on shaking it. She was biting her lip and I could tell she was having difficulty keeping her composure.

"I didn't know," she said finally, "that you had it in you to say what you've just said. I've been thinking such angry, bitter thoughts about you lately, Gary, and now I feel awful."

"Please don't. I know I should've said these things earlier. I know I should've said them on Sunday afternoon."

"Well, that's what I don't understand. Why didn't you? I'd let down my defences. I was drawing you close to me, and you were letting me – at first. But in the end, you couldn't handle it. You had to say something to spoil the moment. Why?"

"I'm so sorry, Sandra. Looking back on it now, I think I was afraid."

"Afraid of what?"

"Of not measuring up to Carl."

"*Really?*"

"It's just that he's so *good* at everything. Loss adjusting. Tennis. Taekwondo."

"How did you know about the taekwondo?"

"I… well…"

"Never mind, it doesn't matter. None of those things were ever big selling points for me."

"But you must see something in him."

Sandra shrugged. "He's a decent person. Responsible. Pays attention to me."

"*I'll* pay attention to you," I pledged.

"Gary—"

"I'll do more than pay attention to you. I'll do everything I can to make this up to you. Carl seems decent enough but… he is a bit of a plastic man, isn't he?"

"That's an *outrageous* thing to say!" she replied, but there was a hint of a smile on her face as she said it.

"Well, tell me this, Sandra: when was the last time he made you laugh?"

After a pause, she said, "No comment."

I shook my head. "You deserve someone with a proper personality. Someone who clicks with you, someone who knows what you're about, someone who can make you happy."

"Maybe so. But – I hate to be all hard-headed and practical about this, Gary – I also deserve someone solid and dependable. No matter how devoted you are to me, this isn't going to work if you carry on tilting at windmills."

"What windmills are these?"

"I'm just saying, if there's always going to be another quest for you to get drawn into, another big project, another surefire money-making scheme... Well, if you end up gambling your family's future on the next one of these things that comes along – that's not something I'm willing to go through again. I can't. I won't."

"There won't be any more mad quests, I promise you. You and Jack come first."

"It's easy to say that, Gary. But the fact is, you're not always in the best position to recognise your risk-taking for what it is. Remember how you got so excited about that company Skyhook Media? You said it was a 'sure thing'. And then you ploughed all that money into it just before the share price plummeted."

"It's interesting you should bring that up," I said.

"What do you mean?"

"I never did get round to unloading the Skyhook shares – which is lucky, because Skyhook is doing extraordinarily well at the moment."

"Is it?"

"Yes, its share price has gone through the roof now that its main competitor is floundering."

"So you're an investment genius?" she asked, with evident amusement.

"That's for posterity to decide. All I know is, I've made a very respectable gain. I can clear my rent arrears with my landlord, pay whatever I need to pay to Southern Electricity to get them off my back, repay my debt to Vincent—"

"You're in debt to Vincent? You never told me that."

"Oh, he lent me the money to buy a new computer after mine gave up the ghost a couple of months ago. Said he knew how important it was for me to have a computer so I could carry on writing my book. That's one thing about Vincent: he may not be perfect, but he's remarkably thoughtful at times. Thoughtful and kind. Anyway, what I'm saying is, I can pay off all those debts and still have more than enough left over for us to afford that family holiday in Rome we'd been wanting to go on for ages."

Again, she shook her head. "You're full of surprises today, Gary. All right, let's just assume our finances are all sorted. What about your book? Is that still going to monopolise your time and energy?"

"Not really. I've all but finished it. It just needs a conclusion. My plan is to end with an inspirational story from my own life, like the story of how I won you back."

She laughed. "You're very confident. You haven't won me back *yet*."

I pulled her close, wrapped my arms round her, and I said, "Please don't disappoint my readers, Sandra."

"Ah, well… when you put it that way, Gary…"

How I'd missed the sensation of Sandra's lips on mine! The kiss went on for a long time. Eventually, we were interrupted by a quiet voice pronouncing the word "So…"

We disengaged ourselves from the embrace and stood facing Carl. He looked as crestfallen as you'd expect someone in his situation to be.

"I'm so sorry, Carl," said Sandra. "I never imagined this would happen."

"I didn't either," said Carl. "I'd assumed… well, it doesn't make any difference what I assumed. Not everything has to make sense to me, I suppose." He paused and looked pensive for a few seconds. Then he said, "What can I say to you other than, good luck. Good luck to both of you. And now I'd better get myself checked in."

"Don't feel too bad, Carl," I consoled him.

"Thank you, Gary. I won't."

"At least you'll get two seats to yourself on the plane," I added.

"Yes, thank you for pointing that out, Gary."

Once Carl had gone, Sandra and I resumed our embrace. She gave me a little tap on my thigh and said, "There seems to be some activity in your trouser pocket."

"Sandra! Please, we're in public."

"No, I meant this." She reached her hand into my pocket and removed my phone, which was vibrating. She looked at the display. "It's *Kim*," she said. "What does *she* want?"

"Oh! This must mean her flight has arrived."

"Are you saying she's here at the airport?"

"Yes, she'd been threatening to fly to London for a 'showdown' with me about how I'm responsible for ruining her life. I never thought she'd go through with it but now she has. She probably expects me to come and collect her."

"I'll let her know she'll have to make other arrangements," said Sandra, and answered the phone. "Hello?"

"Who is this?" demanded Kim. (I could hear her voice very distinctly, despite the handset being pressed to Sandra's ear.) "Let me guess – you're Gary's latest conquest."

"I'm not Gary's latest conquest. I'm the mother of his child."

"You're *Sandra?* Whoa— okay. Sorry, I'm just a little confused about why you're answering his phone. I mean, he ditched you, didn't he? Abandoned you and the kid because he couldn't abide any restrictions on his precious 'freedom'. Classy! Look, I don't mean to poke my nose where it's not wanted, but if you're having thoughts of getting back with him, don't do it. Seriously, that man is a human wrecking ball. Now, if you don't mind, I need to speak to him. He's supposed to be meeting me at International Arrivals and I have no idea where the hell he is right now."

"I'm sorry to have to break this to you," Sandra said, "but you're going to have to manage without Gary."

"Excuse me?"

"He won't be able to come and meet you. I'll let him explain." She passed the phone to me.

"Basically, Kim," I began, "I can't spend any time with

you while you're here. I'm going to be too busy reuniting with my family. But if you ask at the airport information desk, I'm sure they can give you details of hostels and guest houses and—"

"Are you *kidding* me? *Hostels?* This is a joke, right?"

"It isn't. And there aren't any other options. I'd let you stay on your own for a little while in my rented flat, but, well, first of all that would be far too strange, and second I'd be worried you'd smash the place up."

"The way I'm feeling right now, you're damn right I'd smash the place up!"

"So you can't say I'm worrying for no reason. Anyway, it won't be a wasted visit. You can do some shopping, some sightseeing…"

"Oh, well you've changed your tune, Mister Don't-Visit-Any-London-Attractions-Unless-You-Want-To-Be-Set-Upon-By-A-Swarm-Of-Killer-Bees. You *know* my main reason for making this trip. And you've let me down. Again. Anthony, you're not going to believe what he just said to me!"

"Who's Anthony?" I asked.

"He's completely blowing me off, wants nothing to do with me," continued Kim, ignoring my question. "He expects me to stay in a hostel!"

"Nothing would surprise me about that guy," said an American voice in the background. The voice, which sounded like it belonged to someone beefy and muscle-bound, continued, "Seriously, just forget about him. He's a dirtbag."

"But what am I going to do?" said Kim. "Where am I going to go?"

"Stay with me and the other rowing club guys in Putney," said Anthony. "Now that Brandon's dropped out, there's an extra room available. It'll be awesome. Trust me, you're gonna have the best time with us. These guys are so friggin' hilarious, you have no idea."

"Oh my God, thank you," said Kim to Anthony. "But I've still got this unfinished business with Gary. I can't just let him win, can I? I mean, I've come all this way, and—"

"He's not going to win. How can he win? He's a loser. You know what? Put him on, let me talk to him." After a couple of seconds, Anthony's voice boomed in my ear. "Hello, Gary? This is Anthony. I was sitting next to Kim on the plane and she gave me the whole story of how you screwed her over. You're a real piece of work, you know that? If you don't recognise what a beautiful person she is, that's your loss. And I'll tell you what: she can do a hell of a lot better than you. A *hell of a lot* better."

I heard Kim's voice in the background: "Tell him I might still be in touch about the showdown."

So there you have it. As I write this, Jack is shrieking with delight in the next room, where he is defending his sofa-cushion fortress from Sandra, who is pretending she's a fortress-destroying giant. I've been home for three days now. It's so lovely, I could weep. I go to bed at night with Sandra at my side, and in the morning I'm woken by Jack climbing on top of me and singing "Mister Sun" or "If You're Happy and You Know It" at the top of his voice. Let there be no doubt: this is success – this, and the fact that I've managed to produce the book you hold in your hands. Yes, dear reader, I am living proof that the strategies detailed in this book really do work. So get out there and apply them! You have nothing to lose, and everything to gain.

And when success does come your way, don't hesitate to drop me a line! I promise to answer each fan letter individually – at least, until such time as the sheer quantity proves unmanageable.

Field of Stars

Also by Alice Mattison

Stories
GREAT WITS

Poetry
ANIMALS

FIELD

OF STARS

Alice Mattison

William Morrow and Company, Inc.

New York

Library of Congress Cataloging-in-Publication Data

Mattison, Alice.
    Field of stars / by Alice Mattison.
        p.   cm.
    ISBN 0-688-11119-X
    I. Title.
PS3563.A8598F5   1991
813'.54—dc20   91-13005
                                              CIP

Printed in the United States of America

First Edition

1 2 3 4 5 6 7 8 9 10

BOOK DESIGN BY CYNTHIA KRUPAT

FOR MY MOTHER AND FATHER

AND IN MEMORY OF MY AUNT,

CLARE MATLIN

Part One

WHEN SUSAN STERNFELD was three, she went downstairs to visit her grandparents, who lived in the apartment below. It was a two-family house and her grandparents owned it. Susan was allowed to stay overnight that night, and in the morning she didn't go back upstairs. After that her grandmother always told people that Susan was visiting, but her grandfather said she stayed with them because her mother wasn't well. There were times Susan slept upstairs, and her grandmother would mention them as proof that she didn't live with them, she lived with her parents like any normal child, but there was always a reason why Susan slept upstairs. Her grandmother was sick, or the apartment was being painted.

Susan used to say she was visiting her grandparents, but when she had learned to read, she read a book about an orphan girl who lived with her grandparents. She wondered whether someone like the grandparents in the story might carry her off, and she imagined her mother's parents, whom she'd met only twice, coming one day with empty suitcases; they lived in Chicago, and were younger than her father's parents, the ones she knew. Then it occurred to her that she already *lived with her grandparents*, and it was like learning that her name was really Rebecca or Emily, or that Susan, which seemed so dull, was that sort of name. From then on she told friends and teachers that she lived with her grandparents, but only if they weren't likely to come to the house and find out exactly what the arrangement was.

They lived on Hendrix Street in Brooklyn. The house had been built for one family and renovated, and whoever had done the renovation had not taken it as seriously as he might have. The front door locked, of course, and at the end of a short hall on the first floor was the door to Susan's grandparents' apartment, which usually stood open, and was locked only by mistake—people got locked out—or when everyone was away for the day. Upstairs, the door to Susan's mother's apartment also locked, but the bathroom of that apartment was outside the door. Sometimes Paula, Susan's mother, also left her door open, as if they all lived in a large one-family house, and Susan would go upstairs and play or read in her mother's living room. She continued to have a bedroom upstairs, with a few baby clothes in it. Her clothes had never been packed and moved, but had been brought down one at a time as she needed them. Susan didn't go into her old room when she was upstairs. It seemed to belong to someone else, a child from whom she had been called away unexpectedly and to whom she could never get back, as if she were someone in a dream who is prevented, over and over again, by a new interruption or obstacle, from reaching the place where she is supposed to be. Sometimes she made plans to move back upstairs—she thought it might be her fault that everything she owned was in her grandparents' place—but she never could seem to find the time or energy to right things.

When Susan went downstairs her father was away fighting in the Second World War, but he came back a few months later. Something woke Susan one night, shortly after she had fallen asleep, and when she came out of the bedroom she saw him sitting in an armchair, in uniform. He was tall, and even though he sat all the way back in the chair, his knees came out beyond the edge of the seat. Susan stood in the doorway looking at his legs, and at his arms, stretched out along the arms of the chair. Her eyes were level with his knees. Her grandfather was saying, "You could have lost an arm or a leg."

When her father saw her, he called her to come to him but she was too shy. She thought he wouldn't know why she was there. "Grandma read my story," she said, so he would know that she had been put to bed properly.

"Good for Grandma!" said her father. A few days later, he came down and gathered Susan's things and brought her upstairs, but it didn't stick. He didn't stay home. He went on trips—he was a traveling salesman—and when he was home, sometimes he too stayed in the grandparents' apartment. Susan understood that her grandmother was her father's mother, and she knew people often stayed with their mothers. Even when her father was downstairs, her parents weren't far apart: Her mother was right there, except when she went to work. Once or twice she went to stay in a hospital for a time.

"She likes roast chicken," Susan's grandmother would sometimes say, at dinner, with a tiny flick of her chin toward the ceiling. "Ezra, you take a plate up. God knows if she ate." After dinner her grandfather would fill a plate with chicken, potatoes, and vegetables, and carry it upstairs for Paula. When he came down, he would say, "She was taking a nap. I left it on the table."

When Susan was very young, her grandfather would pick her up and turn her upside down. Then he would pretend he couldn't find her head. "Here are her arms," he would say in a puzzled voice, holding her by the legs. "And there"—pointing to her bottom—"is where her head should be, but I do not know what I have done with her head."

"It's down here," Susan would call, delightedly. "It's down here, Grandpa!"

Finally he would leave Susan sprawled on a chair, still upside down. "Leah," he would say, "Leah!" and his face would show a mixture of sorrow, puzzlement, and shame, all make-believe, Susan somehow—righting herself—knew. "Leah, I must tell you something sad," he would say. "I have lost Susan's head."

"God forbid," her grandmother would say. "Even as a joke, you shouldn't say such things."

"Here's my head, Grandpa," Susan would be calling, by now. And he would rejoice and kiss her head.

But he was afraid of Susan's mother, and when Susan went to school, he and her grandmother didn't trust the school or the teachers. They said they were afraid that, although she was a Jewish child, Susan would be asked to sing Christmas carols, and often spoke to her about how she might refuse, and yet be polite and respectful to the teacher.

"Maybe she doesn't know, the teacher," her grandmother said. "She is ignorant—it is not her fault."

In fact, there was not much singing, and when she did have to sing in school, Susan was never certain which songs were the ones her grandmother might object to. Her third-grade teacher was Jewish, but this seemed so improbable to her grandparents that they pushed the information aside, as if only a special sort of Jew was allowed to work for the Board of Education, a Jew who was not really a Jew. Yet this didn't have to do with observance of Jewish law. Susan's grandparents were not observant, and her grandfather was proud that he never went to the synagogue.

Susan saw that school really wasn't Jewish—it wasn't essentially Jewish, even if particular people in it were—but she knew that what upset her grandparents was something else. They were afraid that somehow the school could make Susan move back upstairs.

Susan was afraid her grandparents could forbid her to go. It was hard to understand that other children didn't want to go to school. Susan was not always happy there—often she was embarrassed or frightened, and she lived in dread of misbehaving and being scolded. But in Susan's mind, school was bright and sharp. Its dangerous edges could be seen and avoided. Home was dark, like a drawer that hasn't been cleaned out in a long time and has knives in it so deep under the broken spatulas and tarnished spoons that they have lost their shine and give no warning before the finger touches them.

Yet school was not easy to understand. The one time Susan was sent to the principal's office as a punishment, it was a misunderstanding. A ball had rolled out of the playground across the sidewalk and into the street, and an older girl told Susan to go and get it. She sounded like a teacher, and Susan obeyed her, but the real teacher spotted her outside the fence and sent her to the office.

Still, there was sense to it. The principal told Susan she should listen to the teacher, not to the big children, and Susan saw that that was a rule she hadn't known about, but it was a rule. At home, she didn't know. On her way home from school or from the house of a friend or from an errand, she would try to imagine how her grandmother would behave, whether anything Susan had done would make her angry—angry with Susan or with someone else—and she didn't know. Yet she knew her grandmother was moody. The sense of knives in a dark drawer came from something else.

The apartment really was dark. It had a porch in front, which made the front rooms dark, and her grandmother had heavy curtains, and small lamps with fewer bulbs than sockets in each, no overhead lights. But Susan's mother's apartment, upstairs, was light, especially in the winter, when the trees were bare; it always seemed newly painted, with no curtains and only a little furniture.

"Is your mother crazy?" asked Bernice, who was Susan's friend.

"No," said Susan quickly, and Paula wasn't crazy. Most of the time she went to work, though sometimes she just napped. Susan would go upstairs in the evenings at times and talk to her.

Once Bernice told her she wanted to play a new game, and she blindfolded Susan. Bernice's cousin was there, too, an older girl Susan had never seen before called Janet. Bernice began to chant a poem that frightened Susan.

In the yard
Behind the house
In somebody's garden
Lies the snake.

She sang it faster and faster, louder and louder, and her cousin joined in. The two girls led her somewhere and took off the blindfold. They were in a backyard. She didn't recognize it. Bernice said, "I bet I can beat you up."

She'd never said anything like that before, and now they began to fight. Bernice was stronger than Susan, and Susan could barely return any of her many, hard blows. She was crying. Suddenly an old woman came out of the house. "Private property!" she yelled.

They ran as though the police were after them. Susan couldn't stop crying. When she saw where she was, she ran home, opened the downstairs door, still crying, and went straight upstairs. She didn't think her mother was home, but she could go into her mother's bathroom, out in the hall, and wash her face. If her grandmother saw her crying she would chase Bernice home and shout at Bernice's mother.

Paula's apartment door was standing open. Susan burst in and threw herself, sobbing, on the sofa. Her mother and a man came running in from the kitchen. "What is it? What is it?"

Susan was crying too hard to speak. "Give her some water," the man said. Her mother went for a glass of water and gave it to Susan. It was odd to drink water while she was crying. Her grandmother wouldn't have said to do that, and it gave Susan the idea that the man, whoever he was, wasn't Jewish. In her grandparents' household they didn't usually drink water at all. If they were thirsty, they drank juice or seltzer water with syrup in it.

"Susan, this is Mr. Iannelli," her mother said, as soon as Susan stopped crying. She didn't ask what the trouble had been.

"Art," said Mr. Iannelli. "She can call me Art. Or she can call me Uncle Art."

But Susan called him Mr. Iannelli. After that her mother cooked more. Susan would hear footsteps upstairs and go up and find her at the stove, with Mr. Iannelli sitting at the kitchen table, talking to her. He owned a store, and he would tell her mother about his troubles with the people who worked for him. "Time and again, she says she'll be on time, and still she's late. But once she gets there—perfect. So Paula, what do I do?"

"Don't ask me, Art," Paula would say. "I never had a head for business." Paula had worked for Art for a time, Susan thought. Paula was a saleslady. Now she worked in a different store, selling dresses. She had to bring customers what they wanted to try on.

"It drives me nuts," Paula would say to Susan. "One of them

comes in, and I see right away she's a size eighteen. But she says, 'Let me try this in a fourteen.' So of course it's tight, and she stretches the seams. I say politely maybe an eighteen. I always say, 'They run small.'

"No. She has to try the sixteen. Sometimes if I say they run *really* small, she'll try the eighteen. But I have to say a woman came in the other day who ordinarily wears an eight, and in this style, a four-teen. I make up all kinds of things."

Susan's grandparents had a fight about Mr. Iannelli. Her grand-mother thought Susan should not go upstairs when he was there. "It isn't right," she said.

"But you are jumping to conclusions," her grandfather said. He was reading a book, and he put it down and followed her grand-mother into the kitchen to have the argument.

"What do you mean, I am jumping? A man alone in an apart-ment with a woman. Even if I am not right—but you can see it. You can see a married man from the way he walks, the way he puts his hand in his pocket, the way his shoes look."

"This is foolish, I think," said the grandfather.

"You ask him!" said Leah. She was very angry. "You ask him, you're so smart."

Nobody ever asked Mr. Iannelli whether he was married, but Susan continued to go upstairs when he was there. She liked him. She decided, after all, to start calling him Uncle Art.

Now, when she came into the kitchen of her mother's apartment, her mother would be cutting up a carrot or an onion, or dredging pieces of chicken in flour. Uncle Art would be sitting at the table, near the door, his feet stretched out in front of him. Susan always looked at his shoes to see if he was married, but she couldn't tell. She would say "Excuse me" and step over his feet and go sit at the other end of the table.

Then she would get up and look in the refrigerator. Her mother knew she liked sliced American cheese from a block that came in a wooden box, and a dairy store near where she worked sold it. Susan would find the cheese and take out three or four slices. It was sliced thin. She would eat the slices slowly and listen to her mother and Uncle Art talk. Sometimes she'd eat little scallops around the edge of each slice, making it smaller and smaller, and sometimes she would start at the top and eat down.

Uncle Art always said, "Funny kind of sandwich. No bread." He said it as if it were a clever thing, and it pleased Susan that he noticed what she did, although Susan didn't like that kind of cheese in a sandwich. Either the pile of cheese was too thin, and all you tasted was bread, or it was too thick, and just like other cheese.

A few minutes after Susan had finished the cheese, she would go back downstairs. She never ate with her mother and Uncle Art. She didn't want to ask her mother if she could. This way, it was as if everyone just happened to run into everyone else.

On the Saturday after Susan's eleventh birthday—her birthday was April fourteenth—Paula came downstairs. This was surprising. Susan was reading in her room, and she heard her having a conversation with her grandmother. That night, her father, who lived in New Jersey now, was coming to take Susan to the circus to celebrate her birthday. Her mother might want to know about that, Susan thought.

Then Paula came to Susan's door and invited her to take a walk. Nothing like this had ever happened before. Susan put on her coat.

"Let's get ice cream," said her mother, as they started to walk. It wasn't really warm enough for ice-cream cones, but they walked to the ice-cream parlor three blocks away. Susan bought maple walnut and her mother bought cherry vanilla. When they came out, Susan assumed they would turn toward Highland Park, but her mother said, "Oh, I just remembered something I need from the drugstore." There was a drugstore on the next corner. When they got there, Susan held both cones and Paula went in. She came out with a large bag that seemed to contain a rectangular box. Now they turned toward the park.

Susan was mystified. "If you needed something so big," she said, "why didn't you buy it on our way *back* from the park? Then you wouldn't have to carry it."

"It's not heavy," said her mother gaily.

"What is it?" said Susan.

"Kotex."

"What's that?"

Now her mother told Susan all about menstruation. Susan had had no idea. She didn't like listening, because she was unused to long conversations with her mother, but especially because of the ice cream. It didn't sound like something she wanted to hear about while she was eating. She tried to make the explanation as short as possible by asking no questions and pretending she had caught on when she hadn't. She understood that her mother was talking about something that would happen to her, but she wasn't sure whether, once it started happening, it ever stopped, except when you grew old. It sounded, somehow, as if it happened every day. When she pictured the menstrual fluid her mother was talking about—"a discharge," her mother called it—she imagined something whitish and thick, rather like mucus, something that would be disgusting to see or touch. Her mother said it was important not to get too tired when it happened. She said sometimes it hurt. She explained that once it happened, it was possible to have a baby, but she sounded as if she were straining to find something good to say about it, and Susan didn't think she wanted to have a baby, anyway.

Susan was dismayed, but even more, she was angry because her mother had tricked her. First Paula had probably told Susan's grandmother what she was going to tell Susan. They had had a conversation about this terrible subject, these two women who never spoke to each other.

"I didn't want your grandmother telling you," her mother said now. "God knows what sort of ideas she has—not washing your hair. It's perfectly all right to wash your hair when you have your period, Susan."

"Oh," said Susan.

After she had connived with her grandmother, her mother had deceived Susan. She had pretended she wanted to go for a walk and to have ice cream just so that she could give Susan this unpleasant news. Now they were walking through Highland Park, which Susan loved. She and her friends played there, and in her mind it was a much wilder place than it was. The wooded edges of the park were forests, and the hills were the highlands of Scotland. Susan hated to be there with her mother, who did not understand.

Worst of all was her tricking Susan into asking what Kotex was, so that Paula could pretend she had told Susan all this only because Susan wanted to know. They walked along the path beyond the baseball diamond. It was odd for her mother to be walking in the park at all. She was wearing open-toed shoes with little heels, and a coat with a fake fur collar. Now they walked down the hill and out to Jamaica Avenue and walked home along Jamaica Avenue, next to the park. At least now her mother was willing to change the subject. She began to tell Susan about her jealousy of another clerk in her store. The manager favored the other woman, who was not nearly as good at what she did as Paula.

When Susan had guessed there was a mystery, and her mother was going to tell her something, Susan had thought it would be something she wanted to hear. She thought her mother was going to confide in her as if they were friends or sisters. She thought that somehow the bag with the box inside had to do with the question of whether Mr. Iannelli was married. She had been trying to figure out how the two subjects could be connected, feeling a little superior to her mother, who was going to give away a secret to Susan, who hadn't even been trying to find it out, when her mother began by asking her if she knew what "menstruation" meant. Susan had felt grown up, but now she felt young. She had been fooled, and when she got home, her grandmother would know what had happened. She didn't like her grandmother to know everything that had happened to her. She reminded her mother that she was going to the circus that night—tactfully, she didn't say with whom—and they hurried back to Hendrix Street.

When they got there, her mother went upstairs with her box, and Susan went into the downstairs apartment and straight into her room. She lay down on her bed and picked up the book she had been reading, but she didn't read it anymore, she just found her place in it and then turned it upside down, open, and rolled over next to it. This made her feel very young, for some reason, lying on her stomach like a baby, and she felt that she would like to be a baby. She could remember being a baby, lying in her crib and watching her father, who came over to the crib and leaned down to look at her. She had not been lying on her stomach, she had been lying on her back, playing with her toes. It was early in the morning.

Now she heard the doorbell, and then his voice. As long as he was there, her grandmother would not question her about her walk with Paula, so she went into the kitchen. "Aren't you dressed?" her grandmother said. "It's almost time for you to go."

"She looks fine," said her father.

But Susan had a new dress made of red taffeta, which she and her grandmother had bought at Abraham & Straus. Susan went into her bedroom and took off the clothes she had been wearing, a brown corduroy school skirt and a yellow sweater. She put on her bathrobe and went into the bathroom and washed her face and arms and hands, and then she wanted to be even cleaner, so she took off her underwear and splashed water over her whole body. She didn't bother to use soap because it would have been hard to rinse herself off, and she couldn't take a real bath without making her grandmother curious. Her grandmother took showers at night, before bed, and she thought everyone else should do that, too.

Susan dried herself and put on her underwear and bathrobe, and went back into her bedroom. She was going to wear nylon stockings and a garter belt, and she put them on, and then the dress, but she was damp under her clothes, because she'd dried off too quickly, and it felt as if she had a bad secret. When she was dressed she hurried out through the room where her grandparents were, hardly letting them look at her and comment, and got her coat and went out with her father.

They took the elevated train that passed near the house as far as Eastern Parkway, and took the long escalator down to the subway. They needed the A train. Her father was shy and a little awkward with her. He hadn't said anything about the red dress. When she stepped off the escalator, Susan tripped, because her shoes had little heels, and her father caught her, leaning over so quickly that his hat fell off. He seized her under the arms and held her for a moment. "All right?" he said.

Susan said she was fine and they both bent down for his hat and nearly bumped heads, which made them laugh. She began to talk to him about school. They talked over the loud noise of the train, and then when they didn't talk, that seemed all right, because the train was so loud, nobody could have a sustained conversation on it.

When they came out of the subway in New York, her father said they should get something to eat, and they went to a Howard Johnson's. You couldn't get a whole meal there, just frankfurters, but that was fine with Susan. Her father asked her if she wanted an ice-cream soda, and Susan said yes, even though she had already had ice cream that day. It came with a big wedge-shaped scoop of vanilla ice cream, and having it seemed like a festive, even slightly reckless thing to do. It was the first time in her life she had ever had ice cream twice in one day, but now that she was older, maybe *that* was how things would be.

Then they went to the circus. They were early enough to go into the sideshow. They saw the animals—elephants eating and playing with straw, like elephants in the zoo—and then they saw the freaks. When Susan saw the fat lady she remembered her walk with her mother. The fat lady seemed so much like a grown-up, so little like a child. Then it was time to go into the arena and see the show. Susan had been to the circus before, but not for a long time. She liked the animals best. She liked the clowns, but she knew she was partly pretending about the clowns. She loved watching the tight-rope walkers and the trapeze artists. Some of them were women in tight, beautiful costumes. The costumes were like bathing suits, and Susan remembered that her mother had said that when a girl was menstruating, it wasn't a good idea to go swimming. She wondered if it was a good idea to walk a tightrope or hang on to a trapeze and jump. Susan could see now that what her mother had said was only partly true.

The messy, ugly thing her mother had described had never happened to these women, who wore bathing suits and feathers and turned upside down. She thought that maybe it was something that didn't happen to every woman, after all. Maybe it only happened to people like her grandmother and her mother, people who hardly ever came into New York, people who worked in stores selling dresses. It had probably happened to the fat lady, Susan decided, and maybe it had happened to some of the women she saw around her in the audience—skinny, tired women yelling at their kids, or discontented-looking women with their grandchildren. But there were certainly women who did not experience this mess that must be dealt with by means of pads from big boxes. So there was hope.

· · ·

In New York in the forties, children were allowed to enter kindergarten in September if they were going to be five any time before the end of the following April, and so Susan had started kindergarten when she was not quite four and a half, and first grade a year later, at five. In junior high she was in the S.P. class—"special progress"—which meant that the whole class skipped eighth grade. Susan went to high school at thirteen and graduated at sixteen. She took three years of Latin in high school and won the Latin medal when she graduated.

She was always the youngest in her class, and she became so used to it that as she grew up it was hard to understand that people existed who were younger than she was. She went to Queens College, traveling there daily by train and bus. She lived in Brooklyn, but her grandfather said it was easier to go to Queens than to Brooklyn College. It took an hour, though. In college, Susan's classmates had gone through the New York public schools, just as she had, but still, some were almost two years older than she was, and only a few were her age. Even so, it was when she met people away from the campus, away from New York, that she felt truly young, astonishingly young.

During her freshman year Susan decided she would try to get a summer camp job. She had been a Girl Scout, and now she wrote to some Girl Scout camps. Most of the camps wrote back to say she was too young for a counselor's job, but at the last minute she received a two-line note offering her a job as assistant arts and crafts counselor, at a salary of two hundred fifty dollars, at Camp Robin, which was in the Palisades Interstate Park, not far from New York City, and belonged to a Girl Scout Council in New Jersey.

Camp began on a chilly, bright day at the end of June. Susan's grandfather drove her up and helped her take her trunk out of his car and started to help her carry it down the path to the tent where she would live, but the director of the camp, whose name was Brenda, and who wore a whistle on a lanyard around her neck, just as a camp director should, hurried up to them and told him in a pleasant voice that she would help Susan. Her grandfather kissed her good-bye, standing on the path. He looked citylike. He was wearing a suit and a white shirt and leather shoes, and it was as if he could not be allowed to come any deeper under the trees. He turned and went back to his car.

"We'll take care of her, don't worry!" the director called after him, and then she winked at Susan, who wanted her grandfather gone and the trees as thick as possible.

Susan would be sharing a tent with the nature counselor. The side flaps of their tent were rolled up because the weather was good, and so the tent was both a room and a piece of the outdoors. Setting down her trunk, Susan could see the lake, through bushes. A crisp breeze was blowing, and everything fluttered and glinted in the mixed sun and shade. She would have liked to stay there, but she followed Brenda back to the dining hall, the main building of the camp.

The other counselors were arriving. Susan met the out-of-doors counselor, whose name was Jenny and who had a kind face. Like everyone else, Jenny looked experienced and had long, slim legs. Susan's legs were heavy, and she had to scramble after them all on the paths, which were crossed by tree roots. She helped Jenny take her trunk to her tent, which was near Susan's, and then they went back to the sunny lot behind the dining hall. A car drove up and a thin woman in her thirties with short, tight curls and glittery eyeglasses got out. Jenny introduced them. It was B.J., the nurse.

"Hi, Susan," said B.J. promptly, and shook her hand hard. "I've been here since yesterday," she said then, talking to Jenny. "I just drove into town to mail a letter for Annie. She's tired."

"That was nice of you," said Jenny.

"My tent is all set up," continued B.J. "Do you want to see something new that I have? It's really nice."

"Sure," said Jenny. Susan didn't know whether she was invited, but she followed Jenny and B.J. down the path. B.J. lived with three other counselors. There was a little nightstand next to her bed, not just an orange crate, and on it was a framed picture of a woman's face that had been taken in black and white and later colored in. Susan knew pictures like that were cheap and phony, but in this one, the coloring was delicate. It didn't seem realistic, but it seemed sweet.

"Oh," said Jenny. "Your mom! What a great picture." Susan wasn't used to admiring pictures of people's mothers.

"How do you like the hair?" B.J. said. The woman in the picture had light brown hair that looked as if it had been curled with pin curlers.

"Oh, it's beautiful," said Jenny. "Your mom has such pretty hair."

"Had." B.J. looked hard at Jenny. Her face was thin and her jawbone showed.

"What?"

"Had. My mom died on Mother's Day." Light seemed to flash off her glasses.

"Oh, B.J.," said Jenny. Susan tried to look sad, although it seemed wrong to be hearing this news when she'd just met B.J. She wished she weren't there. Jenny put her hand on B.J.'s shoulder. "I'm so sorry!"

B.J. put the picture back on the nightstand. "I know, Jenny, you're my pal. That's why I wanted to tell you. Some of these people, I'm not so sure."

She led the way back to the dining hall, and shrieked when she saw who had come, one of the waterfront counselors. They began to talk about which of last year's staff was coming back. Susan was cold. It was much warmer in the sun than in the shade. The other counselors all wore shorts, as Susan did, but they didn't seem cold. They were lounging on the steps of the dining hall, which were in the shade. Susan kept trying to move the conversation just a little bit into the sun, but the others didn't notice.

Then it was time to eat lunch. There were two cooks, both black women, and they had set one long table at the end of the dining hall, which was a large open wooden pavilion. It was even colder at the table than down in the yard; the dining porch was in deep shade. Susan pressed her legs together to keep warm.

Nobody would be able to manage quite as well as they had last year, not without a counselor called Skipper; that was clear from the discussion at the table. Susan pictured Skipper as even slimmer and more at ease than these others, and a little larger than they were, in slightly brighter color, as if their photographs had been cut from different pages of a magazine, and the camera had been closer for Skipper's picture. Susan thought that if Skipper were there, she'd have been afraid of her, but also that Skipper might have been kinder to her than these others. Mostly, it seemed, Skipper had played madcap practical jokes.

Lunch was cold cuts and bread and cheese and three-bean salad, which Susan had never eaten before. The cold cuts were unfamiliar too. She was used to kosher cold cuts, though her family wasn't kosher. But when she ate, she felt warmer and less self-conscious. After a while, Brenda said it was time to hold a meeting and make some announcements, and Susan relaxed even more, because she knew she could follow directions and work hard; it was all this joking and chatting that was difficult.

"For the next three days, we'll be setting up camp, as you know," said Brenda. "And then the happy little ones arrive."

"What are *we*, the miserable big ones?" said Susan, with a laugh. Several of the women and girls around the table looked at her, but she was glad she'd spoken, and made a bit of a joke.

"I *hope* no one is miserable," said Brenda soberly.

The cooks were bringing out dessert and B.J. jumped up to help them. It was canned peaches and a plate of cookies. Susan jumped up, too, and helped B.J. distribute the small plastic bowls of peaches, and she felt better yet. B.J. gave her a big, shaky smile.

When the others found out, in the next week, that Susan was seventeen but had already finished her first year in college, they said she must be a genius, and wouldn't listen when she tried to explain about the S.P. class and the April cutoff date and her birthday. By this time the camp season had begun, and the counselors were spending their evenings in the kitchen, where the cooks would leave biscuits or cookies for them to eat, and they would all talk about trying to lose weight (and eat anyway), except for B.J., who was always trying to gain weight and couldn't. On Sundays, B.J. cried about her mother, and it was tricky to talk to her, but on other days she joined in the conversation, although she could be touchy if it reminded her, somehow, of her mother. She quickly became friendly with Susan's tentmate, Mary, which made Susan jealous of both of them. B.J. and Mary sang boisterously together in the evenings, mostly a song whose chorus went, "Roll me over in the clover . . . roll me over, lay me down, and do it again, again, again—" that Susan had never heard before. B.J. sang loudly but her eyes would glint and sometimes Susan thought she was going to cry.

Susan, on those evenings, read Virgil in Latin. She had made up her mind to read the first six books of the *Aeneid* that summer, and she'd sit on one of the kitchen counters, half-listening to the conversation and putting in a word at times, but making herself march along through the narrative, trying to read twenty lines a night.

The other counselors called her Virgie, but Susan didn't mind, even though they meant virgin as well. They were virgins, too; they talked about it enough. In fact they seemed to like her, and she particularly wanted B.J. to like her. She also wanted Jenny to like her, but Jenny was so kind, she couldn't do otherwise. The other person Susan wanted to please was Annie, the head of the waterfront, a calm woman with honey-colored hair who was about twenty-four and didn't look like Susan's idea of a swimming counselor. At the waterfront she was quiet and confident, and her face was gentle, as if she had had a trouble long ago. She said Susan had a nice crawl. The other counselors weren't important.

Once someone said that the boys' camp across the lake was Jewish, and a counselor called Joan said it couldn't be, because she had seen a blond boy there. Susan spoke up right away and said there were plenty of blond Jews. Her grandmother had blue eyes, she said, and had been blond as a child. Joan said she hadn't known, and looked as if she thought Susan was making a big deal of it unnecessarily. It made Susan feel as if she were far from New York. She couldn't imagine anyone from New York saying such a thing.

Susan knew that she was doing the important things right. She was friendly and careful with her campers, the youngest group, age ten. She supervised them when they did their chores—sweeping the dining hall or cleaning and filling the lanterns. In the craft shop, her job was easy, except that Susan didn't approve of the craft shop. The head arts and crafts counselor was Gloria, Jenny's tentmate. Gloria was bossy with the children, artificial and boastful with the counselors. The crafts projects she supervised mostly came in kits, and Susan thought that was shockingly uncreative. The children had to fit previously chosen tiles into a previously designed pattern, and glue them down, or they had to thread gimp—Susan had never before known what that narrow plastic ribbon was called—through holes in a change purse or key case.

Susan liked teaching the children to make lanyards. She quickly learned the different ways to braid them. The lanyards were made of gimp that came not in kits but on spools of many colors, which she and Gloria threaded along a piece of clothesline and hung between two nails in the crafts hall.

Susan tried to get along with Gloria, although she didn't like her. In general, she tried to act as much like the other counselors as possible. She joined the counselors' singing group, though she couldn't sing, but she saw that they'd think well of her for trying. B.J. led the singing, and Susan liked that, and even liked the attention when B.J. occasionally pointed to her, eyebrows raised, as they sang, to let her know she was flat. Gloria, who sang in a fluty, trained soprano that didn't mix with anyone else's voice, was finally asked to keep silent, after long deliberations to which Susan was not invited but about which she was told: B.J. told Jenny and Jenny told her.

Susan knew it was flattering that Jenny had confided in her. In fact, her only difficulty at camp was that she couldn't seem to keep from teasing people. "Anybody drown today?" Susan would say cheerfully to someone from the waterfront staff, or she'd call to a group of campers who were being taught by Jenny how to use an ax, "Kiss your toes good-bye!" It was the kind of thing they had said in her high school—New York humor, she told herself—but not here. She tried to remember not to do it.

One night, as they were sitting around in the kitchen, B.J. announced that the counselors needed to go to bed earlier. They often stayed in the kitchen until close to midnight, she pointed out, and she thought they looked sleepy at reveille. It was a health measure. Everyone got up obediently and filed out, but B.J. sat still, and then she called to Susan to sit down opposite her at the table in the kitchen near the big iron stove. She looked at Susan significantly and Susan realized that her speech was a ploy to get rid of everyone else—apparently with their prior consent, since nobody had protested. She was afraid she must have done something wrong.

"You're an extremely bright, interesting young woman, Susie," said B.J., when they were alone, and Susan realized that though she respected B.J. as a nurse and liked her so much she was unrealistic about her, she didn't think B.J. was qualified to tell her whether she was a bright young woman or not. B.J. went on. "At first, we thought you might have a serious problem," she said. "We were a tiny bit afraid that you might actually be psychotic."

"Why?" Susan giggled, but she was upset.

"The things you say. You probably don't even remember this, but right at the beginning Brenda said we'd be expecting the happy little ones—it's one of her expressions, you've probably noticed by now that she says it all the time—and you said, 'Does that make us the miserable big ones?' "

"I remember that," said Susan, "but I was just joking."

Behind B.J., on the counter, ketchup bottles were being drained. Five nearly empty bottles had been balanced, upside down, on top of five bottles that were half full. The cooks had left them that way when they had finished in the kitchen and had gone off to their quiet tent at the end of camp. Now, every once in a while Susan saw a red blob detach itself from one of the five upper bottles and slide down into its lower counterpart.

"Well, there are jokes and jokes," said B.J., but then she continued, "but what I wanted to tell you is that we were wrong. We were worried about you, but we see now that you're a fine person and fun to work with. And you're being a good sport about Gloria. Gloria will not be back next year, I can tell you that. Anyway, that's what we wanted you to know."

Susan went to bed in a daze. After that she tried even harder to be near B.J. and win her friendship. Near B.J. she could sing, for one thing. Every two weeks, the night before one group of campers went home and another arrived, the counselors dressed up in blue shorts, and at bedtime they walked from tent to tent singing and carrying candles—all but Gloria, who had been asked to stay in the kitchen in case of an emergency during the singing, and who pretended she didn't know why. Later that night, the counselors would gather in the junior counselors' shack and cook hamburgers and onion rings on buddy burners—stoves made from tin cans—and drink Seagram's 7 and 7-Up. The cooking was safe—they never forgot they were Girl Scouts—but the drinking was scary; Susan, who had never had a drink before, felt as if this was exactly what was supposed to happen.

And then she got sick. It was just a cold, but it grew worse. She wanted to go to B.J. to be taken care of, but she couldn't seem to allow herself to line up with the campers at sick call in the evening. B.J. loved to treat colds. She said she did seven things to get rid of colds: She said it gruffly, and then she enumerated. She gave aspirin, put Vick's VapoRub under your nose and Ben-Gay on your chest, she gave cough medicine, she made you gargle, she gave nose drops, and she swabbed out your throat, a legendary gruesome experience. Susan thought it would be lovely to be taken care of that way by B.J., but she was afraid that perhaps she was not sick enough to be given all that care. She might just be talking herself into it. At length B.J. noticed she had a cold and told her to go to sick call, but even though Susan was pleased, she couldn't do it. The next day, B.J. said it again. This time Susan took two girls from her unit and went rowing on the lake after supper, so there was no way she could go to sick call, and, wonderfully, B.J. sent a camper down to the lake to call her in and bring her.

"I gave you an *order*," she said brusquely, and put Susan to bed in the infirmary, a small enclosed room over the dining hall, while she looked after the other sick girls. Then she took Susan's temperature and did all seven things to her. Susan didn't complain, even when she had her throat swabbed.

"I'm going to keep you here tonight," said B.J., "but I think maybe you're a little homesick. We're going to send you home for a day. It will do you good."

Susan was chagrined. B.J. had already talked to her grandmother, it turned out, and her grandfather was coming for her in the morning. Susan had forgotten that she was only an hour and a half from New York. She thought going home might be a punishment for not having come to sick call when she was supposed to, although she didn't mind being punished by B.J., if that was what it was.

She didn't want to go home, though, and the next day when her grandfather came he seemed earthbound, fretful, full of questions and fears. At home it was hot and stuffy. Her grandmother brought her glasses of juice, and she lay on a blanket in the backyard all afternoon, reading a book she had already read. She weighed herself and she had gained five pounds. She vowed to stop eating biscuits at night, but just the thought of those biscuits in the warm kitchen where you went after the campers had been bedded down, because it was cold and dark in the tents, was tempting and comforting. The next day her grandfather drove her back again, and she was out-wardly sullen but inwardly full of humility and sweetness, promising herself that she would do exactly what she was supposed to do for the rest of the summer.

In the early part of the summer, no one could think of practical jokes as good as Skipper's had been, but in August there were more pranks, and then Susan had the idea of inventing an imaginary camper. It was to be a trick on Annie, the head of the waterfront, and on B.J. The other counselors were in on it. The day the last group of campers arrived, Jenny stole a health card and filled it out with the name of this make-believe camper, Jane Strand, and put Jane's name on Susan's list. Sure enough, after a day or two, Susan heard Annie tell B.J. that a girl named Jane Strand hadn't shown up at swimming class, and B.J. couldn't seem to stop talking about it, though Annie said Jane might just be shy and they should wait and see. After another day, B.J. announced at lunch that Annie didn't have to put up with this sort of thing. Annie shrugged, but B.J. walked from table to table, asking, "Is Jane Strand here?"

Susan had been watching them. Now she turned to the girl sitting next to her, whose name was Laura. "You're Jane Strand," she said.

B.J. came to the table. "Is Jane Strand here?" she said, and Susan turned to Laura and asked, "Your last name is Strand, isn't it, Jane?"

"Yes," said Laura doubtfully.

"Is that right?" said B.J. to Susan.

"I think so," said Susan.

"Well, Miss Jane Strand," said B.J., "we've been looking for you. Why haven't you gone swimming?"

"I didn't feel good," said Laura.

"Well, come with me, Jane!"

"Excuse me," said Susan hastily to her group of campers. "I'd better go along to make sure she doesn't beat up the poor kid." B.J. walked Laura over to Annie, and Annie, who didn't recognize her, questioned her calmly and told her to come for a swimming test in the afternoon. "We could have left her alone until she was ready," Susan heard her say to B.J., but B.J. turned away.

"It's a trick," Susan said to Laura, a little guiltily, as they walked back to their table. "You were great." After lunch, she caught up with B.J. and said, "I'm sorry I didn't make sure that kid went to swimming, B.J.," but B.J. looked at her angrily and walked away.

"What's wrong?" Susan called after her.

"I suppose that was another of your jokes," B.J. said tautly, her voice almost shrill. "You don't even remember, do you? You told your table that the nurse was going to beat somebody up."

"Hey, wait a minute—" said Susan, but B.J. turned crisply away. "I have letters to write during rest hour."

Susan walked back to her tent. She was free until the craft shop opened for the afternoon session. She sat on her bed for a moment, then got up and walked along the path past the children's shacks and the counselors' tents and stopped just inside the woods, at the edge of camp, and sat down on the ground. She was sitting between the roots of a pine tree. The needles were slippery and smooth, and she began to break them in her hand, and to sift them through her fingers. They cut into her thighs and stuck to them. She raised her knees, and then she put down her head and hugged her knees and stayed like that for a while. After that, she got up and walked to B.J.'s tent, feeling a little excited and a little frightened, because she was going to apologize to someone who was going to forgive her—and yet there was just a bit of suspense about it.

She found B.J. alone in her tent. "May I tell you something?" Susan said quietly.

B.J. looked up. "Sure," she said lightly, but she sounded brittle.

"It was a joke," said Susan. "Not just what I said—the whole thing. There's no Jane Strand. We made her up."

And she was forgiven, and promised to try not to blurt out remarks anymore. She walked around all day feeling like someone who had escaped danger.

When the last campers went home, the counselors had two days to clean up the camp and put everything away for the winter. Susan felt free, as if she owned the place, swinging along the paths from her tent to the dining hall, where the counselors ate at one long table, as they had on that first day. Mornings they worked; afternoons they swam or sunned themselves on the dock. The first afternoon Susan swam too, but on the second day—the last day before it was all over—she wandered over to B.J.'s tent when she knew that Annie and most of the others were at the waterfront.

"I wanted to get your address, so I can write and remind you that I exist," she said to B.J.

"I won't forget," said B.J. "Do you want to sit down?"

Susan sat on one end of B.J.'s bed, and B.J., who had been lying on the bed reading a mystery novel, pulled herself up and stuck the corner of a tissue into the pages for a bookmark, and dropped the book on the floor. "So you feel good about your summer?" she said.

They began to talk—about Gloria and the other counselors, about the campers, and about their lives at home. B.J. was a school nurse during the year. She lived with her father, now that her mother had died. She had always lived at home.

Susan half slumped on B.J.'s bed, playing with fluff that came off the blanket stretched tightly on it. They'd all made their beds properly as usual, these two days, even though camp was over. Susan was delighted with this afternoon. B.J. talked to her, as if they were friends, for a long time—maybe two hours—but finally she said, "Well, if we're going to fit in a swim before supper, we'd better get down there."

"You're right," said Susan, and ran to her tent to change. When she came down to the waterfront, swinging her towel, B.J. was already there, standing on the dock talking to Annie, who was lying on her stomach, her arms folded in front of her, her head lifted so she could answer. B.J. was not wearing a bathing suit after all, but the same khaki shorts she'd worn all day, although she'd changed into a bathing suit top. "I want to get some sun," she said to Susan. She spread a towel out next to Annie's, but Annie stood up.

"I'm getting so fat and lazy it's disgusting," Annie said. She pulled a white rubber bathing cap over her dark blond curls and dove in, and they all watched—Joan and Mary were lying at the other end of the dock—as she moved steadily away from them, her strong, splashless, even crawl making Susan jealous, as always.

Susan dove in before she could think too long about getting wet—the shock of cold water was hard for her—and swam back and forth in the deep end of the roped swimming area a few times. Then she pulled herself onto the raft that was anchored at the end of the roped area. Brenda was lying on the raft.

"I could watch Annie swim all day," Susan said. Annie had swum far out into the middle of the lake.

"Me too," said Brenda. She sat up on one elbow and glanced back at the dock, where Joan and Mary and B.J. were all still lying. "We have to thank you for what you did this afternoon," she said.

"What do you mean?"

"Talking to B.J. all afternoon," said Brenda. Susan grew warm. Everyone had known what she was doing.

"Of course you know how hard all this has been for Annie," said Brenda. "Really, none of us should have to deal with people like B.J. It's a sickness, her problem. But it made a tremendous difference for Annie to have this afternoon, and I know she's grateful to you."

"But I like B.J.," said Susan. "I liked talking to her." She had never noticed. She had never noticed how B.J. felt about Annie.

"We all like her," said Brenda. "It's terribly sad. Annie's not that way, of course, but B.J. just can't leave her alone. B.J. won't be here next year, you can be sure about that."

She stood up. "I have to go and pack," she said. "I shouldn't have stayed out here so long—now I hate to get wet again. I wonder if Mary or someone would bring a boat out and get me."

"I'll do it," said Susan. "I don't mind getting wet," and she dove into the deep, quiet water. Her crawl had improved that summer, with Annie giving her hints now and then. She tried to think of her elbows now, and her feet. Annie had taught her to position her head straight forward, not to let it duck down, and she tried to do that. The water just lapped the edge of her bathing cap where it cut into her forehead.

Each time Susan turned her head to breathe, and her eyes came out of the water, she saw B.J., like a snapshot: Now she was standing up, her body half turned away, as if she was starting back toward her tent, looking over her shoulder toward Mary and Joan, who were still lying on the dock, and toward the lake beyond them. Again and again, with each stroke, Susan saw how B.J. moved her shoulders and shifted her feet but didn't go, laughing at something Mary was saying, and looking out at the sun-filled lake, the sun glittering off her glasses.

.   .   .

The summer before Susan's last year in college, her mother had a real boyfriend. This man, Lawrence, used to come to the house to call for Paula, and take her to a Broadway show, or, on a hot night, out to dinner at a seafood place in Far Rockaway. Susan's mother would dress up. She had several summer dresses in splashy prints, mostly black and white. They had wide skirts and shiny plastic belts with big buckles. While she waited for Lawrence, she would come downstairs so Susan and her grandmother could look at her.

"Can I get away with this dress?" she'd say. She meant that the dress came down low in back or maybe even in front.

Susan always said she looked great. Her grandmother didn't say much. Susan supposed that it made Leah feel strange that Paula was no longer married to her son, Susan's father, who had married someone else. Susan's mother had lived upstairs in her former in-laws' second-floor apartment all these years. At first there was no choice, because she was not a well woman, as Susan's grandparents used to say, but Susan thought that her mother was acting a little too well these days.

Susan did not get dressed up and go out to dinner. When her mother came through, she'd be hanging around in her grandmother's kitchen talking or helping her fix supper. Her grandmother made a nice salad, and Susan would peel and slice up the cucumbers, slice the radishes and scallions, and cut up the tomatoes. She had been living in her grandmother's apartment since she was a small child, and now that she could move back upstairs if she wanted to—"There's plenty of room," her mother kept saying, as if that were the issue—she was shy with Lawrence, and she felt that she was among her own kind downstairs. Her grandmother wore loose cotton housedresses in summer, and her grandfather always wore baggy pants and an old white shirt; these clothes seemed to blend well with Susan's old shorts from her camp counselor days—too loose now that she'd lost some weight—worn with an old sleeveless blouse. She felt bedraggled, that summer, and that was how she wanted to feel.

And yet she was also generally annoyed with her grandmother. Her grandmother was boring and she made everything she touched boring. She thought Paula's dresses were a bad idea not because they were sexy but because they were too tight to be comfortable. "The skin needs room to breathe," she would say, after Paula had left. "It is not healthy to bottle up the perspiration. The least little breeze, she will get a chill. A summer cold you can never get rid of."

She never asked why Susan had no boyfriends—her mother mentioned it all the time—and partly that pleased Susan, because her life was acceptable to her grandmother, but partly it upset her. Her grandmother simply assumed that Susan would never have a boyfriend, never get into trouble.

"Do you mind, you should set the table?" her grandmother would say, when her mother had gone out in the tight-bodiced black-and-white dress. Susan would take three plates from the cupboard and set the table. One had a gold rim and a small brown design of leaves, another a tiny border of red and blue fruits and flowers, and the third had an all-over design, across the center of the plate: a woods or a garden in pale blue, with a pair of romantic figures emerging from a half-hidden arbor. Leah owned good dishes that matched, but Susan liked these, the everyday dishes, better. She couldn't imagine them new, yet it didn't seem probable that Leah had brought them on the boat from Europe all those years ago. They were cracked, though Susan didn't remember anyone cracking them. She couldn't imagine them not cracked—or more cracked.

Susan didn't have a boyfriend, and she usually stayed home on Saturday nights eating her grandmother's pot roast and boiled potatoes, but she was in love. She had made only two friends in college, both during her junior year, two boys named Peter and Jerry, and now she was in love with Jerry, who was not in love with her.

Peter and Jerry were both tall, skinny boys with glasses. Susan had seen Peter around, but she'd never noticed Jerry until they'd had a class together just this last spring term. They argued about poems, although at first only across the classroom, during discussions. Susan said that Shelley was a better poet than Keats, and Jerry was shocked and scornful. Susan thought Keats was too flowery. At home, she would read Shelley's "To a Skylark" and, when it was over, sink onto her bed and cry. She couldn't say that in class, but she couldn't let this Mr. Goldstein—at that time she hadn't known Jerry's first name—simply announce, in smug agreement with the professor, that Keats was so much better.

After a while Susan had noticed that Peter and Jerry were friends. Peter was in a class with her, too, and when it ended, Jerry would be waiting for him. Susan, who was usually alone, was touched that these boys had found each other and let people see it.

Susan and Jerry first talked one day when Jerry stopped her as she came out of Latin class. He called her "Miss Sternfeld" (though he knew her first name, he said later—he'd once come up behind her to read it off the front of her notebook) and she had to tell him to call her Susan.

"I'm Jerry," he said. Jerry asked her a question about a Latin phrase. She was flattered, and she liked the attentive way he leaned over a little—he was quite tall—to speak to her. They walked up the hill from the classics building, talking, and after that, they talked every Monday, Wednesday, and Friday. When Jerry came to call for Peter after American Literature, Susan walked to the library with both of them. Sometimes they'd find a table and study together.

Jerry was the lively, unpredictable one, and he made Susan uneasy but happy from the first, but it was easier to talk to Peter; sometimes, after classes, she and Peter would leave the campus and take long walks through unfamiliar Queens neighborhoods, finally circling back to catch their separate buses home.

After a while, the three of them began to do things in New York.

Jerry would find out about an old film at the Thalia, or a free concert at the Donnell Library. Susan would tell her grandmother she wasn't going to be home for supper, and she'd take the subway into the city with the two of them, carrying her books around all evening. Once they got standing room at the Metropolitan Opera and heard *Don Giovanni*.

Susan would arrive home late, but her grandmother never protested. She believed that it was good to do things with other people; Leah didn't seem aware that Susan's other people were boys. Susan waited to see whether she would receive warnings about sex, or advice about playing hard to get, but her grandmother spoke of the friendship as if they were all five years old. She was pleased that Peter and Jerry were Jewish. Peter's last name was Klein, and he said it wasn't too surprising that he was Jewish. "I guess I might have been Italian or Irish," he said. "Have you noticed—everyone at Queens College is named Klein, O'Klein, or Kleinarini?"

"Well, she's glad I didn't take up with any of the O'Kleins," Susan said. This was on the telephone, one day during the summer. She and Peter talked on the phone a lot.

"Have you taken up with me?" said Peter. "I didn't know that was the term."

"You and Jerry," said Susan, embarrassed. She didn't want Peter to think she expected him to become her boyfriend, but she thought she'd like it if her *grandmother* thought he was her boyfriend, and she confided that to him. Or to think one of them was. Or to think that someday, somebody might be.

"Of course somebody will be," said Peter. "I'd marry you in a minute, but you'd be bored with me."

"No, I wouldn't," said Susan. She was pleased that Peter had talked that way, although she wanted to marry Jerry. She knew exactly when she had fallen in love with him. It had been during exam week in June. She and Peter had finished the American Literature exam, and gone to find Jerry in the reading room of the library, which was nearly deserted. At a distant table, Jerry had looked up and seen them coming, and Peter, clowning, had pointed dramatically to Susan as if to boast about having brought her along. Jerry stood up and threw his arms wide, as if he wanted to hug Susan. When she got there he was sitting down, and of course he didn't hug her, but she was already in love with him anyway. That day, Peter left early and she and Jerry lingered, sitting in the grass, telling each other that they too should go home. Seeing Jerry's hand pressed into the grass, Susan wished she could pick it up. By the time she went home, she was exhausted with the effort of keeping her hand still.

Now, in the summer, there was more time to do things in New York, though they all had part-time jobs. Susan was helping out in the dress shop where her mother worked, just a few hours a week, hating it. One Saturday, the manager said he didn't need her, and she and Peter and Jerry met at the Metropolitan Museum of Art, in front of the Rembrandt self-portrait. They knew the galleries well, and as they looked over their favorite paintings, Peter began to wonder aloud whether the pictures would look different if they were seen in reverse, and Susan took out a small mirror she kept in her handbag. They took turns walking around the rooms where the Dutch Masters were hung, their backs to the paintings, looking at them over their shoulders in Susan's mirror.

The people who passed through the rooms didn't seem to notice them, but they were gleeful, full of dispute, excited. There was something boyish and charming about Jerry as he peered into the mirror and looked awkwardly over his shoulder to make sure he didn't bump into anyone—even Susan. She was aware of each instant when she and Jerry might have touched, even just to hand over the mirror. If he brushed her arm or shoulder, she couldn't forget it.

Susan was sure Peter noticed. She knew that if either of these two boys was actually going to fall in love with her, it would be Peter, yet Peter didn't love her either. They both wanted to be with her, yet neither minded if the other was there, and at times the two of them went places together and didn't invite her along. She didn't seem to be anybody's favorite, though she was the favorite of the twosome.

When they left the museum it was hot. They wandered into Central Park, where it was a little cooler, and stopped for drinks of water at all the fountains. Little by little, they walked all the way to the bottom of the park, and then they kept walking, stopping for supper at a drugstore. As they walked south and it grew later, there were fewer people, and the light shone strangely off the streetlamps and the manhole covers. Peter began to talk about a girl he'd known in high school named Lillian Gold—"I don't know what made me think of her," he said—and Susan was frightened, because she had known Lillian Gold when she was twelve, at Girl Scout camp. In New York, once you left your neighborhood you never heard of the same person twice. But it was worse, because Jerry said, "But *I* know Lillian Gold. She's a friend of my cousin." It made Susan think they must be about to die, and the lights gleaming off metal things seemed sinister. They were bound together and couldn't stop walking.

That night they walked all the way to the Staten Island ferry, and rode across the harbor, trooping through the deserted terminal in Staten Island to get on again and take it back. It was cold on the boat, and Susan wished Jerry would put his arm around her, which was inconceivable. When they got back to New York they all took the subway home, first together, then each separately, changing to their different lines. By that time, Susan had stopped thinking about exactly where Jerry was at each second, and whether he was near her. She felt misty and sad, and she cried a little, but with satisfaction, alone on the Jamaica el, traveling through Brooklyn.

When Susan woke up next morning, late, she wanted to call Jerry but couldn't think of a good excuse. In the afternoon the phone rang, and she tried to convince herself, as she picked up the receiver, that talking to Peter would be just as good—and that was who it was. In a way it was even better. They talked for a long time, about how strange the Lillian Gold coincidence had felt, and what it was like to ride the subway so late. Then Peter said, "But something's bothering you, isn't it?"

With relief, as if she were agreeing at last, when she ached with weariness, to lie back on a soft cushion, Susan said, "Yes."

"Does it have to do with Jerry?" said Peter.

"Yes."

"Are you in love with him?"

"Yes, of course." She had never allowed herself to think the sentence in words, and it was as if the walls around her opened out a few feet. "It's good to talk about it," she said.

"I didn't know whether you'd mind my asking."

"No, I don't mind." She was delighted that he'd asked. It would never have occurred to her to tell him.

"What are you going to do?" he said.

"Do?" She believed that there was nothing she could do—except that constantly, stubbornly, she imagined declaring herself to Jerry in a far-fetched scene in which it turned out that he felt the same way about her.

"I mean, you mustn't tell him," said Peter.

"Oh, I know," said Susan, trying to sound certain. "I'm afraid it would be all over if I told him."

She waited for Peter to disagree, but Peter said, "I think it might be."

When she could make her voice casual and steady, she said, "You don't think there's any chance that he—" She stopped.

"No," said Peter. "I've been thinking this over. There's no chance."

It could never happen and could never be discussed—except that now at least Susan could talk about it with Peter. She didn't let herself do that too often, but more and more, instead of thinking about Jerry, she imagined herself talking about Jerry to Peter. It was better than the fantasies in which Jerry loved her. Those began to seem thin, always with exactly the same not very realistic dialogue.

As the summer passed, Susan began to wonder whether it was really a bad idea to tell Jerry what she felt. She knew it would ask something of him that he couldn't give, and that wouldn't be fair. One day, though, it occurred to Susan that Jerry might have guessed. If he had guessed, he'd be upset, and the only way to help him—and she loved him, of course she wanted to help him—was to talk about it. If she could change—stop loving Jerry—she could tell him all about it, and he would be relieved that it was over. She went for a long walk in Highland Park to think about this.

It was a cool day with rain in the air. She climbed to the top of the hill behind the playground, and stood looking out, tears blurring her vision. She had to stop loving Jerry for his own sake. She thought of her love as a thick, healthy weed growing up through her heart. She didn't picture a valentine heart, but a realistic one—red, pulsing, four-chambered, with an aorta coming out of it. Stuck in this heart was a plant whose roots grabbed the heart and squeezed it, and which must be uprooted. In her mind, she grasped the top of the plant (it was something like a milkweed, with large leaves, rough to touch) and tugged. Nothing happened. She walked back and forth across the top of the hill, and then, with a burst of determination, ran down the hill and home. She knew she could pull up this pesky plant. She wanted to be free of it, free of wait-ing for the phone to ring and wondering whether it had rung when she was out, free of imaginings, free to love her dull grand-mother instead of finding her contemptible because she didn't guess Susan's secret.

She strode home briskly and was friendly to both her grandparents and offered to go to the store for her grandmother. On her way to the bakery she tugged at the plant in her mind some more. She was enjoying herself now. She began to imagine that the plant shifted slightly when she pulled.

For days, whenever she was alone, especially in bed at night, she pulled at the plant with energy and cool determination. When she was with Peter and Jerry, she was cheerful and almost boisterous, not personal or sensitive. Peter said she seemed better and she said, "Oh, I am. Much better." But she knew that she still loved Jerry—the plant was still in her heart—and she didn't want to tell Peter about this interesting project until she had carried it out.

Not that she would ever tell anyone about the plant. That was childish and embarrassing.

One Sunday, Susan wrote a letter to an old friend who had

moved away. She went out to mail it, and walked to a mailbox about ten blocks away, to give herself the excuse for a long walk. On the way, she pulled at the plant. Of course she did know that the plant would come out as soon as she imagined it out, and then she realized that it was going to come out on this very walk, just before she reached the mailbox. She concentrated on the plant, and the roots began to appear free of her heart. When the time came, she really did tighten her fist and give a tugging motion. Then she looked down at her hand, because it seemed that there might be a milkweed in it, the hairy stem irritating her fingers a little and the white sap coming out where the leaves had broken. Of course she wasn't carrying a plant, but she had been working so hard that she felt lightheaded, a little woozy. She mailed the letter and turned around, and she felt joy. She no longer loved Jerry. It was much better for them to be friends.

Now she began to look forward to the reward: telling him. It would be humiliating to do this, but Susan didn't mind. Jerry didn't like to have personal conversations, but this would be one he could not avoid. By now school had started again. It was their senior year. She and Jerry had a class together, Shakespeare. She knew that Jerry walked to Shakespeare from the other side of the quadrangle, and the day after her momentous Sunday, she hurried out of her own earlier class and ran to meet him, something she could not have permitted herself to do when she was in love with him. Jerry came out of the building alone, his books held to his side as usual, wearing a white shirt with an open neck. Susan went up to meet him.

"Hi," he said. "What are you doing here? Aren't you coming from Psychology?" Psychology met in the opposite direction.

"I came to meet you because I have something to tell you," said Susan.

"What is it?"

"I'm not in love with you," she said.

Jerry didn't say anything for a moment. "That's good," he said tentatively. Then, "Were you?"

"Yes. Did you know?"

"I sort of wondered." She looked up and saw that his ear was red. They walked to class together but neither of them spoke again.

Susan's mother said she was going to marry Lawrence. Now that Susan's father rarely came to the house, and Paula had Lawrence to show for her efforts at living, she came downstairs to talk more often than she used to. She said they were getting married in about a year. Susan's grandmother offered formal congratulations but did not kiss her former daughter-in-law when Paula made this announcement. Lawrence was younger than Paula, although no one seemed to know how much younger. He had been married for a short time to a woman who had died. Susan's grandmother had already told Susan and her grandfather that she thought this was a bad sign.

"I do not think he murdered his first wife," said Susan's grandfather. This was funny, because Lawrence was extremely timid.

They began to talk about whether Paula would at last move out when she got married. By now, they often lived as if they were in a one-family house. The inner doors were kept open, and everyone in the family went up and down freely. This is not to say that Susan's grandmother would have settled down to watch television in front of Paula's set, but she might have gone upstairs when Paula was not home to borrow Paula's iron, if hers was broken. Leah and Ezra treated Paula's apartment like the bedroom of a nearly-grown child, a place they might enter, but only if they needed to. Susan used to study upstairs sometimes, though, especially if her mother wasn't home. When she had a paper due, she would spread out her index cards on her mother's kitchen table during the afternoon, when her mother was at work. Then she would stay up there, even for supper. Her mother would come home and find her. "I was going to open a can of tuna fish," she'd say, or "I was just going to scramble some eggs. I'll go out and get fried scallops." There was a shop a couple of blocks away that sold fried scallops and clams and french-fried potatoes. Susan loved the food, but didn't like to go there because the woman who sold it was pink and fat, as if she drank the frying oil instead of cups of coffee, and it made Susan queasy to think about her. Though her grandparents were not kosher, they had never eaten shellfish, so she ate the fried fish only with her mother.

Susan would write another half page while her mother went for supper. She liked to spread out her index cards in order, and then pile them up as the facts on each one entered the paper. While Paula set out the cardboard containers of clams, scallops, and potatoes, Susan would carefully move her cards closer together to make room.

Sometimes Susan stayed up late, but her mother didn't care. Her grandmother worried if she stayed up late, and her grandfather scolded her for poor planning. When she worked downstairs, he'd appear in her doorway just before his own bedtime and give her a lecture he'd stored up all evening, apparently thinking it was new, although each time he said the same things.

"Aren't you excited about me and Lawrence?" Paula asked, one night when Susan was working upstairs. It was November by then. Susan and Peter and Jerry had less time to do things in the city now that classes were in session, but she heard from them on the phone pretty often. Jerry called her more than he used to, she noted, now that she wasn't in love with him: She was proud of the way her efforts had turned out, and Peter had congratulated her dryly when she'd told him. She hadn't mentioned the plant.

"Of course I'm excited," she said to her mother. She was writing a paper for her psychology course, and she needed to concentrate.

"Lawrence isn't sure if you like him," Paula said.

"I like him." She wasn't sure herself. Lawrence was earnest—he seemed a little simple.

"I know you haven't had a normal childhood, Susan," said her mother. "Spending so much time with your grandparents, because I was divorced and had to work."

Susan wanted to say that that wasn't the reason she "spent time" with her grandparents, and she didn't "spend time" with them, she *lived* with them, but she didn't feel like a long argument about her childhood.

"I've always given them money for you," her mother was saying now.

"Mom, I don't think that has anything to do with Lawrence," said Susan.

"He thinks you're taking out old grievances on him."

"What did I ever do to *him*?"

"You certainly haven't gone out of your way to make friends."

This was true. But Susan didn't have the energy to make friends with someone who found it embarrassing that she lived with her father's parents downstairs from her mother. The one time they'd talked, Lawrence had apologized for taking her mother out "so you have to eat with the folks downstairs."

"He's a little concerned about you, too," said Paula. "He keeps talking about how pretty you are. He wonders why you don't have a boyfriend."

Susan shook her head in irritation.

"He has a cousin he wants you to meet."

"I don't want to meet Lawrence's cousin."

"Don't be like that," Paula said. "We want to take you out to dinner, to celebrate our engagement. Let me tell Lawrence to invite his cousin to come along. It'll be fun—a double date."

"No. Listen, Mom, I really need to work now."

"I don't see what's such a bad idea about it. I'm not asking you to marry the man."

"I don't want to do it." In the end Susan agreed to have dinner with her mother and Lawrence, but only if the cousin, Richard, was not included. Her mother acted a little put out, but she agreed.

Jerry was friendly with a woman who was older than he and Peter and Susan. She had dropped out of college to work for a few years, and she was twenty-four. She lived alone in an apartment in the Village. Susan was a little afraid of her, but she liked her. The woman, Denise, was a poet, and behind her conversation Susan felt the alluring assumption that men and women can be attracted to each other, that even Susan and Jerry might have been. Everyone else they knew seemed to take the lead from Susan's grandmother, acting as if she and Jerry were playground buddies from kindergarten.

Denise patronized Jerry a little bit, which delighted Susan, who was in awe of him because he hadn't fallen for her when she fell for him. Denise called Jerry the Penguin because he wore black and white. Sometimes Susan wondered whether Denise and Jerry had ever tried anything—nothing much, just a kiss or two. She found that she wasn't jealous, if they had. She would have liked assurance that the man who had attracted her could interest someone as grown-up and sophisticated as Denise.

During Christmas vacation, Denise gave a party. Susan hadn't done anything but study for a long time—she had put off having dinner with her mother and Lawrence, along with everything else, though now the dinner, too, was scheduled, and was to be a few days after the party. Susan dressed up for Denise's party. She had to go alone. Peter, who had visiting relatives at his house, couldn't go at all, and Jerry, as usual, was traveling from a different direction, on a different subway line from Susan. Susan tried not to arrive too early.

When she got there, a boy she knew a little let her in. "Hi," he said. "Denise is in the john." Susan could hear the sound of urinating, and the toilet flushing. Denise had a tiny apartment, and the bathroom door opened right into the living room.

"I was just getting in my last preparty pee," she said now, coming out of the bathroom. Susan followed her into the kitchen and asked if she could help, and Denise let her put some pretzels into a bowl. As she did it, she heard Jerry's voice. She carried the bowl into the living room. Jerry was giving Denise a light kiss on the mouth, as if that was the sort of thing he did with women all the time. Then he reached out and touched Susan's shoulder, and flicked her hair— which she was wearing loose, instead of in its usual ponytail—into place; it had fallen forward on her arm. He'd never done anything like that before. He'd hardly ever touched her.

The party ran late and was good. After a long time Denise got a phone call from a friend who had some people at his place, and invited her to come too, and the whole party packed up and traveled, with much glee. Susan had been wanting to go to the bathroom, but she felt shy at Denise's house because the room was so public. Then, by the time they reached the man's house—his name was Jared and he played the guitar and sang—she couldn't seem to ask where the bathroom was.

It was two in the morning when they'd left for Jared's. Jerry walked ahead of Susan, with Denise, and Susan walked with a girl she knew, but halfway there, Jerry rather noticeably scooted back along the line of friends to walk beside Susan. "Sorry," he said, "I needed to ask Denise something."

Jared played folk songs, some familiar to Susan, some new. She grew sleepy, and she wanted to go to the bathroom badly, but while they'd walked, Jerry had said, "We won't stay there long, and then I'll take you home." He'd never taken her home, but it was quite late.

When they finally left, it was cold out, and Susan ached all over. As they walked down the steps in front of Jared's house, Jerry took her hand. She was amused. She was tired, but she wouldn't have stumbled or fallen. He continued to take her hand each time they had to walk: when they changed trains, when they went down a flight of stairs from one subway line to another, when they got off the train in her neighborhood. Then Susan realized that Jerry was holding hands with her. She stored this news in her mind without an explanation, as if it had to do with an exotic foreigner whose actions could be explained only by an anthropologist. When they reached her house, Jerry turned and looked hard at her. He said, "To hell with Plato," and kissed her.

Susan didn't know what he meant. She was so excited it was painful. She'd been carrying her key in her hand since they'd left the train, and when she raised her arms to embrace Jerry it was her fist, with the key inside, that she pressed into the back of his coat. After the kiss, she turned and went into the house. When she opened the front door, Jerry turned away, and he was gone when the door closed behind her. She went upstairs to her mother's bathroom, which she could use without awakening anyone. Then, feeling numb, she went down and let herself into her grandparents' apartment and went to bed.

She did not sleep. After a long time she heard Ezra get up and fix breakfast, and then came Leah's voice. Finally Susan got out of bed. She was tired, but so happy that she was friendly to them. She didn't tell them how late she'd been out, but she described the party, and the second party at Jared's, and she sang one of his songs for them. It had been a long time since she told them much about anything she did.

Talking to her grandfather, she suddenly understood that "To hell with Plato" meant that Jerry didn't want to have a platonic relationship with her anymore. Her throat scratchy and her eyes blurred, Susan helped her grandmother clean the apartment. In the afternoon, she took a nap. Again, she lay for a long time without sleeping, but then she slept.

Susan thought Jerry would call her right away, but when he didn't, that was all right. She moved through the house quietly and simply, as if she were holding a small furry animal in her hand, hidden against her body. The animal slept and she didn't speak of it. She moved slowly, as if she really had only one hand free.

After two days, she began to wonder. It was still Christmas break. She knew Jerry had a long paper to write, but still, he could have called her. She'd have thought he'd *want* to call her. She'd have thought he couldn't wait. Now it was harder for her to be patient with her grandmother, who wanted to talk about the cost of groceries or speculate about Susan's mother and Lawrence. The day before Susan's dinner with Paula and Lawrence was the worst day. Finally she called Peter.

He was talkative. He'd been entertaining his visiting cousins, putting off working on a paper, and now he was worried that he'd delayed too long. The paper was about Henry James, for a course neither Susan nor Jerry was taking. Peter read parts of it aloud to her and asked what she thought of them.

Finally Susan said, "Have you talked to Jerry?"

"Yes. He's changed topics. He's not doing Blake after all. He's doing Dryden."

"Dryden?" said Susan. "Why would he want to do that?"

"Beats me," said Peter. "But why not?"

"When did you talk to him?"

"Oh, a day or so ago. He could have changed subjects again, I guess." He paused. "Why, did he tell you he was going back to Blake?"

"I haven't talked to him."

"Oh." Peter was beginning to sound a little baffled.

"Did he say anything about Denise's party?" said Susan.

"No, was it good?"

"It was great."

"What happened, did the two of you have a fight?" said Peter.

"Not really," said Susan. "Listen, do you think you could call him and sort of mention that I wish I could hear from him?"

"Why don't you call him yourself?"

"I know, I should. . . ." she said.

"No—I don't mind. I just didn't know why you wanted me to."

"Well, we sort of had a thing that night, and I haven't spoken to him since. . . . Listen, don't just call and say, 'Call Susan.' Could you just say—well, you'll know best."

They hung up. Now Susan would never know when Jerry would have called her on his own. The phone rang after fifteen minutes, and it was Jerry.

"Hi," he said. "How are you?"—obviously embarrassed.

"I'm O.K."

"Peter said you sounded funny," he said.

"I wanted to talk to you," said Susan.

"It's not a great time to talk."

"Oh, I didn't mean this minute," said Susan. "I'm all right, really."

"You are? You're all right, really?"

"Yes."

"Let's get together tomorrow," he said.

They agreed to meet at two o'clock in Central Park, specifying which bench. They'd been in the park together—with Peter—so often that it was easy to make a plan. Susan got off the phone and felt better. She went for a long walk in the cold in Highland Park.

The next day, Jerry told her he'd gotten carried away at Denise's party.

"You mean you don't want things to be different between us?" said Susan, picking her words.

"No. I'm sorry if I gave the wrong impression."

She cried. It had been a secret for so long, and she'd worked so hard, getting rid of it. She wasn't rid of it anymore, and this time there was no point in imagining plants growing out of her heart. It was cold on the bench, and they couldn't stay long. She didn't suggest they go anywhere together—it was the one thing she was proud of later—but neither did Jerry. She agreed, over and over again, that they would behave as they always had. Finally he said, "What are you going to do now?"

She was meeting her mother and Lawrence at a restaurant not far away, but that wasn't for four more hours. "I'm going to the Donnell Library," she said at last.

"That's a good idea," he said. He said good-bye and walked away from the bench. She wished she had left first. Then he turned and came back to her, as if he had changed his mind, but he only said, "I'm sorry, Susan," and walked away again.

Susan sat on the bench, growing colder and colder, until an old woman sat down next to her. She stood up then, and she had been in one position for so long that she felt stiff. She walked to the Donnell Library, on Fifty-third Street, where she often came to study when home seemed oppressive. As always, it smelled of books and coats, and she sat down at a table, in her coat, and just sat still for a long time. Then she went to the pay phone and called Denise.

She'd never called her before—she had to look the number up in the phone book. Denise was surprised to hear from her, but pleased.

"Jerry isn't at your house or anything, is he?" Susan said.

"No, why, is he missing?"

"No, I just wanted to make sure," she said. "Are you busy?"

Denise wasn't busy, and she said Susan could come over. Susan took the bus down Fifth Avenue and walked to Denise's house. "Is something wrong?" Denise said, opening the door. "You sounded upset."

Then Susan told her the whole story. It was harder than talking to Peter, because she didn't already know what Denise would think. Denise was older and had had lovers. She might simply be amused. When Susan told how Jerry had taken her hand, Denise sounded gentle. "Did he kiss you?"

"Yes."

"Did you kiss him back?" Susan hadn't thought of it that way. They had kissed. She supposed, now that she thought about it, that it was possible not to return a kiss, just to stand there and feel it. Yes, she had kissed him back.

"And now he's scared?" Denise said.

"He didn't mean to do what he did the other night," said Susan—defending Jerry, she noticed.

"He's scared," said Denise. "But meanwhile he's gotten you going again, right?"

"That's right."

She told Denise about the talk on the chilly bench. Denise had made her tea and she finished drinking it. She felt better. This apartment could absorb her feelings—her own home could not. It would be impossible, in her grandmother's house, to be a woman who loved a man and wasn't loved back. Her grandmother would take her to the doctor for it, Susan decided. Her mother—well, her mother would probably invite Jerry over and try to talk him into loving Susan. She smiled, and told Denise what she was thinking.

"I've loved so many men who haven't loved me," Denise said.

"How do you stand it?"

"I think I'm better off than they are," Denise said.

"It makes me sick," said Susan.

"Well, yes, I know what you mean," said Denise. "But in the long run it's sort of—*satisfying*." She was talking as if she were much older than Susan, but then she told Susan about the man she loved right then, and even though they had slept together, it wasn't so different.

"Do you want to spend the night here?" Denise asked. "You could call your grandmother."

"I can't," said Susan, touched. She explained about the appointment with her mother and Lawrence.

Denise said she was brave to go. "I'd have taken the excuse to go to bed."

Susan didn't want to go to bed. She thought she'd like a good meal. She felt like meat—roast beef, maybe. She told Denise that she felt better, and set out, in the dark, for the subway and midtown. Halfway there it occurred to her that she should have dressed up, for she was wearing a school skirt and an old sweater. She didn't care. It was better this way—she'd been through a lot; mud-stained khakis would have been even better.

The restaurant was near Broadway, a place that wanted to look fancy, with pillars that had little gold tiles glued to them, except that there were places where the tiles had come away. Susan spotted her mother, wearing a bright green dress, as soon as she arrived. Susan joined her and Lawrence—and there was someone else at the table, too, a man. She had forgotten about Lawrence's cousin. She had been so certain she didn't want to meet him that she hadn't thought about him since she'd told her mother not to invite him. Now Paula looked at her brightly as Susan shrugged off her big duffel coat and arranged it on the back of her chair.

The gilt pillar opposite her had tiles missing in a pattern that looked like a ladder, except that one leg of the ladder wasn't there. That was the first thing Susan noticed, and in the confusion of greeting Lawrence and meeting his cousin, Richard, she felt as if she were somehow supposed to give the ladder more attention than she could. She wanted to go over and break off some more tiles so the two legs would be even. It looked as if the tiles would come out easily, as if the material into which they were stuck was soft and elastic, but that might not really be true.

At first Susan thought Richard was about Denise's age—maybe twenty-four—but then she began to think he might be older. She could tell at a glance that Richard was not like herself and her friends. He would not look over his shoulder into a mirror to see paintings behind him. He had a deep voice. "I love you," she imagined him saying. That was shocking. He had barely said hello. She couldn't imagine Jerry's voice saying, "I love you."

"I kept worrying that you wouldn't remember where to come," said Paula.

"No, I remembered all right," Susan said. "I'm sorry I'm not dressed up. I've been in New York all day."

"You look fine," said Lawrence. "Just fine."

Richard nodded solemnly.

"I did tell you Richard was coming, didn't I?" Paula said, nodding her head to prompt Susan. "I know we talked about how busy he was, and that he might not be able to make it. But did I ever tell you he was coming after all?"

"No," said Susan. She didn't want to be there, and even thought about running away, but she was hungry. She wanted that roast beef. "So you two are cousins?" she said to Lawrence and Richard. "How are you related?"

She always wanted to know exactly how people were connected to each other. She was not at all shy that night, she found. She was angry with her mother for deceiving her, though not too surprised, and her anger seemed to justify anything. She even felt angry with Jerry, for the first time. It was a startling emotion, cleansing her body like a swift wind sweeping sand off a boardwalk. The other feeling would come back—she would drown in sand, she was afraid—but meanwhile, how light she felt.

"Our mothers are sisters," said Lawrence.

"You're not so far apart in age," Susan said. That was what wasn't supposed to be said. Lawrence was younger than Paula—an unknown number of years that could not be specified; Paula always shrugged hopelessly when asked, as if the number were not fixed, and it was pointless to calculate it at any particular time, or as if it *couldn't* be calculated. Lawrence was younger than Paula, and Richard was really quite a bit older than Susan. This party did not consist of two young people out to dinner with two older people; Richard and Lawrence belonged to a middle generation between the mother and the daughter, and Susan wondered why Lawrence had wanted to include Richard.

"He's ten years older," said Richard. It was more than she'd thought. Lawrence had moved his hand quickly, though, as if to stop him, and now he relaxed and pulled it back, as if he was relieved at what Richard had said.

She wanted to know more, maybe just to catch them in the lie.

She didn't care about either of them. It was ridiculous to describe Lawrence as her future stepfather. She could have no stepfather.

Paula was asking her if she wanted a drink—well, that had certainly never happened before. Susan had a drink: sherry.

"Are your mothers close?" she asked. "Are they still alive? Did you live near each other when you were children?"

Suddenly Lawrence seemed to crack and grow, as if a tight cellophane wrapper had been squeezing something larger than it appeared to be into a smaller space. "We lived in Flatbush," he said. "We'd see each other every weekend. We'd go to our grandmother's for dinner."

"Sometimes Larry's father took the two of us to a ball game," said Richard. It took Susan a minute to realize that Larry was Lawrence.

The sherry tasted bitter, but Susan enjoyed drinking it. Then the roast beef came.

Susan had no cousins. Her grandmother had had a sister, but she had died before Susan was born. Her mother had relatives, but they were far away, and nobody seemed to be in touch with them. They'd been scared off in the early days by the strange things that had gone wrong with her mother, Susan suspected, the doctors and hospitals. Then there was the question of Susan herself. Maybe nobody in the house had company because they would have to talk about why Susan lived downstairs.

The thought of Lawrence's grandmother's house, to which cousins came—there were six or eight of them—made Susan envious, nostalgic, and happy. She wanted to be one of the girl cousins, tired of the rough play of the boys, maybe, sneaking off to read and being followed by one of the younger ones. "Susan, couldn't you watch Teddy for me?" an aunt would say—a young, querulous, pretty aunt, who couldn't possibly manage her children without Susan's help.

Lawrence and Richard really did tell stories of the Sundays at the grandmother's. She'd made rugelach and honey cake for the Jewish New Year, hamantaschen for Purim. The children had played complicated card games; Richard and Lawrence couldn't agree on what the rules had been. Once the two of them had played ball in their grandmother's living room and broken a little figurine—they must have been closer in age even than Susan had imagined—and their mothers took them off into separate rooms to spank them, to the great interest of the other cousins. Lawrence laughed at the memory, and seemed to grow bigger still.

"My parents used to take me out to a restaurant on Sundays," said Paula. She stopped and they all waited. "I always got a dessert that came in layers—cake, and ice cream, and some kind of custard. Always the same dessert."

Susan was embarrassed for her. They hadn't been talking about childhood Sundays, or about desserts, but about *cousins*—or, at least, other people. She had nothing to add, herself—that went without saying. There had been no other people.

"What were the names of the other cousins?" she asked Lawrence and Richard, ignoring her mother.

"Well, there was my sister, Jeannette," said Richard. They went on and talked about the others, reminding each other and then explaining to Susan: what had become of them, which were stupid and boring and which were interesting and fun to be with. They laughed a lot. Susan began to feel, to her surprise, that she would probably have agreed with Lawrence, if she knew his cousins, about which were the good ones and which the dull ones, although she had always thought *he* was stupid and boring. When the meal was over, her mother's laughter had become forced. She seemed to be laughing all the time. Lawrence and Richard said they would go and get Lawrence's car and bring it to the restaurant. It was parked blocks and blocks away, Lawrence said, and that made Paula laugh some more, about how far they had walked. Soon Paula and Susan were left alone, at opposite sides of the table. Susan pulled her arms into her coat, but Paula said it would be a while before the men got back.

"I knew you'd like Richard," she said to Susan.

"I do like him," said Susan. He was no date for her, though—he was too old—and Lawrence was no date for her mother, either—too young—and she knew that now he knew it. That was why he'd gone off with Richard. They could all have walked together to the car.

He'd begun to think of Paula as an older person, for whom the car should be brought around. They would break up, soon, and it would be Susan who had done it, just by asking questions, but Paula would never be sure how it had happened, and Susan wouldn't tell her. She liked Lawrence better now that she knew he would not be her stepfather. She felt like a powerful woman. When she thought of Jerry on the bench, it was surprising that at the time the weather had seemed so cold, and the wind so much keener than her coat had been warm.

Part Two

SUSAN STERNFELD was an English major in college, but she took three psychology courses, and on the strength of that, when she graduated she went to work as a clerical assistant at a clinic for children with problems. She didn't want to be a teacher or go to graduate school like her friends Peter and Jerry. "You're a girl—you can get a job," said Peter bluntly. They were afraid of being drafted; they had to keep up their student deferments until they turned twenty-six. Peter went to the University of Minnesota and Jerry to Berkeley, both on scholarships. Now Susan would never again know as much as they did.

Problems meant emotional problems, but sometimes it turned out that the children who came to the clinic couldn't hear or see well. Susan typed reports and wrote up notes for the three social workers and sometimes she answered the phones and explained things to parents who were supposed to bring their children in, but more and more, she became the person who tested the children's sight and hearing. She was good at it. She was patient if they didn't understand what they were supposed to do, and friendly when they didn't speak English.

Once a little girl lied to her. She read off five letters from the chart, fluently—all wrong. Susan knew she was faking because the letters she'd chosen didn't resemble the actual letters, the way "A" and "H" do, nor were they the correct letters in reverse.

Susan laughed. "I'll bet you fooled the school nurse," she said.

"Yes," said the little girl, shyly. But it wasn't Susan's job to find out why she had lied.

She liked talking to the children and testing them. Mostly they did well on the tests, which was sad: Everyone at the clinic was relieved when the children did badly on the hearing and vision tests. That explained everything, and they'd be sent off for glasses or a hearing aid. But it was sad for Susan when they did badly. Many of the children rattled off the letters on the eye chart proudly, in a great hurry, and raised their hands promptly whenever there was a sound in the hearing test, sometimes with a quick smile at Susan, as if the sound in their ears was a secret between them and her. When someone stood silent, frightened, and motionless, it made her feel bad—not that she thought wearing glasses or even a hearing aid was tragic. It was that they'd given their secret away so soon, the first morning in the clinic. She couldn't help being proud of the jaunty, self-possessed children who read off the bottom line on the eye chart instantly, in a strong voice, and who might never tell the patient social workers what was really wrong, what sorrow or confusion had made them do whatever had driven some exhausted teacher or principal to send them there.

It was a small clinic, with three social workers whom Susan, who had no aunts, thought of as auntlike—older than her mother, younger than her grandmother. At first she wished they *were* her aunts, and she had to work hard not to confide in them. It didn't seem like a good idea—she wanted it too badly. Two of them were Jewish—the clinic, on the Lower East Side, had been set up years earlier to serve the immigrant Jewish children, and it still had a Jewish feel, although most of the clients now were black or Puerto Rican—and the third, Catherine Donnelly, had an Irish name because she'd married an Irishman, but was Italian, with one Jewish grandmother. "Hitler would have considered me Jewish," she told Susan cheerfully.

Catherine was called Cat. She lived in Connecticut and came in only three days a week, and she was going to quit altogether pretty soon, she said. She had five big children. Susan, who loved hearing about families, got Cat to tell her their names and ages: Douglas, Frank, Tony, Cathy, Claudia. Douglas was twenty-eight and Claudia fourteen. Frank was named after Cat's husband, Tony after her Italian father, and Cathy after Cat herself, a custom that seemed intriguing to Susan, but impractical. She didn't see how they kept from being mixed up all the time. Cat was always called Cat, and Cathy was always Cathy, so that was all right, and Cat insisted that when her father had been alive, it had been perfectly simple to tell him apart from his grandson Tony, a baby—but Susan kept catching Cat as she spoke of her husband and son in the same sentence with the same name. Susan teased her for it. "Now, wait a minute, didn't you just tell me that Frank was too busy to meet you at the train so Frank was coming?" she'd say.

"No, Frank can't, it turns out—Cathy's coming," Cat would say, straight-faced. Her son Frank had been Frankie as a child, but he'd become impatient with it. But it wasn't a problem. "Mostly when people say Mister, they mean Frank," she said, as if *that* was the issue. "I mean *Frank*—my husband Frank."

Cat was leaving the clinic because she thought her youngest child, Claudie, needed her around more. Cathy was in college and the others were out of college—Doug had a job in California, Frank was in graduate school, and Tony was in the Air Force—but Claudie was home, going to high school. "She gets low," Cat said. "I'm looking for something closer to home."

It took two years before Cat did leave. Susan had hoped she never would. She and Cat talked, at times almost intimately, though always standing up, in a hallway or in the doorway of Cat's office, and always hurriedly, though sometimes for half an hour, after the clinic had closed at night. They planned to have lunch or coffee together, and once Cat even said that Susan should come and see her in Connecticut, but none of these things ever happened. Sometimes Cat was distracted and vague, but at other times Susan caught an affectionate look in her direction, or Cat took time to explain something Susan wanted to know. The other social workers, Bea and Helen, weren't as easygoing, and they seemed to be watching Susan quietly as if to make sure that she herself didn't turn out to be one of the children with problems.

Susan sometimes thought they might be right. She was too conscientious, too demure—she was sure they thought that. She had hardly any friends. She lived with her grandparents and she didn't have a boyfriend. She did date at times, though, she reminded herself. A year after college she had a swift, painful three-week affair with a man she had met at the Metropolitan Museum of Art. She'd been there alone, had let him talk to her, and had gone to his apartment, quite aware of the risk she was taking. The man hadn't raped or murdered her. She'd let him seduce her, and he was embarrassed to discover that she was a virgin.

While they were seeing each other, she'd encouraged him to meet her at the clinic after work, so the social workers would stop thinking she was a baby. They went to his apartment on the Upper West Side—she couldn't take him home to Brooklyn. He always insisted he wasn't hungry enough for a meal, so they'd make love on his floor or his bed and eat peanut butter and jelly sandwiches. Susan would leave about nine, and buy a pretzel or a hot dog from a vendor to eat in the subway. Her grandparents thought she was being taken to fancy restaurants.

After it was over, Susan thought of this episode with discomfort, although she was glad she had lost her virginity. Her lover had smoked, and he always smelled of it, not just of smoke but of tobacco, as if he crumbled cigarettes over his clothes. He said he was a graduate student in art history at Columbia, but he didn't like talking about paintings and he thought Susan's opinions were childish. His apartment was filled with art books, but they weren't textbooks or scholarly books. He said Susan wasn't a particularly interesting person. Susan somehow managed not to fall in love with him—though he was tender in bed, and nibbled her breasts, talking to them inaudibly—possibly because of his smell, and so she didn't imagine that he was right about how interesting she was, but was healthily angry. Still, she kept the relationship going for a week after she decided she disliked him, just because of the sex, or, rather, so she could tell herself she was having sex with someone, and that was what troubled her later.

Susan hadn't thought she'd stay long at the clinic, but she did, gradually being given more interesting tasks, continuing to travel in from Brooklyn on the subway every morning. A few months after Cat finally left, Susan moved out of her grandparents' place. She found an apartment—one big room and a tiny kitchen—in a building on Fourteenth Street and Fourth Avenue which her grandparents considered all right because it had a locked front door and an intercom over which visitors could announce themselves. "This is Ezra and Leah!" her grandfather shouted regally, the one time they visited. "Your grandma and grandpa!"

Susan could just manage the rent. She brought her bookcase from Brooklyn in a taxi, but bought a second-hand single bed and a dresser and a small table and two chairs. She bought picture frames at M. H. Lamston's and prints of her favorite Dutch paintings at the Metropolitan Museum. She made curtains. Moving in was like a second job or an affair—for weeks, it took up Susan's time and attention. Each time she consulted her bankbook and allowed herself another purchase—dish towels (for color, not because she dried dishes) or a lamp—she decided that *now* her apartment looked like the actual home of an actual person, as if, in her grandparents' place, she had not been quite real. Her grandmother gave her plates and some pots, and Susan bought a ceramic teapot and a supply of Constant Comment.

When Cat left, she'd told Susan that her son Tony was getting out of the Air Force and moving to New York, and he wanted to call her. Susan was surprised, but she quickly began to think this would be a fine thing—men called her rarely—though she also felt nervous about him. He might have barbarian right-wing politics; he might think she was impossibly naive. Tony didn't call, and gradually she forgot about him. Then, one evening at the new apartment, the phone rang.

"Tony Donnelly?" the voice on the other end began, interrogatively. It took her a moment.

"Oh—right. Hi," she said.

"I got your number from your mother," he said.

"Grandmother," said Susan.

He didn't ask her out, nor did he deliver a message from Cat. He acted as if they already knew each other and he'd called to say hello—as if they knew each other well enough for him to call without an excuse.

"You're not too far from here," he said, when he found out where her apartment was. "I don't know if I'm going to last here," he went on. "It's a little complicated for me." There were people who actually lived in the apartment, he explained, and people who were just staying there while others who lived there were away—except that they weren't completely away. "I'm always seeing new people and they act as if I've broken in," he said. "When I come out of the bathroom in the morning, somebody is always glaring at me—usually somebody I've never seen before."

"I know *just* what you mean," said Susan, which was what she used to hear herself say on the phone to Peter, except now she was a little more nervous, a little more alert (she was playing with the cuff of her blouse, opening and closing the button on the hand that held the receiver). "Didn't you get used to being glared at in the Air Force?" This was the son who had been in the Air Force.

"That was different."

"Why did you join the Air Force, anyway?" Susan asked, leaning back a little in her chair and letting her free hand fall into her lap. "Are you a military type—I mean, a hawk?"

"No," said Tony. "I enlisted so I wouldn't be drafted when I got out of college. Also to upset my father and my brother. I wanted to be a writer and I figured I'd write a novel about the Air Force."

"Did you?"

"I have a few pages."

"So *are* you a writer, now that you're out?" said Susan.

"No. I didn't want to earn money the way writers do—typing, waiting on tables. I'm working in a law firm, to see if I want to go to law school. I hate it, though. Maybe I'll get a job on a newspaper."

"I guess you could still write the book, even if you do something else," said Susan.

"It's not too good. I'll show it to you sometime," he said. She was pleased that he spoke as if they were going to know each other. After a while he said he'd better hang up and go out and do his laundry, or he wouldn't have a clean shirt to wear the next day. "See you," he said, although if he did, Susan reflected, he wouldn't recognize her.

"I forgot to give you my phone number," Tony said, the next time he called, three days later. He waited while she got a pencil. She didn't want to say that she couldn't think why she would call him. Anyway, it wasn't as if she didn't like him—she just didn't know him. Of course, by now she almost did know him, except that she didn't know what he looked like. They talked, this time, about brothers and sisters and pets, none of which Susan had ever had, and about summer camp jobs—she'd had one, he'd had three. He told her a little about the Air Force. She wanted to talk about books, but she hadn't read most of his favorites. His favorite book was Catch-22. He liked to read plays, and he thought he might try writing one.

She told him about the clinic, which was fun because he already knew about it, but Cat had said such different things, it was hard to believe it was the same place. When she mentioned Bea and Helen, he wanted to know which was the one with the limp and which was the one with the nephew, and Susan, who had now worked with them for almost three years, had never noticed a limp or heard about a nephew. It was Helen who limped—she watched for it the next day—so it must be Bea who had the nephew.

"What sort of nephew?" she asked, the next time she and Tony talked.

"Troubled nephew. Jail or bankrupt or his house burned down. I forget."

He'd called after a thunderstorm to ask her what it had been like where she lived, a few blocks away. He'd been sure the thunder and lightning had been right above his head, and he wanted to know if it had seemed slightly distant to her. Susan hadn't noticed. "Don't you count the seconds between the lightning and the thunder?" Tony asked.

"No, why would I do that?"

"To see how many miles away the storm is. Didn't your parents teach you that?"

"I don't think so."

"My brother Doug taught me to count during thunderstorms," Tony said. "To calm me down."

Susan could remember being afraid, but her grandparents had been more afraid than she was. Her grandfather would race through the house slamming down windows. There would be clothes on the line, and her grandmother would rush to the window to take them in, while her grandfather shouted, "Leah, Leah, let them be—close the window!" Leah would whip the rope toward her on its pulley, barely taking off the clothespins, just snatching the clothes and jerking—as though, if the rain touched them, the clothes would be dangerously enchanted. Susan realized that without thinking about it she had assumed that there were no thunderstorms in Europe, that her grandparents thought thunder and lightning were a hostile American invention. Not Jewish.

She had a clear picture of Tony in her mind as he counted the seconds between the lightning and the thunder: thick straight hair that fell across his forehead and was parted on the side, blue eyes, a broad face. When she saw someone like that in the street, she began to wonder if it was Tony.

Someone new had come to work in the clinic, Cat's replacement (except that she came full-time)—a woman named Lennie. She was Susan's age, and on her first day at work, she asked Susan if she knew a good place to have lunch, and suggested that they go together. Bea and Helen always brought their lunches and ate in the waiting room between appointments, and Susan often brought hers too, and ate at her desk. Sometimes she went out, though. She was entitled to an hour, and she liked being by herself and going for a walk. She'd usually eat at a little luncheonette in the neighborhood.

The day Lennie came, Susan had brought her lunch, but she pretended she hadn't. She suggested the luncheonette, and Lennie agreed, but while they were walking over there, Lennie spotted a pizza place she wanted to try. "I want to eat in every restaurant in New York, sooner or later," Lennie said. "We'll go to your luncheonette tomorrow."

"How many have you tried so far?" said Susan.

"Not many. I just moved here." Lennie was from southern Illinois. She'd gone to Radcliffe and then taken a master's in social work at the University of Michigan. Now she'd come to New York, found a job and an apartment, and was trying the restaurants and learning the subways. She found it charming that Susan had grown up in Brooklyn.

"I'll take you to meet my grandparents," Susan promised. Lennie was tall, and she had red hair. Those traits might interest Susan's grandmother, although you never knew. Possibly a tall, red-headed peddler had cheated Leah's great-grandfather in the middle of the nineteenth century.

And Lennie was perhaps a little *too* tall. She was taller than everyone in Susan's family, even her grandfather. She had a loud laugh, and she laughed at herself. "I'm great to take home," Lennie said. "I put my foot in my mouth when I meet families. When my rich roommate at Radcliffe took me home, I asked her mother whether she was a descendant of one of the robber barons. I'd been taking a course—on I went."

"Was she?"

"You know, I think she might have been. It was a touchy moment."

Susan loved the dark red sheen of Lennie's hair. It was short and just a little curly. Outdoors in the sun the ends looked gold. Lennie had had more experience with men than Susan had, but she was tentative and uncertain about them anyway. She'd had a steady boyfriend in high school and they'd gone to her prom, and she'd had two affairs, one long, in college. She liked to talk about men. She asked Susan's advice, and Susan found she could give it. Just now Lennie was interested in a man called Jeff, and Susan was called upon to interpret Jeff's behavior. Lennie wasn't sensible about him.

"What would you think if he were a client?" Susan asked.

"You mean if he were a child? Say if Jeff was ten and one day I asked him a question and he didn't answer, which is what happened last night?"

"Yes, what would you think?"

"Oh, I wouldn't take it too seriously."

"So pretend he's a kid," said Susan, and Lennie laughed, but she couldn't think about Jeff the way she did about her clients.

She was a good social worker. She talked about work as much as about Jeff. Sometimes she called clients at night, or met them in a playground or on the front steps of their houses. She'd walk around the neighborhood with some eleven-year-old, asking questions— finding things out, she said—while both of them licked ice-cream cones. Susan thought Bea and Helen would probably object, but Lennie was in her office so much that they didn't notice. Lennie worked extra hours.

She loved New York—her clients' New York (she wanted to find out about gangs, she said innocently) and Susan's New York. She got Susan to take her to the Cloisters, the Frick Collection, and the Metropolitan Museum. On these trips she carried a notebook.

One day Susan told her about the ferry to Staten Island. "It's what New Yorkers do, isn't it?" Lennie said. "Not like the Statue of Liberty."

Susan said they could meet at the ferry on Saturday afternoon and ride over and back. Then they'd walk to Chinatown and have dinner. She explained to Lennie how to get there from her apartment on the West Side. Susan knew that her grandfather would have been able to tell Lennie whether to get on at the back or the front of the train, so as to be close to the right staircase when she got off, but Susan couldn't do that. Still, Lennie loved hearing Susan talk about the subways. She'd lean back on her heels and sway slightly and grin, whenever Susan explained about the shuttle to Grand Central or some other subtlety, the way she might have reacted if she heard someone from Pennsylvania Dutch country talk in dialect.

When Susan reached the ferry terminal on Saturday, she didn't see Lennie. She was surprised: Lennie always arrived first. She figured out how much time each step of a trip was going to take, and added on fifteen minutes here and there, just in case. Susan walked around reading newspaper headlines and watching people, not looking at the clock. When she did, she was alarmed—Lennie was more than half an hour late.

Susan had not known Lennie long, but she'd heard about her life in Illinois, where she had been a cheerleader and editor of the high school newspaper, and her years at Radcliffe—unhappy at first, then better. Lennie could do things. In college she'd acted in plays and had an affair with a violinist who was now a little famous. Lennie had once brought a review of a performance of his to work with her. She was clearheaded about him, even though he had broken up with her. "He said I distracted him from practicing," she said. "It was true."

When Lennie was an hour late, Susan called her house, but there was no answer. She thought she shouldn't leave. Lennie might have misunderstood the time. Yet it seemed silly to stand there, watching wave after wave of people going off on ferries, disembarking from arriving ferries. Susan sat down on a bench and searched through her purse, as if she might find something helpful in it. She found a used envelope on which, two weeks earlier, she'd written down the starting time of a movie she and Lennie had gone to see. On the other end of the envelope was Tony Donnelly's telephone number. It would be a good idea to get advice. She went back to the phone booth where she had tried Lennie before. Again, there was no answer. This time she put in her dime and called Tony.

Someone else answered, and Susan wondered whether she should give her name if he wasn't there, but he was. "I'm not sure why I'm calling you," she said. "I'm worried about a friend and I thought you could tell me whether it makes sense to worry."

"I'm good at that," said Tony.

"And I can't call my grandmother," said Susan. "She'd say *definitely* I should worry, before she heard the story."

"I get it."

"I'm in the Staten Island Ferry terminal," she said. She told him about her date with Lennie, and how late it was—almost an hour and a half, by now.

"Is she the sort of person who'd just not show up?" said Tony.

"Definitely not. She has your mother's job," said Susan, realizing that that was why she'd called him. "She's the sort of person Bea and Helen grabbed onto when they couldn't have your mother."

"Oh," said Tony. "Well, I think we should worry, but I don't think we should call the police yet."

Susan hadn't even thought about calling the police. She loved Tony's "we."

"I think we should go to her house," he said. "Is she the sort of person who might be a secret depressive who is lying in the dark considering whether to take pills?"

"Oh, I don't think so," said Susan. "She'd have invited me over to talk her out of it."

"I think we'd better go to her place anyway."

Susan told him where Lennie lived, and he said they'd meet in the Fourteenth Street station of the IRT.

"We'll never find each other," she objected.

"Of course we will. I know where the uptown train comes in," he said. "You be in the first car, near the first door. When you get to Fourteenth Street, get out, and I'll be standing right there."

She laughed at him.

"What?"

"How will we know each other?"

"Oh, honestly, Susan," he said, almost seriously. "All right— what are you wearing?"

Now she felt self-conscious. "A pink blouse and a brown skirt."

"Gotcha." He had her wait another twenty minutes, to give him time to get there. After she hung up, she wondered what she'd do if Lennie arrived during the twenty minutes, but she didn't come. When Susan stepped off the train at Fourteenth Street, sure enough, there was Tony—of course it was Tony—and he took her by the arm and pivoted her back inside. "There," he said, looking down at her, seeming excited, as the doors closed. "We don't even have to wait for the next one." They'd spotted each other instantly, as the train pulled in, and Susan had felt herself flush.

Tony looked exactly the way she'd pictured him—blue eyes, straight, thick hair, broad face, glasses—which seemed so odd that Susan couldn't speak for a few minutes, realizing that people *never* looked the way one had imagined them—which didn't matter; one just stepped over the discrepancy and moved on. Thinking rapidly about people she'd spoken to over the phone, and then met, she saw that in some cases she could still bring to mind the wrong face she had imagined. She hadn't *known* how Tony looked. The only one of her children Cat had described was Claudie, who had hair so long she could sit on it. Cat said strands of Claudie's hair got stuck in the vacuum cleaner.

Susan and Tony tried phoning Lennie once more, when they got off the train. Tony handed Susan a dime for the phone call. He looked sober, standing in the doorway of the phone booth, his arm braced above his head, watching Susan dial the number. Meeting Tony had distracted Susan from her fear, but when there was still no answer she went back to worrying about Lennie. Lennie was like people one read about in the newspaper, found murdered. She was from out-of-town and she liked New York too much. If someone had offered her a ride or pretended to have a problem, Susan wasn't sure that Lennie would know enough to turn away. Susan's grandmother could pass among sidewalk vendors, beggars, people thrusting petitions at her, and not look at any of them (except the man who sold hot chestnuts, for some reason), her manner somehow suggesting that Jewish people didn't *notice* the Sabrett's hot dog man, or the pretzel vendor. Susan now bought pretzels and hot dogs. Lennie bought anything.

She and Tony met Lennie on her own block, hurrying toward her house. "*Susan!*" Lennie said, stopping, looking startled and guilty. She touched Susan's arm. "I can't believe what I did. You must be very angry."

She looked at Tony, and Susan introduced them. Lennie gave a glint of interest and surprise—she had been hearing about the phone calls—that came through even though she was upset.

"We were worried about you," said Susan.

"We came to identify your body," said Tony pleasantly.

"Oh, I'm so embarrassed," said Lennie. She brought them up to her apartment and made coffee. She'd been on a walk with Jeff. He had called in the morning and wanted to see her for a few minutes— and she had gone, telling herself that she could easily be back in time, but she hadn't brought along her watch—and then she and Jeff had had a fight, and she had let the time pass, trying to resolve it.

"I knew what I was doing, Susan," she said abjectly, right in front of Tony. "You don't have to forgive me. I knew I was wasting your time. I kept telling myself it wasn't that late—but I knew it was. I just couldn't bring myself to leave him. I stood you up in the worst way. Even the other cheerleaders would be mad at me, and they thought you could do anything to a girlfriend if there was a boy involved."

"But didn't you know I'd be *worried*?" said Susan, sounding like her grandfather. Being made to stand in the ferry terminal didn't seem so bad if it was in a good cause. If Lennie had said, "Please go wait in the Staten Island Ferry terminal for an hour and a half, and it will fix things up between me and Jeff," Susan wouldn't have minded at all, but it was different because Susan had *worried*. Lennie didn't have the right to make her worry. "You could have called me this morning, after Jeff called, and said you weren't coming," she said.

"Oh, at that point, I *was* coming," said Lennie.

"What did you think I'd think?" Susan persisted. She didn't say it angrily, and more and more, she didn't feel angry with Lennie, but she did feel curious. She would not have had the *freedom* to leave a friend waiting for her; she couldn't have done it unless someone was dying, she decided, and she wanted to know how it was possible that Lennie could do it. Susan would have walked away from Jeff, feeling betrayed by both him and the friend she was meeting.

Something told her it was all right to be curious in front of these two people—that Lennie would not be too embarrassed about Tony's presence, and that Tony would not decide that Lennie was a bad person, even though he had just taken the train all the way to Eighty-sixth Street for no reason.

"Well," said Lennie, "I didn't think you'd worry. I thought you'd wait for a while and then decide I wasn't a very nice person, and go home. I pictured you angry, not worried."

She was bringing in two mugs of coffee, and she stood still, the white mugs in her hands, as she said this. Then she put one down in front of each of them, Susan's on a little table and Tony's on the edge of a bookcase, and went back to the kitchen. She had looked careful and *bright*, somehow, holding the mugs. She was wearing a blue-and-white checked shirt and she was watching her hands, to keep from spilling the coffee. Now she stayed in the kitchen, getting her own mug, longer than Susan would have thought, and when she came back her face looked odd, and Susan realized that Lennie had been crying.

"I forgot to ask you if you wanted milk and sugar," she said, and on the last word, her voice broke. "I'm sorry," she said, crying for real. "It was just so *friendly* of you," and she turned back to the kitchen, and came out again with the sugar, a container of milk, and some spoons. She set them all down on the table next to Susan's cup, and then she reached out to Susan and half-hugged her head, pulling it close to her. Susan relaxed against her lanky body, and stood up so she could hug Lennie back.

"I forgive you," she said, laughing a little bit.

Lennie sat down on the floor, cross-legged, and began to drink her coffee. "I didn't even get through to him," she said. "We're still having the fight."

Then she looked up at Tony. "It was nice of you to come," she said formally. "I mean, you don't even know me."

"Hell, he doesn't even know either of us," said Susan. "He's just free and easy about his social life, I guess."

"I wasn't busy," said Tony seriously. He looked happy, drinking his coffee and leaning over to read the titles on Lennie's bookshelves. "Everybody I know has the same books," he said. "*Intro-duction to Western Civilization. A Farewell to Arms. Psychology.* Some people have a book called *Introduction to Psychology* instead, but I have the same one as yours."

"I have different books," said Susan, remembering her conversation with Tony about books. *A Farewell to Arms* was one of the books he'd mentioned, but she hadn't read it. She wondered whether Lennie and Tony would fall in love, since they had the same books. Tony had been in Lennie's house when he hadn't been in hers—he'd gone searching for Lennie—in some ways he was already closer to Lennie. Swiftly she imagined how the two of them, married, with children, would explain her presence—their old friend Spinster Sue—at their dinner parties. "We *met* because of Susan," they'd say.

She took herself through this fantasy lightly but curiously, almost lazily, as she sat back in a worn overstuffed armchair and drank coffee, relieved of worry, and then she wondered for a moment whether she had no feelings for Tony, if she could simply release him in her mind to her friend. Lennie was still her friend, she discovered, as she followed the thought. More than ever. Susan had liked something, and when she examined the day's events, followed everything Lennie had said—Lennie and Tony were still talking about books, and now they'd begun to talk about records—she saw that it was that Lennie couldn't break away from Jeff and come to Susan. Lennie seemed more interesting to Susan than she had been, as if someone had handed Susan a pair of glasses that enabled her to see cracks and shadows in a surface that appeared plainer.

But that wasn't why she didn't worry about Lennie and Tony. If she wanted Tony, she thought, she could have him. She had never felt this way about any man or boy in her life—any person. She didn't know where the feeling came from.

Now Lennie went back into the kitchen with the cups and Tony came over to her chair. "Shall we invite Lennie along to dinner?" he said in a low voice, leaning over her from behind and picking up her hair, then dropping it again, idly, as if he'd done it before.

"Yes," said Susan, and wasn't jealous. Tony marched into the kitchen to make the invitation, and Susan sat in Lennie's coffee-colored armchair and recollected that she had *planned* to have dinner with Lennie, it was *Tony* who was being invited along, except that—well, it was clear to her, too, that they were having dinner together.

Lennie got her purse and the three of them went down to the street. It was a summer day, but not too hot. They walked along Broadway for a long time, not choosing a restaurant yet, just looking into windows and talking about what they saw. Tony was fascinated by a hardware store. He said he liked to look at tools and learn their names. Lennie knew them all, and said she knew how to use most of them, too. She knew the difference between a socket wrench and a monkey wrench, and Tony knew a Phillips screwdriver from an ordinary screwdriver. Susan knew nothing. "My grandfather bangs on nails with his shoe," she said.

They began to talk about how their families earned their living. Lennie's father was a high school gym teacher, and her mother was the secretary in the same high school, which was where Lennie had gone to school. Tony's father worked in a printing company owned by a cousin. It had been in the family for three generations, and was a pretty big firm, Tony said, but nobody closely related to him had made much money from it. Susan had never known this—she had never thought to ask Cat what her husband did.

"Do they print books?" she said.

"No, not usually. Sometimes brochures and circulars. Sometimes books—not books you'd see in a bookstore, much, but catalogs and manuals. Sometimes they do stationery. It's a good place—they do fine, accurate work. They just expanded. My father liked it better before—he's spent his life avoiding being important." The company was in Bridgeport, Connecticut, where Tony had grown up.

"Did you ever think of going to work there?" asked Lennie.

"No," said Tony. "That would be a defeat."

They walked for a while in silence. Susan thought about her own family. Her mother sold dresses. Her father worked for a company that made children's clothing, and he traveled, mostly through New Jersey and Pennsylvania, selling children's clothing to stores. Her grandfather had worked in the men's haberdashery department of Gimbels before he retired. They didn't *know* anything, Susan felt.

The three of them browsed in a bookstore and Tony bought a novel by Thomas Mann. Then they got hungry, and came to a Middle Eastern restaurant, and Lennie was entranced—she had never tried Middle Eastern food. They went in and sat down, and then Lennie got up to go to the ladies' room. Susan was looking at the menu, trying to decide if she'd like falafel, when Tony leaned across the table and covered her hands with his. "I'm really happy," he said. "I thought I was going to be this happy, and I kept putting it off, because I thought maybe I wouldn't be, and then I wouldn't have it to look forward to. But I'm really happy." He stopped and gave her her hands back. Then he said, "You, Susan, are you happy?"

She had just met him. It was his idea—it was as if she had agreed to enter a story he was making up. But what was flooding her body might well be happiness. Tony was looking at her, and she thought that she probably looked pretty good: Her hair fell around her face in a loose, relaxed way that she hoped was not too messy. She liked the soft color of the pink blouse, which was open at the neck, and she had on a string of dark beads she'd bought in the Village.

She smiled and shrugged. "What can I tell you? I'm happy," she said. She felt grown up.

SUSAN SAID SHE AND TONY were walking out together, as if they were in a book about Ireland, because they walked together more than they slept together, although they did that, too, and quite creditably, Susan felt. They walked, she pointed out, exaggerating, on every street in New York. Susan was not much shorter than Tony, and her hair was thick, almost bushy. It was light brown. She wore it in a ponytail held together by a rubber band, although her mother said that would damage the hairs. The ponytail gradually came loose during the day, and by the time she saw Tony in the late afternoon or early evening, the rubber band had slipped down, and her hair swelled out softly and then was caught on her shoulders. Sometimes she lost the rubber band altogether. Tony claimed he had dozens of them around his apartment, each one with a few brown hairs twisted through it.

Tony's hair was thick, too. From the start he said they'd have a set of bushy-haired children. They discovered that when they walked, if Tony put his arm around Susan and bent his head just a little, he could rub it against hers, and she'd rub her own past his ear and cheek and the temple of his glasses.

After a while Tony had moved out of the house full of unidentified people and into his own apartment. He'd kept his job at the law firm, and still talked about law school, some time or other, but he said he hated the job. It was nothing much, he said, mostly running errands. Some days he said he had definitely decided not to go to law school, and to try to get a job at a newspaper, or even to go to work at his father's company—he always said that with a short laugh, as if he expected that Susan would be laughing and he was joining her.

One Thursday in November he called to say that his youngest sister, Claudie, was coming to visit him the next day, but that the law firm was sending him out of town and he wouldn't get back until after her arrival. He wanted to know whether Susan could meet Claudie at the train station and take her to his apartment. She agreed readily. Again she would have to find one of this family without knowing her. "She looks like my mother," said Tony. "But she's little."

"Tell her I'll meet her at the information booth."

When the time came, Susan was late. As she hurried toward the information booth from the subway station, she spotted a tiny girl in blue pants standing near it and felt a sudden, unexplained excitement, as if Claudie was someone she'd wanted to meet for years. Claudie moved closer to the booth, then away again, turning to look for Susan in every direction. She had short brown wavy hair, and when she saw Susan she turned her back on her overnight bag and smiled widely, a childlike, delighted smile which was like Tony's smile, although her face was sharp and thin. It was as though she and Susan already knew each other, and Susan ran up to her and took both her hands, knowing the gesture was excessive. "Wait a minute, it's really you, isn't it?" she said. "I'm Susan. I thought you had long hair."

"I cut it off. It's me."

Susan took her hands away and pulled the overnight bag closer. Then she bundled her own hair back into the rubber band, which had been about to fall off.

"Tony said you had a red coat," said Claudie conclusively, as if there were no other red coats in New York. Susan looked at her boyfriend's sister's lively face—a little, rabbity face.

"Are we going to your place?" said Claudie.

"We're supposed to go to Tony's." Susan had had a key to Tony's apartment from the time he'd first moved in. "But he won't be home for a while. We could go to my place. It's easier to eat there."

"I've starving," said Claudie. It was suppertime. "I'd love to see your apartment. I really like seeing people's houses. I'm always trying to get my friends to invite me. I *need* to see their rooms— you know, whether they're messy, what they put on the wall, what they throw in the wastebasket. Whether their parents have fights."

"I'd love to take you to my apartment," said Susan. "I live alone."

"Where do your parents live?"

"My parents are divorced." Susan usually came to this information more slowly with a new person. They were just walking down the subway steps to the Lexington Avenue line. "It's a little strange. My father is remarried and lives in New Jersey. I hardly ever see him. My mother lives in the same building as my father's parents. They brought me up—my grandparents."

"They live in an apartment house?"

"A two-family house in Brooklyn. My grandparents own it and my parents went to live there when I was a baby. Then my father left, and my mother just stayed."

"They didn't throw her out?"

"No," Susan said. "They wouldn't do that." She felt as if there were a spotlight on her. They were standing on the subway platform, and now she heard the train coming.

"How is your mother?" she said, over its noise, though she could have asked Tony about his mother at any time and usually didn't. She was conscious that Claudie was Cat's daughter, and felt almost as if Cat were watching them and could overhear them. She had never felt that when she was with Tony. She could imagine Cat and Claudie talking about her.

Claudie knew New York, that was clear. When they got off the train at Fourteenth Street she began to tell Susan about trips she'd made to the Village alone or with friends. Susan was happy to be taking her home. She questioned Claudie about what she liked to eat, and they stopped to buy spaghetti and chopped meat and tomato sauce, as well as vegetables for a salad.

"I guess I can't offer you wine," she said. It was new for her, too, to have wine with her dinner, and sometimes she had to show identification to buy it.

"Well, if you did, I'd drink it," said Claudie.

"Maybe a little." She stopped and bought a bottle of chianti with a straw basket around the bottom.

"So your grandparents brought you up?" said Claudie, in the elevator. "That must be funny. Do you think of them as your parents? I mean, are they the ones you call up and everything?"

It was hard to explain. "I do call them up, but it's not as if they're my parents," said Susan. "My grandmother wouldn't like it if I confused her with my mother. But my mother gave me away." To have a mother who sends you downstairs to live, she explained to Claudie, was like having one's part in a play written out by the playwright. She remembered her professor at Queens pointing out that in *King Lear*, the Fool disappears halfway through the play. "I'm the Fool," said Susan. Claudie was happy to talk about Shakespeare. She had read two plays, she said—*Romeo and Juliet* for school, and *The Tempest* for herself.

"Somebody told me it was about magic," she said. "So I read it."

"Did you like it?"

"Parts."

She threw herself onto Susan's bed, and they kept talking. It was half an hour before Susan found time to stand up and start supper.

"I'm very difficult," Claudie said. Susan had gone into the bathroom, and now, as she came out, Claudie seemed subdued, as if she'd been thinking about this difficulty of hers.

"You don't seem difficult to me," said Susan.

"Well, talk to my shrink," said Claudie. She was looking at Susan almost defiantly. Susan wasn't shocked, though neither Cat nor Tony had told her that Claudie was seeing a psychiatrist. Cat herself, after all, was a social worker who worked with disturbed children, and would be matter-of-fact, not flustered and superstitious, about sending her daughter to a psychiatrist.

Maybe there wasn't much wrong, Susan decided. Maybe Cat—being in the profession—would jump to doing something like that long before anyone else would think of it. She had a picture of Cat in her mind, shading her eyes to look at Susan. Her desk had faced a window when she worked at the clinic, and she never would be bothered to pull the shade or put up curtains. In the afternoon, the sun would stream in, and Cat would squint and shade her eyes, peering into the sun at her client or anyone else who came through. That was how Susan imagined her, her hand to her forehead like a sloppy sailor saluting.

Susan was playing house, cooking with Claudie. She opened the wine and Claudie accepted a glass. Susan felt guilty about that but she didn't stop her when Claudie drank some of what she had and took a little more. It was a small galley kitchen, and the two of them kept bumping into each other, and soon they were teasing each other, as if they were the same age.

"You get in the way, like my sister," said Claudie. "Cathy can't fix a sandwich without knocking you down three times."

"Is that any way to talk to your hostess?" said Susan.

Claudie giggled. She was washing lettuce and patting it dry with a paper towel, and then she cut up a tomato. The dish Susan was cooking was simple, but she liked it and was proud of it. It was the sort of thing her grandparents would never eat. They thought of spaghetti as foreign, but Susan ate it constantly. It was Lennie the midwesterner who'd first fixed meat sauce for her.

"I think about my grandparents and my mother in a pile," she said to Claudie, thinking aloud now, not bothering to make much sense. "They're on the bottom, in their apartment, and she's on top, in hers. It's like a dollhouse and I can look in and see all of them. They watch me." She had to keep reminding herself that Claudie was only in high school. It was easy to talk to her.

"All the time? Oh, I know what you mean!" said Claudie.

"No," said Susan honestly. "Not all the time. But since I moved here, sometimes I see them that way, looking me over, watching."

"Do they disapprove?"

"Really, or in my mind?"

"In the dollhouse."

"Sometimes," said Susan. "My grandfather hardly ever does, but my mother does. Sometimes, though, she just faces the other way, with her back to me." Susan didn't look to see whether Claudie was following what she was saying. "Mostly my grandparents are afraid of what I do."

Claudie had her back to Susan, tearing the lettuce, but now she dropped her hands and turned around, eyes bright. "Oh, that's just like my parents!" she said.

Susan couldn't imagine Cat being afraid of her children. "Let me tell you what I mean," she went on. "It's not like your parents—not like your mother, at least. Now, your mother's a good example. My grandmother couldn't believe that I could be friends with your mother, because she's older than I am, and she was in charge, while I was the employee." She paused. "She wouldn't be able to imagine that I could be friends with you, either, because you're younger."

"I'm not that much younger," said Claudie.

"Anyway," Susan went on, "whenever I said I had disagreed with your mother about anything, when we worked together, my grandmother would get nervous. Or even if I told her I'd just given my opinion. She thought I should always be making sure I wasn't going to get into trouble."

"It's funny to think of you working with my mom."

"I guess that's why they're afraid," Susan continued, feeling that Claudie understood her remarkably well, though she was too absorbed in what she was saying to stop and make sure. "I don't mean because I worked with Cat—because I *didn't* get into trouble. I must be magic."

"You seem sort of magic," said Claudie. "Are you in love with my brother?"

Susan looked over at her. She had a bad sore on her arm that

Susan hadn't noticed before. She took Claudie's hand. "How did you do that?"

"The cat," said Claudie. It was wide, not a scratch, but Susan, who had never owned a cat, did not question her further. She felt obscurely that Claudie would not want Susan to think ill of her cat.

Susan carried the food into the main room of her apartment, where the table was—a card table; she wanted to get a real table but so far she hadn't done it—and ran back for napkins. There was a chair at the table already, where she always sat, and she brought her desk chair for Claudie. She had two more folding chairs, in case she had extra people in. Once Lennie and Tony had come together.

Her grandparents had come once, as well, but it was during the afternoon and they hadn't stayed for supper. She had made them coffee. They had brought fancy cookies from a bakery, in a box tied with blue-and-white string.

Then Claudie said again, loudly—as if she were calling to someone across the street—while Susan ran back and forth, "Are you in love with my brother?"

Susan laughed. "Yes." She sat down and looked at Claudie and looked at the food. "It's wonderful having you here," she said. She felt enchanted. She didn't want to tell Claudie that.

"I know, I know," said Claudie vigorously. "I don't think I ever got to feel this way with someone so fast." They laughed. It was odd but it had happened.

"Yes, I guess I'm in love with him," Susan repeated slowly. She felt solemn about saying it. She and Tony had said it to each other, but not to other people; at least *she* hadn't. She had told her grandparents and her mother that she was seeing him, but not that she was in love. In fact, she hadn't been sure she *was* in love. There wasn't enough pain in it. It had come easily, and she had never worried, never lain in bed waiting for the phone to ring. It had rung and rung. And if it didn't, she concluded that Tony had tried when she was out, and she called him.

"I'm close to your mother," she said to Claudie, "but please don't tell her this." She was surprised that she'd said she was close to Cat, and wondered whether Cat would agree. Probably not. She began to tell Claudie how she and Tony had met, and how quickly they had come to feel at ease together. She tried to remind herself that Claudie might never even have had a boyfriend yet, but Claudie said, "I once went out with a boy like that"—a little sadly, like a woman beyond her prime discussing the lost past.

"Where's Tony's place?" she asked now. "I've never been there—he just moved in, didn't he?"

"A few months ago," said Susan. "It's not far—in Chelsea." It was a basement apartment in a brownstone. "We can walk there."

"Listen, Sue," said Claudie. "You don't have to come with me. You've been so great—I mean, I love seeing you, and I'd really like to just stay here, but as long as I'm going to Tony's, I can go by myself. I can walk over easily."

"Oh, no, I don't mind. I promised Tony."

"That's the sort of thing I mean about my parents," said Claudie abruptly, and her voice was hard. "Nobody trusts me."

"Of course people trust you," said Susan. "I trust you. But I promised Tony I'd stay with you—to keep you company, not to be your baby-sitter."

"You do see me as a baby, then?" Claudie said. "See. I knew you did." She had been twirling a last strand of spaghetti around her fork. Now she put it down.

"Of course not," said Susan. "I said *not* to be your baby-sitter."

"But you used the word, Susan. You did use the word. You wouldn't use the word about someone you trusted."

Susan was suddenly overwhelmed with frustration. She didn't feel as if Claudie were a baby, but, all at once—though Claudie was now acting childish—as if she were older than Susan and had power over Susan, as if she knew how to say things Susan couldn't answer. There was no answer to this.

"Look, I say things," Susan said, and her voice shook. "I blurt things out." She paused. "I'm sorry. Forgive me. I don't think you're a baby." She wasn't used to saying, "Forgive me." It was dramatic— maudlin, but she would have said more to calm Claudie.

It was getting late. Tony would be home soon, or maybe he was home already. She stood up to telephone him, but he wasn't there. While she was dialing, Claudie took their plates into the kitchen and put them into the sink. "Well, I guess we ought to go," she said. "Thank you for dinner. It was delicious."

Susan wanted to put her arms around her, but she didn't, nor did she take out a package of cookies and suggest that she make tea. She went over to the window to draw the curtains. She had made blue burlap curtains, hemming them herself by hand. The clerk in the fabric store had shown her how to make pinch pleats by sewing a strip of special white material to the backs of the curtains. The material had a series of fabric tunnels woven in, and there were metal hooks that went up the tunnels and curved around a rod, some with several prongs and a clip, to make the pleats, others single hooks at the end of each curtain. Susan had been mixed up, and had sewn the first strip on upside down, but then she ripped it off and did it right, and she thought the results looked quite professional. Now as she pulled the curtains together it seemed that one corner was sagging a little—she might have left out one hook after all.

As they walked to Tony's house, they held Claudie's overnight bag, which had two handles, between them, and sometimes it bumped against their legs. Susan felt better again. Claudie did not continue the quarrel; she said little. The city was full of light and movement, and it was a cold night, but Susan felt warmer as she walked. Claudie made jokes about Susan's long stride, and complained that Susan was bumping her with the bag, and she swung it against Susan's legs, rather hard, and pretended it was an accident and laughed.

When they got to Tony's they were giggly and foolish. He was there—he opened the door as Susan was opening it with her key, proud that Claudie saw she had a key. "Hi," she said. "I love your little sister!"

"Well, that's nice," said Tony. "I got home and you weren't here and weren't at home."

"Were you worried?" Tony never worried.

"A little. But I'm glad you're here. Did you eat?" Now Susan was suddenly shy and thought she should drop Claudie off and leave, but something in Tony's voice was upsetting and she had to stay and figure it out.

"Are you angry with me?" she said, coming in and taking off her coat. "Was that all right, taking Claudie home? I couldn't leave you a note or anything, because I wasn't here."

"It doesn't matter. I was just afraid my parents would call and I'd have to tell them I didn't know where she was."

"Well, surely they wouldn't think she'd been kidnapped," said Susan.

"They wouldn't like it," said Tony soberly. Claudie said nothing. Tony made coffee. Claudie asked for a glass of milk, and sat quietly in the corner of Tony's sofa drinking it, while he told them about his day.

"I approve of Susan," she said at one point, when Tony paused. "Do as you will with her."

"As I will!" said Tony, but he laughed, and Susan was pleased, though she said, "Good grief, girl."

"So what are we going to do tomorrow?" Tony said. He sounded more like himself, and he looked around at both Susan and Claudie, apparently assuming they would all be together.

"We could go to a museum," said Susan, who still had her Brooklynite's love of them. Now she had passionate attachments to paintings and sculptures, but what she liked best was what she'd liked first—she was allowed in; the museums were grand houses in Manhattan that she owned.

"No, that's boring," said Claudie. "Though the planetarium is good. My mother used to take us there. What I'd really like," she said, "is to go to the beach."

"But it's November," said Tony.

"Not to go swimming, just to walk around. I'd like to see water."

"I don't know where to find the beach in New York," said Tony impatiently.

Suddenly it seemed to Susan that anybody truly alive would want to go to the beach, not a museum. "I know how to find the beach," she said, though she didn't. "We could go to Brighton Beach— that's my grandmother's favorite." She hadn't been there since she was old enough to keep the subway lines straight in her mind, but she could look at a map.

When Susan left Tony's place, she thought he might still be angry with her. She wondered if he minded her quick friendship with Claudie. He wasn't close to her himself, though he'd invited her down for a weekend. Claudie said she was closer to her sister, Cathy, and to Frank.

In the morning they met at the subway station. Tony and Claudie walked over to Susan's neighborhood. She was early, and watched them coming toward her. They were both wearing pants and short heavy jackets, and both had their hands in their pockets. Tony seemed twice Claudie's size, and she looked as if she was hurrying to keep up with him. She looked at him more often than he looked at her. It was interesting to see him with another woman. He wasn't chivalrous, although Susan felt that he was protective of Claudie in some larger sense: If something had threatened her, Tony would have hurled himself against it.

Claudie put her hand out and touched Susan's hand when they met. "That was great last night," she said. She seemed to have forgotten her outburst about trust.

"It was pretty amazing," Susan said. "It usually takes me a long time to make friends."

It was a long subway trip and then a ride on an elevated train to Brighton Beach. They passed small houses and small yards, remains of gardens inside fences. Susan and Claudie sat together. Susan began to tell her what she remembered about being taken to the beach by her grandparents. It had been a long trip from their house in Brooklyn, too, with changes of trains. Her grandmother brought food.

Tony sat by himself with his arms folded. He looked bored. She leaned over to him. "Do you think this is a bad idea?"

"No, it's a good idea."

"Are you tired from yesterday?" she persisted.

"Yes." It was the first time she'd felt this way with him, as if she were scrambling. She couldn't *help* scrambling, though—she couldn't just wait to see what he'd do.

Brighton Beach was windy. Susan liked the neighborhood where they got off the train, full of little stores. They walked under the elevated tracks for a while, looking at the stores and the women shopping. Then they turned down a side street to the beach. The boardwalk was deserted. As they walked along it, in the wind, Tony put his arm around Susan's shoulder and pulled her toward him as usual. She leaned her head against him. He didn't put his head down to meet hers.

Claudie was loitering behind them and occasionally catching up. "She's wonderful," Susan said.

"She has a lot of problems," said Tony. "It's good that she was wonderful yesterday."

"You shouldn't worry so much about her," Susan said. "Teenagers have problems. You should have seen me at sixteen."

"It's complicated."

Claudie came along and said, "I guess this was a bad idea. Are you cold?"

"No, it was fine," said Susan. "A fine idea. I'm not cold."

"Then do you want to go down to the water?" Claudie said.

They went down the steps from the boardwalk and walked in the sand to the edge of the sea. The waves were fairly high and noisy. Susan was elated. Claudie began picking up shells and putting them in her pockets. Tony stepped forward as if he was going to stop her.

"What's wrong?" said Susan.

"No, nothing—I just thought they could break, and the edges would be sharp," said Tony.

"They don't break easily," said Susan. "And anyway, people don't get hurt on them. People come here barefoot."

"That's right," said Tony.

Claudie had started to listen to him, and then turned away down the beach.

"Look, did you notice her arm?" Tony said to Susan abruptly, in a low voice.

"What about her arm?"

"She has a sore—a wound on her arm."

"What do you mean? Do you mean she tried to slit her wrists?"

"No," said Tony. "On the top. Not where you'd cut your wrists."

"I don't know what you mean," said Susan, irritated, and then she remembered the sore. Claudie had said the cat had done it.

"She hides it," said Tony. "But she liked you so much, I thought she might have told you. She did it to herself."

"I did see it," Susan said. "She said the cat did it."

"No."

"She made a wound on her arm?" she said. "She did it to herself? On purpose?"

"Yes. Just above the wrist. It's awful."

"I didn't realize," said Susan. It hurt to think about it. "What did she use?"

"A paring knife."

"Oh, my God," said Susan.

"They decided not to hospitalize her," Tony said. "But we all get scared every time she goes near anything sharp. And of course there are sharp things everywhere."

"She cut up the tomato with a paring knife last night."

It was the last time they were able to talk alone. Susan looked at Claudie's wrists, but they were covered by her jacket. She was angry with Claudie, as if their meeting yesterday had not been quite real. She turned and walked away from them, along the shore in the direction they'd come, while Tony and Claudie walked on together. The waves crashed, large and frightening, making her feel alone. This brother and sister had been through something important together. She could never catch up to them, could never mean as much to either of them as they did to each other.

She turned back. They were striding side by side along the shore, away from her, a scarf Claudie had tied around her head billowing and flapping as if to wave Susan away. She followed them slowly, so she didn't catch up to them. She had never had the impulse to cut herself with a knife. She couldn't imagine wanting to do that. She found herself wondering whether Tony and Cat sometimes thought about cutting themselves with knives. Maybe it didn't seem quite so exotic to them.

She was angry, but she wasn't angry at Claudie, she realized—she was indulging herself in this anger, and it was at Paula, her mother, who had given her away, who had caused her to be alone. Probably her mother and father had brought her to this beach when she was a baby. She could picture it—her mother in rompers, which Susan remembered from old snapshots, and a bathing suit underneath. They'd have spread out a blanket and sunned themselves, then run daintily into the water, she and her mother, her mother lifting each leg high, like a show horse, as she darted in, because the water was cold, while Susan flung herself into the swollen tops of the waves, trying to swim. But when it was time to go home, Susan imagined that her parents had gone off together by themselves, arm in arm, in a rare good mood, hurrying toward the subway without her, forgetting her. She could see herself—able to walk and talk, maybe two—following her parents at a distance and wondering whether they would think of her.

It had to be the ocean that was doing this to her. It was gray and cold and apparently limitless. It was making her feel desolate, but she let the desolation come. By the time Tony and Claudie stopped and waited for her to catch up, as they were even with the rides at Coney Island (Susan could see the parachute jump and the ferris wheel, looking abandoned these days), she was letting tears run down her face. She didn't wipe them away as she approached Tony and Claudie.

"Are you all right?" said Claudie, as Susan reached them.

"Sure," said Susan, but she went on crying. "I'm sorry. Something made me think of bad stuff." And then she leaned against Tony and cried into his brown corduroy jacket.

It felt luxurious. She couldn't exactly remember wanting to cry and suppressing the wish—but something in her had been longing for this. Tony would assume she was feeling bad about Claudie, but Susan knew that her crying was selfish and almost recreational. He put an arm around her—not both, but even so—and waited. After a while she stood up straight again.

"That was about my mother," she said.

"Oh, your mother. Her," said Tony. He hadn't met her mother yet.

They turned away from the beach and went up into Coney Island. The rides and souvenir stands were closed for the winter, and much of the place was closed altogether. It felt sad, and Claudie, whom Susan kept close to her side, now *seemed* unhappy—now that Susan had been told; the skin of her cheeks seemed transparent, as if it had been stretched painfully to cover her sharp bones. Still, Susan felt happier than she had before.

Nathan's was open. They were hungry. They had to wait on separate lines—Susan waited on the french fries line, Claudie on the drinks line, Tony on the hot dog line. Tony and Claudie liked the food even though they weren't Jewish. "See?" Susan said to her grandmother, in her mind.

When Claudie raised her hand to sip her drink, Susan caught a glimpse of the sore on her arm, red and deep. Then the jacket fell back into place. She didn't know if Claudie had seen her looking, but maybe Tony had told her they had discussed it. Claudie looked at her.

"Listen, Sue," she said after a while, as they were still eating. "I don't want to use you."

"What do you mean?" said Susan. "How could you use me?"

"You were so friendly yesterday. I took something from your house—while you were in the bathroom. I climbed up and took it." She reached into her jacket pocket and handed Susan a drapery hook, one of the single kind, with one sharp point. It had been at the end of the curtain that had sagged.

"Please don't be angry with me," said Claudie.

Tony looked as if he might cry. "I'm not angry," said Susan. She put the hook into her own pocket. They finished eating, and Claudie said it was so good she wanted another hot dog, so they bought her one, liked pleased parents whose child eats well, and walked on either side of her to the subway while she ate it.

AFTER SUSAN MOVED OUT of her grandparents' house and into her own apartment, she was angry with her grandmother all the time. She chided herself, because she didn't know why she should be angry. Her grandmother had given her a home for twenty years when her parents had not, and she would have kept Susan with her for the rest of her life if she could. Her grandmother now seemed grasping, small-minded, even ugly. She had almost no contact with her son, Susan's father, and Susan blamed her for that, though she knew it was out of loyalty to her that her grandmother remained aloof from him. In the weeks after she moved out, Susan visited her father twice in New Jersey, where he lived with a second wife and two daughters. He was kind, and his wife, Sonia, was generous and friendly, but they had wall-to-wall carpeting and a color television set and Susan could not bother herself to discover whether there was anything in them she could respect. Her two small half-sisters entertained her in their room before dinner, and Susan grimly noted the evidences that they too were money-conscious and in love with possessions. Her father wasn't certain whether the American presence in Vietnam was a necessary thing or not. Yet Susan knew she was being self-indulgent when she dismissed them all.

She would have preferred to go northeast to Tony's home in

Connecticut, but she had not been invited, despite her old friendship with his mother. She imagined the house in Connecticut as a low-ceilinged farmhouse with clattering wooden floors and maybe a few worn braided rugs on which children had tumbled. She loved Tony's stories about his childhood, or the stories she made up from his hints. "Frank had all the stitches and Cathy the broken bones," he said once. "One time I fell out of the tree and got cut, and Doug called my father to come home from work and take me to the doctor's, but Dad was so used to taking Frank, he got three blocks away from the house with him in the backseat before he figured out what Frank was saying to him. Meanwhile I was lying on the bathroom floor with gauze on my forehead. I still have the scar."

Susan's grandmother would have wept for a week if Susan had ever needed stitches. Her grandfather would have been deeply troubled, too, but she wasn't angry with him these days. She found that she forgot about him, or thought of him like someone in a story, a kindly and dignified Jewish patriarch. His faults—he was a snob and a bit of a bigot—seemed understandable, given his background, though at other times in her life they had driven her to angry tears at almost every dinnertime, or whenever he mentioned "the colored."

Her mother no longer lived in her grandparents' house. It seemed like proof that huge change was possible, along with the election of President Kennedy and then his abrupt death. Years ago, Paula had applied to live in a middle-income project on Linden Boulevard. No one thought anything would ever come of her application, but finally an apartment became vacant and she had moved into it. Her main interest was men. She dyed her hair light brown, lighter than Susan's.

Lennie wanted to know all about Susan's childhood in Brooklyn with her grandparents, so different from her own in Illinois. Susan had once promised to take her to visit her grandmother, but she and Lennie had been friends for almost a year before it happened. Finally she arranged the visit to punish both Lennie and Leah. She'd mentioned Tony on the phone and her grandmother had claimed she didn't remember who he was, which was nonsense—she had met him: Susan had brought him once, and they'd all had coffee.

And when Susan told Lennie the story, Lennie wasn't sympathetic to her, but to Leah. First she thought that Leah might be genuinely forgetful, because of her age. When Susan insisted she wasn't, Lennie began to see it differently, in a way that irritated Susan even more. "What must it be like for the poor lady?" she said. "You spend all your time with me or Tony and neither of us is Jewish."

"That's not important to my grandmother," said Susan, though she had often tried to explain to Lennie how important—illogically, since her grandmother wasn't an observant Jew—it was. "She's just being difficult."

"How could it not be important to her? You see the Spanish women at the clinic, and how much it means to them if I use a few words of Spanish?"

Susan did not like to think that her immigrant grandmother was like the women who brought their children to the clinic. "You think that's the source of all my problems?" she said testily, and Lennie backtracked, though Susan saw that she couldn't follow Susan's train of thought.

"I'm sorry," Lennie said. "I shouldn't make up advanced sociological theory about your family. I don't even know them."

Susan said it didn't matter, but she was still annoyed, and on the phone that night she asked her grandmother if she could bring Lennie for dinner. She hung up thinking she had done something kind and friendly to everyone, to make amends, but then she realized she was assuming the dinner would go badly and had arranged it on purpose to see *how* badly. Maybe her grandmother would somehow discover that Lennie had some German forebears and call her a Nazi.

Lennie brought a box of chocolates to dinner. It actually had a red bow on it. Susan told her in the subway that she had been silly to buy something so expensive. She thought her grandfather would look down at Lennie because the candy was Whitman's, which he considered inferior to Barton's, or, best of all, Barricini's. He could not literally look down at Lennie, however, because Lennie was taller than he.

Her grandmother was polite about the chocolates. She had made chicken soup with *knadlach*—matzoh balls—which Lennie said was the most delicious thing she had ever put in her mouth. "Is this Passover, then?" she asked, when it was explained to her what matzoh balls were. But it was December.

"Passover is the same as Easter," said Susan's grandmother, with rare ecumenicism. Although Leah was scornful at times of the infinitude of rules and distinctions made by her own religion, Susan was not used to hearing her acknowledge the existence of others. "The Last Supper is Passover." Susan couldn't imagine where her grandmother had learned that.

"Of course," said Lennie. "I knew that. What an idiot you must think I am, Mrs. Sternfeld."

"I would be stupid to think you are an idiot," said Susan's grandmother. "I know you are a graduate of Radcliffe College, a social worker. Such people are not idiots."

"Well, we all have our dopey days," said Lennie.

"*I* do not remember ever feeling dopey," said Susan's grandfather. He laughed, but Susan thought he was serious. He pronounced the word "dopey" in an odd way, and Susan thought he had probably never said it before.

"I feel stupid all the time," she said, and then fell back out of the conversation, because her grandmother remembered that *she* was in charge of Susan and her brains, and said, quickly, "How could you think that? With honors, you graduated. What about that report you wrote, that the professor mentioned to me at graduation?"

She leaned over the table toward Lennie, holding her collar (which was long, made of elegant-looking cream-colored stuff, with a bow at the neck) out of the soup. "So many students," she said, "but he had to tell me in person how brilliant was my granddaughter's paper."

"Mrs. Sternfeld," said Lennie soberly, also leaning forward, "your granddaughter is a certified *genius*."

Leah had dressed up for Lennie's visit. It was only now that Susan noticed the blouse. She was touched. "You look pretty, Grandma," she said. "Is that a new blouse?"

Her grandmother's face, powdered pink, was deeply wrinkled,

which made the silky cloth seem even smoother. Susan wondered if dressy fabric is smooth because it promises smooth skin beneath it: an advertisement—in her grandmother's case, a false one. Everyday cloth, Susan went on to think (entranced with her idea)—wool, corduroy, denim—is rough. Go away, it says, I prickle. She felt the thick, nubby weave of her own heavy woolen skirt. She almost never wore smooth fabric, she realized—she didn't like nylon stockings and preferred tights or lumpy, textured cotton stockings. She wore sweaters or corduroy shirts instead of blouses. She looked around the table, almost as if she were going to confess these thoughts, feeling her sweater as well. She didn't even like *angora* sweaters.

"I'm afraid of sex!" she'd say, in horror, though she'd been proud of herself because she was *not*, even if she didn't always have orgasms: She liked sex, and that was the important thing.

Her grandmother was serving the pot roast. She'd been pleased that Susan had said she looked good, and had begun to tell the story not of her blouse—which was not new—but of her blue suit. It was a *suit*, she was pointing out, though she wasn't wearing the jacket right now. She had bought it on the Lower East Side, and she explained the exact location of the store. Susan was bored but Lennie was enchanted. She had heard about shopping on the Lower East Side, but the one time she'd ventured into a store, she had been too confused to buy anything. "The man started shouting at me. I wanted a sweater, and I asked him if the one he showed me was real wool, and he was insulted."

"Of *course* real wool!" said Susan's grandmother, as if the man were her cousin.

Lennie had been unable to buy the sweater. The man wouldn't give her a chance to think.

"Think!" said Susan, who went to impersonal department stores on purpose.

"Mrs. Sternfeld," said Lennie now, "would you let me know, the next time you're going shopping there? Do you think I could possibly go with you? I'd be able to buy something if you were there, I'm sure, and I bet you have good taste, too."

"I would be delighted," said Mrs. Sternfeld, with a formal nod.

"Susan could come along, too," said Lennie. "Do you think we could do it on our lunch hour? Those stores aren't far from the clinic."

"No, thanks," said Susan. "I like to shop alone."

"She has a mind of her own," said her grandmother apologetically to Lennie, as though Susan were a child, and Lennie smiled and said, "Don't I know it."

"Boys like a mind of your own, and then again they don't," said Susan's grandfather softly.

Susan tried to joke. "I think I'm a rather compliant person, actually."

"Boys," said her grandmother, so swiftly that Susan was almost dizzy with the shift in the conversation. "For a friend, they like a girl who speaks up, but not for a wife."

"But Susan speaks up, and she has a boyfriend," said Lennie. "Not like me. I had a boyfriend but we broke up."

"Who? What boyfriend?" said Susan's grandmother.

"His name was Jeff."

"No, *Susan*," said Leah.

"Tony," said Lennie, uncertainly.

"Just a good friend," said Susan's grandmother quickly. "An army man."

"Wait a minute!" said Susan. Lennie might step in and argue for her, but she didn't have the patience to wait and see whether that would happen. "Grandma, I can't stand this. He's my boyfriend. What's going to convince you? I'm afraid we don't go in for handing over fraternity pins, not that he has one. And he was in the Air Force."

"This war—I am not holding him responsible," said her grandmother.

"Of *course* he isn't responsible! He wasn't in Vietnam—it hadn't started when he enlisted," said Susan, trying to remember when the first Americans had gone to Vietnam.

She suddenly thought she might cry, and that was unthinkable. This was the way she remembered arguing as a teenager. It would become so important not to lose in a discussion with her grandfather, she'd go on insisting something she knew could not be true. Maybe Tony wasn't really her boyfriend. Maybe, in his mind, it was pleasant, casual, and temporary. She had not been invited to visit his family. He was offhand—she always thought this was because it was a settled matter between them, but it could be because what was between them was quite small indeed. Maybe he had a real girl-friend somewhere else, and thought of Susan as a buddy with whom he had occasional not very interesting sex.

"This Johnson," said her grandmother to Lennie, now. "Roosevelt would have known what to do."

"Oh, F.D.R.?" said Lennie. "Were you for F.D.R.?"

"Yes," said Leah serenely, as if she were announcing her real religion. "We were for F.D.R."

"My grandmother hated him," Lennie said, but Susan inter-rupted her.

"Grandma, I'm not going to let you get away with this," she said. "Do you think I'm lying to you about Tony and me? Is that what you're accusing me of?"

"Lying!" said Leah. "Of course not. But this young man—he was in the army, he grew up somewhere else, not New York. A girl isn't such a big deal for him. A very nice young man, but not with our ideas."

"Can't you let me judge for myself about Tony's ideas?"

"Of course you judge for yourself. Now I think we should have dessert and not let Lennie think we are people who are always fighting."

Susan knew that they weren't convinced, or that if they were, they would never say so. Lennie smiled at her and got up to help clear the plates, but Susan stayed put. To stand up and carry plates into the kitchen—they were eating in the living room, which meant they were important company—would be to fall back into girlhood, to become a person who couldn't possibly have a boyfriend, cer-tainly not one with a gentile name like Tony Donnelly.

"Grandma," she said, "is it just that he isn't Jewish?" but she knew what the answer would be and it was.

"Susan, you should know better than that. We are not narrow-minded people. Jewish is not the whole world. When the time comes, you pick a man you love, and I don't care what he is."

"So you think I don't love Tony?"

"I think your kind of boy does not join the army."

"But Grandma," she said. "He's *against* the war. He marched in a peace march. What do you think, he voted for Goldwater?"

"God forbid," said her grandfather.

"Lennie," said Leah, "Lennie darling, do you drink coffee or tea?"

Lennie drank coffee. So did Ezra, even though he was so old. He laughed at people who said coffee kept them up late. He was sitting back in his chair, watching Lennie and then Susan with interest. Susan felt more attractive when she saw Ezra looking at her. He was dressed in a white shirt and a tie and a jacket, and she always thought of him as a man in control of things, but she realized now that he must be about eighty, and he made a sound when he breathed. He had done that for a long time, though—when she thought about it, it seemed that that sound had been a part of her life for years, and that without knowing it she had been homesick for it since she moved away. She wasn't angry with him, even though he seemed as determined as her grandmother to insist that Tony, somehow, wasn't real. It was that, she thought, later, as she and Lennie were walking back to the elevated train: They insisted he was imaginary. And Susan could be dissuaded from believing in Tony. When she got home, she'd want to call him and it would be difficult, almost as though he might not recognize her name.

Lennie, who still didn't sympathize with Susan about her grandmother, thought it was charming that Leah didn't believe in Tony. She thought it was an interesting way of solving a problem. She looked at it as a social worker, which irritated Susan, except that social workers don't love their clients, and Lennie loved Susan's grandparents and immediately made plans to see them some more. She and Susan would have a joint dinner and invite them: They would throw a party.

"My grandparents at a party?" Susan didn't want the parts of her life to connect that way. Seeing her grandparents and her friends at the same time would have been like meeting her dentist at the opera. Meanwhile the dinner had put Susan into a worse mood, and she wanted something from Tony to make her feel better.

"A ring?" said Lennie.

"Don't be silly." She wanted him to take her home to his family. She wanted to be welcomed and hugged and taken into a big warm house by Tony's mother, Cat—whom Lennie had met once and didn't like. "I just can't believe that," said Susan.

Three days after the dinner with Lennie and her grandparents, when Susan was alone in her apartment in the evening, she decided that people should solve their own problems and she would call up Cat herself. They'd known each other for years, after all. If Susan *hadn't* met Tony, she might well have called Cat by now. She had the number.

She opened her address book to the right page, and weighted the book with a snapshot in a small frame that she kept next to the phone—a picture of her mother—Paula in a billowing coat, her hand holding the collar closed, a nervous, windblown smile on her face. Susan liked it because the photographer—one of Paula's boyfriends—had caught her unawares.

Leaving the book open next to the phone, Susan lost her nerve. Finally she poured herself a glass of wine, to drink *after* she made the call. Then she was able to dial.

"Oh, *Susan*," said Cat, immediately, in a relieved voice, as if Susan had finally called her back after she'd left repeated messages. "I've been anxious to get your opinion. Did Tony tell you what's happening?"

"I don't think so," said Susan.

"Well, it's this plan to send Claudie to boarding school," said Cat. "Her psychiatrist agrees with me that it might be a good idea. Claudie doesn't want to go. She's accusing me of wanting to get rid of her. Susan, it meant so much to all of us—she hasn't sounded so happy in months, talking about meeting you. I don't know what you said to her, but it was helpful."

"I just liked her," said Susan. It had been exciting, meeting Claudie, but since then, she had to admit, she hadn't thought much about her; Claudie was delicate, frightening, and wonderful, but still a child. There was a thrill about being with her, a little uncertainty—but of course Susan couldn't call her up and talk about her day-to-day life.

"I've been meaning to ask you up here since I stopped working in New York," Cat went on. "Do you think you could come on Saturday? It would mean a lot to Claudie."

"You mean, without Tony?" said Susan. It was as if Cat didn't believe she was Tony's girlfriend any more than her grandmother did.

"Could Tony make it?" said Cat. "Doesn't he have some huge thing to write?"

The law firm had been giving Tony more to do, and yes, he'd already told Susan he couldn't see her that weekend. He'd signed up for law school at night, starting in February. Susan was confused about that because he had been so sure he didn't want to do it, and he didn't like the research and writing that was being required of him now, either. He was silent and impatient with her about law school, as if people weren't *supposed* to do what they wanted.

The Donnellys lived in Bridgeport. Susan had never been able to remember which Connecticut city it was. She took the train there on Saturday morning, and was met at the station by Tony's brother Frank, who was easy to recognize because he looked so much like Tony—but here she was again, she reflected, expected to find these people as if she already knew them. Maybe, she decided, there were so many of them, they couldn't remember what it was like not to know a person. Frank explained that Cat was marketing, Claudie was—well, unavailable.

Frank's wife, Judith, was with him. She seemed pleased to meet Susan. "We're here for the weekend," she said. "We live in Boston."

Susan fell into step with them, more at ease than she had expected to feel. "Did you grow up in Boston, Judy?" she said. "Did you like it?"

"*Judith*. I grew up in Brooklyn, like you."

"Oh! Where did you go to high school?" said Susan.

"Midwood," said Judith. She was a thin young woman with dirty blond hair that was pinned up but fell into her eyes. "I can't believe Tony's going out with a Jewish girl. I feel as if you're a relative!" Susan would never have said that.

She didn't have much sense of Frank, only that he was older than she was, and that he walked too fast for her. His silence seemed familiar.

Judith drove. "Brooklyn girls don't learn how to drive," she said to Susan. "I bet you can't." Susan couldn't. "I just learned, and now I do all the driving, because I know that if I stopped for even a day, I'd lose my nerve. Pretty crazy."

"That sounds hard," said Susan.

"Life is hard," said Judith, with a shrug Susan could see from the backseat, and a Yiddish intonation.

The Donnellys lived in a small wooden house on a crowded street. It had a big porch and a small, bare yard. The house was being repainted. The walls, which were green, had been scraped, so there were big, unevenly shaped pale patches here and there, and the white trim had been scraped even more—but the painting project seemed to have been abandoned, perhaps because it was winter. The house looked startled, Susan thought. Judith pulled into the driveway.

It was still early in December, but a Christmas tree, not yet decorated, had been placed in the living room, and it was the first thing Susan noticed. It looked wild, as if a piece of the woods had been brought in. A gray cat came from the back of the house to examine her, and rubbed itself on Frank's legs. The floors were covered with worn green carpeting with a few throw rugs on top, and in the hall were three layers—the carpet, a runner, and, near the living room doorway, a round rug with a large pink rose on it. The rugs looked as if they hadn't been vacuumed in a while.

Judith took Susan's coat and Frank led the way into the kitchen, where a gray-haired man sat reading at a big table. When he stood up, he looked stiff-legged.

"Have you met my dad?" said Frank. "Dad, this is Susan Stern-feld."

"I'm told you're a Latinist," said Frank Donnelly, Senior, shaking hands, and then Susan noticed that the book he was reading was a volume of Seneca's letters.

"Not since college," she said. She still took the *Aeneid* out of the bookcase every so often, but she never got more than a few lines into it.

"We'll read together," he said. "How about it?"

"Dad's suffering because they're starting to have the mass in English," said his son. "He needs a certain amount of Latin in his life."

"I do," said Mr. Donnelly. Still standing, he smiled at Susan. He looked like someone smiling in the wind, on the deck of a ship, gamely waiting for a photographer to figure out how the camera works, so he can go below decks and get warm. Then he said again, somewhat wistfully, "We did think you'd read Latin with me."

"I'd like to," said Susan. She wasn't sure when this was going to happen. She hadn't moved in, and didn't live in the neighborhood. She put her purse down on the table and asked Judith where the bathroom was. "Upstairs," said Judith. "There's one here but it's broken."

When Susan climbed the stairs, she saw a row of closed and open doors, but then one of the closed ones opened, and suddenly Claudie was upon her, hugging her and crying, burying her face in Susan's shoulder. Susan was startled, but then she had time to think, because Claudie stood still, quietly crying. Susan put her arms around the girl's shoulders, patted her back a little shyly, and stood there, Claudie's brown hair in her eyes, just able to see over the top of Claudie's head. Many minutes seemed to go by. Susan noticed that this hallway, too, was doubly carpeted. All the carpets were worn. There were patterns she could scarcely make out and, tying them together, islands of dark color that might have been blue or gray, except that where the light came through a small window above the landing in the staircase, Susan saw that they were dark green.

She said, "Let's sit down, Claudie," and sat cross-legged on the floor, and Claudie slid down, too, and leaned her head against Susan's shoulder. Susan put her arm around Claudie. She could see sores on both Claudie's arms, which were at least as bad as the one she'd seen before, but somehow, less frightening here.

"So how are you?" Susan said at last.

Claudie sat back against the opposite wall of the hall. "I'm pretty bad, but *really*, I'm all right," she said, "no matter what Mom says. I thought you'd never speak to me again after New York."

"Of course I'd speak to you!" said Susan.

"Wasn't that wonderful, Sue?" said Claudie, mercurially, abruptly brightening. "Did that really happen? I mean, it was like love at first sight, except we're girls. Do you know what I mean? I don't mean love exactly. . . ."

"I know what you mean," said Susan quietly. "But you don't *seem* all right."

"Well, I never am," said Claudie. "I don't need to go to boarding school. Would you tell her that?"

"She'll listen to me?"

"Oh, sure," said Claudie. "She thinks very highly of you."

While they were talking, Susan heard a door open, and then a new voice—Cat's voice. She should go downstairs. She wanted to, but it seemed that it would hurt Claudie, who was telling her in detail why her mother and the psychiatrist thought she should be sent away to school.

Below Susan were all the voices: Frank Senior and Junior's, Judith's, Cat's voice—did Cat love Judith? Susan needed to hurry down the stairs, not to plead for Claudie but to make sure Cat preferred her to Judith. She thought she might have liked to fall upon Cat the way Claudie had fallen upon her, and this was surprising. But she sat still, and then she heard someone mounting the stairs, and Cat's squarish face appeared, open and harried and between things, just as it had looked when she was at her job in New York, where she was always walking through the office with a pencil in her hand, aimed at a piece of paper two offices away on which she was going to mark down an appointment.

"Susan, you are great to come see us," she said. She didn't seem to think it was strange that Susan was sitting on the floor with her daughter. "And it's nice to see *you*," she said to Claudie, a little sharply. "We haven't seen this girl for some time. That locked door, Claudie. . . ." She smiled at Susan. "Now we'll have lunch."

She and Claudie waited while Susan was in the bathroom, as if to block an escape, Susan found herself thinking, and then Cat led the way downstairs and Susan and Claudie followed her. Mr. Donnelly put his arm around Claudie's shoulder as she came into the kitchen.

"Feeling better, Claudie?" said Judith, who was setting the table with blue and white dishes.

Claudie didn't answer, and Mr. Donnelly, who was still holding her shoulder, didn't say anything to her. But Claudie looked all right—very little, Susan thought.

"So you're Jewish, Susan," Mr. Donnelly said. There was lunch, suddenly. Cat had made a salad earlier, or maybe Judith had made it, and there were platters of ham and cheese and bread and rolls. Cat was rummaging in the refrigerator. "I have some cold roast beef, too, in here," she said.

"Yes," said Susan. "I'm Jewish."

"We didn't know if you ate ham," said Judith. "I eat ham. But you can still be in the family, I'm told, even if you don't."

"I eat ham, too," said Susan. Her grandmother had never served it, but it was one of the things Susan had discovered when she grew up. "But I like roast beef, too," she said. "Either would be fine."

"And I wanted to ask you," said Mr. Donnelly. "Do you read Hebrew, as well as Latin?" His light eyes grew brighter and Susan felt bad about disappointing him.

"My family isn't observant," she said. "I never learned Hebrew."

"It's just as well," said Judith. "I did, but it's not enough for him. He wants me to explain the finer points of the Old Testament."

"I can't *stand* Latin," said Claudie now. "It's nothing but killing."

"Oh, Claudie," said Cat. "Don't be silly."

"You must have read Caesar," said Susan. "I don't know why they give that to kids who are just starting out."

But Claudie wasn't listening to her. She had turned to her mother, and her voice was abruptly so shrill and urgent that everyone in the room stopped moving. "So now I'm silly," she said. "I'm silly, I'm crazy, I'm stupid, I'm disgusting, I'm emotionally disturbed. . . ."

"Claudie," said Cat, wearily, but also with fear. "Claudie."

Claudie sat down at the table and jerked the paper napkin out from under her fork with a gesture that seemed likely to tear it in half. It disappeared into her lap. Her elbows, in a white shirt with the sleeves rolled up, looked sharp and angular; she seemed all acute angles as she sat there while everyone else stood around her.

"Let's sit down," said Mr. Donnelly. "I'm glad you're not actively against Latin, Susan. I'm used to opposition, though. Nobody else around here even goes to mass."

Cat asked Susan to start the plate of meat and cheese around the table. She wasn't sure whether she was expected to make a sandwich of her cold meat, or just eat it with her knife and fork. She wanted a sandwich and decided to go ahead with it. Frank, sitting next to her, wordlessly passed her the mustard, and Susan, who usually refused mustard, spread some on her bread, she was so anxious not to break any rules.

"So where in Brooklyn?" said Judith, and Susan began to describe the quiet neighborhood in East New York, near Highland Park, where she had grown up. Talking about it, she felt homesick for it for the first time in her life.

"It's not like anyplace in New York that I've ever seen," she said. "Wooden houses. Houses like this, except not one-family. Some of them used to be one-family. In fact," she went on, "I grew up in a house that really *was* like this, now that I come to think of it, except that it had been divided into two apartments. So going upstairs still seems like taking a trip."

"You lived downstairs?" said Mr. Donnelly politely.

"Yes," she said. "In some ways it was one house, because my grandparents lived downstairs and my mother upstairs. . . ."

"Then you lived upstairs," said Frank briskly.

"No."

"You lived downstairs and your grandparents lived downstairs?"

"Yes," said Susan. "I lived with my grandparents."

"Susie, I never knew that!" said Cat, looking up. Susan was a little disappointed. She had pictured them talking about her— though in truth it now seemed hard to imagine them talking about anyone except Claudie. "Imagine your working with us all that time, and I never knew it," Cat went on. "You have to understand that to a social worker, such things are terribly interesting."

But Susan couldn't believe that Cat had never known she had lived with her grandparents. She had forgotten, that was all. "It *was* interesting," she said.

"So did you have two mothers, in effect?" said Judith.

Susan put down her sandwich and looked across the table at Cat. Cat's gray-streaked light brown hair stood away from her head—she had had a permanent, Susan speculated, but it had grown out, and she hadn't gotten around to doing anything about it. She seemed more like a mother than anyone Susan had ever known, and yet she was not like a mother at all, because—why?—because, like her daughter, she needed to be helped. "No," said Susan, nonetheless. "I think in a way I didn't have any mother."

Then a wave of courage—from then on, mustard would always taste like courage to Susan—passed over her. "Would you like another daughter?" she said. "I still need a mother. A third mother."

"Join the crowd," said Cat. She reached across the table and Susan, biting her ham sandwich, had just enough mustard-courage left to reach out and put her hand over Cat's and hold it. She held it a moment longer than she thought Cat would expect her to.

JUDITH INVITED SUSAN AND TONY to Boston to celebrate Frank's birthday, which was a week after Susan's, in April. Susan and Tony had planned to attend a march in New York that weekend, to protest the war in Vietnam. At first Susan hadn't gone on these marches because she felt self-conscious, but when she joined one for the first time, she was relieved, and even elated. She liked the simplicity of having an opinion she was sure of, and letting other people know it. She liked walking in the middle of the street. She felt less helpless about the war, though that didn't make sense.

Still, they agreed to go to Boston. Judith said they should come for dinner on Saturday and spend the night. Judith and Frank didn't have an extra bed, only a narrow sofa, but they'd drag the mattress from their own bed into the living room, and sleep on the box spring themselves. Susan hadn't seen Judith since her visit to Bridgeport when the family was thinking about sending Claudie to boarding school—now a forgotten idea, just months later—and then she'd felt a little uncomfortable with her, but Tony was unhappy, taking law school classes at night and working in the law firm, days, and Tony wanted to go.

"Frank's having a hard time with his thesis," Tony said. Frank was a graduate student at Harvard. "We can be miserable together. Life feels easier when your big brother is having trouble."

Tony had two brothers, but he always spoke of Douglas as "my brother Doug" and Frank as "my brother." Doug had been living in California for several years. He had been in architecture school but had quit as soon as he turned twenty-six and no longer needed a student deferment to avoid being drafted. Now he worked for a landscaping firm. "Plants things," said Tony. "Prunes trees. Frank says Douglas's middle name should be Fir. He'd like us all better if we were trees."

Susan and Tony took the train to Boston and the Boston subway to Frank and Judith's house in Somerville. Susan had never been to Boston before. She was interested in the subway, which had short trains and a simpler map than the New York subway, and had a different feel and sound. When they came out into the street, the houses weren't quite like houses in New York, and the street signs were different, and even the trees: In New York, the leaves had come out on the trees, but Boston was a week or so behind.

Susan had visited Tony's family in Bridgeport twice now, the second time with Tony, and on that evening they'd driven to New Haven and gone to a play. Bridgeport, too, and New Haven, she supposed, had bus stop signs of a slightly different design from New York's, but she had never thought about it.

Frank and Judith lived in a second-floor apartment and Judith came down the stairs to let them in. As she led the way up, she called over her shoulder, "We have additional company. I hope you don't mind. This *stray* from my family." She spoke in a loud, joking voice and Susan, coming ahead of Tony, could see an open apartment door before her, and then the doorway was filled with a big, grinning man in a sweater who had dark hair and dark clothes but round rosy cheeks like a child's. He turned out to be Judith's cousin, Dan Tobin, a resident in pediatrics at Yale. He was in Boston on a quick trip to see his girlfriend, but she'd come down with a cold and refused to let him in.

"She goes to Wellesley," he explained instantly. "I thought I could sneak into her dorm, but when I got there she sent her roommate out to shoo me away, and then when I wouldn't go, she turned up in her bathrobe and insisted she had a fever and I had to go back to New Haven. So I came here."

"Did you think she was making it up?" said Susan, concerned.

"You think she's just breaking up with me?" Dan said. "I think it's half and half."

"So aren't you upset?" said Susan.

"Of course I am." Dan laughed. They'd been standing up, all this time, as though whether Susan and Tony stayed depended on what Dan said. Susan had brought an overnight bag that had once belonged to her grandmother. It was a satchel made of heavy plastic that was supposed to look like leather, and it had two handles, which had been biting into Susan's hands until finally she picked up the bag and carried it in her arms like a bag of groceries. She'd been holding it, all this time, meeting Dan. Now, at last, she put it down, and Tony put down his small suitcase, and they took off their coats.

Judith and Frank, Susan saw, had actual bookcases, being married—not just bricks and boards—but Frank's desk was a door resting on two file cabinets, just like Tony's.

She followed Judith into the kitchen. Frank was at the library, but Tony sat down and began to ask Dan about medical school, probably to assure himself that he wouldn't be happier there, Susan thought. She could hear them in the next room.

Judith had prepared a tray of crackers and cheese, and now she poured glasses of red wine. "You could bring this out," she said, and Susan removed her own glass from the tray and carried the tray out. She put it on the floor, because there was no furniture near the two men, and then thought better of it and handed each of them a glass of wine, but then she went back to the kitchen and leaned against the old-fashioned, much-painted kitchen cabinets, which reminded her of her grandmother's, her glass of wine in her hand. Judith was slicing mushrooms in a way Susan didn't know about—vertically, through the stems.

"I love mushrooms," Susan said.

"Me too," said Judith. "So how do you like the *goyim?*"

"What?" Susan couldn't understand for a moment; she thought Judith meant something about food.

"This family I've married into and you seem to be about to marry into," Judith said. Judith had bad posture, Susan noticed. She was hunched over the cutting board so that her head hung down. She had to keep tossing it to get her hair out of her eyes. "When you turned up," she went on, "it was like Robinson Crusoe spotting Friday—someone else of my own species! I never thought it would happen."

Susan was offended, especially since Judith had said something like this when they first met and didn't seem to remember, but interested that Judith thought she and Tony were going to get married. But she didn't want to be the same species as Judith and a different one from the Donnellys.

"Claudie and I are pretty close," she said.

"Watch out for Claudie," said Judith. "Have you met Cathy?"

"No."

"I like her better," Judith said. "She's independent—doesn't come around much. But I like them all, actually. They're different from my family. I have one intense sister. She has big breasts and I have small breasts, so according to family myth, she's the sexy one and I'm not—and sure enough, I never had a date in college, and she got married at the end of her freshman year and already has two kids. In the Donnelly family, at least the myths go in more directions than that. It's freer."

"I think so, too," said Susan, intrigued despite herself. It was true that Judith was flat-chested.

They heard Frank come in and they went out to the living room to say hello. Tony sat down on the floor and emptied his suitcase to take out the birthday presents he had brought for Frank: a wide-brimmed hat Tony said looked just like Frank, and a crucifix, the kind that hangs on a wall, made of heavy dark varnished wood with a small metal figure nailed to it.

"I don't understand," Susan had said. "Is it a joke?"

"Sort of."

Frank shook his head over and over at the presents. "Now what am I supposed to do with this?" he said, about the crucifix.

"You could put it over your bed," Tony said, shrugging. "You could use it as a paperweight."

"Did you buy one for yourself, too?" said Frank.

"I already have one," said Tony.

"You do?" Susan had never seen a crucifix in his apartment.

She saw Dan watching the brothers. She could see that he was trying to make it out. All of the witnesses were Jewish, she reflected. No one could say what was Donnelly and what was something broader.

Judith made beef stroganoff for dinner. Susan watched so she would be able to try it herself. The beef was cooked quickly, and sour cream was added. They ate it with a salad and more red wine, sitting on the living room floor and leaning on pillows, while candles, stuck into chianti bottles so colored wax dripped on their straw baskets, lit the room.

Dan said, "I got what I deserve, coming to see Eileen on my only day off. I should have gone to New York to see my grandmother, but I don't like her."

"Is she sick?" said Judith. He meant the grandmother they didn't share, apparently. They were first cousins, she'd told Susan.

"Yes, she's failing fast," he said.

"Why don't you like her?" said Susan.

"She's not very nice. I know, you're not allowed to say that about an old person, but she isn't. I should feel sorry for her. She should have been a scientist, instead of having seven kids she never liked—but then I wouldn't have existed."

"Do you see her often?" said Susan.

"Hardly ever."

There followed a discussion of grandparents, and when they had all last seen their grandparents. Judith won: She had seen her grandmother—also the one she didn't share with Dan—just two weeks earlier. Susan hadn't been to see Leah and Ezra for far longer than that.

"You're lucky," said Dan to Judith. "You have two good grandmothers. Now Bubbi—I'd go to see *her.*" Bubbi was the one Dan and Judith did share.

"She yells at you," said Dan. "She wants to know who I'm going out with, what they're teaching me in medical school, what's wrong with my patients. Usually she thinks I'm not doing the right thing for them." And then, impulsively, to Judith, "Let's call her up."

And so they did, right then, on the phone in the kitchen, as their food grew cold on the plates on the floor.

"Bubbi, Bubbi," Susan heard Dan shout. "You know who this is? Danny. Isn't that a surprise? And Bubbi, you know where I am? At Judy's. How do you like that? Judy, in Boston. Yeah, Judy who got married." Susan watched them through the kitchen doorway, Judith waiting for her turn, grinning, while Dan, who was a little fat (that was what made him seem big), talked to Bubbi. He wasn't tall, he was Judith's height. His hairline was starting to recede. All the time he was explaining to his grandmother where he was, he was pointing at Judith, jabbing his finger in the air as if poor Bubbi could see it. Susan sipped some more wine and ate her dinner slowly, thinking about each piece of beef, each slice of mushroom, each noodle. She wanted this evening to pass slowly, as if there was something about it she was supposed to notice.

That night, Dan slept on the couch and she and Tony slept on the floor in the same room. They each undressed in the bathroom and got under the covers right away. Then Susan wanted to talk, but when she said something—"What a good dinner that was!"— neither man answered her. She was aware of Dan, and she began to think he didn't like her. She'd said some bad things about grandmothers, in that discussion, and even though he didn't like one of his own grandmothers, he surely disapproved of Susan. He had been friendly at first, but then, she thought, distant.

She had trouble falling asleep. At last she got up and went into the kitchen for a glass of water. She tiptoed in her bare feet on the cold floor, but she was hoping she'd awaken Dan—not Tony, to her surprise—and that he'd come talk to her. Probably, she argued with herself, Dan had barely noticed her at all. He was understandably upset about the girl at Wellesley who was breaking up with him. She swallowed the water, got back into bed beside Tony, and tried to forget where she was and who was in the room with her. It was fairly unusual for her to spend the night with Tony, and it had certainly never happened before without their making love when they got into bed. This made him seem more like a stranger.

She thought she had never fallen asleep, but she must have, because she woke up when Dan, dressed, tiptoed past their bed on the floor—not looking at it—picked up a bag, and then opened the apartment door and went out. From her place on the floor, Susan could see the last of him, and see the door close slowly behind him, and then she heard the snap lock find its opening with a small, sharp noise. He had said he had to leave early, but he hadn't said how early, and she'd assumed they would have breakfast with him. It wasn't important, except that he didn't like her. She would have been friendly at breakfast.

She couldn't fall asleep again. Finally she got up and took a shower and dressed. When she came out of the bathroom there was still no one else awake. It was Sunday morning—at home she would have eaten breakfast and gone out to buy the *Times*. Here she curled up on the couch, which Dan had straightened before leaving. A madras spread was arranged over it. Susan had a book in her bag, but she didn't feel like reading it. She chose another book from the bookcase—*Tom Jones*, which she had always meant to read—but she didn't like it. She was cold.

Finally she heard Frank get up and use the bathroom, and she followed him into the kitchen. He made coffee and she offered to help fix breakfast. She was hungry by now.

"It's already nine o'clock," said Frank. "I was going to go to a museum with you guys, but that was if I got up at seven and put in some work on my thesis. Now I'd better stay here." Tony and Susan weren't going back to New York until late afternoon.

"Tony says you don't like writing it," said Susan.

"Hell, it's not even *true*," Frank said. "I don't even believe what I'm writing anymore. I set out to prove something and it turns out to be wrong."

"So are you giving it up?" said Susan.

"No, I'm proving it anyway. It's about Erasmus. Nobody will read it, nobody will care. It wouldn't make sense to prove it's *not* true—nobody but me ever thought it *was* true."

"Are you going to be a professor when it's done?" asked Susan.

Frank laughed, and began stirring frozen orange juice. "Ask me in two years," he said. There was a pause and he added, "I presume you're going to be around in two years?"

"I'll be around," said Susan, and then she remembered something. "I thought none of you liked Latin," she said. "Didn't your father say none of you studied Latin?"

"Oh, I've had decades of Latin," said Frank. "But I don't like to spend my Sunday afternoons reading Cicero with Dad, for some reason."

"But you wouldn't mind if I did?" she said. "I mean, if it ever happens."

"Be my guest," said Frank.

He made her feel better, and she was sorry he couldn't go to the Museum of Fine Arts with them. She went with Tony and Judith, and they didn't have a good time. Her throat felt scratchy, and she thought she might be coming down with a cold, or maybe it was only lack of sleep. Tony was restless, and hurried from painting to painting, looking as if all of them reminded him of something troubling. Judith talked about Frank's thesis and her job—she worked for a science journal. Susan would have wanted to see the paintings if she hadn't been so tired, and she was disgusted with herself because she couldn't get interested in them. She was glad when it was time to leave.

In the train, late that afternoon, Susan leaned against Tony and fell asleep as soon as they began to move. She woke once, resettled herself, and slept again. When she really woke up, Tony was gone. She looked out the window. It was getting dark, and they were passing bare fields and a little woods, then a house, then more bare fields. She heard someone say they would be in New Haven soon, and after a while she noticed buildings—she thought she might have slept again—and in the growing dark, they pulled past streets that looked like the edge of a city. Susan looked out, just in case Dan, home now, happened to pass near these tracks. When the train stopped, the lights went out, and the conductor said they were changing from diesel to electric power. In the dark, Tony came back. He had gone to the snack bar and had bought a sandwich and coffee.

"I didn't bring you anything because you were asleep," he said. "You can have mine, if you want. I'll go back for more, once the lights come on again."

"Why can't I go myself?"

"No reason. I'm just being the guy. Do you want to? You look sleepy."

This annoyed Susan, for some reason. Of course she wanted to go and choose her own food. She wanted to find the bathroom and wash her face, too. She waited until the lights were on and the train was moving again, and then she climbed over Tony and walked through the swaying train to the snack car. She bought a tuna fish sandwich and a container of milk, and as she accepted her change, she knew she was going to have a fight with Tony, and that there was no good reason for it, but in another moment she had forgotten this was going to happen, and when she started asking him why Frank persisted in writing his thesis when he was so unhappy, a few miles later, she didn't remember that she was asking questions with any other purpose than to find out the answers.

"He's not that unhappy," Tony said. "He likes to sound dramatic."

"He sounded pretty unhappy to me. He's writing a thesis he doesn't believe in. That's terrible."

"You're being naive," said Tony. "People don't always get something to do that's absolutely perfect. You think everybody has to have some sort of ideal life."

"I didn't mean *you*," said Susan. "Although I certainly don't understand why you're going to law school when you hate it."

"Look, I thought I wanted to be a lawyer."

"You've never liked anything about the law firm, not one thing," she said. "You don't like it any better now that you're in law school, and you don't like law school. But you keep forcing yourself to go there."

"So what do you think I ought to do, if you have everything worked out?" Tony said.

"I don't have everything worked out."

"You have yourself all worked out," he said. "You want to get your M.S.W. and save the poor."

This was more or less true. Susan had been talking about going to school at night, too, but she knew she'd never see Tony if they both had evening classes, maybe on different days, and she had put it off. But she was stung by the way he'd said it.

"I'm not walking around in an idealistic fog," she said. "I don't think there's anything wrong with trying to help people."

"If you don't use them, there isn't."

"What do you mean, use them?"

"Look," he said, "I don't know how you are with the people at the clinic, but I look at the way you idealize my family and *simplify* everything—now you want Frank to quit graduate school, of all things. Do you know what it took for him to get as far as he has? Do you know how my father would feel if he quit?"

"I just thought there was no reason to write a thesis he didn't believe in. It's worse than that," Susan said. "It's dishonest."

"And Claudie," said Tony. "You think your own family is the only crazy family. But my father hangs around at the edge of everything—and my mother's just frantic—and there's Claudie. *Look at Claudie.* You think my family is so fantastic, but you refuse to look at Claudie."

"I don't. I don't refuse to look at Claudie. I love Claudie."

"Oh, you just like to say that. You barely know her."

This was further than they had ever gone. Susan felt as if she had put her hand to her hair and it had all come away. She was too angry and afraid to cry or talk. She dug her book out and didn't read it, but kept it open.

"I'm tired," said Tony, in a slightly softer tone. "I don't think it's a good idea to talk now." That made Susan want to talk, but he rolled his coat into a pillow and put his head back against it, his face turned away from her. He didn't move until their train arrived in New York. Then they walked down the platform, almost in silence, and headed for the subway. Susan thought that Tony would go straight to his own place, but he seemed to be taking her home. She was tired and didn't care. They went to her apartment and as soon as they got in he took off his shoes and lay down on her bed. "Do you have anything we can eat?" he said. "I'm starved."

It was nine o'clock. "You could have said something before," Susan said. She cooked some eggs and toast. They were eating, still not talking much, when the doorbell rang.

"That's funny," said Susan. "Maybe it's Lennie," although that didn't seem likely. It could be Dan, she fantasized wildly—"I wanted to tell you that I didn't dislike you and so I called up Judith and got your address and took the train. . . ." No. Judith didn't even know her address, only her phone number. She couldn't just buzz to admit this person, and the intercom to the lobby didn't work. In her slippers, she went downstairs. Tony offered to go along but she shook her head.

It was her mother, now rattling the doorknob and going back to the doorbells to push the bell once more, accompanied by a man Susan didn't know. The inside door was glass, and as Susan came from the elevator she watched Paula, who was dressed in a short skirt and a black jacket. Her mother patted her hair and tugged her skirt with a half-conscious, eager gesture that Susan liked, and so she opened the door with more amusement and affection welling up in her than she might have felt otherwise.

"All right, what are you doing here?" she said, as if Paula were her errant little sister.

"I know, I should have phoned—I'm sorry. I had to introduce you to Jay."

The man had come up behind Paula. He was taller than she was, balding, wearing a brown coat with a gold-colored collar. It looked cheap to Susan, who had never thought previously for one second about men's clothes except her grandfather's pants, so baggy she had hypothesized that he bought them at an Old Man's Pants store.

"This is my daughter, Susan," said Paula, and Susan and Jay did not shake hands but smiled at each other. "Susan, Jay is a wonderful man, and I wanted you to be the first to meet him. We've known each other only a few weeks, but we've just decided to get married."

"I made her come here," Jay put in now. "I don't know how late it is"—actually, it wasn't all that late—"but I said to her, 'Paula, I can't wait another minute before I meet this wonderful daughter you keep talking about.' "

"You'd better come upstairs," said Susan. Her hand on the open door was trembling. She held it farther open for Paula and Jay, but Jay took it out of her hand and closed it firmly behind them all. When they reached the elevator, he pushed the button. Susan knew it had been Paula's idea to come, not his. She tried to smile at her mother in the elevator. "So, congratulations, I guess," she said.

"You guess?"

"Congratulations."

Tony had finished his supper, she saw when she opened the door of the apartment, and he was lying on her bed reading a magazine. Her own half-eaten plate of food was still on the little table she kept in the main room of her apartment.

"Oh! Did we interrupt your supper?" said Paula. Then she saw Tony, who was getting up and coming toward them. "And you have company."

"This is Tony," said Susan. "I told you about Tony." They had talked about him many times.

"Oh, *Tony*," said Paula. "What a pleasure! Oh, I've heard all about *you*."

"How do you do, Mrs. Sternfeld?" said Tony.

"Paula," said Paula. "And this is Jay."

"Jay and my mother," said Susan, and she found herself needing to suppress a nervous giggle, "have just decided to get married."

"Oh," said Tony. "Oh, well, isn't that great?" Then he shook hands with Jay. "Can I get you a drink?" he said. "Though I'm not sure Susan *has* anything to drink."

"Coffee," said Jay, and Susan went to prepare some, glad to have something to do. Paula followed her into the kitchen.

"I'm just so excited I can't stand it," she said. "I'm not going to ask you what you think. I know you've only just met him."

"What does he do?" said Susan.

"Oh, Susan, he's in a lovely business. He's going to open a pet store."

"Really? What does he do now?"

"He's had a lot of jobs," Paula said. "He's been working for a company that makes pet food, that's what gave him the idea. He's going into business with a friend of his, who's lending him the money."

Susan made coffee, and then she asked Jay about the pet store. It was going to be in a little shopping plaza in Queens, he said. He began to talk about the animals he would keep—fish, kittens, puppies. "Birds, I guess," he said. "Definitely birds."

"Do you know how to take care of birds?" said Susan. "It must be complicated. Don't they get sick a lot?"

"No, it's not too complicated," said Jay, who was a quick-moving middle-aged man with glasses, and eyebrows that arched above them. "I have a knack for that sort of thing."

Susan was warming her hands on her mug of coffee, not drinking it. She turned to Paula. "So, I haven't seen you for a long time," she said. "How did you and Jay meet?" She thought that if she was polite for a little while, she could then say it was late, and all these people—Tony too—would leave. If she were alone, maybe she'd feel better. But first she had to ask three polite questions that weren't hostile.

Paula and Jay had met at a wedding—a friend of Paula's had married a friend of Jay's. They had danced together, and begun to talk. Being at a wedding had started them talking about weddings and marriage, even that first night.

"This time I want a nice wedding," said Paula. "Your father and I—well, it was dull."

Jay was talking to Tony, and under cover of their conversation, Susan said to her mother in a low voice, "But are you sure you want to marry him? You only just met him." Then she saw that it wasn't a polite question.

"Oh, I was afraid you'd say that," Paula said. "That's why I brought him, so you could see that this is the right thing. I thought maybe you'd see. But you have so little experience about these things. Trust me."

"You're in love with him?" said Susan. She had abandoned politeness.

"That's what I *mean*, honey. I don't think you know how it feels, when you actually meet the right person. I hope you find out soon."

"I have feelings," said Susan, sorry that she had told her mother how easy and quiet things were between her and Tony. Her mother made her feel pallid, not adventurous, not passionate.

Her mother looked at Tony, who had stood up and was carrying Susan's plate into the kitchen. He could be heard scraping the uneaten food into the garbage.

"You know, sweetheart, you asked about birds," Jay said now, turning to Susan. "Maybe you'd like a little parakeet for your apartment here. Sometimes the landlord doesn't let you have a dog or a cat, but it's nice for a single girl to have something to come home to. A little blue one or a green one. Sometimes you can get them to eat out of your hand."

Susan stood up, carrying her coffee mug toward the kitchen. She wanted Tony to stop cleaning up. She knew he was doing it to get away from Paula and Jay, and although she too wanted to get away from them, she was angry with him. "I loathe parakeets," she said as she walked across the room.

"Oh, well, it was just an idea," Jay said.

"I must say," said Susan, in a high voice, "I'm a little surprised at the way you're talking about these animals. It doesn't sound responsible at all. You talk about them as if they were a bunch of mops or boots or something. You don't seem to have any feelings about animals, and as far as I can tell, you don't know anything about them. They'll all die the first month." She knew that wasn't fair; Jay had said very little.

"Well, you have to expect some losses," Jay said quickly, uneasily. "That's true of any business."

"Susan," said Paula.

Susan carried her mug into the kitchen. "Would you stop it?" she said to Tony in a loud voice. "You're just showing off, trying to make my mother think you help me when you never do." Then, in tears, she turned back to Jay and Paula. "You're both appalling. You're both absolutely appalling. You don't know what feeling is."

They left quickly after that. Paula did not try to make up with her. "I'm sorry we came at an inconvenient time," she said. When they were gone, Susan lay down on the bed, sobbing. She kept thinking she was going to stop, but then she cried some more. At last Tony came over to her and sat down on the bed next to her. He put his hand on her back and began to stroke her. "You didn't like him," he said.

"I don't care about him," said Susan.

"You must. What a stepfather."

"It's not important."

"Then what's wrong?"

"I don't know," she said. She got up and went into the bathroom and washed her face with cool water. When she came out, Tony was still sitting where he had been.

"It's you and me," she said. "It's what happened on the train."

"Oh, Susan. I was so tired. I didn't know what I was saying."

"I want you to be excited about me," said Susan.

"But I am," Tony said. "I've always been excited about you. Don't you know that?"

"Do you think—" She lay down on the bed and looked up at him. "Do you think we'll ever get married?"

"Of course. Of course we're going to get married," said Tony. It wasn't the first time the word had been mentioned, but it was the first time he'd said it directly. "Don't you think so? Don't you *want* to get married?"

"I'm as crazy as my mother," said Susan. "I'm tired of being sensible. Let's get married."

"All right," said Tony. "Tomorrow?"

"No," said Susan. "In three months. Let's get married in three months."

"Fine," said Tony, "but there's one problem. I've been trying to think how to tell you. I should have told you on the train. I'm going to quit law school and quit my job, and I want to leave New York."

"Leave New York?"

"Would you leave New York? Would you live somewhere else?"

"Sure," said Susan quickly, thinking of the bus stop signs in Boston, and of her grandparents. She would turn her back—joyfully—on her loving grandparents, who had raised her. She would leave New York.

"Where do you want to live?" she said.

"I don't know. Let's go to bed. Let's talk about it later."

Again, they didn't make love. They were too tired—Susan was glad Tony didn't seem to want to, because she was exhausted. In the morning, Tony had to hurry home to change before work. They didn't talk at all. Susan wondered how real the conversation of the night before had been. Could she tell Lennie? She decided she could tell Lennie, but no one else. She told Lennie exactly what had happened, and asked for her opinion, and Lennie thought the conversation meant that Susan was going to marry Tony.

TONY SAID HE WAS GOING to buy a rocker, and Susan could go along, if she liked. It was Saturday morning and she was glad to go, but she didn't like the sound of buying a rocker. A rocking chair, he meant. It had taken her a second to understand. She'd seen Tony only once during the week since they'd gone to Boston, and he hadn't mentioned getting married. Maybe he had thought it was all a joke. It hadn't been a joke for her, but if he was buying furniture, he might be planning to stay put after all.

They went to an unpainted furniture store on Third Avenue. "Why a rocking chair?" Susan asked.

"I like them," he said. Then, "I feel like working on something. I'd buy lumber and *make* something, but I don't have tools."

"Like Kennedy," said Susan.

"Kennedy?"

"President Kennedy used to sit in a rocker. For his back."

"You'll see," said Tony. "I'll never get you out of it."

He didn't like the quality of workmanship of the furniture in the store. It looked fine to Susan, but Tony pointed out how edges didn't quite meet, and how the dowels in the back of the rocker didn't fill the holes in which they were placed. They went to another store, a few blocks away. There Tony approved of what he saw and Susan could see the difference as well. They rocked the pale pine rocking chair, back and forth, to make sure it was balanced, so it wouldn't travel, Tony said.

Now they had a long way to carry it. "It's a good thing you came," said Tony. They held it between them by the thick dowels under the armrests. It was difficult to walk, and they had to hurry across streets. "I feel as if we're carrying someone frail and important," said Susan. "My grandmother."

As they were mounting a curb, Tony said suddenly, "Do you think we could live in New Haven?"

"New Haven? Why New Haven?" Susan found herself looking around, as if they'd somehow wandered from lower Manhattan to New Haven, Connecticut. She thought of Judith's cousin, Dan, but they hardly knew him. He was no reason to live in New Haven.

"It's not a bad place," said Tony. "There are bookstores and theaters and restaurants. Yale is there."

"You mean when we get married," said Susan; in her imagination her grandmother slid off the rocking chair and was left behind on the sidewalk while Susan departed, a bride.

"Of course." She supposed it would be possible to move the rocking chair to New Haven. They would have other things to move, of course, and they would rent a truck—Tony could drive—or even call a moving company. They could move anywhere.

"If you want to leave New York," she said, "we could live somewhere exciting. Chicago . . ." She thought of San Francisco but that seemed extravagant. "Maybe you should look for a job at a newspaper."

Tony didn't answer for a while. Then he said, "I'm thinking about going to work at the printing company."

"For your *father*?"

"Well, with him. He's not in charge of much of it. It wouldn't be *for* him."

"You don't want to do that!" She stopped, and the chair knocked against the sidewalk.

"I think maybe it makes sense," he said. "No, I think maybe this time it *is* what I want—but I don't want to live in Bridgeport. It's too close to them. New Haven is better."

Susan had been in New Haven once, and had the impression of muted yellow dappled against gray—leaves and the Yale buildings, and sycamores with varicolored bark: a dappled city.

"Are you sure this isn't another thing like law school? I can't believe you want to work with your father," she said.

He didn't answer. She was thinking she might like living in New Haven—she liked being surprised by Tony, and she hadn't thought this was coming. In New Haven, it seemed, he would be someone she couldn't quite know. She liked that.

"I need to go into this store," said Tony, pausing. "I need a brush, and stain for the chair."

"Paint it red—or maybe black," she said.

"No, I think a walnut stain." She waited outside the store, a hardware store, holding the chair, but it was heavy, and after a few minutes she set it down and sat in it. She rocked back and forth gently on the sidewalk. She tried to imagine Tony working at the printing plant. He would come home from work, and she would be rocking in this chair—walnut—in their living room, with sycamores outside the window. "No one in that firm can line up paper properly," he'd say.

"What would you do there?" she asked when he came out. Come to think of it, he didn't mean he'd run a printing press himself.

"They need someone to oversee the bigger jobs they've been getting," he said. "They're doing more complicated stuff, and nobody keeps track." He laughed at her because she was still sitting and rocking, while he stood before her, as if presenting himself to a receptionist. Now he gave her the parcel from the hardware store to carry, and he took the chair, carrying it upside down by its arms. "Things run by themselves until there's trouble," he continued. "I hate hearing Dad talk. He just lets things happen." He put down the chair while they waited for a light to change. "But I'd like to get ink on my hands, too," he said, looking at his hands.

She watched him for much of the afternoon while he sanded and stained the chair. She liked the way it looked. When she left him, late in the afternoon—she was meeting Lennie—he was almost finished. His hands were stained walnut like the chair.

A few days later, on the phone, Tony said, "Can you handle a Catholic wedding? Can you deal with a priest?" Susan had assumed they'd get married at the Municipal Building, in a civil ceremony. There had been no evidence that Tony still thought of himself as a Catholic, except the present he'd given to Frank.

"But would a priest marry you to me?" It was something else about him she didn't understand. It made her proud of herself, that a man she couldn't understand wanted to marry her.

"A priest I know, not just any priest. He's excited about it."

"You *told* him?"

"I called him."

Susan liked the thought that Tony had told someone they were getting married. She didn't care whether or not she was married by a priest—it seemed so unlikely that it had to be more fascinating than upsetting. Mostly, she was glad it was time to tell people. If Tony had told some priest, she could tell her mother, and she called Paula now, who was cold about the idea, and seemed to think that Susan was trying to steal the attention of the family by getting married before she did, not that there was a family to care. When Susan called her father's house, his wife, Sonia, was the only one home, and she was thrilled, as if she and Susan had been through prom corsages and acne together. She asked Susan many questions about Tony, and seemed to approve of the answers almost before she heard them, religion and all. Susan was uncomfortable. She didn't know how she *wanted* these people to behave.

Her grandparents had to be told in person, and Susan went to see them one Sunday afternoon. They had lunch, and in the middle of it, Susan said, "I have something to tell you. Tony and I have decided to get married."

"To get married?" her grandfather said. "Such a big step! You have enough money? You like his family?" He sat back in his chair.

His eyes looked happy, though they looked as if they hurt, Susan thought now, and there were red veins in them. He squinted at Susan under his eyebrows.

"*Mazel tov*," said her grandmother, who had just given Susan a cup of her weak coffee and a second slice of cheese danish from the big ring in the middle of the table. Her grandmother did not sit down again, but began to carry things out to the kitchen, while Susan drank her coffee. She looked over her shoulder when Ezra talked to Susan, and shook her head quickly, without speaking, when Susan offered to help, as if it would be impossibly trouble-some for her to help, as if Susan didn't know where everything was kept. Her grandfather was fascinated by this prospective wedding, and wanted to know everything. Susan even told him about the priest, which troubled him—he wouldn't have objected to a civil wedding, but he worried about Catholics. Still, he listened and asked questions about that, too. He wanted to know whether Susan was expected to convert, and Susan told him that she wasn't going to convert, whether she was expected to or not.

Leah had a faded apron tied tightly over her dark skirt and white blouse. She walked with a pronounced stoop, slowly, and some-times stopped to rest, leaning her hand on the table or the sideboard near it. Then she would carry something else back into the kitchen: the plate of lettuce and tomatoes, the bowl of tuna and egg salad, the whitefish, the bagels. Each time she came and went again, while Susan chattered about Cat and Claudie and the rest of Tony's family, and about the advantages of living in New Haven, and how easy it would be for her to come on the train and visit, Leah looked less and less like someone who knew Susan well. She hardly said anything, so it was not what she said. It was an air of formality, Susan told Lennie later.

"At the beginning of the lunch," she said, "someone watching who had never seen us might have known that I had lived there. By the end, someone watching would have thought I was a stranger."

"No, Susan," said Lennie. "You're not fair to your grand-mother." Lennie had remained friendly with Susan's grandparents.

She'd once gone to see them alone, and she occasionally called them on the phone. Mother's Day had just passed, and she'd sent a card ("To My Friend's Grandmother"—they actually had such cards in the drugstore) to Susan's grandmother. Susan had never sent a Mother's Day card to anybody.

Susan waited for Cat to call and congratulate her (though her own mother was certainly not planning to call and congratulate Tony), but there was no phone call. Cat welcomed her with a hug when she and Tony went to Bridgeport for the day, late in May. "When is this wedding, anyway?" she said. "I'm so exhausted, Susan. You don't want a big party or anything, do you?"

"Of course not," said Susan. "Doesn't the bride's family do that, anyway?"

"Oh, we'll do something," said Cat. "I'm really happy. I'm really, really happy." Susan didn't like all the really's.

Claudie smiled at her and then left—she was going to the beach with friends.

"At least she has friends," said Cat. She rested a hand on Susan's shoulder and Susan felt better. It was as if Cat was saying, "*You* understand what I'm up against."

Then Cat left Susan and Tony alone and went off to the store to shop for dinner. Mr. Donnelly was working in the garage. He came in and shook Susan's hand warmly, murmuring something she couldn't hear, and put his arm briefly around Tony's shoulders. Then he went back outside, turning for a moment in the doorway. "There are things I should show you," he said to Tony, "now that you've made this decision. Tedious documents. But maybe they won't be tedious to you." He left the room, and they heard the back door close. Susan decided he was pleased that Tony was coming to work with him, even if he had an odd way of showing it.

Susan and Tony made cups of coffee and took them to Tony's old room, where, feeling gleefully reckless, they made love in his narrow bed and then tried to straighten the bedspread the way it had been before.

During dinner, Frank called, and both he and Judith spoke to

Susan and Tony. They sounded happy, especially Judith, who said she wasn't surprised. "You're going to live in New Haven," she said. "You'll have to look up my cousin Dan."

"I met your cousin, remember?" said Susan. "I don't think he liked me."

"Oh, he liked you all right," said Judith. "Let me give you his number," and Susan wrote it down. They knew little about New Haven. Maybe Dan would be able to tell them where to look for a place to live; maybe he could recommend a dentist.

Paula married Jay during the summer, and Susan and Tony attended the wedding, with a lunch afterward at a restaurant. Susan found she was unable to maintain an acknowledged fight with Paula, though they weren't getting along well—but Paula had married first, and that helped. Neither Susan nor her mother referred to the evening at Susan's house, and Susan bought her mother a broiler pan and a double boiler for a wedding present.

She and Tony decided to get married in October. By the end of the summer, they were almost living together at his apartment in New York. They went to Bridgeport one day and visited the priest, Father Michael, who turned out to be someone Tony had known all his life. He'd gone to school with Tony's brother Doug.

"We used to play basketball," Tony said.

They met Father Michael at his rectory and went to supper at the International House of Pancakes. Father Michael claimed that all the flavors of syrup were the same, with different food coloring added. "You think you can tell the difference," he said, "but it's an illusion. Try the blueberry syrup and the strawberry with your eyes closed. You won't be able to tell them apart."

"They taste different to me," said Susan, sipping them off her coffee spoon, and she was startled, a moment later, when he said, "How do you feel about marrying a Christian?"

She didn't think of Tony, who didn't go to church, as a Christian, but she didn't want to say that to the priest.

"I feel fine about it," she said, and he didn't ask her any more questions.

Susan was spending those weeks thinking not of Tony's religion but of leaving the clinic. She had never expected to stay this long, but now she found that she was fond of Bea and Helen, and could scarcely imagine life without seeing Lennie every day. She liked the work, too. She'd have to find a similar job in New Haven. She didn't know where to start, beyond writing letters to clinics on a list she had found at the library. She thought of calling Judith's cousin, but that seemed pointless—what would he know about jobs for Susan?—but then one day, having told herself again that it was silly, she called him. Dan remembered her and sounded glad to hear from her, and he even had some ideas. He knew a woman who did similar work. He would talk to her, and perhaps Susan should talk to her too, he said. She should come to New Haven. "You ought to come and look at the place, anyway, if you're going to live here," he said. He had a day off, a week later, and Susan agreed to take a vacation day and go to New Haven.

"I don't have a car, so I'm going to give you a walking tour," Dan said, when he met her at the train station, as promised, a week later. "How far can you walk?"

"I like to walk," said Susan. It was a cool summer day and she was full of energy. Dan didn't say much about jobs, except to give her a list of names his friend had provided—which he could have mailed to her. They walked through downtown, and crossed and recrossed the green, and then Dan took her to Wooster Square, an old-fashioned neighborhood with brownstones around a park. He said pizza had been invented in New Haven and they ate some for lunch. Then he said, "You're probably already tired, but what I really wanted was to take you up East Rock. Can you walk another thousand miles?"

Susan was happy. "Two thousand."

They took a bus to East Rock, after all. It was a red cliff sitting in the middle of a park, hugging the city on the northeast. They walked through the park. Dan knew how to find a path that took them through the woods. "You can climb up the front of the hill, but we won't try that today," he said, looking at her feet. Susan was in a skirt and sandals. Even on the fairly level paths in the woods, the sandals gave her trouble, but she was able to keep up with him. She liked the look of his sturdy body moving along deliberately just ahead of her on the narrow trail. He moved like a doctor, she found herself thinking, just like a pediatrician, which is what he was, and she decided it was thoroughness she was observing; he looked at everything and talked about it. To Susan the woods felt like country—or Girl Scout camp—cool and shadowy.

At last they emerged into a meadow. They had reached the top of the rock. There were benches ranged along a walk, near the edge of the cliff, and they could see the city and the harbor beyond it, and Long Island Sound stretching away from them. Behind them was a Civil War monument. They sat down on a bench, and Dan pointed out the street on which the bus had brought them, far below, and showed her where Wooster Square was, and the train station. He thought he could find his house but he wasn't sure. "Do you see that roof with all the chimneys?" he said. "It's a school. Now jump your eye over that green roof. . . ."

"I see, I see," said Susan at last, though she wasn't sure. Then he showed her the hospital where he worked and lots of Yale buildings.

Dan wasn't dressed for the woods either. He was in a white shirt and neat dark pants. He sat calmly on the bench beside her, pointing out places as he recognized them. Susan had been exhilarated all day, and here she was sitting next to Dan on top of a mountain, which seemed remarkable, even more remarkable than sitting opposite him at lunch or walking behind him in the woods. She wanted to think, and she stood up and walked around, leaving him there, taking pleasure in the thought that the day was not over yet, that she would go back to him on the bench.

She walked over to look at the monument, and then she walked around it. When she returned to the spot where she had begun, she saw that Dan had stood up and was walking along the line of benches, stopping to look at the view. Then he turned.

"Susan!" he called. "Susan, come here, I want to show you something." She hesitated and he must have thought she hadn't heard him. "Hey, Sternfeld," he called, a little louder. "Star-field!"

No one had ever called her that, but Susan had known for a long time that her name meant star-field. She pictured stars above a meadow, a wide meadow not too different from the one she was crossing now, to return to Dan.

"Hey! Hey, field of stars!" he called now, loudly, playing with the name, making enough noise that a woman walking with two school-age boys turned around to look at him, and then looked at Susan, and smiled at them. When Susan reached Dan, he put his arm around her, and moved her to where she could see what he'd spotted—a boat in the harbor—and then he kept his arm around her. "I'm awfully glad you came up," he said.

A bad thing had happened. Riding back to New York on the train, Susan saw that she was in love with Dan. He had kissed her when they separated, and then said, "I'm sorry. Don't think about this." Love of him and longing for him seemed to drench her and change her. She was afraid she would cry out his name as she sat on the train. She thought that maybe she already had. Her hands ached to touch him. She thought that she had never been this happy or this unhappy before.

She didn't hear from Dan, and she didn't mention him to Tony or anyone else. For a week—a hot, sticky week in which everyone at work was difficult, Tony was moody and quiet, and Lennie was unavailable because she had just fallen in love and it was going well—Susan felt torn in half. She didn't know what she wanted. She kept reminding herself that she was not yet married to Tony, that she had done nothing irrevocable. She could break up with him and call Dan. She wasn't sure what Dan would say, if she did that. Something in her argued that he had behaved as he did only because he knew she was getting married and nothing could come of it. Then she made a different argument: Dan was a conscientious man; he wouldn't act that way toward an engaged woman unless something important had happened to him.

At the end of the week, Claudie came to see them. She brought a kitten with her. She had smuggled it onto the train, hidden in a tote bag.

"Didn't it cry?" said Susan.

"Yes, it mewed. People kept looking around. I looked around, too," said Claudie. "I just kept looking accusingly at the woman behind me."

Tony, sitting in his rocking chair, laughed and laughed at her.

The kitten, a calico, was named Rain because Claudie had found her under a friend's porch on a rainy night. "I couldn't leave her home," said Claudie. "Mom would have dropped her in the garbage disposal by mistake."

"Your mother would *never*—" Susan began.

"Silver doesn't like her," said Claudie. Silver was the Donnellys' cat. "They fight."

"But that doesn't mean your mother would get rid of her," Susan persisted. The kitten, purring loudly, curled up on Susan's lap, and she stroked it. It seized her finger in its claws and licked it with a scrap of rough tongue.

"I'm glad you're going to be living nearby," said Claudie seriously, as if rescues were going to be necessary.

Tony was brighter than he'd been all week, thinking up ways to entertain his sister. It was too hot to do most of them, and finally they just went out to dinner in a restaurant with air-conditioning— that was the main treat—but he was careful and kind with her. At night Susan heard Claudie crying from her bed on Tony's couch. As she lay and listened to her, she felt married to Tony. She didn't have to make a decision.

The day Susan and Tony were to be married, they dressed in the morning in their wedding clothes. Tony wore a suit, and Susan a short white dress with long sleeves. Then she put on her regular lightweight coat, a tan trenchcoat, and she and Tony took the train to Bridgeport. Lennie was to be the maid of honor, and she met them at Grand Central Station.

They were to be married at Mr. Donnelly's church by Father Michael. Susan's father and Sonia were coming, and so were Judith and Frank and Cathy and Claudie, along with Tony's parents. Doug had sent a friendly letter from California. Paula and Jay were on vacation in Florida, and Susan's grandparents were too old to come, though she had sent them an invitation and instructions, so they wouldn't feel left out.

It was the first time Susan had been on the train since her day in New Haven with Dan, and she noted that she did not feel sentimental and odd about it. She was glad the day had taken place but that was all. Tony seemed solid and untroubled beside her, though he looked out the window and they didn't say much. In Bridgeport, Frank met them at the station, and they all gathered at the Donnelly house, where Sonia, weepy and bright-eyed, fussed over Susan's hair and dress. Susan met Cathy for the first time; she was a pleasant young woman who looked like her father and who would clearly never burst into tears and hang on anyone, as Claudie was in the habit of doing. Cathy was a physical therapist who lived in Philadelphia. In her presence, Susan noted, Claudie was quieter, listening intently to conversations. Cat, today, was wearing high heels and looked as if she might fall, and she almost forgot to turn off the stove when they left—she'd been giving people coffee all morning. It was she who herded them all out to the sidewalk, and figured out who should ride in which car. She was friendly and businesslike with Susan's father, who was shy, and with Sonia.

At the last minute, as they were climbing into the cars, Susan looked down the street and saw an old man walking toward them who reminded her of her grandfather, and then she realized that it was Ezra himself, in a dark suit and a white shirt and a hat, a newspaper under his arm, stumping along this street in Bridgeport as if he had lived there all his life. For a moment she didn't say anything, wanting, for some reason, to deny it to herself. If they stepped quickly, they could get into the cars and be gone before he reached them.

Then she saw that Lennie was looking down the street as well, and Susan managed to speak first. "Isn't that a rather *familiar* old gentleman coming along?" she said.

Her father ran to scold his father for coming without letting them know. "You could have driven up with Sonia and me!" he said.

"I had business in the area," said Ezra, a nonsensical notion. He had taken the train and then a city bus, having asked for directions at the station. Susan put her arms around him, but then she started to sob, and all she could say was, "Grandma didn't want to come?"

She had been telling herself that it was such a small wedding, and Leah and Ezra were so frail, it was not significant that Leah had scarcely listened to her descriptions of where and when.

"Oh, your grandma," said Ezra. "A foolish woman."

Her father gave her away. Her grandfather studied everything in the church, and Susan thought he had probably never been in a Catholic church, or any church, before. He walked up and down the aisles looking at the stained glass windows, the names on the memorial pews, the votive candles. During the ceremony he stood still a few yards off and watched. The church was almost empty, and Father Michael obviously thought Ezra was a wonder. It didn't matter that he never sat down.

Her father took the entire crowd out to lunch. Susan clung to Tony. She kept wishing she could take her hair down. It was pinned up in a French twist, something Lennie had taught her. Tony was quiet but gradually began to smile as the day wore on, and smiled more and more. He had dimples—Susan was always forgetting that. Every once in a while, he reached out to stroke the center of her back, a series of little pats.

At the restaurant, they were all seated at one long table. Susan wasn't hungry; the meal seemed to go on for a long time. After a while she realized that one chair had been empty for fifteen minutes or so, and then that it was Claudie who was missing. She glanced at Cat and couldn't tell whether Cat was worried or not—she was nervously moving her hands, talking politely with Sonia. She looked as if she were interviewing Sonia, and she looked strong and able, except for the nervous hands.

Tony was sitting next to Susan but he was listening to Frank, who was on his other side. "When we got married," Frank was saying, "I was *glad* Judith wasn't Catholic. I told her, anything but the Catholics. Anything but Dad's church."

"That's not how I felt," Tony said.

"Guess not," said Frank. "You're a puzzle."

Tony was grinning, looking as if he were trying to decide what he could say that would puzzle Frank some more. Susan wanted to lean over and join this conversation, but she was concerned about Claudie, and not sure Tony and his brother didn't prefer just to talk to each other. She stood up and went to the ladies' room, and there was Claudie, smoking a cigarette. She held up her hands to Susan. She was in a short, tight dark green dress with long sleeves that clung to her arms and made them look even thinner than they were.

"What?" said Susan.

"I'm just smoking it. I'm not burning myself."

"My God, Claudie, the things you think about." It had not occurred to Susan. Nonetheless, she took the cigarette and stubbed it out on the sink and threw it away. She put her arm around Claudie and Claudie buried her face in Susan's shoulder, while Susan, looking down past Claudie at her own white shoes, silly in October, cried a little. "Dan," said her mind, rhythmically: "Dan, Dan." And she held tight to the girl who was now, according to law, her sister.

SUSAN WAS ALWAYS ASLEEP on Sunday mornings when Tony got up to go to mass. This bothered her; she wanted to be up first, to see him awaken, get out of bed, dress, and go off to church.

If she had awakened first, maybe he would have told her where he was going. She knew—St. Mary's Church in downtown New Haven—but he didn't say. Nor did he talk about it afterward, except obliquely and reluctantly. Later he would admit to knowing what the weather had been like in the morning, but that was almost all. Sometimes when he returned to their bedroom to dress, after his shower, Susan would wake up. "Are you going to church?" she would ask.

"Yes." He never invited her to go along. She was curious about mass, and she didn't want him to think that because she was Jewish it would upset her, so she was tempted to ask to go. On the other hand, she didn't want to intrude on something private, and that was how it felt. It was surprisingly difficult to ask questions about it. Other than his departure for church every Sunday she wouldn't have known that Tony was a Catholic, except that while putting away laundry, Susan found a crucifix—a small one, not like the one he had given Frank—in the bottom of his shirt drawer.

She didn't think he went solely to please his father. Her father-in-law never urged anyone to go to mass, as if it were his private domain, and it was possible, Susan thought, that he didn't know Tony went. She didn't think Tony ever went to the church in Bridgeport, half an hour away, that her father-in-law attended, where they'd been married, despite his friendship with Father Michael.

Tony would come back, smelling of the cold and the outdoors, when Susan, in her bathrobe, was drinking coffee and looking at the Sunday paper. Then he would settle down with his own cup and his own sections of the newspaper—they still bought the *Times*, not the New Haven paper—and the day, which had seemed to start early with energy, would become slow; Susan would grow restless long before she could get herself to shower and dress.

But then they would take a walk, no matter what the weather. She insisted on it. Once, they walked all the way through their neighborhood and downtown, and then out to the park where Susan and Dan Tobin had climbed that hill—East Rock—during the summer. She and Tony did not climb it. When they reached the base, they turned back; they had a long way to go, and it was cold and late. By the time they'd started their walk that day, it was afternoon.

Of course Tony had known that Susan had come to New Haven when she was looking for work, and had seen Dan, but now she was uneasy, when she recognized East Rock, a red cliff that seemed to wrap an arm around the city below it; it felt peculiar that she and Dan had climbed it together, not the sort of thing one did on a day devoted to seeking employment. But as she walked away from the park with Tony, she wanted to talk about that day.

"Remember Dan?" she said. "He took me there, to East Rock, when I came in the summer."

"Up to the top?" said Tony.

"No," lied Susan, "we went only a little way up. We didn't have much time. We took the bus—it was different from today; I almost didn't recognize it. Winter makes it different."

Yet it was not different: Bare red ridged basalt rose above woods, and there was the Civil War monument on top. She had remembered it perfectly. She didn't think she had ever lied to Tony before. Now, as they walked in the growing twilight, their boots ringing on the cold sidewalk, she told him how she and Dan had gone just far enough for her to see how countrylike the park was, how different from the city around it, and then turned back because Dan was in a hurry.

The sun was shining in her eyes, but then they came to a street with taller buildings, or maybe the angle changed a little, and suddenly they were in shade. She'd been squinting but now her eyes relaxed. It was colder, though. Walking had made her hot and she'd taken her gloves off, but now she put them on again. After a while she took Tony's gloved hand in hers. There had been nothing to hide—Tony wouldn't care whether she climbed East Rock with Dan—but he might be upset that she'd had such a good day, an adventurous day, with anyone but him. She had lied to shelter Tony.

She thought about Dan at bus stops. She had a job—she had found one easily, as it turned out, just after they had moved to town—and the job required that she travel about the city. They had bought a car and Tony was teaching her to drive, but so far she walked or took buses. Standing at a bus stop, trying to concentrate on being warm, she would think she saw Dan at a distance, walking toward her. When the man she was watching passed her before the bus arrived, he usually didn't even resemble Dan, but sometimes the bus would come before she could see him clearly, and she would climb on feeling bereft, as if she had actually missed Dan. It made no sense and she knew it; yet the next time, she would find herself again spotting a stranger and thinking he might be Dan.

She was working for a research project being run by a Yale psychology professor who was studying the families of children with disabilities or serious illnesses. Susan had a long list of families who had agreed to be interviewed, and she had to visit each of them every two months and ask questions. She typed up what she'd learned in a little office at Yale, and sometimes one or two other women, who worked on similar projects, were there typing as well.

Susan liked being outdoors and learning the geography of New Haven, a place so much simpler than Brooklyn that taking in its basic structure was like cracking open a walnut and seeing its lobes at a glance. She didn't mind going into people's houses. The families were expecting someone to come, and at times they seemed to look forward to it.

Some of the families didn't seem to have noticed that they had a disabled child. Susan liked them best, at first, the mothers who didn't understand what she was talking about. She was suspicious of those who could say immediately and in detail how a child's problem had changed everything.

One woman she interviewed had a son who'd been born with a badly deformed leg. He'd had operations, but still walked with difficulty. At first the mother of this boy couldn't think of any way in which his deformity had changed their lives, then she remembered that she had to travel to a special store to buy shoes for him. But maybe she was just turning her back on her problems. Susan wasn't sure she liked this woman after all. She tried to suppress all these thoughts. She knew she wasn't supposed to have any opinion of these mothers, she was just supposed to write down what they said.

One woman, an immigrant with a strong accent, Polish or Hungarian, tried to make Susan sit down and drink coffee. The first time, Susan refused, and she could see that the woman was not just hurt but baffled. Susan's second visit was on a cold, windy day and she was tired. This time she didn't argue. The woman sent her daughter, who used a wheelchair because of cerebral palsy, into the next room for the cream and sugar, and the little girl wheeled back with a wooden tray balanced across her chair, the creamer and sugar bowl on it.

"You forgot a spoon," said her mother, laughing, and the child, who was about eight, laughed too and wheeled back into the kitchen, though Susan was calling after her that she didn't take sugar and she didn't need a spoon.

Susan knew she idealized this woman, who was so sure of herself she might possibly do harm at times. She was religious, and Susan was tempted to confide in her about Tony and the church. The woman seemed to think that God had made her child handicapped to give them good, challenging puzzles to figure out.

"God sent us to this apartment," she said, "but the bathroom is so small, Charlotte can't turn the chair around. When she is little, we just carry her in, but it's not nice, a big girl, her brothers carrying her to make pee-pee." The woman had gained permission from the landlord to make changes, and now a flimsy but useful extension to the bathroom, built by her husband and sons, stuck out into the kitchen. Susan described this addition in her report and included a drawing of it. These people didn't seem to need help, and might even help her. She drank their coffee gratefully. She was lonely, and had no friends if you didn't count the families in the study.

One Saturday Susan went to Malley's department store to see if she could find something warm to wear to work. When she stepped off the escalator on the second floor, she saw Dan walk past her. "Hello, Dan," she said, but he didn't hear her and she didn't run after him. She turned away, as sad as if he had told her he was leaving the next day for a distant place and she would never see him again. She found the dress department and slid the dresses past her hand, one after another, looking for a warm one. She felt as if Dan were watching her critically, thinking she cared about nothing but clothes, but of course when she turned around he wasn't there. She did buy something—a maroon plaid wool jumper that fell in gathers from a yoke and was tied with a soft black rope belt. There was something comforting about the way it didn't catch at the waist or under her breasts, something old-fashioned. She called Lennie that night to describe the jumper, and told her about seeing Dan in the store.

"Should I be scared about this?" she asked. She had finally told Lennie about the day she and Dan climbed East Rock.

"No, you're just lonely," Lennie said. "I'll come for a weekend." Lennie was still in love, but now it wasn't going well. She'd gone to see Susan's grandmother and had told her all about it. Susan couldn't imagine such a thing.

"Sex?" she said.

"Yeah," said Lennie. "Well, sort of. I mean, there is sex, and I sort of mentioned it."

Susan pictured Lennie at her grandmother's table, stirring her coffee—Lennie took lots of sugar—and glowing, her hair lit from underneath the way it sometimes seemed to be, when the sun was in the room in a way that was not obvious. In her fantasy, Lennie towered slimly above her short round grandparents, and they were openmouthed, listening to her talk, but the teacup Susan pictured wasn't her grandmother's, it was Charlotte's Polish mother's teacup, and it was Susan who was stirring and stirring—to use well the spoon that Charlotte had brought—and talking.

She loved to talk, but hardly did these days. On most Sunday evenings, she and Tony had dinner with Cat and Frank (her father-in-law, not her brother-in-law; Susan still couldn't get used to having two Franks in one family). After dinner, she and Cat did the dishes, sometimes with Claudie mooning around, sometimes alone. Susan would have liked it if she somehow knew her way around Cat's kitchen, just by instinct, but she was always opening the wrong drawer or awkwardly staring into a cabinet, and Cat didn't teach her. "Just leave it on the counter," she'd say.

They had become almost formal, she and Cat, even she and Claudie. She talked about the families she visited, and Cat sometimes gave her advice about putting them at ease or modifying a line of questioning. She was a social worker, after all. Cat still seemed tired, and Susan would try to bring something to dinner—banana bread or macaroni salad—but sometimes she thought Cat didn't like that.

One evening in March when she came home from work the phone was ringing, and when she picked it up, she heard Dan's voice. "Hello, Sternfeld," he said. "I got your number from Judy. How are you? I want to have lunch with you. Are you too busy?"

She said she wasn't too busy, and suddenly it seemed ordinary and easy for them to meet for lunch. She could have called him. They agreed to meet at George and Harry's. "So now we're cousins," said Dan, first thing, when they met and sat down.

"In a way," said Susan. She didn't want to be Dan's cousin, but it was better than not knowing him at all. He was thinner than she had remembered. She thought of Dan as a big man but he really wasn't. He was dark, though, the way she pictured him. He had a high forehead and small, tight curls. He was wearing a plaid flannel shirt and she thought she remembered that that was what he'd had on the first time she'd seen him, at Judith's, in Boston. He opened his blue down jacket, but didn't take it off.

"I'm a doctor," he said. "You know that?"

"Of course I know it. How could I not know it?"

"I thought maybe you forgot." Susan was offended. How could she forget?

His schedule was a little easier this year. "When you're on call every third night," he explained, "you can sleep the second night and actually enjoy the third night." After a bit, though, he became quiet. Then he said, "This is silly, but I feel guilty about seeing you because you're married, even though I have lots of married women friends. My two best friends at the hospital are married women. And then I also feel insignificant, as if I couldn't possibly matter to you at all."

Susan shook her head. She wanted to say that he mattered, that maybe there was a reason to feel guilty. "People can be friends," she said instead. "People can have lunch."

"I got a little carried away when you came up last summer," Dan said. "My girlfriend was jealous of you."

"I didn't know you had a girlfriend."

"Oh. Yes." They were eating their sandwiches now. She didn't want him to have a girlfriend, even though she was married.

"Tell me about her," she said.

"Oh, sure." Somehow he never did tell Susan about his girl-friend. The subject was changed and Susan couldn't remember later, how. She began to tell Dan about the families in her study, one after another. It had never occurred to her that he might know some of them, but of course he was a pediatrician, and it turned out that he did know two of them, although not the ones Susan was most interested in. He didn't know Charlotte. He wanted to hear all about the families. He was curious about what was wrong with the children, what was being done for them, and how the mothers talked.

Dan sat across from her at the scarred wooden table in the dim room, listening. The room emptied. They'd met at one-thirty and Susan thought it must be three or later. When they finally stood up, he became more distant. He said good-bye to her on the sidewalk in front of George and Harry's, as if he were certain they were going in different directions.

Susan shook hands with him, her face hurting as she smiled and smiled, nodding her head up and down until the rubber band slipped off her hair. She bent to pick it up and put it into her pocket, where there was already another one. When she stood up with the rubber band, he touched her shoulder lightly and walked away, and she, following his script, walked in the other direction, which was not the way she was going.

Her afternoon was free. She was supposed to visit two families, but both had canceled. She could have gone to the office to type reports but it was late, and no one would care if she didn't. She walked—she was on Temple Street—until the street ended at a large intersection. Across it was a small triangular park, and she thought that even though it was cold, she could go into the park and sit there for a while. She stood waiting at the corner for a few minutes, as if she was going to cross, but then she turned and began to run back in the direction in which she had come.

She couldn't be sure Dan had stayed on Temple Street, but she kept going straight ahead for several blocks, and when she reached the green she spotted his blue jacket ahead of her, and she ran until she caught up to him. The green was cold and windswept, and her hair was in her mouth, but she was hot; her face was hot. He heard her coming and turned to meet her and put his arms around her. She hugged him and stepped back and apologized.

He was saying, "What is it? Is something wrong?"

"I don't want to lose you," she said.

"Hey, Sternfeld," he said to her. He put his arm around her

shoulders and they kept walking. Neither of them said anything for several blocks. Then he said, "You're the one who got married." She didn't answer. She thought about Dan's body next to her: his torso, which would be short and a little thick—it would have volume—his arms. She imagined his penis inside his clothes, warm and big. Her mind kept returning to his thighs.

"I want to see you anyway," she said.

"Oh, me too, me too," said Dan, but then he was silent. After a long time, he said, "I don't like secrets."

"It will be all right," she said—a block later—not knowing what would be all right, or how anything could be all right. Then she began to talk. She told him she'd seen him in Malley's, and he said he'd been shopping for a birthday present for his mother. She told him about thinking she saw him at bus stops or when she was walking. He seemed amazed. They were in an unfamiliar poor neighborhood now. Sometimes cars passed them with loud radios. There were little stores, but none Susan recognized. Finally Dan steered her around and after a while they turned down a side street and eventually came to the highway, and then she recognized the streets. "I have to go now," he said.

"I can take the bus home."

"Call me." He took out a notepad and wrote down his telephone number, pulled out the page, and handed it to her, and she stuffed it into her pocket, though she knew his number already. He kissed her cheek, then her other cheek, and then he walked away. She walked to the bus stop and waited for the bus, feeling disconnected from the buildings and people around her, and from the day, as if her photograph had been superimposed on a picture of a scene where she had never been. When she got off the bus at her corner, she stopped at the supermarket and bought a chicken, and when she got home she cooked it in an elaborate way she had never tried before, out of *The New York Times Cookbook*, reading the recipe carefully and making sure to follow all the steps. She felt that it didn't matter how long it took her, and that she would be able to do it very well.

Tony talked about his work that night. He had been given responsibility for some large projects, and he was pleased, but nervous that they would turn out wrong. He'd made some mistakes. She liked listening to him talk. She thought about calling Dan that night, though—and she thought about it every day for weeks. Walking, she'd play with the rubber bands in her pocket, and the piece of paper that had his phone number on it—"Dan Tobin," he'd written, as if to say he had nothing to be ashamed of. She left it in her pocket.

She called Lennie often, but didn't tell her she'd seen Dan. Lennie didn't want to leave the city, because of Chuck, the man she was seeing, but finally, in April, she came for a weekend. Things were still going badly with Chuck, she said. She came on a Friday night and Susan cooked the same intricate chicken dish she'd cooked the day she saw Dan. It had mushrooms and sherry in it. Lennie loved it. They drank wine and stayed at the table for a long time, and then Lennie slept on Susan and Tony's couch.

On Saturday morning, when Susan came out of the bedroom, Lennie was just awakening. Tony was still asleep; it might be the only time they'd be able to talk alone, but Lennie still needed to talk about Chuck. They had decided not to see each other for a month. Lennie thought he wanted to see someone else, but all he would talk about was time to think things over.

"I can think things over in one shower," she said. "Two showers for a major life decision. What does he need a month for?"

Susan had made coffee and now she brought in two mugs. "I put in half the sugar bowl, just the way you like it," she said. Then, "I know what you mean."

"I guess I just have to feel bad for a while," said Lennie.

"I wish it was better." Then she waited, but Lennie, sitting in the rocker and rocking slowly, was silent for a long time, and Susan decided she was done. "I saw Dan," she said, finally.

"You did? When? You should have told me."

"More than a month ago. We had lunch."

"Why didn't you tell me?"

"I don't know. I feel stupid," said Susan.

"What's stupid about it?"

"I'm married."

"So you had lunch. So what? Are you in love with him?"

Susan stood up and untied the belt of her bathrobe, which had loosened. She smoothed her nightgown and pulled the right side of the robe snugly over the left again, tied the belt, and sat down. "Yes."

"Oh, dear. And what about Tony?"

"I'm in love with him, too."

"You're sure?"

"Yes," said Susan, trying on the idea to see if she was in fact in love with both of them.

"So what are you going to do?"

Susan laughed a little. "Feel bad, I guess."

"You'll get over it." Lennie sounded a little uncertain, but Susan could hear Tony getting up, so the conversation was over. She stood up again and went into the kitchen to make breakfast. She'd thought it would be fun to have pancakes, and she'd bought pancake mix and maple syrup.

In the kitchen, she took out a bowl and got started, then stood back, waiting while the griddle heated up, listening to Tony say good morning to Lennie. She thought of Dan kissing her cheeks. Tony, in his bathrobe, came into the kitchen now and began to set the table. Lennie came in, too. "I love having pancakes for breakfast," she said. "Sometimes I even make them for supper, on bad days." She sat down.

Tony had sat down too, and now he turned his chair a little to face both Susan, who was at the stove, starting to fry the pancakes, and Lennie. "Is life treating you badly?" he said to Lennie.

"Just the usual stuff," Lennie said, dipping her red head a little. "Men are hard."

"I'm sorry," said Tony.

"It's not your fault."

"Oh, we're a bad lot," he said.

Lennie laughed. "The ones I keep falling for certainly are," she said. "It's not good. My mother thinks I'm going to hell, and she's not even sure I'm sleeping with them."

Susan had been putting pancakes on a platter, and now she had enough to bring them to the table. "Does your mother think you're still a virgin?" she said.

"Sort of," said Lennie. She took some pancakes onto her plate and buttered them. "It's incomprehensible to her that I might not be. She has to think if I'm not, I was raped—or at least tricked."

"You just get into bed with these guys, in a friendly way," said Susan, "and then you're totally surprised by what they want to do there."

"Right. But mostly she asks me whether I've found the right church yet." She passed the syrup to Susan.

"So have you?" said Tony.

Lennie looked up quickly. "No, of course not."

"You don't go to church at all?" Tony persisted.

"No."

"You don't believe in God?" He leaned over a little toward Lennie, listening. Susan watched him. She had never heard him talk this way.

Lennie shrugged. "Frankly, I'm not sure I ever did. I ask myself— Did I ever think an actual deity cared whether I prayed to Him or not?"

"What denomination are you?" said Tony.

"Baptist. I was baptized. Immersed. I guess I believed in God then. I remember now that when the pastor pushed me under, I was quite sure that I felt something come over me—something besides water, I mean." Susan and Tony were laughing. Susan remembered hearing Lennie talk about her baptism. She hadn't known about total immersion until Lennie told her about it, and she'd asked many questions about embarrassment and hair and splashing. Lennie had assured her that, at least in her particular church, whatever else was going on, the baptisms weren't funny.

"So when did you stop believing in God?" Tony asked. He was holding his knife and fork, waiting for the answer.

"Oh, I don't know," said Lennie, looking uncomfortable. "I suppose it was gradual. I suppose that one day I realized that I hadn't meant it for a long time. When I went to college, I stopped going to church more than once every couple of months, and I didn't miss it."

"Do you pray?"

"What is this? No, Tony, I don't pray. Do *you* pray?"

"On occasion," said Tony. Susan looked at Lennie, because she'd become so shy about Tony's religious life, she couldn't quite look at him. Lennie was facing the window and squinting a little, although the sun wasn't out, and she seemed amused and slightly charmed, looking down her long neck at Tony, smiling because he'd let himself say something surprising. She was wearing a pale blue satin bathrobe and the color set off her hair. Her eyes were intensely blue, and so were Tony's, and yet they weren't the same blue at all.

"So you believe in God?" she said.

"I think so," said Tony.

"And you think God cares what you do?" She swallowed and took a sip of coffee and kept talking. "I mean, there's Vietnam. How many deaths is it now? I suppose no one even knows. I can't bear to watch the news anymore. Do you think in this context there could be a God who could actually be aware of what we are doing *there*— and also of us three *here*, right now, and whether we're *sinning*? Whether I am sleeping with this guy who is breaking my heart?"

"I don't think God wants you to have your heart broken," Tony said sympathetically.

"So you really think He knows?"

"I don't know," said Tony. "Maybe not. But I think it could be—I can't imagine a God like a large person who knows everything. That seems childish. I can't imagine that God is leaning over listening to us have this conversation as though He were the lady upstairs overhearing us. But I think it could be that—I don't know how to put it. It could be that there is in the universe a great kindness—a great kindness and sorrow. I can believe in that."

"Tony's been going to mass every Sunday," said Susan quietly. Then, to Tony, "I hope that's not a secret."

"Of course not," said Tony. "Quite a few people have seen me do it. The entire congregation, in fact."

"But *I've* never seen it," said Susan.

"You think maybe it isn't true?"

"No, I think you go," said Susan, "but—this is silly—I didn't think you wanted me to talk about it. Or go with you."

"You can talk about it," said Tony. "You can come, if you want to. I didn't think you'd like it."

"Why not?"

"Well, it wouldn't solve anything," he said, and she was taken aback, but he went on. "It wouldn't tell you anything important. It's just—well, the priest holds up the Host. There's nothing to see. It looks like a cracker. He says, 'The body of Christ.' Maybe it isn't."

"I'd like to go along sometime," said Susan.

"Fine."

Lennie had stood up to pour herself another cup of coffee. "So," she said, "God is kind—does God also care what we do?"

"Look," said Tony, "if you go on sleeping with this guy when he breaks your heart—well, I think that really might be a sin, Lennie. Not that I think fornication is a sin, or stuff like that—but I think to go on doing something that makes you unhappy is like—well, it's like when I was going to law school. It's a sin. And I think it makes everything a little worse, it makes Vietnam easier, in a way, for people to perpetrate."

"You think my sleeping with somebody makes Vietnam get bombed? Hey, wait a minute, Tony."

"I don't mean that exactly," said Tony. "No, of course not. But well, yes, I also do mean it."

"But it's because it makes me unhappy? If it made me happy it would be all right?"

"I'm not as smart a guy as you need for this conversation, Lennie," said Tony. "I can't answer that." He ate pancakes quietly for a while. Then he got up and walked out of the room, and after a time they heard the shower running.

"Did I make him angry?" said Lennie.

"I don't think so," said Susan. "I think he's worried about you. He could tell that you were trying to see what to do."

"I'm trying to see what we should both do, Susie," said Lennie. "You and I both."

"Oh, I'm different," said Susan. "Nothing I do is interesting enough to think about"—and that seemed true, although Lennie laughed, at the time, and Susan did too. She thought about Dan constantly, during those weeks, and wanted to see him, and yet when she told herself she was a married woman and should think only about Tony, she shrugged that thought off. "It isn't like that," she'd tell herself.

One day in May she walked home from her last interview and when she arrived she called Dan. "It's time to have lunch again," she said. They met on a Wednesday. It was noon, and George and Harry's was crowded. There were no empty tables.

"I live near here," said Dan. "Shall we go to my house? I'll make you a sandwich."

"Fine." He lived in a small third-floor apartment in a frame house on Orange Street. It was surprisingly tidy, but a little stuffy, and when they came in, Dan opened the windows, and the bright fresh air streamed in—and then it was slightly cold, but airy and pleasant. He went to the refrigerator and began taking things out of it, piling them on a counter, naming them.

"Ham. Cheese. Mayonnaise. Mustard." Susan stood still, in the middle of the room, and watched him. She'd been wearing a sweater, which she'd taken off, and her arms were bare and cold. It was the first day in spring that she'd worn a short-sleeved blouse. She'd put her sweater and purse on a chair and her hands were empty. Her palms ached, and she pressed them together. She wanted to touch Dan's head and arms. He was wearing a T-shirt and his arms were hairy. He put the mustard on the counter and turned, and she let her hands drop, facing outward in the gesture that says "Here I am" or "So what can we do?"

He came toward her and grasped her elbows, murmuring over her shoulder, "I don't want to screw up your life. I don't want to screw up your life," and at last Susan pressed her hands into his back, his neck, and touched his head, his arms, his back again.

"It's not your fault," she said. "I need this to happen. I need you."

"I want you so much," he said. He undressed her, standing up, and she undressed him. They kissed. It was cold, with the breeze coming in, and they got into his single bed. He was a caring, fumbling lover—but so excited, so happy that it was hard to say what sort of lover he was. He couldn't stop kissing her, caressing her, and talking. "I wanted this so badly," he kept saying. "I want it so badly. You'll never know how much."

"Since the time we met, in Boston?" They were lying on their sides, now, quiet, facing each other in the narrow bed.

"Well, no—" and he laughed. "I didn't think about you much that time. But when you came here and we climbed East Rock. It was all I could do not to turn around and grab you. Susan, *why* did you get married?"

"I wanted to," she said quietly, shifting her body slightly. She thought of Tony, at the printing plant in Bridgeport, his sleeves rolled up, working out some difficult idea with the assistant plant manager, saying, "Well, that could be, that could be. But if you look at it *this* way . . ." She took Dan's hand in hers. "I'm not sure it wasn't the best thing to marry Tony," she said in a quiet voice.

"Maybe it was." He stood up and began to dress, silently.

She knew he was hurt, but she couldn't think how to fix things. She dressed and they kissed, hard, at the door, and she left. Halfway down the stairs she realized they had never had lunch. She was hungry, and she wanted Dan some more, she wanted to talk, but she had to hurry to her next appointment, and it was not with a family that would offer her something to eat. They were Puerto Rican people who barely spoke English. Usually she thought they were shy, but today they seemed suspicious, and Susan didn't blame them. She thought that what she had done was probably visible on her face. The family was religious. Pious pictures hung on the wall, and the mother wore a medal around her neck; she touched it occasionally as they spoke. Susan was afraid the woman could hear her stomach growling.

When she left she went into a small store, thinking she'd buy a piece of fruit, but all she saw were bananas with too many brown spots on them. She walked up and down the aisles of the store. Everything looked dusty. She could buy crackers or raisins, but she was afraid the boxes of raisins would have worms in them, the stock looked so old. She left without anything, and went to two more interviews, then to the office, where she wrote everything up. There she had a cup of coffee. At home she cried and told Tony she hadn't had lunch. "You shouldn't skip meals," he said. "You aren't the sort who can do that."

He went out to a Chinese restaurant and brought back food, and they ate with chopsticks, a wedding present (along with a wok, which they'd never used) from Frank and Judith. Watching Tony, in a light blue long-sleeved shirt that was coming out of his pants, cross the room for glasses and bring them back, filled with water, Susan felt that she had done right to marry him. She pictured him older, his hair silver like his father's. But more than anything else, she wanted the phone to ring and the call to be from Dan.

"I don't know what you want," Dan said to her, when she called him, almost a week later.

"I want to see you."

"I want to see you, too." They met on Wednesdays (not every Wednesday), which were his easiest days. He was never quite as excited as he had been the first time, but she loved him more and more, and, in bed with him, was happy, free, and passionate. Summer came, and they would lie together, naked, on the bed, for a long time after they made love, sometimes talking. Dan needed to talk before lovemaking too; sometimes he'd propel her to his bed and begin working her shirt over her head, talking about a patient, or about his colleagues. "I *knew* he hadn't been paying attention," he'd say of one man he distrusted. "I *knew* it." And then he'd break off, kissing her, his hands reaching urgently toward her crotch, saying her name again and again.

Sometimes Dan was silent and troubled, and then she was unhappy until the next time; once, three weeks went by, and she thought it was over, because she couldn't bring herself to phone him, but at last he called, and when they met the next day, he called her "Star-field" and kissed her all over her face and body, as if he would never be satisfied.

She had her driver's license now, but she usually walked anyway. Tony said he could take the train to Bridgeport, but she insisted that he use the car. She liked walking, and the walks were her happiest times, happier, even, than the hours with Dan. Sometimes she felt waves of joy come over her that were so strong and sweet they made her gasp. She had not known it was possible to feel so happy. She and Tony were beginning to make friends in New Haven, and to attend antiwar demonstrations and civil rights speak-outs. There was a meeting at a high school, and a rally on the green. Susan went gladly and cheered loudly, reminding herself that all this mattered far more than her personal life, but she knew that what gave her the calm and confidence to identify her opinions was happiness.

On other days—without any reason—she wasn't happy at all. She felt needy and incomplete, as if nothing could help, as if she were heading into waves of pain from which there would be no release.

It was surprisingly easy not to tell Tony what she was doing. During that summer, she kept another secret from him, one that didn't matter, and somehow, having one secret made it simple to have two. The second secret was a drawing class. Susan had always wished she could draw, and one day she had noticed a sign on a bulletin board announcing a private class given by an artist in her studio. The class was held on Thursday mornings, and the professor in charge of her study said Susan could come to work late on Thursdays, and stay later in the evening. Tony often worked late, and he never asked why Susan came home late on Thursdays.

In the drawing class were only three students besides Susan, two retired women and a young mother who came while her child was in day camp. At almost every meeting she remarked that it was fortunate that the class hours coincided with the short period when she was free. She rushed away when class was over, and the two older women, who were friends, left together, always offering Susan a ride, which she refused.

Susan loved drawing. She wasn't as bad at it as she expected, and the teacher, a woman named Adrienne, was clever and kind, and gave the little group assignments that Susan enjoyed. They were learning to see, Adrienne often said. They had to draw eggs in an open egg carton, a sneaker, half laced, and other ordinary things that were somehow not ordinary. Susan began to carry a sketch pad, and when the weather was good, she'd buy a sandwich somewhere and eat lunch on a park bench—sometimes in the little triangular park where she'd almost gone to sit the day she'd first had lunch with Dan—and draw.

She didn't show Tony her drawings, or talk about the class. Keeping it secret was an interesting task. Keeping Dan secret was easier, especially once Susan went on the pill. The first time she'd made love with him, she hadn't been wearing her diaphragm, and had relied on the fact that it wasn't her fertile time, and she was lucky. But—as she explained to Tony—she'd never liked or quite trusted the diaphragm, and now she went to a doctor and had the pill prescribed to her. Almost immediately, she gained some weight. "My punishment," she told herself.

She felt guilty about the secrecy, although not about sleeping with Dan. She examined her feelings on that subject scrupulously. There was something lacking in her, some moral hole. She did feel guilty about concealing the drawing class, and was relieved when it ended, in the middle of August, though she missed it.

One Friday evening in the fall, Susan had a quarrel with her mother on the phone. Paula had called just as Susan came in from work, and was talking about Jay and his pet store—which had really come about; it was open and Paula said it did well. Listening, Susan was restless. She was tired and edgy, and she didn't like the assumption that she had a bond with Jay and should hear about his pet store. She interrupted to ask whether Paula had talked to Leah and Ezra.

"Susan, they are your grandparents, but they are not my parents.

I don't know why you think I owe them something. I was divorced from their son close to twenty years ago."

"You lived in their house for years after Dad left. They raised your child."

"I was a tenant."

"You were a lot more than that."

"Which was entirely their doing," said Paula. "I had plenty of stress in my life, and there were my ex-in-laws on top of it, making sure I felt guilty because they had to baby-sit my daughter. Most of those years, you looked after yourself, Susan."

Susan was sorry she'd changed the subject. Her mother made it seem as if she had been alone, as a child. She wasn't sure. She didn't remember it that way.

"Tony's doing well at work," she said, trying a new subject again. "I think he likes it. He's working on the catalog for an art exhibition at a museum in Hartford—the firm hasn't done anything quite like it before."

"I always feel funny about a man who works for his father," said Paula.

"Oh, for God's sake," said Susan angrily, suddenly unable to control herself. "It's a big place—he hardly sees his father when he's there." She thought that might not be true. "But that's a stupid thing to say, anyway," she went on.

"Why is it stupid?"

"Tony can take care of himself."

"Whatever I say, these days, you jump down my throat," said Paula, and then, suddenly, in a different voice, "There's no *trouble*, is there, between you and Tony? I mean the basic things?"

"Of course not," said Susan, needing to get off the phone in a hurry. Paula knew nothing—it was like the flash a light bulb gives just before it burns out, a meaningless scattering of clairvoyance. Susan hung up quickly, and then she heard Tony coming in. They were going out to dinner and on to a film in a series at Yale, *Rashomon*. Susan hurried into the bathroom and washed her face.

"Frank is leaving graduate school," Tony said, first thing, as they got into the car. "He's coming to work in the firm."

"Will they move here?" She was overcome with dread. Judith would find out about Dan and tell Frank, and Frank would tell his brother.

"They're thinking of it. Here or Bridgeport, and they don't want to move to Bridgeport."

"That's good," she said reluctantly. "He didn't want to stay in graduate school."

"It's great," said Tony with glee. "It's wonderful." He meant it, she saw—for a second she thought he was being sarcastic, he was so flamboyant. She thought maybe it made him feel better about his own choice to work with his father. If Frank did it, it must be all right.

"I like Frank and Judith," she said. "It will be good to see more of them." They talked about Frank and Judith and the firm all through dinner.

As they waited to go into the film, one of the older women from the drawing class came along and stood behind them on the line. She greeted Susan enthusiastically and looked expectantly at Tony until Susan introduced him. "I'm from Adrienne's class, the drawing class," the woman said chattily to Tony.

"Oh, right," said Tony vaguely, as if he hadn't heard and was trying to conceal it. Just then it was time to pay and go inside, and the woman, who was alone, said she liked to sit close to the front of the room at a film, and left them. Susan and Tony sat down, and Tony said, "But he must feel terrible about that thesis. He's filled so many sheets of paper. Just to throw it away—"

"Maybe some day he'll go back to it."

"If he leaves, I don't think he'll ever go back."

The film began. Susan had known it would be about different versions of a crime, but it was stranger, harder to predict than she had expected. The print was poor and the sound harsh, and sometimes the titles flickered; by the end of the movie she was absorbed in it, but she had a slight headache. They walked around for a few blocks, and bought ice-cream cones, and she began to feel better.

"What did that woman say?" Tony said suddenly, after a silence. "How is it you know her?"

Susan didn't answer for a moment. She had bought a chocolate cone, and the flavor was strong and somehow dear, as if it were the last sweet thing she would taste for a while. She licked the cone and turned it and licked it again. Then she told Tony about the drawing class, how she'd seen a notice on the bulletin board in the basement of the Yale Co-op, and had called Adrienne and then bought the necessary materials and located her studio. She talked about the other students, and about Adrienne's hard, interesting assignments.

"And do you still go?" said Tony, a little hushed, when she stopped.

"No. It ended in August. She's starting again in a couple of weeks. I might do it again, I think."

"And do you ever draw?"

"Yes. I have two sketch pads, a small one—it's here in my purse— and a larger one at home."

He was silent again. "Do you think I could see?" he said then.

"Yes." She took the sketch pad out of her purse, and they stopped under a lamp post. He ate the last of his cone quickly. She watched him while she finished hers, as he turned the pages. She had drawn things she'd seen outside, mostly in the little park where she had lunch: a man reading a newspaper, a squirrel, even a trash can.

"You're good at it," he said.

"I'm better than I thought I would be," said Susan soberly.

He handed back the pad and she put it into her bag. He watched her, and when she snapped the bag shut she had the sudden thought that he was going to strike her. They walked toward their car.

"Why didn't you tell me?" he said, finally.

"I don't know." Then she said, "You don't tell me about going to mass."

"But you knew I go. Does it bother you that I go?"

"No, it doesn't bother me." He was silent.

The next day she showed him the larger sketch pad, and when they went for a walk on Sunday, she took it along. "I should have told you," she said. In East Rock Park, she sketched some children playing.

One of the children came over to watch her. "He loves to draw," his mother called to them. "He's very impressed."

"As if I were an artist," Susan said to Tony.

"How old is he?" Tony said. Susan thought he was about three, and Tony was impressed that his mother would let him come over to their bench by himself. "That's how I want to be when I have a child," he said. "Give him a little freedom."

Susan sketched the little boy as he stood there. "What's your name?" she said to him.

"Luke." She wrote "For Luke from Susan" on the bottom of the drawing, tore it off the pad, and gave it to him. He ran to show his mother, and she nodded and smiled at them, and called a thank-you as she lifted him into his stroller.

"Luke is a good name," said Susan, as the woman wheeled her little boy out of the park.

"Too sissy," said Tony. "I should warn you. When we have a child I'm going to have to insist on calling him Frank." He spoke with mock seriousness. "We just don't have enough Franks in this family."

"Not enough frank*ness*." She knew he was teasing. "Jewish people don't name babies after someone alive," she said. "It makes the older person drop dead."

"Well, my father is doing fine, and Frank is past thirty."

"That's just because they're not Jewish. If he was Jewish, he'd be dead."

"Is that a law or a superstition?"

"I don't know. A superstition, I guess—because I have it, and I don't follow the laws."

Going home, they walked past Dan's house, and she was uneasy, yet she kept sneaking looks at his front steps, hoping despite herself that he would open the door and come out as they passed. It would be unpleasant—she couldn't imagine what it would be like—but worth it.

On Wednesday, though, she went to his house, as she'd agreed to do the previous week. Dressed, she sat down in his chair. "We have to break up," she said.

He was walking toward her, holding a book. "No," he said. Then, "Do you want to break up, Susan?"

"No," she said. "I don't want to."

"Did Tony—"

"No. But still." Maybe he had been about to show her the book. He put it down. He sat down heavily on the bed, and then he slumped over on his elbow, looking at her. He had gained some weight again. For the first time, he looked awkward to her, frightened, not like a doctor.

"You must know," he said, and sounded cold. She began to talk, but she didn't give him any reason. After a while she went and sat on the bed next to him, but he stood up and shook his head.

"I think maybe you ought to leave now," he said.

She stood before him for a few minutes, holding her bag. She was afraid to try to kiss him. She reached her hand out to touch his cheek, just as he stood suddenly, and her fingers touched his lips and his teeth. She said, "I'm sorry," and hurried to the door and down the stairs, as if she were going to feel better when she stepped outside; but when she did, she was beginning to go away from Dan.

She walked to her next appointment, which was with Charlotte's mother, who served Susan a cup of coffee, without asking, as usual, but this time Susan thought she was bossy and too full of herself, not delightful. Charlotte went to a school that had a ramp, now, and so she wasn't there. The mother told Susan she believed it was her husband's fault that Charlotte had been born with a disease, that he wanted to have sex too often.

The next morning, Susan called Dan. "I made a mistake," she said. "I can't stop seeing you. I want to keep on seeing you."

She could hear him breathe. "No, it's better this way," he said. "I'm sorry."

"I'm going to die," she said.

"No."

"I want to die."

He wouldn't talk long and he wouldn't change his mind. He told her he loved her but it didn't help. She'd called first thing in the morning, as soon as Tony left—she'd phoned her first appointment and said she'd be late—and now she lay down on her bed in her nightgown and cried for a long time. She remembered Claudie cutting herself, burning herself, and understood why she had wanted to do that, why it might be a relief, a good thing, to feel physical pain. She missed one more appointment—she called and said she was sick—and then she took a shower and dressed and went to her next one. She heard herself sounding sympathetic and intelligent, talking to the mother, who was unusually troubled, a woman whose child had been hurt in a car accident a few months before, and who might never walk normally again.

"I have no children," Susan said. "It must be so hard—knowing she's in pain."

"It helps to talk," said the woman. "I'm glad you came."

AFTER JUDITH AND FRANK moved to New Haven, where they bought an old house that needed work, Susan and Tony saw them often. The four of them went out for pizza, or had dinner at one house or the other. Sometimes Susan spent time alone with Judith, and she began to think of her as a close friend, maybe her best New Haven friend. Judith was pregnant, and they shopped together for baby things, and refinished an old oak chest for a changing table. They talked, but Susan didn't tell Judith she had had an affair with Judith's cousin Dan, and Judith mentioned him only now and then.

Sometimes Susan imagined that she would come home from work and find Dan sitting on her front steps. She would imagine this on her way home, and she'd look quickly to see whether he was there, but of course he never was. Susan was busy. She was working, and a few months after Frank and Judith moved to New Haven, she started going to school at night. She had to drive to Hartford, but by now she was used to driving, and they'd bought a second car. She was studying for her master's degree in social work at the University of Connecticut.

She found that she was happy with Tony. She surprised herself, one day, thinking for a second that their bed had grown, that they weren't as cramped in it. Their house *had* grown: They had bought a two-family house around the corner from where they had lived in an apartment. Now they lived in a big, sunny second-floor apartment that had three large, light, indeterminate rooms in front, all in a row, which became a living room, a dining room, and a room for their desks. An older Italian couple, tenants, lived below and had come with the house. There was an unfinished third floor which Tony said they'd renovate one of these days. He and Frank would do it.

Tony flourished, having Frank around, and was always going over to Judith and Frank's on weekends to help fix or build something. Frank, unlike Susan, was not too shy to ask Tony about going to church. "I guess you just missed feeling guilty," he'd say.

"Something like that," Tony would answer genially. He still wouldn't *talk* about it, but continued to go, although sometimes he went to Frank and Judith's on a Sunday morning instead. When the baby was born, a boy, he drew Tony even more. He was not still another Frank but was named James Anthony—his middle name was after Tony—and called James.

Susan thought there was a good quiet about Tony, lately—an improved quiet. There had been something muffled about him, before, as if his arms and legs were wrapped in invisible quilts. When she had drawn him, his outline was rough, but now, in the sketches of him she found in her drawing pad, it was smooth. It seemed as if she had to reach a little farther, through clean, well-organized, crisp air, to reach his arm.

Susan went to see her grandparents in New York every few months. As long as Leah was well, she moved slowly but sturdily through her apartment, and when she had occasion to talk about Susan—to her new tenants, for example, the people who'd come to live upstairs when Susan's mother finally moved out—she didn't say she had brought Susan up. "It was almost as though she lived with me," she said to the woman from upstairs, in Susan's hearing.

"I know what you mean," said the woman. "I'm close to my granddaughter too."

"But Grandma, I did live with you," said Susan. Lennie had asked her many questions on this point, and Susan had admitted that when she was growing up, it was her mother who took her shopping for new winter coats, and her mother who went to Open School Week. But her grandmother had bought her sweaters and socks and all but a few dresses, and had washed her hair, fed her, and done her laundry.

"Did your grandmother bawl you out?"

"Yes." Her grandmother had never hit her, but at times she had taken Susan by the shoulders and shaken her hard, over and over again, scolding away. This happened when Susan had been wasteful, when she had left a container of milk on the table instead of putting it back into the refrigerator, so that it spoiled, or when she had refused perfectly good food.

Now Leah had had a stroke and could no longer speak. She had been taken to a hospital, and then to the Jewish Home, where she lived on the hospital floor. Asked if she would ever come home, Ezra wouldn't say. Leah stayed in bed, and couldn't walk.

On a Saturday in April, a few days after her birthday, Susan took the train to New York from New Haven and took the subway out to Brooklyn, to her grandparents' house. Ezra prepared lunch for her— canned soup and rolls from the bakery. He moved back and forth deliberately from the table to the refrigerator to the stove.

"Grandpa, use a pot holder," Susan said, watching him. "Not a dish towel. Grandma keeps the pot holders in that drawer." She jumped up and showed him.

"I know where. I like a dish towel."

"I'm afraid it will catch fire," Susan said. "It dangled near the flame."

"I'm careful."

She washed the dishes with pleasure, recalling the feel of her grandmother's things and how Leah worked—with a dish cloth, not a sponge. From the time Susan had said she was marrying Tony, Leah had never let her help here. Then they took a taxi to the home. It was Susan's second visit, but the first time, her grandmother had been so weak she hadn't seemed to notice her. Now Leah recognized Susan and grinned at everyone, kissing Susan's hands over and over again. She pointed to her own mouth.

"I know," Susan said, sitting down on the edge of the bed. Ezra was in the chair. "I know you can't talk, Grandma."

Leah touched her heart, then pulled Susan closer by the arm and patted her cheek. When a nurse's aide gave Leah a glass of juice, Leah pointed at Susan, nodding and smiling. "Well, *you* must be special," said the nurse. She was a black woman, and Susan imagined that she had a warm and affectionate family life.

"I'm her granddaughter," said Susan. "She raised me. I lived with her." Leah was holding her hand, and she didn't let go, nor shake her head in disagreement.

"Lucky grandma, lucky grandchild," said the nurse. Yet Susan didn't feel triumphant.

Susan wanted to take a taxi back to the apartment, and offered to pay for it, but Ezra said that he could manage the bus and train one way, and that was how he wanted to travel. It took a long time. Ezra breathed audibly, climbing down the steps of the elevated train, and when he got home, he was glad to rest for a while.

Then he said, "You should do me a favor." He wanted Susan to clean out Leah's closet and get rid of her clothes. Susan was taken aback.

"But doesn't she need clothes? She won't be in bed for the rest of her life."

"Perfectly good things she will never wear," he said. "Maybe you can use them. A good coat, very warm."

He followed her into the bedroom. "This I bring." He showed her a pile of housedresses, nightgowns, and sweaters. "But not this."

He meant the suits and woolen dresses, what Leah had worn when she had company. Susan was surprised to see how much there was. Some of it was in plastic bags from the cleaners. These were the clothes in which her grandmother had served her meals, once she was grown up. "Do you want to send this stuff to Goodwill, or what?" Susan asked.

"You do not want it?" Susan couldn't bear to put the clothes into grocery bags. Her grandmother had saved brown bags from the market for decades, and Susan hated to think that this might be why, for her clothes to be carted away as if Leah were dead. She went through everything. She told herself that she was obligated to take only a few things back to Connecticut. Her grandfather didn't seem to have thought about size, and Susan was taller and heavier than her grandmother, but Leah had worn her clothes loose, and so some things looked as if they might fit Susan. Others, she thought, she would keep—just to keep. She did want them.

She took the good coat, though it was heavy, and she'd have to ride the subway to Grand Central Station and then the train to Bridgeport. She was meeting Tony there for a dinner at his parents' house to celebrate her birthday and Frank's. Once she had chosen the coat, it wasn't hard to pick other things—the dress her grandmother had worn to Susan's college graduation, Leah's two good suits, a couple of blouses. It was like selecting clothes for a museum, as if her grandmother had been an important public figure, and that, she saw, was something like what Ezra had in mind. He didn't seem to care that many of the clothes remained in the closet when Susan had finished.

One of the suits was bright blue. She remembered it. The jacket had a low neckline and was double breasted, and the top button had come just above her grandmother's bosom. The jacket had a peplum. "A peplum is a nice touch," her grandmother had said. She'd been proud of how she'd looked in it. Holding it up, folding it, Susan felt as if she had restored her real grandmother, and, at least in part, done away with that gushy woman at the home who kissed Susan's hand and didn't object to anything she said.

Her arm around a bundle of coats and dresses and a shopping bag in her hand, Susan made her way down the aisle of the train to Connecticut, late that afternoon, and then she spotted Claudie at the back of the car, slouched against the window, apparently looking out into the darkness of the tunnel through her own reflection. Claudie was living in New York. Now she had a suitcase on the seat next to her. When Susan came closer, she saw that Claudie was asleep, or pretending to be asleep so no one would ask to sit there.

"Claudie." She shoved what she was carrying into the overhead rack, and put Claudie's suitcase up there, too, as Claudie looked around, startled. Susan sat down.

"What are you doing here? I'm going to your party," said Claudie.

"Me, too. How are you?" Claudie had graduated from high school the previous year. At one point she had spent a week in a psychiatric ward, but the doctors said she would be all right. She had enrolled in college and completed one semester, living at home and going to the University of Bridgeport, but then she dropped out and moved to New York, where she was living with a friend. "Are you working?" Susan asked.

"I've been doing some modeling," said Claudie.

"Art or clothes?"

"Art," said Claudie. "You can make good money, modeling for art classes."

"Not modeling clothes?" Cat had told Susan that Claudie was working for a clothing manufacturer, modeling bathing suits for visiting buyers. Cat had been afraid of that. "They're call girls," she said. "That's all they are. I've known of cases. And she admits she's smoking marijuana."

She might be just as upset if she found out Claudie was modeling in the nude for art classes. Claudie closed her eyes again, as if she were bored with Susan's questions, without asking her where she'd been or why coats and dresses were stuffed into the rack above their heads, but then she patted Susan's shoulder as if she were testing its weight and strength, turned her face, and went to sleep, leaning against Susan like a child.

Susan was tired, too. She closed her eyes, once the conductor had come by for the tickets, but didn't sleep. She wondered whether Claudie might like one of her grandmother's blouses. It was nothing like what a young woman would wear, of course—she was thinking of a shell pink blouse with tucks—and it would be much too big, but it might please Claudie anyway.

Tony met the train. "Look who I found," said Susan.

"I know," Tony said. "Mom said Claudie was coming now. We hoped you'd find each other."

Claudie noticed what Susan was carrying. "Your grandma was an elegant lady," she said.

"She's still alive."

"I didn't mean she was dead. Let me see." They were putting the clothes into the trunk of the car. "Look at all this," said Claudie. "I love your family, Susan. There's something strange about all of them, as if they'd been around the world."

Susan shook her head. "They're just different from yours."

Claudie had found the bright blue jacket. She was wearing a huge dark green raincoat, and she took it off and tried on the jacket. It was supposed to be fitted, but on Claudie it looked as if it was supposed to hang loosely, just the way it did. Claudie left it open. "This is great," she said.

"You can keep it," said Susan. "Do you want the skirt?"

"No, I never wear skirts. But I'd like to have the jacket."

"Was it a hard day?" Tony asked, as they drove. He glanced at Susan, next to him, and she nodded.

"My grandmother kept kissing my hand," she said.

"She was glad to see you?"

"Yes."

Tony said, "Frank and Judith are at my parents' place already. I've been there for half an hour." Tony worked with Frank all day now, at the printing company, but they still looked forward to seeing each other in the evening. "And did you know that your mother and Jay are coming?" he said.

"My mother?" said Susan, startled. "Of course I didn't know. Why is she coming?"

"My mother invited them, because of your birthday. It's supposed to be a surprise, but I thought you might like a minute's warning."

"It certainly is a surprise."

"I've never met your mother," Claudie said from the backseat. "Don't you want to see her?"

"We're not close," said Susan. This was not precisely true. She and Paula talked once a week or so, sometimes about personal subjects, but they didn't see each other often, and Susan didn't like Jay. She didn't want either of them to come to her birthday party. Paula had met Cat herself only once, briefly, at Susan's house. It was going to be awkward.

Tony touched Claudie tentatively on the shoulder, following her into their parents' house, with Susan coming last. Claudie punched the doorbell and then tried the door. It was open, and they all went into the lighted living room together, where for a moment they were barely noticed. Paula and Jay had arrived in Tony's absence, and Paula was admiring James while Cat stood waiting, smiling, ready to take her coat. Judith stood with James in her arms, also smiling, and as Susan and Tony and Claudie came in, Paula reached her arms out and took him, and Susan saw that she was an older woman, that she looked like a grandmother.

Paula had gained weight since her marriage, and although she still dyed her hair, it was a different color, a soft brown that was probably meant to make her look younger than the harsher color she had used before, but made her look older—or at least, more domesticated. Jay was hearty and gray and a little fat, too, and Susan remembered that he *was* a grandfather—he had a daughter by an earlier marriage who had had a baby sometime in the past year.

James stared soberly at Paula's face, or at a shiny pin at her neck, and didn't cry. He was a dark, small baby with lots of hair, and his face looked too dignified for his light green terry cloth suit, which had an appliqued kitten on the chest and yellow pompoms at the feet. He was trying to focus his eyes.

"He likes me," said Paula.

"He must," Judith said. "He's hungry, and usually when he's hungry he hates everything but my breast."

Paula turned to Susan, still holding James, and Susan leaned past James, and gave his foot a wiggle while she kissed her mother. "Surprise!" said Paula, a little nervously.

"It was nice of you to come," Susan said. "Mother, have you ever met Claudie?"

Paula still had the baby in her arms but she somehow reached out under him to touch Claudie's arm. Now James did start to whimper, and Judith took him back and sat down to nurse him. Susan's father-in-law had gone to fix drinks for Jay and Paula, and now he brought them, and the younger Frank came in with him from the kitchen and began to talk to Tony, quietly and intensely, as if they hadn't seen each other for weeks. Cat had disappeared and Susan followed her into the kitchen. "Lots of people," she said.

"I don't mind lots of people."

"You'd rather I didn't help?"

"Susie, of course I'd love you to help!" said Cat. "Aren't you exhausted? How's your grandmother?"

Susan began making a salad and after a while Paula came into the kitchen. "You have handsome children," she said to Cat. "Every one of them. At least, all that I see here."

"Thank you. Claudie's looking better. For a while there, she wasn't so pretty."

"Oh, I can't imagine that," said Paula, and Cat exchanged glances with Susan. "She's a beautiful girl. Does your other daughter look like her?"

"A little," said Cat. She bent over the oven door to check the roast chicken, and then straightened up. "Your own kid's all right," she said.

"Thank you," said Paula primly. Susan was uncomfortable, but not as uncomfortable as she would have expected to feel. Cat handed her a bowl that was in her way, as if she didn't need to say what Susan was supposed to do with it. Susan had always known that Cat was grateful to her because of her famous closeness to Claudie, which was mostly myth anyway, but often Cat was distracted and almost impersonal. Now Susan basked in the attention she was getting, or, rather, the matter-of-factness she was getting.

At the dinner table, Jay was the center of the conversation. Claudie had found out that he owned a pet store, and she was enthralled. She had a cat, and had always wanted a dog, and she was delighted to hear that Jay sold puppies. She wanted to know who fed the puppies when the store was closed, whether they were ever taken outside. "Every Christmas, when I was little, I longed for a puppy," she said, glancing at her mother, "but there never was one. Is that just something I saw on television, kids getting Christmas puppies—or does it really happen?"

"Of course it does," said Jay. "One couple came in on Christmas

Eve this year. Mostly people arrange it in advance, and I open for an hour on Christmas morning so they can pick them up. But these people showed up Christmas Eve, just before closing, and they fell in love with a collie pup. We put a red bow around his neck and out he went."

Susan hated hearing about the pet store. She assumed it was not properly run, not clean, that the puppies got sick. She didn't like to think even about well-run pet stores. What happened to the puppies that didn't sell, for example? What happened to those that were bought on a whim and improperly cared for? She tried to change the subject, and asked Judith whether she expected James's hair to fall out—Susan had heard that that happened. James was asleep upstairs.

But Claudie kept talking about the pet store. "Do you have a parrot?" she said. "How do you train them to talk?"

Jay had had a parrot, but he said someone bought it. Susan wondered whether that was true or whether it had died.

"Well, if you ever need someone to work in the store, I'd love to do that," said Claudie.

"Claudie, that's a wonderful idea," said Cat, suddenly leaning into the conversation. "But it's all the way out in Queens, isn't it?" Then she stopped. "I shouldn't jump in like this. You probably have all the help you need, Jay."

"No, I don't," said Jay. "I have a kid who comes in, but he's not reliable. Your daughter would be an improvement."

"Where is the store?" said Claudie. "Where is it exactly?"

"Oh, I don't think you'd like it," Susan said.

"Now, I know you're still doing that modeling," Cat was saying, "but maybe, for a start, part-time . . ."

Susan looked at Judith. Somehow she thought Judith would see that Jay was not to be trusted.

"It must be a difficult business," Frank, her father-in-law, was saying. Judith didn't look interested in the conversation. Now Frank and the younger Frank and Jay began to talk about seasonal peaks and lulls in the pet business and the printing business. Susan was seated near Claudie but far away from Cat—who was near the door so she could run into the kitchen—and she wanted to get Cat's attention, to warn her. She stood up and began collecting dirty plates.

"Jay's bad news," she said to Cat, when they met in the kitchen. "You don't want Claudie to have anything to do with him."

"Women often feel that way about their stepfathers, you know," Cat said. "It's hard to get any objectivity in that relationship."

"Oh, that's nonsense," said Susan, more harshly than she intended.

Cat glanced behind her to see if Claudie had followed them in "Look, do you think I can sleep nights as long as she's a model?"

"She says she's posing for art classes," Susan said. "That's not so bad. There are unwritten rules. The students don't rise up and rape the model."

"She's also modeling bathing suits," said Cat. "She told me on the phone this morning. She says she likes it. And there are no unwritten rules there. Besides—modeling in the nude at an art school—would you do it?"

"I don't know. I suppose I might," said Susan.

"Oh, don't be stupid, Susie," said Cat. "And if they don't rape the model, they certainly give her grass to smoke." She sounded angry now. She hurried back to the dining room.

Paula was making friends with Claudie. She couldn't stop commenting on her looks. Claudie had taken off the blue jacket and under it was wearing a black leotard. "I've sold dresses all my life," Paula was saying. "I notice figures. Yours is lovely."

"Thanks," said Claudie. "I inherited it from my dad."

There was laughter, and then Cat brought in a large birthday cake with Frank and Susan's names on it. They had to stand up together while everyone sang, and blow out the candles in unison—a great many candles. Cat said she hadn't counted, she'd just put all she could fit on the cake.

Blowing the candles out, Frank seemed to expand a little. He'd looked grave all evening. "Well, I had a good year this year," he said, "and the next year should be pretty good, too."

"You became a father this year. It's hard to outdo that," said his own father.

Judith was sitting back and grinning, and Paula looked nervous but pleased. Cat brought in presents. Frank received a power drill he'd been wanting, and Susan a copy of Ovid's *Metamorphoses* in Latin. She knew that was her father-in-law's doing—he'd been after her for months to read Latin with him. "Now we'll be all set," he said.

It was a good party, Susan decided, as she helped cut the cake and distribute the slices, even if Cat—who was probably right about Jay—was a little angry with her; maybe *because* Cat was angry, just as if Susan were her own difficult child. She'd wound up in the right place—in this old dining room, which had faded tan wallpaper and walls that looked as if they weren't straight up and down—or maybe it was the floor that wasn't quite right—or maybe it was just the rugs on top of rugs. Susan remembered how badly she had wanted to be invited to visit Tony's house—Cat's house—when she first met Tony. She had received something she wanted. She'd forgotten how keenly she'd wished for it.

Somewhere in the middle of eating her cake, Judith said, "Oh, I almost forgot. What's everybody doing this summer? Who wants two weeks in Vermont?" Relatives of Judith's owned a summer cottage. They were spending August in Europe, and had offered it to Frank and Judith. "We just want it for the first two weeks," Judith said. "It's available for the last two weeks. It's on a lake. It's fantastic. I used to go up all the time for weekends, when I was a teenager. One of my cousins—"

Susan became uneasy at the mention of a cousin of Judith's, but she relaxed as the cousin turned out to be a girl, not Dan. Sometimes Susan forgot about Dan entirely, and then something would remind her of him.

"That would be *great*," said Tony, as soon as Judith finished her explanation. "Susan, wouldn't that be great?"

"It's quiet," said Judith. "A small lake—they call it a pond."

It was settled that they could have the cabin for the second half of August.

"It's cold then," said Frank.

"We don't mind cold," Susan said.

It was another birthday present, a big one. It gave her something to look forward to. She had almost never been in the country, not since Girl Scout camp. It made her remember that she liked to be active, to swim and hike. She and Tony had gone away for a few weekends, but this would be their first true vacation. It was like buying the house—it made her feel more substantial. She was glad her mother was there, to see what she had been given.

After supper, everyone stayed at the table, but the chairs were shifted as someone got up to clear or to go to the bathroom, and in his absence someone else moved over. Frank came to talk to Susan, and she found herself telling him about her visit to her grandmother.

It upset Frank. "Having James," he said, "I'm so conscious of dying. Sometimes I catch myself about to say 'When James died' instead of 'When James was born' as though the two things were the same, or connected."

"It makes you more aware, I guess," said Susan, who didn't like what Frank was saying.

"You look at people like us, people in the middle of their lives," Frank said, "and you don't think of them as future dead people. At least I don't." He shifted his chair around to take in the other people at the table: Claudie—still talking with Paula, Jay and the senior Frank, Judith and Cat. Tony had gone into the kitchen for a second cup of coffee, and now he returned and sat down by himself, his chair pulled back from the table, just like Frank's, also looking around the room, as if his thoughts were the same as his brother's.

"I can't stand it to think that some day James has to die," Frank said. "I just can't stand that, but I can't stop thinking about it."

"I couldn't even say it," Susan said. "I don't like thinking that my grandmother has to die, and she's so old."

"Do you think she's going to die soon?"

"I don't know," she said. "I suppose people can go on like this for a long time." She was vowing to visit her grandmother at least once a month—every two weeks, she had thought at first, and then, no, that was unrealistic, once a month.

Frank stood up. "I hear him," he said, pointing upstairs. "He's objecting to our cavalier discussion of his mortality. Have a baby,

Susan. It's worth it, but it's not easy." He patted Judith's shoulder in a concluding sort of way, as he squeezed past the chairs and headed for the stairs—and shortly after that, the party began to break up.

Susan did not visit her grandmother once a month that spring and summer, but she did go once more—in June—before it was midsummer and suddenly almost time to go to Vermont, and then it *was* time. When she visited the home in June, she didn't see Ezra. It was easier to take the subway directly there, and then go right back to Manhattan. She and Lennie met at an Italian restaurant and talked about work and men and babies—Susan was thinking that she might stop taking her birth control pills—until it was time for Susan to take the train home. On that visit, Leah had not been quite as excited to see Susan, but once again, she had taken her hand and held it.

When Susan and Tony drove up to the house in Vermont, they knew that no one at all would be there, because Frank and Judith had been planning to leave early, and had told them where to find the key—in the drawer of a wooden table on the porch. Still, they were startled by the silence, startled by the solitude. There was really no one there but themselves. Driving in, they'd passed the only nearby house, and it was not being used that summer—the dock was drawn up on the beach and the porch furniture was covered. The house where they were staying, a little farther down the road, had a short wooden dock and a rowboat, but it was almost as silent, as drawn back into itself. It had a large room with a stove, sink, and refrigerator at one end and a sofa bed at the other, two little bedrooms, and a bathroom. The house was filled with books, mostly old novels and mysteries and Reader's Digest Condensed Books, and copies of *National Geographic*. The furniture—the sagging sofa bed, a table with four unmatched chairs—had obviously been bought at tag sales over the years, or brought from someone's house because it was old. Susan dragged a suitcase onto the screened porch and then went to look at the lake.

It was raining, though not very hard. The lake was quiet and gray, and the sky above it was a similar gray. The lake *was* a pond, not large. She walked out on the short, tilted dock and sat down at the end of it, hugging her knees. The lake was surrounded by tall evergreen trees, and their shadows were almost black.

The thought that came to her was that she had to do only one thing at a time, so she could concentrate. Now the task was to carry in suitcases. Then they would make the bed. Next, they would drive into town and buy groceries. All this seemed pleasantly challenging, but not hard. When she walked up to the cabin, Tony was sitting on the porch waiting. He said, "I'm trying to think of a poem to quote."

"Which poem?"

"Just a poem." He put his arms around her and began kissing her, and before bringing in the suitcases, they took off their clothes and made love on the old sofa. "Well, that's a fine thing," Tony said, afterward, and he strode naked across the room toward the bathroom, swinging his arms, as if his clothes had hurt all his life.

Tony walked around naked a lot in the next days, or wearing nothing but bathing trunks, though it was cool—too cool for Susan to swim, though Tony went in, while Susan stood on the dock in her sweatshirt watching him. He had a slow, easy breaststroke, and his arms made wide, innocent circles, away from the center of his chest, when he swam, as if he were showing himself to someone over and over again. From the dock she could see ripples spread around him. He would swim straight out into the middle of the pond as if he were going to go on forever, and the sight made Susan sad, watching the back of her husband's head as it moved steadily away from her. Then he would turn on his side and sidestroke, first in a wide circle, then back to the dock. When he came out he'd be cold, and Susan would hurry to the cabin to make coffee.

There was a small charcoal grill, and Tony grilled chicken on it, the third night, while Susan made a salad and then came out to watch him. It had been raining, but it had stopped. They'd bought corn at a roadside stand and Susan brought it out for Tony to cook, and brought him a glass of red wine. In front of the cabin were ferns growing, now beaded with rainwater—but the sky seemed to be clearing. Susan sat down on the bottom step of the porch to drink her own wine. He turned and looked out over the lake. "Judith doesn't want to have James baptized," he said.

"I wondered what you were thinking about," Susan said. She drank some more wine. "I suppose Judith would feel a little funny about that—but it isn't important to Frank, is it?"

"I don't know," said Tony. "I think Frank thinks Dad cares, but he doesn't want to discuss it with him."

"Does Frank still tease you about going to church?" Susan asked.

"Sometimes," said Tony. "But if I stopped, he wouldn't like it."

He didn't say anything else for a time, and Susan said, "So I guess it isn't a problem for them. Baptizing James. They can wait and see what James wants when he's older."

"That's what Judith says."

Susan watched a bird high in the sky above them, maybe a hawk. It was starting to get dark. Soon the mosquitoes would begin to bite. "What made you think about it?" she said.

"I was thinking about whether we'd have a baby," he said.

She waited and spoke carefully, as if he might step sideways into the woods and disappear. "Do you want a baby?" She'd brought up the subject once or twice, but she couldn't tell what he wanted.

"I've been thinking about it," he said. "I think about Claudie. My parents are decent parents. My mother is a social worker who helps people with their kids. All the rest of us turned out all right, but Claudie's full of all kinds of trouble. I don't know how they could have prevented that."

"Well, my parents weren't so hot, and I'm all right," said Susan.

"You mean there's no way of telling."

"You're afraid we'll have a baby and it will turn out like Claudie?"

"Not that there's so much wrong with Claudie," he said quickly. "She really seems fine." Just a few weeks before, Claudie had gone to work in Jay's pet store. She talked about it enthusiastically, and Susan reminded herself that Cat had wisdom. Claudie was nursing a sick puppy back to health.

"I want a baby," Susan said. "I think we should try it. You could pray to raise it right, how about that?"

He sighed, turning the chicken. "I know you think my religion is nonsense," he began.

"No, Tony, I really don't. I was just teasing," she said. "Let's not talk about the religion part. Unless you're going to want to have *our* baby baptized—is that what you're getting at?"

"I don't know, Susan, I just don't know," he said, and she wasn't sure whether he was talking about baptizing the baby or having the baby at all. She waited, and after a while he said, "I thought you might not want to have a baby with me. I thought you might not be happy. With me."

"Oh, Tony," she said. "Oh Tony. I'm happy. I'm very happy. I want a baby. Lots of babies. O.K.?"

He nodded, but didn't answer. "I'd better take that inside," she said, holding the plate while he put chicken on it. She needed to go into the cabin for a moment. She set the table, and then went out again. Tony was in shorts, and she sprayed his legs with insect repellent—his big legs with their light, plentiful hair—as he stood there. Then she sat on the step waiting for the corn to be done, with her wine and her bug spray, as if the mosquitoes were wild animals who might come out of the woods and harm Tony—as if, armed, she could be ready.

In the next two days, the weather warmed up and they swam a lot. She was glad to be alone with Tony, but by Thursday she wanted to show off the cabin—and maybe even the two of *them*, alone in it— and so she drove into town and called Lennie, to invite her to spend the weekend with them. Lennie resisted at first, but then she said it was a good idea, she was getting low, it would do her good.

"Do me one favor," Susan said. "I just tried to phone my grandfather, but there was no answer. Could you wait a while and try? There's no phone at the cabin—we can't be reached, and it makes me a little nervous."

"Sure." Lennie had remained friendly with Susan's grandparents. She'd gone to see Leah in the nursing home.

Lennie left New York early Saturday morning in a rented car and arrived in time for a late lunch. It was sunny, and in the afternoon they went swimming and then lay face down on the tiny beach, warming themselves. Then Lennie and Susan dressed and went blackberry picking down the road.

"I love this place," said Lennie. "You were so smart to get it lent to you."

"Apparently more of the houses are used in July," Susan said, "but I like it now."

They had brought a saucepan from the cabin, and they found a bush heavy with ripe blackberries. They passed the saucepan back and forth, filling their hands and then emptying them. The berries were soft and firm, fat and juicy. Susan stopped to eat some.

"Oh, by the way, I couldn't reach your grandfather," Lennie said now, coming around a bush and holding the thorns back to talk to Susan, her red head glowing over the top of the bush. "I forgot to tell you."

Susan had forgotten to ask. "How many times did you try?"

"Twice. I suppose he was visiting your grandmother."

"He might have gone to the store," Susan said. She was frightened, although she explained to herself that she was worried only because she had no phone, not because it was likely that anything had happened at just this time.

Lennie began to talk about her own life. She wasn't seeing a man. "I'm getting old," she said. "I never imagined I'd be this old and not married, no children—when I planned my life. Did you plan your life?"

"I didn't think anybody would marry me," Susan said.

"And here you are married, and I'm not."

Lennie had always liked Tony, and at dinner they all three talked about work and families and men, as usual, and then she and Tony began to argue about Christianity, as they often did. Susan half listened, not saying much. They'd made chicken and corn on the grill again, it had turned out so well the other day.

In the night, there was a thunderstorm. Susan woke up and took Tony's hand, in the dark. She listened to the thunder, feeling bad for Lennie, alone in the other bedroom. They all slept late on Sunday, and when they woke up it was cold and rainy. At breakfast Susan said to Tony, "Do you want to go hunt for a church?"

"There's a Catholic church in town," he said. "I noticed it the other day. Mass is at 10:30. I thought I might go. Do you want to come?"

Susan had been to mass only two or three times, and she didn't want to go in a strange place. And it was raining. She wanted to keep warm and talk to Lennie, to sit on the porch drinking coffee and looking at the lake. Lennie was driving back to the city in the late afternoon.

They straightened the cabin and then Tony left. "While you're in town," Susan said, "would you call my grandfather?"

"Sure." He wrote down the number.

"If there's no answer," she said then, "call my father and Sonia in New Jersey. I want to be sure everything's all right."

"No problem."

She and Lennie settled down on the porch, watching Tony back the car onto the road. "You seem good together," Lennie said. The car drove off. Raindrops hit the lake. Over on the other side, Susan could dimly see a green house. She was glad she'd brought two warm sweaters—she'd lent one to Lennie. She wished she had something to do with her hands. The weather made her want to knit, something she hadn't done since she was a child, when Leah had taught her.

"We are," she said. "We're thinking about having a baby."

"That's what you told me last time."

"Now we mean it," said Susan. "I think we mean it."

"Do you ever think about Dan?" said Lennie cautiously.

"Oh," said Susan. "Of course. Of course I do. But only once a day, and mostly, it doesn't hurt anymore. Mostly it's good. I'm glad that happened, Len."

"I know what you mean. Do you hear from him?"

"No," she said. "It would be strange to hear from him. I wouldn't have an affair with him now—but I wouldn't be indifferent. Maybe he'd like to marry Claudie or something. Then I could love him safely. Or maybe *you'd* like him."

"He doesn't sound like my type," Lennie said. "I like them more unreliable, unfortunately."

"Everyone's unreliable sometimes."

"I suppose. Wouldn't that bother you, though—someone you'd

been involved with? When I break up with someone, I never want to hear his name again, and I wouldn't like seeing him with another woman."

"I don't think it would bother me."

Tony was gone for a long time, past lunchtime. The rain stopped and Lennie and Susan went for a walk along the road and back. When they returned, they were hungry, and Susan made grilled cheese sandwiches with tomatoes. They carried them out to the porch. After a while they heard the sound of a car, and then Tony pulled carefully into the wide place next to the house. He got up and looked up at the house quickly, and then he began to run toward them.

Susan stood up. "What is it?"

"Why is he running?" said Lennie, who had gone into the main room for coffee and was just coming out.

Tony looked at Susan in a strange way as he caught sight of her through the screen. He stopped. "Susan, this is terrible," he said. "Your grandfather died. Ezra died. He died on Thursday and they've already had the funeral. Your father feels terrible. He didn't know how to reach you—but if he'd called my mother, she'd have sent Frank. Susan, I don't know why he didn't do that. I'm so sorry this happened." He couldn't stop talking, standing below her on the wooden steps of the porch, as if he were a messenger who might not be admitted, who might be sent back with a return message—a denial, a refusal.

Susan sat down. "Ezra died? *Ezra?* Not my grandmother?" She started to get up and run to the car in the rain, which had begun again.

"Come back," said Tony, catching her. There was no hurry. There was time to bring along a suitcase, to make plans, to stop and phone for more information. He had died in his apartment. The tenants had heard him fall, and called an ambulance, but it was too late. His heart had stopped. The tenants had called her father. Everything had happened the way it had to, without her.

"Why didn't they come and find me?" she said to Tony, after she had talked to her father. She hadn't asked him.

"He said he didn't know how. But Frank would have come—if he'd just called my parents."

They drove to New York and went straight to the home, where Susan took her grandmother in her arms and didn't say anything, forgetting that *she* could still talk, and that the old woman could hear. After another day or two—they couldn't decide whether Leah understood what had happened—Susan and Tony decided to go back to Vermont. They had left their things there, and no one in New York needed Susan now. Sleeping at their house in New Haven was painful; the place was too neat, organized for their two-week absence.

They drove back. The last two days of their vacation, the weather turned hot, and they swam twice a day. Susan had never swum so well in her life. As she swam, she heard Ezra's slow, formal, ironic, accented voice—talking, talking to her. *He* had found her. At the end of the week, before they went back to New Haven, Susan took her cardboard container of birth control pills, each one in its plastic bubble, and stuck it into the garbage with the sweepings from the cabin and all their vegetable peelings and empty milk containers. She drove home while Tony dozed next to her. She was full of plans, anger, sorrow.

IO, A YOUNG WOMAN, had not only been turned into a cow by Jupiter (he'd raped her, then panicked when his wife, Juno, came along), but she *knew* she was a cow.

Conatoque queri mugitus edidit ore
pertimuitque sonos propriaque exterrita voce est.

Susan looked up from the Latin at which she'd been staring, as if she were coming up out of deep water.

Susan's father-in-law had talked about reading Latin with her from the day he found out that Susan had studied Latin in high school and college, but even after he'd given her Ovid's *Metamorphoses* for her birthday, it had taken them a year before they got around to beginning. Finally, this fall and winter, they had started to meet at the Donnellys' house once every two or three weeks. Frank was taking days off occasionally, now that two of his sons were in the business. Tony was doing well, and Susan had quit her job to finish her M.S.W. Her field placement, three days a week, was in New Haven. She had to go to Hartford for classes on the other days, but not until afternoon. There was time now and then for Latin.

They didn't read many lines at once, because Susan had forgotten some of what she'd learned. Frank read Latin more easily, but he obligingly went at Susan's pace. She had begun in order to please him, but by now she was interested.

"When she tried to complain," she said slowly, "she put forth moos with her mouth, and she was afraid of the sounds, and terrified by her own voice." She looked at Frank. "She *knows*. She knows what's happening to her," and what she had said reminded her of a phrase she had read, more than once, in one of the pregnancy books—five books about having a baby that she'd bought during the year it had taken for her to become pregnant. Now at last she was in her fifth month, and she read and reread them, a kind of daydreaming, when she was supposed to be studying. "If the woman knows what is happening to her body . . ." said one of the books. She couldn't remember what came next.

"That's right," said Frank, "but she's resourceful."

Io's father didn't recognize her when she showed up as a cow, but she told him who she was by writing in the dust with her hoof. Frank hinted that eventually she'd do even better.

"You mean she'll be changed back?"

"She'll be changed back." If he hadn't been her father-in-law she would have said she felt like a cow herself, and she wondered if *she'd* be changed back. Sometimes when she stepped on the scale the thought went through her mind that maybe she wasn't pregnant at all, maybe it was a mistake, and she was simply getting fat. She was getting appallingly fat, then. She had begun to gain weight right away, although her doctor had said she wouldn't for a while. She was going to see him today, after a little more Latin, and he would tell her again that she was too fat.

The sun came through the venetian blind in the dining room window and showed up the spotted places on the green carpet. There were three small rugs on top of it. Sometimes Susan pictured Cat running through the house with armfuls of rugs, depositing them where they were needed—to pad things. It was too bad the rugs couldn't pad people: Everyone in this family was thin. When Frank stood up he swayed, as if he were in danger of being knocked down by the dust motes in the air, though he was a healthy man.

He moved to the window and adjusted the venetian blind. The sun had been shining in Susan's eyes. As his back was to her, he said, "You'll make a good mother for my next grandchild, Susie." He sounded a little gruff. Susan, pleased, bent her head to the next line of the Latin poem. Now Io, still a white heifer, saw herself reflected in the river where she had played as a child, and she ran away in terror.

"*Pertimuit*," said Frank. "Ovid uses the word twice."

"I suppose the *per* means through," said Susan, quite moved. "She's frightened through and through."

"Something like that."

She was speaking lightly but she was afraid she might cry about Io, and that would be perfectly silly. It wasn't that sort of book. The stories followed one another, blending easily as if to emphasize that they were not being told in order to move or change you. But this white heifer staring into the river in fear at what she had become . . .

"How did you learn Latin?" she asked.

"I taught myself. I had a year or two in high school, of course, to start with. Then I read for years and years."

"I wouldn't have read this on my own," said Susan.

"Well, you don't have to. We'll keep at it. After the baby comes, we'll meet at your house, so it will be convenient for you."

When they'd begun, that day, he'd made himself a cup of instant coffee. Susan wasn't drinking coffee because it made her feel sick, now, and without it, she had tried to explain to Lennie, the days seemed softer and slower and somehow puffier. Frank had long since finished his coffee, but now and then he raised the cup to his lips as if he might find more in it after all. He read the Latin aloud. She could tell that it made him happy to read with her, though happiness always seemed equivocal for him.

It was cold in the house, and she felt like picking up one of the rugs and tucking it around him. He was most moved by Io's father's lament, when he realized that the beautiful white heifer was his missing daughter. Reading, Frank seemed almost ready to break down, and Susan wondered if he was thinking of Claudie, who was not lost, and not changed to a cow, but who was not what he had thought she was when she was little. They read a few more lines and Susan looked at her watch. "I have a doctor's appointment," she said shyly. When she left, she was conscious of the faded colors and slight dustiness of the Donnellys' house, because the air outside was so bright, and she drove along the turnpike, which she usually disliked, not minding it much, feeling freed. It was the middle of the day and the road wasn't crowded.

As she drove, she wondered what Frank Donnelly and her obstetrician, Dr. Fall, might think of each other. She liked the doctor, who wasn't much older than she was. He was the newest and youngest member of a group practice, and sometimes she thought of Dan and wondered whether he had Dr. Fall's air of trying to seem older than he was. Dan was probably in a practice, now, but she didn't know where. She had known when his residency was supposed to end, and around that time, ugly brown drapes appeared in the windows of his old apartment. When a new phone book came out, he wasn't in it.

When Susan arrived for her appointment, the nurse weighed her and took her blood pressure. She didn't comment on Susan's weight, although as usual Susan said she felt bad about it, so the nurse wouldn't think she was indifferent.

The doctor had detected the baby's heartbeat at her last checkup, a month ago. This time, as she lay on his table, her belly sticking up, he stopped at his desk and stood, his back to Susan, studying her chart, slouched to one side as if he was thinking about something.

"Aren't you going to give me the fried foods lecture?" said Susan. She couldn't tell whether this doctor minded jokes. She had been to see him four times before, and twice the doctor himself had joked, but once he had seemed lost, and had glanced at her face as if he were surprised to see *her* in the room along with her abdomen.

Now he was silent, and then he came to the table and began to palpate her midsection. When she spoke ("Does it feel like a boy or a girl?" she said, because it made her nervous that he was so silent), he glanced at her as if to ask her to be quiet. Then after a minute he said, "I can't tell about the sex, Susan," as if she'd been serious. He had never before called her Susan—always Mrs. Donnelly, although in fact she still used the name Sternfeld.

Now he took his stethoscope and began to listen at various places on her abdomen. He did it again and again, over and over. "Is the baby all right?" said Susan, suddenly worried. "Can you detect the heartbeat?" Suddenly she was flooded with panic—had the baby died? She had read about that. It sometimes happened. It was mysterious.

"Oh, yes," he said, more cheerfully than before. Then he took the stethoscope out of his ears and held it in his hand, bunched together as if he was going to put it into his pocket. "Susan, you've got two babies in there," he said.

"What do you mean?" said Susan, sitting up quickly, and she knew she sounded angry.

"Twins. You're having twins."

"But I don't know what you *mean*," said Susan crazily, knowing that wasn't what she was supposed to say, what she wanted to say. It was as if he'd awakened her abruptly.

He laughed at her. "Surely you've heard of twins, Susan. Two babies. It does happen. I've been wondering, because you've been gaining weight rapidly, and today I can feel two heads, and hear two heartbeats. One baby's head is here—and the other—well, I can't exactly feel the other head, I think this is the buttocks. But the heartbeats are plain. I'm pretty sure. There's a test—don't worry, it's perfectly safe. You'll have to go over to the hospital, just for an hour or so. That will confirm it."

"So you're not sure?" said Susan, who had heard almost nothing. She felt slightly dizzy.

"No, I'm sure," he said. "I think the test is a good idea, but I'm sure."

"But will they die?" Susan said now.

"From the test? Oh, no."

"No, I don't mean from the test." She had lain down again.

"Why should they die?" he said.

"I don't know. Don't twins die, sometimes?" She didn't know whether she wanted to have twins. She felt that it was a mistake, as if he had gone into the wrong examining room. She should apologize—maybe *she* had gone into the wrong examining room. It was a woman in another room who had twins.

"I realize this is a big surprise," the doctor said now. He was trying to be kind, to calm her down. "Financially . . ." he said. "That is, I don't know your exact financial situation, but . . ."

Susan pulled her sweater over her stomach and sat up, swinging her feet over the edge of the table. It was important to say something sane. "I can't help getting scared about them," she said quickly, tasting the word "them" as she said it—the plural—as if it were a pebble in her mouth, like some of the Latin words that seemed clearer and more definite, once she knew what they meant, than words in English. "What if they're born early and they're so small that they die?"

"Oh," said Dr. Fall. "Well, that does happen, but mostly they're all right. Don't worry. You're a healthy, big woman."

"I'm big?"

"Your pelvis is big."

"I've known people who were twins," Susan said, almost to herself, as if to prove that not all twins died. She didn't know why she was quite this frightened.

When she told her friends, in the next day or so, they said it wasn't great that she was having twins. She told everyone who'd listen to her. Each person knew one or two women who'd had twins. Mostly the babies had not died, although a woman in one of Susan's classes admitted, when Susan persisted, that she knew a woman who had lost one twin. Susan nodded. The woman apologized for telling her, though Susan had forced her to. She needed to find out. But the dominant message was that twins were *hard*. They both cried at once, they were always hungry, they used unimaginable amounts of laundry.

Susan was impatient with this line of argument. She had read so many books, she knew that babies weren't easy, and although she wanted a baby she had been expecting to be overwhelmed and quite miserable, even with just one. She didn't see how two could make her feel that much worse. What somehow seemed significant was that she herself was an only child, but now neither of her children would ever be an only child. They would be more like Tony, who was one of a group from the start, and that made her feel shy with these babies—who were actually inside her. They already knew something she would never know, a secret known to Tony, and secret signals about brothers and sisters would pass among the three of them whenever they were together.

She didn't deserve two babies. Of course, she wasn't sure she *deserved* even one baby. She didn't know how people earned babies, but her ordinariness, as she walked around New Haven, or drove to the market, in the days after the news was given to her, seemed so demonstrable as to present a convincing argument that the doctor was not telling the truth. It was unusual to have twins, and she was not unusual. When she looked in the mirror, at her brown hair slipping out of its ponytail, her round face and brown eyes, she thought the doctor would laugh at her, on her next visit, for believing him, for imagining that something as odd and interesting as twins could happen to her.

Tony thought it was good news. He wouldn't listen to the people who said twins would be hard. "If one baby is good, two are better," he said. "It'll save a pregnancy."

"I wanted twins and I never got them," Cat said on the phone— they were discussing it daily. Susan had finally done something that fascinated Cat. "I thought twins would be funny. Seeing babies together always makes me laugh."

When Susan got off the phone she went back to the conversation with Tony that had been going on, whenever they were together, for days now. "But I'm still afraid," she said. "I shouldn't have told anybody." And then she began to know what she was afraid of.

First, she was afraid the babies wouldn't like being twins. She was sure *she* wouldn't have liked it, which was interesting, because she'd always wanted a sister or a brother. When she thought it over, she decided she would not have minded a twin brother. Having a twin sister would be harder, and having an identical twin sister would be the hardest of all. She wanted to be the only one of her, and surely these children would feel the same way.

"Wouldn't you *hate* being a twin?" she said to Tony.

"I could be a twin with Frank," he said. "Not Doug."

"But it might be the wrong person and you'd be stuck with him. Or her."

"I suppose you get used to the person you have. Sometimes I feel as if Frank and I *are* twins," he said. "Sometimes I forget that I don't know what he's thinking. If a call comes for him at the office when he's out, without meaning to I find out what the guy wants and tell him what Frank would say. I forget I'm not him."

Susan could not imagine this. "You literally forget you're not Frank?"

"Well, not literally. Although if he has something wrong with him—say if Frank had a cut on his cheek, and I felt my cheek, I might be surprised not to feel a cut. That's happened. But I *know* what he'd think. I forget I'm not supposed to know what he'd think."

"Do you get it right? Does he get mad?"

Tony thought about that. "I sort of get it right. Last week the production people wanted permission to change a print run, and I said no for Frank. I was right, but I had the wrong reason. I knew he wouldn't say to do it, but I didn't know why."

"You can read his feelings but not his thoughts?"

"I guess so."

At first she was interested, but then she was upset. They'd been getting ready for bed. Brushing her teeth, she found herself angry with Tony for not minding this sloppiness he seemed to live in with Frank.

"That's *worse* than being a twin," she said, berating him, scolding him. He had gotten into bed beside her. She was curled on her side—she couldn't lie on her back—facing away from him. She cried about it, which made no sense.

"What's worse?"

"What it's like with you and Frank. That's worse. It's as if you don't know where your edge is. I'd *hate* to live like that. I think that's sort of *sick*."

Unperturbed, Tony said, "I kind of like it."

"It really is worse than being a twin. At least twins are two people. One of them can go live in Australia and the other can stay here."

"I'd hate it if Frank went to live in Australia."

"Tony, don't be stupid. You know what I mean."

"I like Frank."

"It's as if you're *Siamese* twins," said Susan, and then she knew what she was most deeply afraid of. She was afraid her babies were Siamese twins.

The doctor would not even discuss it. He tried to explain to her how rare it was to have Siamese twins. "But what is happening to me *is* rare," she said. "Twins are rare." Once she had broken out of usualness, she reasoned, anything could happen.

"Twins aren't that rare. The likelihood of twins is about one in ninety, I think. Siamese twins are probably one in a million." He was a little impatient with her. "I could look it up if you want me to, but honestly, Susan, this is one worry you should cancel."

She couldn't think of anything worse than being attached to another person. She was still going to school, and writing a paper, but in the library she'd wander to the section where she could find books about pregnancy and, now, about twins. Beyond a certain point, the books would not tell you anything. If she knew a doctor to *talk* to, she thought, just to talk to. The only doctor she knew was Dan.

She had been thinking about Dan, in fact. She always thought about him—she had not stopped loving him, and she thought probably if she hadn't stopped by now she never would. She was always slightly aware of his existence. Now she found herself discussing these twins with him in her mind. After all, he was a pediatrician. Surely there were things he could tell her. She still didn't know where he was—Judith never mentioned him, but Susan didn't see Judith often these days.

Judith had gone back to work part-time at a scientific journal connected with Yale, and with a group of other parents, she and

Frank had founded a parent cooperative day-care center, where James spent his mornings. Each week Judith and Frank both spent time there looking after the children.

"I was working my turn. . . ," Judith was always saying, when Susan and Tony did see her. The day-care center was a good place, according to Judith, where healthy food was served, sexist stereotypes avoided, and where daddies changed diapers. Judith had been urging Susan to meet her there one afternoon, so she could see how well run it was; they could pick up James and take him for a walk in his stroller. Now Susan called and said she'd like to see the place, and they met there on a sunny spring day. Susan was excited. She liked seeing the children, who looked happy and untrammeled; some were naked, and she found that delightful.

"Oh, yes, Judith's pregnant sister-in-law," said the woman who greeted them, who was carrying a child into the nap room. "I hear you're having twins. I hope you join, although twins are a bit of a drag, here—two kids coming in at once. We're short of adults. You don't live in a *ménage à trois*, I don't suppose?"

"Don't shock my sister-in-law, Frances," said Judith. She explained that Frances was the only paid teacher; except for her, parents staffed the place.

"We don't need experts in child psychology to raise our kids," Frances said sternly to Susan, looking her over, Susan thought, to make sure she wasn't an expert in child psychology. "We do it ourselves."

James wasn't wearing his shoes, and Judith sat down on the floor to put them on. "Here's Aunt Susan," she said.

"Susan," said James clearly, and when Susan leaned down to greet him he touched her belly.

"There are two babies growing there," said Judith. "Your cousins." They put him into his stroller and began to walk toward East Rock Park, a few blocks away. "Let's take the path to the waterfall," Judith said. "I want him to fall asleep. If he doesn't nap, he's insufferable."

The park still made Susan miss Dan, though she'd been there many times since the day they'd climbed East Rock. Now she and

Judith set out along a path near the river. It had been a wet spring, and the ground was still spongy. Judith had trouble pushing the stroller, whose wheels were small. She stopped and swore and dug the wheels into the ground in her impatience.

Their little group seemed clumsy to Susan, though she was elated; the dogwoods were in bloom and the grass was dark and lush now. But she herself seemed awkward lately, and she thought anyone she was with looked funny next to her. Her jacket didn't fit and she was wearing an old one of Tony's in which she felt like a clown. Judith was round-shouldered, grouchy, and too thin. She couldn't help but overpush the stroller. Susan trotted beside her—a fat puppy.

Judith talked about the day-care center, which was always good for twenty minutes of conversation, Susan had learned. The parents there took turns cooking, and Judith had just had a food week. Someone had criticized her. "She said I didn't have enough protein," Judith said, "but the kids *ate* my food. It's no good bringing in soybean casserole if the kids don't eat it."

"I've been meaning to ask you," said Susan, feeling suddenly daring, watching birds swoop toward the nearby river. On a rock, a dark shadow could have been a turtle. "How do you like your pediatrician?"

"Oh, she's great. Have you picked someone yet? I'll give you her phone number. I suppose with twins there's a lot to talk over in advance."

"I don't know," said Susan. "But speaking of pediatricians, how's your cousin Dan?" She sounded stilted, rehearsed—but Judith didn't seem to notice.

"You can't use him, he's too far away," she said.

Susan's heart turned over. "Where is he, exactly?"

"Yonkers. Were you going to drag your twins to New York to see him?"

"No, I didn't mean that," said Susan. She intended to say that since she knew Dan, through Judith, she thought she might call him and ask him some questions about twins. She thought she might tell Judith that she had an irrational fear of having Siamese twins, and that Dan might be able to reassure her, but suddenly she couldn't say that. Judith, she was sure, never entertained irrational fears. And of course as a pediatrician Dan wouldn't know more about the incidence of Siamese twins than any other doctor; he wasn't an obstetrician. Probably he had never seen Siamese twins in his practice. She didn't need to be told they were rare.

So instead, and partly because the day was soft and warm, and partly because she wanted to feel like a woman instead of a puppy, Susan said, "Dan and I once had an affair."

"You are *kidding* me!" said Judith. Susan didn't answer. After a moment Judith said, "There *were* a couple of things that made me wonder."

"What?"

"Once I mentioned him and you looked as if you were about to say something, but you didn't."

"I would like to call him now," said Susan slowly. "My life has changed so much. It's totally over, of course—but I'd like to call him."

"You want me to give you his phone number?" said Judith. "It's at home."

"If you're sure he's in Yonkers, I can probably get it from Information." Then she began to worry. "Judith, Tony doesn't know," she said, "and I don't want him to know. You wouldn't tell anyone, would you?"

"Of course not."

"Not even Frank. Please."

"Not even Frank, if that's what you want. Though don't you think Tony would be better off knowing?"

"Why?"

"I don't know," said Judith. "People are better off knowing the truth."

"No," Susan said. "Please. No."

"Oh, I wouldn't tell him," said Judith. "Don't worry about me. I just meant maybe *you* should."

"I don't think so," said Susan. It would be terrible for Tony if he knew. She hadn't the least intention of telling him. But she wasn't sorry she'd told Judith. In a moment Judith would ask her something about the affair, something that would remind Susan that she had not always been simply a pregnancy.

"Did it go on for a long time?" said Judith, and she sounded respectful. Usually she spoke as if Susan were years and years younger than she was, or more naive. "I've never had an affair," she said. "I'm probably the only married woman in the state who's never had an affair."

"Oh, I don't think that's true," said Susan. "It went on for a few months. Not very long."

They reached a place where the mud worsened, and there were puddles, so they turned back. James was asleep. Judith walked Susan to her car. Her own car was parked nearby.

"I can still fit behind the wheel," said Susan, "but not for long, I'm afraid."

"Be good," said Judith, with a laugh, as they parted.

Dan's office number, but not his home number, was available from Information. That was just as well, Susan thought. In the morning, she phoned his office and asked if Dan could call her back.

"Certainly," said the receptionist. "Is your child a patient?"

"I don't have any children yet," said Susan. "I just wanted to ask him some questions. I'm an old friend of his."

"Oh, sure." She took Susan's name and number, but after Susan hung up, she was sorry she had given it. After all this time, she didn't want to talk to Dan in the middle of his morning, between cases of chicken pox. She called the receptionist back and said she'd be out all day and Dan shouldn't bother to phone. "Maybe I'll try again later," she said. "How late will he be there?"

Dan's last appointment was at 5:45. "Maybe I'll catch him before he goes home," Susan said. "Thanks."

She hung up and calculated how long it had been since she and Dan had broken up: two years and five months.

She was done with school; her last exam had been a few days earlier. She left a note for Tony saying she would be having dinner with a classmate, and suggesting he heat some leftover meatballs for his supper. Then she took her car and drove to New York State. It was strange that Dan was so close—it had seemed as if he must be many days' travel distant. She didn't get lost. She stopped in a gas station, looked up his office address, and got directions from the attendant. She had time to go into a Friendly's and have a glass of milk.

Dan's office was in a wooden building in a poor neighborhood. She was glad it was not forbiddingly modern. At five to six, she walked into a waiting room where toys were strewn on the floor. A young woman was picking them up and straightening the magazines. Susan explained that she had found herself in the neighborhood, and decided to stop by and see Dan. "I called this morning," she said.

"Oh, I remember," said the woman. "Sit down. He'll be free in a few minutes." Then, glancing again at Susan, she asked, "Are you looking for a pediatrician?"

"I live too far away to use this office," said Susan. "I wish I could."

"They're *excellent*," said the woman, straightening up to say it. Susan had noticed that there were three doctors in the practice. "You could meet them all, ordinarily, but the others are out. But you already know Dr. Tobin?"

"Yes." Now a woman carrying a baby came out of the back part of the offices, and the receptionist hurried into her cubicle to schedule another appointment for her. When the woman was ready to leave, she laid her baby gently on a chair near Susan. Susan saw that there were two sweaters on the chair, and the woman put on her own, then leaned over to dress the baby. She was a tall black woman. She worked the baby's arm carefully into one sleeve of the sweater. Meanwhile, the receptionist, now wearing a raincoat, snapped out the light in her cubicle and came through the waiting room. "I told him you're here," she said to Susan. "He'll be right out," and then she left.

The baby cried a little when he was stuffed into his sweater.

"I know," said his mother conversationally. "You hate that." She picked him up and smiled at Susan. "They just hate putting on sweaters."

"I guess it's uncomfortable," said Susan shyly.

"When are you due?"

Susan looked down at herself. "Pretty soon."

"You bet."

She didn't want to say she was carrying twins and had many weeks to go. It seemed like boasting, when the woman had such a nice single baby of her own. And Susan had begun to worry again. With twins, would such a simple thing ever happen—dressing a baby in a sweater? Would the babies be sick, and unable to be taken outside . . . or would they die? And where did you put one baby while you dressed the other one? She wasn't sure she could carry two babies around, and what about those puffy snowsuits they wore in the winter? It wasn't easy for this woman to carry even one baby, she saw, as the woman hoisted him onto her arm, reached for a large tote bag, and then had some trouble managing the doorknob.

Susan sat quietly, alone now. There were many toys in the cluttered waiting room, and posters on the wall—antiwar posters, signs about meetings of the La Leche League, a recruitment poster for a day-care center. Susan approved. Then the door opened and Dan came out. He looked different.

"You have a mustache," she said.

"You're having a baby."

"Two babies."

"Oh, Sternfeld, *twins,* I can't believe it!" and he hugged her as if he were her brother; then he sat down next to her and reached out to hug her shoulder again. "Lynne told me you called this morning. I couldn't believe it. What made you come?"

"I wanted to talk to you."

"How did you find me?"

"Judith."

"Judith," he said. He turned silent now, for a moment, a little embarrassed, and then laughed and touched her shoulder again.

She didn't want to go to bed with him—it would be as though the children, the twin babies, would be watching—but her arms felt liquid with a wish to hold him. She asked him if he was married, though she was sure Judith would have said; he'd been living with someone, he told her, but they had broken up.

"Dan," she said seriously, "I want you to talk to me about Siamese twins."

"Siamese twins?"

"Imagine being attached to someone," she said. "I couldn't bear it if it happened to my babies."

"It's almost unheard of," he said.

"I know, but I think about it all the time."

"I once saw Siamese twins," he said. "When I was in medical school. They were attached at the hip. There was this guy—Hansen was his name—he was doing state-of-the-art surgery on them. It was exciting."

"But it's such a terrible thing," she said.

"But rare," he said. "How do you feel, anyway? Is it a hard pregnancy?"

"They seem so deep inside me," Susan said. "And yet I keep thinking they have to get out, somehow." Two small wiry creatures clutched her insides—her intestines, her liver—with spidery fingers and toes, and the cords in their navels were attached to her. She shook herself involuntarily, as if to shake them free, but they were solidly connected to her, and then, although Dan had not given her new information, she stood up and walked a few steps, shaking her legs as if she'd been in one position for too long, and she suddenly understood that she was the Siamese twin of the babies, and that was what she had feared—what had happened.

"There are these people inside me," she said, smiling—not saying the thought that had come to her—and they both laughed. She was in a knot with two strangers, and she was the different one. She wanted to get away from them.

Dan started to speak, one hand raised to gesture, but then he stopped and waited. She stood before him, looking at him—at the back of her mind was the worry that this might not be Dan, that although he was a great deal like Dan he might be an impostor, a double she'd never heard about—and the sense of being trapped with the babies grew and felt overpowering and then she was able to stop thinking about it and listen to him.

He couldn't tell her whatever it was she wanted to know, but he talked. He gave her the name of a pediatrician in New Haven, in case she didn't like Judith's, he talked about babies, and then he told her everything he could think of about twins, talking fast, as if it were information he'd been wanting to give her for years. In the middle he paused for breath and said, "We don't have to sit here," and they took his car and went someplace to eat, a little Italian place. He told her about all the twins he could remember seeing, one pair after another, and every once in a while he'd remember another set. Some of them had problems. One set was retarded— that was hard to hear. "I have twin boys in my practice now who are about three," he said. "One of them gets ear infections all the time, the other never does. Go figure." Finally he drove her to her car, and just before she got out of his, he put his hands on her shoulders and kissed her.

"I'm going to love you for my whole life," she said.

"Me, too."

"How do we know?"

"These lifetimes loves," he said. "People can tell."

When she stopped on the road to call Tony, she told him that she had remembered that Judith's cousin Dan was a pediatrician. She knew he must have experience with twins. She had been so worried about the babies, she said, that she had found out from Judith where he practiced and had driven two hours to see him. "Now I know everything about twins," she said.

"I thought you were having dinner with Barbara," said Tony, and she remembered the note she had left him.

"She canceled," said Susan. "I should have changed the note."

"Where are you?"

She estimated when she would get home, and she took even less time to make the trip than she had expected.

It was one of the last days when she was able to do what she liked, freely, and when she thought about it later, that was how she remembered it, not the day when she'd seen Dan but the day she drove a distance, sat in whatever chair presented itself, ate in a restaurant. Soon she was so large it was hard to do anything. Houses seemed badly designed, and she couldn't walk past furniture without bumping into walls. Food disagreed with her, she was tired, and she couldn't sleep. She stopped reading Latin with her father-in-law; she couldn't concentrate.

In the summer, the doctor had her stay in bed most of the time. It was hot. Experimenting, Susan learned that she was most comfortable on a bare sheet, wearing one of two cotton nightgowns that were cut so wide they never stopped fitting her. She washed one every night, and sometimes washing the nightgown was the only thing she could definitely say she had done that day.

She was impatient with Tony, and he seemed distracted. He often ate at Frank and Judith's and brought home a plate of food for Susan. She didn't mind his absence—she wanted to be alone. The babies tumbled and kicked and punched inside her. Sometimes the wildness of it amused her, but at other times it wore her out. Sometimes she'd lie on her side with her hands on her belly, feeling them pound her until she fell asleep.

One afternoon she awoke knowing that for some time, in her sleep, she'd been hearing someone moving around in the kitchen. She lay and listened. There was something tentative about the way this person moved, but it was not like a burglar, she thought, though she had never lain in bed listening to a burglar. It was someone going about her business. Judith and Frank had a key to the house, and the footsteps sounded like a woman's, but it couldn't be Judith, who would never just come in and start moving about. Cat might, she decided, and although Cat ought to be at work now, it seemed possible—and exquisite—that she had taken the key from Judith and come to take care of Susan. Then the footsteps came down the hall toward her, and she knew it was Claudie just before her sister-in-law appeared in the doorway, smiling, carrying a glass of iced tea—which turned out to be for herself.

Susan sat up. "How did you get in?"

"It wasn't hard."

"Did you ring the doorbell?"

"I thought you might be sleeping."

"You broke in?"

Claudie smiled and shrugged. "You should have a better lock. By the way, I brought my cat. Can I feel the babies?" She knelt next to Susan's bed, pressing her small hand against Susan's abdomen. Then she put her ear down. "Are they asleep?"

"One of them is assaulting me," Susan said, guiding Claudie's hand.

"Oh, right!" said Claudie, looking up, her eyes bright. "I didn't know it would be so definite. Is this one a boy?"

"I keep thinking they're both boys," said Susan. "They seem so different from me, and I'm a girl." They seemed totally different. One night she had dreamed that she gave birth to two small animals with teeth, weasels or otters. But she did imagine boys, and she'd been trying to decide whether it would be worth it to persuade Tony to let her name one of them Ezra; she didn't like the name, but she missed her grandfather badly. "Your brother calls the babies Frank and Tony," she said.

"I hope he's kidding," said Claudie. "We have enough Franks and Tonys."

"It's tricky, though," said Susan, drawn into the conversation though she was irritated with Claudie for showing up like that. "Nobody in your family gets a name that doesn't belong to someone already, I notice."

Claudie nodded rapidly. "I'm named for Aunt Claudia," she said, "and there's a great-aunt Claudia. It's like having to share my underwear, not having my own name. When I have kids, I'm calling them Sascha and Natalya." She paused. "You don't want to smoke a joint, I suppose?"

"No," said Susan. Then she added, "I didn't know you wanted kids."

"Oh, definitely," said Claudie. "I won't make a good mother, because I'm such a fuck-up, but I don't think that matters. I have a prize-winning mom and I can't stand her. I'd like her better if she drank or something. It's going to be easier on my babies."

She began to tell Susan something Cat had said, the last time they'd talked on the phone, that had upset Claudie. As usual, Susan and Claudie were talking—almost breathlessly—before anything had been figured out, before Susan understood how Claudie came to be there, or how long she was staying. Susan resented it that Claudie was more interested in talking about herself than in finding out about Susan, even despite Susan's engrossing predicament, weighed down on the bed by babies she estimated at ten pounds each. Still, it was a relief to think about something else, even somebody else's problems. Soon Claudie was telling her about the pet store, where she was now working full-time. In fact, she was living with Paula and Jay.

"You're living with my mother?" Susan said. "Even *I* never got to live with my mother. What's it like? How did you manage to get her to let you do it?" She was making a joke of it, but she felt as if she'd been slapped. Paula hadn't even told her.

"I got thrown out of where I was living and she took me in," said Claudie. "She's good to talk to. We're pretty close."

They were close but Claudie had been given an indefinite period of time off. Susan couldn't tell whether her mother and Jay felt that Claudie had earned a break, or whether they were tired of her. "I'm supposedly staying with my parents," Claudie said, "but Rain doesn't get along with their cat. I thought maybe you'd want me here. I thought I could help."

"That would be wonderful," said Susan, responding to something in Claudie's voice that seemed almost to plead with her, though she wasn't at all sure it would be wonderful.

"And there's so much going on in New Haven," Claudie went on with excitement. "Have you been keeping track of everything? You know about the Black Panther trial?"

"Of course," said Susan, though she didn't really know. She knew that important events were going on, rallies and demonstrations. Her neighbors were frightened, afraid of black riots, apparently, and friends of hers were attending marches and writing petitions—but she couldn't pay attention.

Claudie moved in, and she went to some demonstrations herself, and told Susan about them. Her cat spent her days on Susan's bed, curled next to her, or bumping her hand with her head, asking to be petted. Sometimes Susan scooped her up and dropped her on the floor, but sometimes she pulled Rain closer and scratched her behind the ears so she'd stay. Claudie was best at distracting Susan with talk, filling the bathtub so Susan could get in without waiting for it to be full, and answering the telephone. She refused to let anyone talk to Susan, but Susan didn't care; she didn't want to talk. Claudie was also willing to go to the library and bring books home, and except for listening to Claudie, and taking baths, Susan couldn't do much more than read during those weeks. Once Claudie went off to a rally on the green and disappeared for a day and a half. Tony was frantic, thinking she'd been arrested or kidnapped, but she turned up the next day and laughed at him. "It wasn't like that at all," she said. "Not where I was."

One day she was sick, and she confessed to Susan that she'd taken mescaline and was having a bad trip. They both lay on the bed all afternoon, and Susan held her, stroking and scolding her. Claudie cried. "I'm supposed to be helping you," she said. Susan didn't tell Tony.

She lasted to within two weeks of her due date. Every day she stayed pregnant was hard, but in the morning, she was proud of herself when she opened her eyes and it was light and she was still pregnant. She knew that the babies would do best if they stayed inside her as long as possible. As the months had gone by, Dr. Fall had become more and more cheerful, and now she was cheerful too. Claudie and Tony shopped for diapers and a bassinet—they already had James's for one baby—and people dropped by with presents and loans of baby clothes and receiving blankets.

Susan's water broke one night just after supper. Tony and Claudie were both home. Claudie thought it was funny, but Tony became extremely serious, and insisted on calling the doctor himself, instead of letting Susan do it. Claudie stood on the porch waving, her cat in her arms, when they drove off to the hospital. She'd given Susan a damp, teary, sweaty hug but now she smiled brightly.

"She thinks I'm going to die in childbirth," Susan said.

"Of course she doesn't," said Tony severely, and she saw that he was worried about that too.

In the end she had to have a cesarean section. The doctor was not satisfied with the babies' position and when he tried to shift them, they moved back. Susan was in pain, though she had been doing the breathing exercises she and Tony had learned in Childbirth Preparation class, and she was secretly relieved when the doctor said she'd need surgery. She was given an injection, and the pain stopped. Everything was still. Her fears returned, but they were underneath a great quiet, the sense that she just had to do exactly as she was told, like a character in a fairy tale given precise but enigmatic instructions. Not to raise her head was apparently the main thing.

Tony wasn't allowed into the delivery room. She had never seen him look more unhappy than when she was wheeled away. She knew it wasn't just that he had expected to witness the birth; he had been unhappy throughout this long night. He moved as if at any moment he might raise his arms in a primitive supplication.

She felt the delivery as a strong tug, as if the doctor had to pull very hard—and then another strong tug. There was a crowd in the room—teams of pediatricians, an anesthesiologist, nurses, all with things to say and do. She heard them say "her" but wasn't sure whom they meant.

"Are they all right?" she called, as if she were communicating out a window to the people grouped around her screened-off abdomen.

"They're fine, Susan," said Dr. Fall quickly, turning his masked face toward her.

"Are they boys or girls?"

"Girls."

She felt a great euphoria take hold of her and raise her, as if something were cutting strings that had tied her to earth, and she was a helium balloon. "They're both girls?"

"They're big and beautiful," someone said. "What are you going to call them?"

It was the anesthesiologist, a kind, fat woman who was holding Susan's head. Susan rolled her eyes up to try to see her. "Eliza," she said, "and I think Amy. I have to talk to my husband."

"Those are good names," said the anesthesiologist. "The last set of twins I worked on were Anna and Tanya. Can you believe it? I kept calling both of them Anya."

Susan slept, and dreamed that the hospital required that the babies be named Anya and Tanya, or else they could not be born. "Those are the only birth slots left," a clerk told her. When she woke, Tony was there. "Don't pick up your head," he said.

"There really are two babies," Susan said.

"I know. I saw them. They're great."

"Where are they?"

"They're being warmed up. They have a sort of oven."

"Maybe they weren't done yet."

"They have hair."

"I know," said Susan. "The nurse showed them to me. She came and stood there with the two babies. I reached out and grabbed a foot."

"Whose foot?"

"Eliza's." She didn't want Eliza to be the main baby, just because she was named for Ezra. Amy was just as important. But when she saw them again, she didn't know which one Eliza was, and when they were named, she wasn't sure whose foot it was she had grabbed.

Susan had read that it might take some time before she loved her babies, and she must not worry about that, but she loved them instantly. As Cat had predicted, together they seemed funny. They were not beautiful, but charming, and they made a sort of baby package, a matched set, that pleased Susan mightily. She lay on the bed and played with them and compared them. They looked alike. Tony, lying at the end of the bed, across the bottom of it like a big dike across Holland, was happy again. It took him longer than it did Susan to tell the babies apart. He liked to call them by their full names, Eliza Marie and Amy Leah. Susan had given Amy her grandmother's name as a middle name, although her grandmother was still living. "It's a roomy name, they can both fit in it," Tony assured her. "And it makes sense to my family." Marie was both Cat and Claudie's middle name, but Amy—a name Susan loved—was new. There had never been an Amy.

Susan went home after a week, although she still felt crampy and exhausted from the surgery. At home, the babies cried and cried, whether she nursed them or not. Occasionally one of them would take a bottle, but mostly Susan tried to nurse them. She lay in bed and Tony or Claudie brought her one baby or the other, or both, though she didn't like nursing both at once. "It makes me feel like a factory," she told Claudie.

Tony had found Claudie crying more than once, and sometimes she disappeared for many hours and slept for a day when she returned. But usually she worked hard. Neither of them had ever seen her work before. Susan thought she'd learned from taking care of the puppies in the store, for she seemed to have picked up a sense of routine. She washed the babies' clothes, straightened the house a little, and figured out, every day, what they'd do about dinner, early enough that they could do it before they were ravenous. She'd show up in Susan's bedroom at about three. "Do you want to get take-out tonight, or should I cook?" she'd say. Once she roasted a turkey. She remembered to change Rain's litter box most of the time, and to feed her. She assured Susan she smoked dope only now and then, and she hated hard drugs. "I've learned my lesson."

Paula came for a weekend and wasn't much help, though she liked holding the babies, who stopped crying when she walked them. She made Susan anxious. The next weekend, Lennie came, and she was truly useful—she knew how to change diapers, it turned out, and give babies baths—but she didn't love the babies as much as Claudie did.

One afternoon, Tony was at work and Claudie had gone somewhere. Both babies started to cry and wouldn't stop. Susan tried to nurse them but they turned their faces from her breasts, and she thought she might not have any milk. She put each in turn into her bassinet, and rocked the other one in the rocking chair, and she tried rocking both together, one in each arm.

She had not had ten minutes away from them all day. She was still in her bathrobe, which wasn't clean, and she had never taken a shower. Now she paced the living room with her daughters, crying herself. Finally she stopped and laid both babies down on their backs on the dusty living room rug, though she knew you weren't supposed to put them on the floor, and lay down herself, between them, on her stomach, her face cradled on her arm, and sobbed. Rain came over and sniffed all three of their faces. The babies screamed, face up, on either side of her, and after a while it began to seem not tragic but stupid.

"You're both impossible," she said, rolling over and sitting up. She scooped them up abruptly—usually she held them gingerly, as if they were borrowed—and carried them into the bedroom, where she snatched a blanket from one of the bassinets, stuffing it under her arm. In the bathroom, she laid Eliza down on the bare floor so she'd have a hand free. She spread the blanket on the floor and placed both babies, still screaming, their stomachs drawing in and out frantically, on the blanket. "You can't fall off the floor," she said gruffly, as if they had inquired.

She filled the bathtub, took off her bathrobe and her sweaty, milky nightgown, and climbed in. As she lay there, out of breath, Amy stopped crying and looked around, staring at something, possibly the shiny metal curved drainpipe under the basin. Eliza continued to cry. Susan tried to stop herself from thinking about holding each of them, briefly, under the water. She washed thoroughly and climbed out and dried herself, standing with her legs spread over her daughters. She was still fat and she wondered how she looked to them from below—her pubic hair, her belly, her breasts. It had seemed that as long as they cried, she had to keep them with her.

She put them into their bassinets while she dressed. She had one pair of pants that fit, with an elastic waist. She wore Tony's shirt. Eliza was still crying, and now Amy had started again, but less fiercely. Susan left them while she took a beer out of the refrigerator and put it next to the big chair in the living room. She also brought a package of crackers and a package of cheese, which she sliced. Finally she carried both babies into the living room. Leaving Eliza on the floor again, she nursed Amy, who fell asleep after about a minute. The tingle and pressure of her milk letting down brought tears to Susan's eyes, and she felt her shoulders relax. She waited, to make sure Amy was truly asleep, then slipped her finger into the baby's mouth, to detach it from the nipple, and stood up carefully. In the bedroom, she eased Amy into her bassinet.

Eliza nursed long and hungrily while Susan ate and drank; then she too slept. Eliza often woke up when she was lowered into the bassinet, and Susan didn't try; she sat still, in the big chair, with her sleeping child, until Tony came home. Her fantasy, as she waited, was of life with only one baby.

Claudie stayed for a long time. Sometimes she talked to Paula on the phone, and Susan was not always called to take her turn in the conversation. Once or twice she heard Claudie's voice raised. Finally, in the fall, Claudie said she had to go back. She seemed reluctant and Susan tried to persuade her that she needn't go, but it wasn't that exactly. In some ways, she wanted to go. Tony said he thought they could all drive to New York together. They packed the babies into their car seats in the backseat, with Claudie between them and Rain on her lap. The trip wasn't hard.

It was a Sunday, the pet store was closed, and Paula and Jay were both home in their small house in Queens. Susan had been there a few times. It smelled of cooking; she couldn't get used to the thought that her mother now cooked. She didn't like the furniture, which ran to gold tassels.

Paula was deft and amiable with the babies, which irritated Susan, and Jay kept pointing out how gifted Paula was with babies, which irritated Susan some more. Paula put both girls to sleep by carrying them around and singing, and that was unheard of. Then she served coffee. Claudie, who had kissed Paula when they arrived, had carried her suitcase off to a bedroom to unpack—she really did live there. Now she came back, as they sat down to coffee and cake. "Did the inspector come?" she said.

"What inspector?" said Susan.

"The state. It's just routine," said Jay. "Of course he came. It wasn't a big deal."

Claudie ate a large piece of the cake Paula had bought, though she had hardly eaten anything at Susan and Tony's house. Susan refused cake, though she wanted it.

When she and Tony left, both babies were crying, but they fell asleep in the car. Susan rode in the backseat between them. She was afraid to leave them alone there for the long drive to Connecticut. She was tired. Tony's head looked square and competent in front of her, the unquestioning head of a taxi driver or a bus driver, not of someone she could talk to.

They drove along a road in Queens near the East River. It was a bleak, chilly fall day, and suddenly, as vividly as if it had happened, Susan saw how her two babies would look if she got Tony to pull over onto the shoulder and stop the car, and they carried them across the waste land on the side of the road, and laid them on the bare ground near the river. She and Tony would walk back to the car, get in, drive away, and leave them there. She pictured their two blankets—one a yellow knitted crib quilt sent by a relative of Tony's, the other a pink flannel blanket, a baby present from a classmate of Susan's. The corners of the blankets would flutter in the dank wind as Susan and Tony drove away, and she could look out the window and see her babies there alone in the vast, dirty, cold margin of the city. She was so frightened that she rubbed her hand across her face to clear her mind, and leaned over each baby in turn, kissing their wide blank foreheads.

SUSAN THOUGHT THAT CAT AND FRANK were probably sending money to Claudie every month, but even so, it was hard to imagine that the pet store supported Jay and Paula, and Claudie as well. The one time Susan had seen it, a dusty place in the corner of a small shopping center, with shelves full of items she couldn't picture anyone buying—decorated perches for canaries, feeding bowls for dogs and cats with unfunny jokes printed on their sides, and tank after tank of tropical fish, a few fish in each tank, plus paraphernalia to go into the tanks (rubber octopi, small figures of divers, plastic chests of pirate gold)—she had not wanted to linger there. It was called Pet Village, but it was dark. A village, Susan considered, should at least be sunny.

"It's a front for something," she said to Tony. "Pet Brothel." At the time, besides the fish, there had been cages with ten or fifteen puppies in them, and a few kittens. "The puppies didn't look right."

Now she guessed there were fewer puppies, but it was hard to tell. She never talked to Jay unless he answered the phone, and then he inquired heartily after the babies and turned Susan over to her mother. She hardly ever talked to Claudie either. In the months after Claudie returned to Paula and Jay, she never seemed to be free to come to the phone, and she didn't come to Connecticut to visit, even for Eliza and Amy's first birthday.

When Paula spoke of Claudie, something in her tone startled Susan—they'd grown too used to each other. Paula complained that Claudie didn't eat breakfast, and that she expected Paula to do her laundry. She bought cotton shirts that had to be ironed. "The gorgeous easy-care things you can get now," Paula said, "and she turns up her nose." Claudie forgot to change Rain's litter box, and Paula had to do it.

"How *is* Claudie?"

"Fine."

There was some problem about the store, some trouble about a license, or an inspection, but Susan couldn't tell what it was and she didn't want to find out. Claudie stayed late to take care of the animals, and apparently sometimes she slept overnight in the back room. ("Don't tell anyone," Paula said.) Susan didn't visit Paula. She was busy, and she didn't want to come upon her mother ironing Claudie's shirt.

"My mother feels funny about it too," Tony said.

"I thought she was glad Claudie's doing something respectable."

"With a different mother."

He was more buoyant, these months, after a long period when he seemed sad and far away. He was proud of the babies, and liked doing things for them. "I'm glad you're twins, I'm glad you're twins," Susan heard him singing operatically to them, one Saturday morning. He was changing both their diapers at once—he'd lay them side by side on the bed and do it assembly-line style, exaggerating each gesture, which made them laugh. She tried to decide whether she was glad the babies were twins. She couldn't have done without either of them now, but that was a different question. The first year, she hadn't been glad, but now she sometimes was. They were active, interesting babies. They intrigued strangers—she thought many mothers of twins must hate that, but she liked it.

At a year, the babies had begun spending their mornings at the parent cooperative day-care center James attended, and Susan had found a part-time job as a social worker in a convalescent home in East Haven. She stayed home with her daughters in the afternoons, except for Fridays, when she worked her turn at the day-care center, and they stayed and napped there. Tony had to work at the center too—he went in on Wednesday mornings.

One Friday, Susan was late leaving the convalescent home. Her favorite patient, a woman of eighty-four named Miss Keenan, had a niece who was always consulting Susan, and the niece kept her. Miss Keenan was a small, sprightly, depressed woman who wore tailored suits, sometimes in red. "I never married, but I had fun," she once said. She'd worked for the phone company all her life. She found Susan amusing, but her amusement was like a lace handkerchief thrown over a heavy brown blanket. She had broken her hip. Every week she promised to try to walk again, but she didn't try.

Her niece, also an old woman, was angry. "Auntie, you're just making trouble!" she said with surprising savagery. They were all in Susan's office, Miss Keenan in her wheelchair. "She's making me pay the rent on that apartment—but she can't go back there. Auntie, I'm going to tell the social worker what I found you eating, last winter."

Miss Keenan glanced at Susan, who didn't want to know. Miss Keenan was not like Susan's grandmother—who had died six months earlier when the babies were so little Susan barely had time to grieve for her—but she reminded Susan of Leah.

"She has never faced up to anything," the niece said furiously, as she left. The niece was a disheveled woman who spoke raucously, not delicately and grammatically like Miss Keenan. "Do you know how she broke her hip?" she said. "Scatter rugs. All over the place. I throw them away, she buys new ones. If at least she bought *good* ones, but junk, she gets, so they slide."

Miss Keenan's niece gave Susan a cheerful wave when they met again, a few minutes later, in the parking lot. "Take it easy, honey!" she called, and Susan wondered which of the two she'd have preferred if the niece had been her client instead of the aunt. Now Susan had no time even for a sandwich in the car. She was on her way to day-care to work her turn.

She hoped there would be food around the place, but lunch at day-care, it turned out, had been macaroni and cheese and it was all gone. Susan was hungry all afternoon. The children had two snacks—strawberry yogurt after their naps, and apples late in the afternoon—and she ate some yogurt and an apple. She spent the first part of the afternoon reading to some of the older ones, who didn't take naps. Susan often spent hours at day-care leaning against cushions on a big mattress, her shoes off, a pile of books in her lap, but today the children were restless. She tried finger painting, then blocks, but it remained a noisy, edgy afternoon—the phone kept ringing; the babies woke up cranky.

At a little after four, the adults began cleaning the center. Today it was Susan's job to vacuum the carpet. She was grateful. Pushing the vacuum cleaner, she could hear nothing but its motor; she felt alone. It took a long time. Occasionally, out of the corner of her eye, she'd watch the other people on the turn—Frances and a father named Dick—talking to the children or trying to get them to put away toys and blocks, but it was all pantomime.

The phone must have rung again. She saw Dick, his long legs in jeans stretching over two children who were lying in a heap on the rug, run to answer it. He listened, frowned, pointed at Susan. She turned off the vacuum cleaner.

"Susan, I hate to have to tell you this, but I knew you'd want to know." Paula.

"What's wrong?" Susan said. "I didn't know you had this number."

"I called Tony at work, but I didn't tell him what happened. I thought it would be better if you told him."

"Mother, what happened?"

"She took pills, she slit her wrists—Susan, I don't know why she did this. It wasn't *her* responsibility. Nobody was blaming her for anything that was happening. Susan, I had no idea what a disturbed young woman— She—well, I shouldn't tell you. She put the puppies to death."

"Claudie," said Susan, trying to understand.

"This I can't make sense of—I mean, if she did it because she was upset—"

"Mother, are you telling me Claudie is dead?"

"Claudie— No, I'm not telling you Claudie is dead," said Paula. "The puppies are dead."

Susan shouted as loudly as she could, really a scream. "What's wrong with Claudie?"

Everyone came running. A three-year-old, William, was holding her legs.

"Susan, I'm trying to tell you. She took pills and she slit her wrists. Jay found her. He called an ambulance."

"Where is she?"

"Jamaica Hospital."

"Is she going to live?"

"My God, I hope so. I don't know," said Paula. "I'm sorry—I thought you were the one I should tell."

"Cat doesn't know?"

"No."

"I hate you," Susan said, sobbing. Then she said, "I'm sorry, I'm upset. Jamaica Hospital. I'll call Cat."

She hung up, and turned to find herself crying in Dick's arms. "Is there anything I can do?" he said.

"I'll do it." She called Cat, except that she called the house and Cat wasn't there yet, so she had to tell Frank.

"I see," he said, over and over again. "I see. I see. I'll pick up Catherine and drive to Jamaica Hospital. Do you know where it is, dear?"

Susan knew. A friend had had a baby there, and Susan had visited her. She heard herself giving Frank directions in a clear, rational voice. It was as though she were someone else, watching herself speak. "Now I'm going to call Tony and Frank at work and tell them," she said, and she did. She asked for Tony and got him right away.

When she told him, he said, "I'll go, too. Susan, go to the house and wait for me there. I'm going to leave now, right from here. I'll tell Frank. Take the girls and go to the house. The house in Bridge-port."

She obeyed him. It had never been so easy to get Amy and Eliza ready to leave. It was not that things were simpler, but Susan was like steel. Amy had no shoes on, and Susan quickly found the shoes and put them on. Eliza had a wet diaper and wet overalls. As Susan undressed her, Frances was already handing her a clean pair of overalls from somebody's cubby. Frances dressed Amy in her coat and Susan dressed Eliza. Then she put on her own coat, was hugged by the people on the turn and the parents who were starting to arrive for their children—there was a blur of concerned faces, sober frowns close to her own face—and then she slowly walked Eliza, the better walker, out to the car, with Amy on her arm.

On the road, with the babies strapped into their car seats in the backseat, she began to imagine that it might not be true. What if this was her mother's fantasy and Susan had terrified the family for nothing? But she could remember the gray, ragged sound of her mother's voice. Her mother had sounded irritated with Claudie, not concerned, and that had made Susan angry, but Paula was scared; she was trying to make the trouble go away. Susan couldn't understand what Claudie had done. It sounded as if she had killed the puppies in the store, then tried to kill herself. She couldn't imagine how Claudie could kill the puppies.

Frank and Judith's car was in the driveway of her mother- and father-in-law's house. The front door was not locked, and she walked in, hauling Amy again, and guiding Eliza. James met her in the hall as she was taking off the babies' coats. "Tony's not here," James said. "We're going to have chicken."

Judith came hurrying from the back of the house. "Frank's on the phone with the hospital," she said. "Of course, they won't tell him anything. Just getting through to a doctor is impossible."

Susan looked up from the floor where she was sitting, undoing Amy's coat. Eliza had wandered into the living room, touching chairs and tables for balance, and while fumbling with Amy's things, Susan was watching Eliza, out of habit, and eyeing the room for hazards. "She's at Jamaica Hospital?" she said.

"Oh, she's there," said Judith. "They confirmed that much. But

Patient Information won't tell us anything, and nobody's home at your mother's house."

"She's probably at the hospital." Susan stood up and moved to embrace her sister-in-law, who hugged her back, but distractedly.

"Anyway," said Judith, "we have to feed all these kids. I thought I'd go out for Kentucky Fried Chicken. Will yours eat that?"

"A little," said Susan. "Don't worry about them."

"I'll be right back, then," said Judith.

"I want to come," James said.

"Not this time," Judith said. "I'm a little frantic, Jamie. Leave me alone this time."

"You can help me with Eliza and Amy," said Susan, and James followed Eliza into the living room and dragged her back into the hall, holding her under the arms. Behind Susan, the front door closed. Amy lay on the floor on her back, where Susan had left her. Both coats and Susan's bag and the car keys were on the floor. Susan was sitting cross-legged. Something about James carrying Eliza (it was such a makeshift way to carry a baby), and her own situation, sitting on a rug over a rug, as usual in Cat's house, where surely she had sat on floors far more than in any other place, made her suddenly able to weep quietly, her head down over her knees. Scatter rugs—she was laughing as well as weeping—why did people insist on scatter rugs? Maybe Cat could explain Miss Keenan to her, or to that impatient niece. Partly Susan was crying because—of all things—she felt left out, as though what Claudie had done would be easier to understand if Susan were a Donnelly.

Frank came in from the other room, and Susan scrambled to her feet and blew her nose, and carried Amy into the living room. "I'm sorry, Frank," she said.

"Thank you," he said, as if she were apologizing, or as if what had happened was more his trouble than hers—and that was true, she supposed.

"Can you find out anything?" she said.

"The doctor's going to call us back."

He sat down on a chair in the living room and leaned forward, then as Eliza passed him he reached over to pull her overall strap, which had slipped off her shoulder, back into place.

"Why did you call the doctor?" said James.

"Aunt Claudie is sick."

Susan sat down opposite Frank and took Amy onto her lap. "I just don't understand," she said.

"Claudie's had problems all her life. We knew that."

"Well, we knew it, but it seemed that she was better," Susan said. "But I *have* been worried. I never thought it was a good idea for her to be with my mother and Jay."

"It seemed like a nice job for her," said Frank meekly, and now it was he who sounded apologetic. "We all feel responsible for her all the time," he said. "Maybe that's as much the problem as anything. When the rest of us were that age, nobody sat around and worried about us."

"Frank—could you tell from what they said—is there any actual danger?"

He glanced at James, who was sitting on the floor turning over the pages of a magazine. He liked old magazines, and his grandparents kept a pile of them for him.

"Of—fatality?" he said. "I'm not sure. They wouldn't say anything. And I don't know—if she took a lot of pills, I suppose there could be brain damage. I don't know what she took."

"I guess we don't know when we'll know, either," said Susan.

"No." He picked up one of James's magazines, an old *National Geographic*, and turned the pages quickly and then more slowly.

Amy was starting to whine and cry. Susan said, "I'm going to see if I can find something to feed them," and went into the kitchen. She found a box of oatmeal, and cooked a portion for the babies. She felt like eating oatmeal herself, not fried chicken, but if she ate oatmeal for supper she felt, oddly, that she'd be claiming a greater sorrow than Frank and Judith had—as if oatmeal were the food of mourning or of penance.

Cooking, meanwhile hushing the babies with crackers to eat and pots and pans to play with and bang on, she was seized with the certainty that Claudie was dead, her thin, childish body limp and still, and Susan thought that this would be a greater sorrow than any of them could bear. God let her live, God let her live, she whispered, comforting herself with the rhythm of the words, while she put Amy into the single high chair here—Cat was always saying she'd get hold of another one—and sat Eliza on a chair, pushing it close to the table so she wouldn't fall. She usually used two spoons when she fed them, but she was too tired and miserable. Dipping a spoon into the bowl of oatmeal, she sat between the babies and inserted it first into one mouth, pulling it out between Amy's teeth, then into the other, from which it came out more easily, because Eliza, for some reason, didn't clamp down.

God let her live, she kept whispering, and timed her dipping of the spoon into the bowl to her words.

When Judith arrived with the chicken, Susan astonished herself by being eager—almost happy—to have it. Suddenly it seemed as though Judith had done something wise and generous, providing this chicken, and as if everything would be all right if Susan were only allowed to put this warm food into her mouth. There were cole slaw and biscuits as well.

The doctor didn't call back. Frank tried again and got nowhere. It began to be time to expect his parents and Tony to call. It would have been better if they had traveled together—they were in separate cars—and Susan worried about that. The Donnellys' car was old, and her father-in-law was an erratic driver.

"I can't stand this," Judith said, following Susan into Frank and Cat's bedroom, after they all ate. Susan had decided to try to put the babies to sleep. There was a crib in Cathy's old room, and she had put Eliza, who was harder to get to sleep, in there. Now she was sitting with Amy on Cat and Frank's bed, stroking her back and humming to her. "Eliza's yelling," Judith went on. "Do you want me to go in to her?"

"I think she'll stop," said Susan. "Does it bother you?"

"It's not *that* I can't stand, it's this waiting. Doctors talk only to other doctors. Listen, I'm going to try to call Dan. Maybe he can get through to these people."

Susan's hand, stroking Amy's back, became heavy and stiff. She was sure Judith could see that it was no longer a real hand stroking, but a mechanical device. "That's a good idea," she said.

"Uh—you don't know his home number, by chance, I suppose?" said Judith.

"No." Susan felt warm.

"I guess his answering service can get him," said Judith.

Susan had not been in touch with Dan since her visit to him when she was pregnant, except that she'd sent him a birth announcement and, to her embarrassment, he'd sent the children presents, two beautifully made stuffed animals, a dog and a kangaroo. She'd written a short, warm thank-you note that was just like the ones she wrote to other friends who sent gifts.

"I think he ought to be able to learn something," Judith said, "even if he just calls and announces himself as 'doctor.' "

"I'm sure that's true," said Susan.

Judith left the room and turned back. "I just wanted to say, I hope it's not a personal thing for you anymore."

"Oh, no, of course not."

"Because I'd do it anyway, if it were," said Judith. "He's the only doctor I know, and he's my cousin—but I'd just as soon not make you feel bad."

"It's not important anymore," said Susan.

Judith went downstairs, and after a while, Susan heard her voice on the phone, as Eliza's cries diminished and stopped. It must be Dan she was talking to. She couldn't hear Judith's words. The old gray cat came into the room and curled up on the bed, next to Amy. Amy seemed to be asleep, but for a long time, whenever Susan stopped stroking her and raised her hand, Amy stirred and lifted her head.

At last she did sleep, and Susan stood carefully, her body stiff, and went quietly downstairs to join Frank and Judith in the living room. They'd put James to bed in Claudie's room, but he kept coming down and fretting. "Lights come on the ceiling," he said.

"Is it when a car passes in the street?" said Judith.

"It goes in lines."

"In lines? Oh, because of the venetian blinds," Judith said.

He went back upstairs. Then he came down again. "Will I still be here in the morning?"

"I don't think so," said Judith. "I think we'll pick you up and take you home and put you in your bed."

"If Aunt Claudie comes, she has to go in her bed."

"She can't come here tonight," said Judith. Again he went back up to the bedroom.

When he stopped coming, there was silence for a long time. Finally the phone rang, and Frank ran to answer it. "Hello? . . . Yes, Tony—what?" He stood in the dining room, nodding quickly, over and over again, then he looked at Susan and Judith, and Susan tried to know what that could mean.

"Do they know what she took?" he said at one point. Then, "Judith called—well, her cousin." He glanced at Susan, who was trying to tell from the way he moved, the way he held himself, whether Tony was saying that Claudie was expected to live. The glance in her direction meant something else, she felt—without making sense of it—but she shook it out of her mind to make room for her intense scrutiny of Frank.

"How long, do they think?" he said then, and Judith stood up. "Will you tell us what's going on?" she said sharply.

"Tony, one second," he said, then turned to them. "She's not conscious, but they pumped her stomach and they think if she makes it through the night, she'll be all right, but she might not wake up for days."

He went back to the conversation, then hung up and turned once more to Judith and Susan, while he continued to stand near the phone. "They really don't know anything yet," he said. "She's not conscious. Apparently the health department has been threatening your stepfather with closing down the place—there's been some sort of epidemic among the puppies, and today she was alone there and an inspector showed up. When he left, she killed them all, and then she took the pills. She'd been hoarding antidepressants—I suppose you knew she was on antidepressants?"

Susan shook her head.

"Well, neither did anyone else, I gather, except your mother."

He looked at Susan as if Paula were her fault, and Susan felt that this was so.

"How did she kill the puppies?" she said.

"She put a plastic bag over their heads, one by one."

Susan started to cry. "How many puppies?"

"I don't know."

Then he turned to Judith. "Was your cousin—was Dan going to go over there soon?"

"He said he'd drive down right away, but it would take him a while."

"That's very kind of him," said Frank formally. He had continued to stand next to the phone, reporting the conversation to Susan and Judith. Now he walked rapidly to the front of the living room and straightened a drape that had caught on the back of a chair and was bunched oddly there, as if it had been bothering him for a long time. When he turned around again he spoke in a different voice— hurried, deeper, as if he was uncomfortable and angry to be made uncomfortable. "Susan, you probably think I'm totally boorish," he said, "talking about this guy, but I'm afraid I'm just not used to the level you apparently live at."

"The level?" said Susan stupidly.

"Of sophistication or something, I guess. I'm not used to it. I'm a pretty simple person."

"Frank, what are you talking about?" Susan said.

He stared at her, still standing. "I'm talking about your relationship with Judith's cousin. Your sexual relationship."

"You know about that?" she said. She was suddenly breathless.

"You told Judith."

"And that means you know?"

"I didn't tell him right away, Susan," Judith said. "But after a while, it felt corrosive. You just can't ask a wife to keep something like that from her husband."

"But you said you wouldn't," said Susan.

"And I didn't, for some time," Judith said.

Susan was silent. She was afraid to speak. Then she said—making sense of the way Frank had spoken to Tony on the phone—"Do you mean Tony knows?"

"You don't know he knows?" said Frank.

Susan got up and left the room. She was so stunned she couldn't cry, as if her body might break. She walked quietly and mechanically upstairs, and checked on all three children. They were asleep. Eliza was uncovered and she covered her. The only person in this family she wanted, right now, was Claudie, and Claudie might be dying.

Finally she went back to the living room and sat down. She didn't know what else to do. She wanted to know how long Tony had known, but she didn't want to ask Frank—who sat brooding over the *National Geographic*—any more questions. She wanted to see Tony.

Claudie did not die. Tony came at midnight and hugged Susan, and then they all four brought the children downstairs, turned out the lights, and locked the house, carrying the children to the cars with blankets around them, waving to each other, not calling out, so as not to wake them up. Cat and Frank spent the night at the hospital. In the morning, Susan called Lennie. She didn't tell her about her conversation with Frank and Judith, just about Claudie. Lennie promised to go to the hospital and see her—she was still working in New York, at a different clinic now—and she went three times during the weeks Claudie was hospitalized. On one of the visits, she told Susan on the phone, she had met Dan at Claudie's bedside.

"He's sweet," she said. "I never knew what you meant about him."

"I'm glad you met him," said Susan. Then she told her—it was a week later—what Frank and Judith had said.

Lennie listened seriously and quietly, asking only the questions that would give her a more precise understanding of what had happened. It was the social worker, the careful listener in Lennie that Susan was hearing. "So have you and Tony talked about this yet?" she said when Susan finished.

"Not yet. He's barely conscious." She had been thinking and thinking about it, about Claudie and about Dan. Tony and Frank had both known, maybe for a long time, and not said. It was a year and a half since she'd talked to Judith about it.

Claudie was now in a psychiatric ward. She sent word to everyone that she was glad to be alive, after all, that she was sorry she had killed the puppies, but that at the time it had seemed like the only choice. The store had failed inspection after inspection, and had been on the point of losing its license to sell live animals. An inspector had visited. All the puppies had worms and there were signs of distemper. What he had found that day—insects, dirt—did not mean the puppies would die, but somehow Claudie had felt certain that they would, and she wanted to help them by making it quick. There had been seven puppies, and it had taken longer than she thought to kill them. Partway through, she realized that she didn't know what to do with their bodies. This seemed to change everything. She thought she had to die with them. She had been saving pills, just in case, she said, and she took other things too, medicine that was there for the animals. She had been at the store all night, and it was early in the morning, hours after the inspector left, when she did all this. Jay had taken the day off, and Claudie had had to face the inspector alone. He took the next day off, too, and nobody knew that anything was wrong until early afternoon, when the woman who owned the store next door began to wonder why the pet store was closed, and phoned Jay.

Tony went to see Claudie every few days. "I'm not as worried as you'd think," he said to Susan. "Now we know the worst. Now she can start to change. Probably that doesn't make sense, but it's how I feel."

"Where will she go when she gets out?"

"Not to Paula and Jay's."

Paula felt blamed, unfairly. She hinted that she blamed the family, including Susan, for not warning her about Claudie. Susan was angry with her. "You could see she wasn't just some little conventional, happy type, couldn't you?" she said. There was no point in talking to Paula about it—she didn't answer.

The night of one of Tony's visits, as he and Susan were getting ready for bed, he said, "Judith's cousin went to see her yesterday."

"Dan," said Susan.

"Yes. He's been helpful. He's sorted out a lot of things, and he made it possible for my mother to talk to the doctors right away."

"He's gone several times?"

"Yes, he's visited her twice since that first night. Claudie said he was decent to her. She said, 'He didn't act like I'm a piece of shit.' "

"Does the staff treat her badly?"

"I don't think so, but I guess they're pretty patronizing."

Susan wanted to say, "Dan isn't a patronizing person," but she didn't.

The next day was a Wednesday. On Wednesdays, Tony brought the babies to day-care and worked at the center from nine until one. Then he'd go to Bridgeport, to work, and Susan would pick the girls up and take them home. Sometimes she'd see Tony leaving as she arrived, although sometimes, in a hurry to get to work, he'd leave before she came.

The entrance to the day-care center was a big white wooden door in the yard behind the church. The door always looked locked to Susan when she came along. It was hard to think how much went on behind it. It was a heavy door. This time, when Susan opened it, she heard no one. Frances must have put the all-day children down for their naps a little early.

Several children left at one o'clock, and Susan realized that she was a few minutes late, and all of them except Amy and Eliza were gone. The big room seemed empty, and then she spotted Tony, over on the other side, on his knees. He was sorting books in the bookcase, and he had a pile of books to one side of him. His back was straight and the soles of his shoes—winter shoes, with ridged soles—showed. There was something innocent and open about the way their pattern was revealed: ridges around the edge and raised dots in the middle.

"Hi," said Susan, coming up behind him. Tony jumped and then stood up, a book in his hand—it was *In the Night Kitchen.*

"I got involved in doing this," he said. "I didn't realize how late it was."

"Where are the kids?"

"Amy conked out at noon," he said, "so Frances and I decided to put Eliza down, too. She thinks they're exhausted."

"They've lost a lot of sleep this week."

"The older kids went on a trip to the Peabody Museum, so nothing's going on here. Frances is in the nap room. She said to tell you she'll keep the babies until three."

"That's nice of her," said Susan. "I'll come back at three."

The center was hushed. They'd been speaking in soft voices, and they continued to do that as Tony put down the books he'd been sorting and went for his coat. When they stepped outside, Susan stopped. She didn't know what she was going to do with her two hours. She felt like going for a walk, even though it was late November and cold. It was too bad Tony worked in Bridgeport. She'd have liked to ride with him to his workplace, then walk back.

"What?" he said, stopping too.

"I'm trying to decide what to do now," she said.

"I'm late for work," said Tony.

"They're expecting you."

"Yes, of course." But he kept standing there. "I don't know how I got started sorting books," he said, "but once I began, I wanted to keep going."

"Do you want to go back and finish?" she said.

"No."

"Do you want to come for a walk with me?"

"You're going for a walk?"

"Well, they won't surrender my babies," she said, smiling.

"A walk would be good," said Tony. "I feel as if I've been cramped up for weeks."

"Will they mind at work?"

"I'll call Frank," he said. He had been half turned back toward the door, as if he'd thought all along that something like this might happen. Now he went back inside. Susan waited. She wanted to talk about Dan. She hadn't known that until now. Now she was afraid it wouldn't happen. Frances would call out to Tony that Amy had waked up, and they would have to return to their regular Wednesday afternoons.

But in a few moments he came out again. "Not a long walk," he said. When they reached the gate at the edge of the yard, they put out their hands at the same time, and bumped into each other. Tony's arm touched Susan's shoulder and dropped again as she undid the latch and then closed the gate behind them.

They turned left and walked to the park, and in the park, they headed for the path in the woods near the river. It was cold—a raw, cloudy day—and they were alone. There were brown leaves on the paths. They didn't speak for a long time, and Susan felt that Tony was so far away, she might not be able to bring him back, even if she spoke. "Are you thinking about Claudie?" she said as they entered the woods.

"About Claudie and other things," he said.

She was afraid. She was suddenly more deeply afraid than she could ever remember being—afraid that he would leave her. It didn't entirely make sense. If he wanted to leave her for having an affair, he could have done it when he found out. But she must have been pregnant then. Maybe he had decided to wait until she brought it up, as if that would be the signal that she could manage on her own, that she was a person who could speak again, not just a pregnant body or someone frantic with infant care. Tony was so ethical he could never have left her as she had been a year ago. She could imagine him telling Frank, "I'll wait until the children are a year old, settled in day-care. When she can get along without me."

She thought, obscurely, that even now she could postpone her fate if she didn't speak. If she spoke, she herself would be giving the signal—yet it seemed as if she had to, even as if it were somehow for Claudie's sake.

"Tony," she said, as they walked, he a half step behind her. The river was next to them, beyond the nearly leafless trees.

"Yes."

"A long time ago," she said carefully, and paused, "something happened."

"Yes."

"I know you already know, but I want to tell you."

"Why?" he said.

"Why?"

"I already know."

"I know you know," she said. "Don't you want to talk about it?"

"I guess I might," he said.

"I fell in love with Dan," she said. She had made up her mind to use those words, because she had *loved* Dan—did still love him. "I slept with him for several months."

"Why are you telling me this now?"

She paused. "I don't know. Partly because Frank told me he knew, and you knew. I guess he told you. Maybe I'm jealous that you and Frank knew you knew, and I didn't—"

"If someone's going to be jealous about secrets—" he said.

"I know. I know. I don't mean it." But she wanted to cry.

"You don't have to talk about it," he said, and it sounded like a warning.

"Tony," she said, and she turned his body with her two gloved hands to face her. He felt stiff. She wasn't sorry she had had an affair with Dan—she still wasn't sorry. But the man before her, in his brown coat, standing on the path near the bare, dry shrubs, was the person who ought to be there. "I'm afraid you won't want to be married to me anymore."

She started to put her arms around him, and stopped. She couldn't beg. He put his arms around her neck, resting them on her shoulders as if they were tired, and began to sob. She had never heard him cry before. He made a sound—*eeeh, eeeh*. In some ways it was like someone imitating a crying person. It was without guile or protection, as if he were alone.

He disengaged himself—she had put her arms around his waist—

and stepped to the side, where there was a tree, as if he were going to hide his face on it, and then, wandering again, he came back to her. They sat down heavily on the ground, in the dead leaves, and then he put his arms around her.

"I love you, I love you," he was saying, in a high, choked voice, and she, in tears, said it too.

They sat there for a long time, leaning toward each other. A dog, a cheerful white mongrel, came along the path and stopped to sniff them carefully, as if she might learn a specific fact. Susan patted her smooth head, and the dog moved on. "I'm cold," she said, her face still wet from tears.

Tony stood up and brushed himself off, and they began to walk again. "Maybe when the kids are bigger," he said, "we could get a dog."

"I love dogs," said Susan. Then she said, "When you first found out, why didn't you say something?"

"Why didn't you tell me?"

"I don't know," she said. "I was afraid you would leave me."

"I was afraid if I talked about it, you'd leave *me*," said Tony.

"You weren't angry?"

"Yes. I was very angry."

"Are you still angry?"

"Yes. I wouldn't have done it and I don't think you should have done it either."

She took that in, and didn't answer for a long time. She supposed he was right. At the time she had seemed to have no choice. She couldn't answer; she couldn't speak for the person she had been. Finally she said, "It was wrong of Frank to tell you."

"He didn't," said Tony. "I read it on his face. I knew there was something—and in a way, I'd known for a long time that there was something. Once he knew, I guessed so much that he had to tell me."

She could imagine it.

"Once I knew, I felt a little better," said Tony. "It was like going to the doctor with a pain, and being told, yes, you have a disease. At least you know."

"You were alone with it." He had been in pain, for a long time.
"Yes."

They had reached the footbridge over the river, and were standing
on it, looking out at the river and the swampy land around it. The
ground was dark and the vegetation was brown, but it was beautiful.
"When did Frank tell you?" she said.

"I don't remember. When the babies were little, I think—or just
before they came. When Claudie was with us."

"Claudie doesn't know."

"Oh," he said. "I wondered."

"Did he make it clear that it had been over for a long time?" They
had crossed the river, and continued along the path on the other side.

"Yes," he said, "but I knew you'd seen Dan when you were
pregnant."

"But it was over then."

"Yes, but still—"

"It had been over for a long time."

They walked farther along the path, and then he glanced at his
watch and without speaking they both turned around. Now the river
was on their right. Walking silently beside it, Susan thought that it
was like her mind, which moved along as it had been moving since
she was a child. The water shone darkly and she couldn't see into it,
and no one could see into her mind, either. She took Tony's hand.
"I'm sorry," she said, at last.

When Susan was a child, it had pleased her that her mother knew
only part of her, and her grandmother a different part; because they
didn't live together, and didn't get along, they could never combine
their knowledge and figure her out entirely. In her adult life, Dan
had been a secret for so long, she hadn't been sure she could stand
and walk without—not him, but the thought of him; it had been a
walking stick. She thought that probably she would still think of him
and she wouldn't report that to Tony. Truth-telling—exhaustive
truth-telling—had never been the stuff of her life, or theirs together,
and it never would be, but this way, when it came it shook them and
made a difference. Maybe what the white dog had learned when she
sniffed their faces was that they were married to each other and

wanted to be. Susan cherished Tony down to the crumpled tissues in his pants pockets, but she didn't want him to know everything she was thinking.

They kissed at the edge of the woods and then Tony seized her again and held her so close to him she was breathless; they stood in each other's arms for a long time. Then they hurried back to the day-care center, where she went in and collected their babies, thanking Frances for the respite, while he jumped into his car to hurry to Bridgeport. Arriving home with Amy and Eliza, maneuvering them into the house, Susan pictured him there, carrying his white coffee mug as he moved through the building in the late afternoon, the lights bright and the windows darkening (so that safety seemed to be within), asking questions of people, ticking off each answer in his mind, nodding and listening.

"FRANK AND I COULD PAINT the house during our vacation," said Tony, at the beginning of summer the year Amy and Eliza were turning three. He meant the inside of the house, which did need painting. He and his brother had done a lot of work at Frank and Judith's on weekends and during short vacations. They didn't seem to mind working in hot weather—or working at all when they could have been enjoying themselves, as long as they were together. Now Tony explained that they could paint the house in a week, but not if Amy and Eliza were around. Frank and Judith had the use of the cabin in Vermont again, and it would be free, once more, at the end of August. If Susan took her vacation then, she could spend a week in Vermont with the children while he and Frank painted, and he would join her for the second week.

He wanted this, Susan saw. He and his brother would transform their house into a draped, spattered site for their half-jokes and incomplete arguments, sometimes resumed hours later when a ladder was moved or a new can of paint opened. "But it depends on what you *mean* by original sin," Tony would say, passing through a room, and—half a day later—"Original sin, well . . ." Frank would reply.

Tony was most at his ease, as a religious man, in a debate with

Frank. "You and Frank should have been named Maybe and Maybe Not," Susan said once. Together, they were like two men in a three-legged race: Tony had a leg in the church, Frank had one firmly outside, and the other one was in a sack in the middle, making Tony three-quarters a Catholic, Susan calculated, and Frank one quarter. James had never been baptized, though Frank still talked about it sometimes. When Amy and Eliza were babies, Tony had mentioned baptism once and Susan had lightly offered to let him baptize one of them. In the end both babies were baptized in a ceremony that included Jewish prayers read by a rabbinical student whose wife was a friend of Susan's. Susan was uncomfortable.

Susan would have preferred to leave the house unpainted and spend both weeks in Vermont with Tony, but then it occurred to her that Lennie could come for the first week, and she arranged that. Then, a few days before the trip, Susan phoned Judith and suggested that she also take James. Judith was pleased. She and Susan were still friends, though not intimate friends. When Claudie recovered, Frank had returned to his old manner with Susan—serious, respectful, and a little remote, but he was friendliest talking to Susan about the children. She liked James, who was five. He'd keep Amy and Eliza happy in Vermont.

Susan was alone with Tony the evening before she left. Amy and Eliza spent the night in Bridgeport, at Cat and Frank's, so the painting could begin as soon as Tony got home from work on Friday afternoon. He spent Friday evening moving from room to room, patching holes in the plaster, and Susan spent it packing. It was strange to be in the house without the children. She and Tony could talk without interruption or self-censorship. The babies had learned to talk and listen, and Amy, especially, lately, wanted to know everything because she already seemed to know everything.

"I like the way you sound when you're on your way to get something heavy," Susan said. She was in the children's room, packing their shirts. "You walk differently. I can tell. It's a brave walk."

"The things you think," said Tony, but he continued to sound brave.

They went to bed late, tired and sweaty, but woke up early; Susan woke to the feel of Tony's chin exploring her face and neck and shoulders. They made love. Quickly, they packed the car and Susan said good-bye and set off for Bridgeport.

When she drove up to Cat's house, she spotted Amy playing in the grassless front yard. Cat and Eliza were sitting on the porch steps watching her. Cat was in shorts, and her knobby knees were bare. She was turned toward Eliza with a hand in her own unruly light brown and gray hair, listening intently, as if Eliza were a colleague at a meeting. Eliza's legs were fat and short, bent over the step on which she sat. She too looked like someone at a meeting—she was making a point. Amy, who was in long pants because she didn't like shorts, even when it was hot, was stepping slowly and deliberately along an imaginary line on the ground, her head bent, apparently talking to herself. She looked up when the car stopped, and ran to meet Susan. Susan picked her up and kissed her and balanced her on her hip. The pediatrician said they were the same weight, but Amy always felt heavier to Susan.

Cat looked up at her, smiled and squinted. Her face looked thin, Susan thought, and her eyes were large and a little anxious, but they seemed at rest when she watched Susan and Amy come up the walk.

"You look as if you've just decided that I probably won't drop her after all," said Susan.

"No, I was thinking you look pretty."

"Pretty!" She was dressed in a T-shirt and jeans, and her hair was already coming loose.

"You look good with a child on your hip," said Cat.

Susan put Amy down. Eliza hugged her leg and Susan leaned over to smell her hair and kiss the top of her head. "How did it go?" she said.

"Fine. Eliza was just telling me that I make French toast wrong, though."

"Is there more than one way to make it?"

"I don't know. Claudie always said the same thing. She'd never eat my French toast."

"You haven't heard from Claudie?" said Susan quietly. She'd been wanting to ask for weeks, waiting for Cat to mention her name.

"No." Claudie had moved to Boston shortly after she was released from the hospital. She'd been working. A few months ago she'd called to say she was moving to a new apartment, and promised to call soon, but she never did. No one knew where she was. "I think she's all right," said Cat. "I think this might be the way it's going to be." She said it in her office voice, Susan thought.

"You don't mean we'll never hear from her again?"

"No, I mean that sometimes she'll need to be out of touch."

"Yes," said Susan, and she thought that Cat, too, needed to be elsewhere, out of touch, occasionally. This morning she was not out of touch. She rested her hand on Susan's arm, standing up, and then she laughed at the children's concerns. They were suddenly certain that Susan had not been capable of packing their things, did not know the way to Vermont, would not have food or plates when they got there. "And pots, Mommy?" said Eliza. "Are there pots at Vermont?"

"There are pots."

"And *beds*?"

"There are beds."

Susan hugged Cat good-bye and watched her walk swiftly back into the house. Her back looked like the back of someone who was already alone. But Frank was home, probably—reading upstairs.

It was late in the morning by the time Susan had met Lennie at the train station, and picked up James, and they were all together on the road, James belted in the middle of the backseat between Amy and Eliza, in their car seats, Lennie beside Susan in the front, excited to be on vacation, looking New York-y, Susan thought, in a loose denim sundress.

"I hope you brought other clothes," she said.

"Of course. Flannel shirt. It's cold up there."

"And hot. Bathing suit."

"Bathing suit."

When they stopped for lunch, Lennie was quiet and Susan hoped she was not regretting her decision to spend a week with three children. They were good children, and they all ate at least some of their lunches and didn't quarrel, but they were unmistakably *present*. They talked all the time. "My mom and my dad never come to this restaurant," said James. "They go to the restaurant with the blue horse"—and none of them could figure out what he meant, though he seemed to need badly for them to understand, and they asked all kinds of questions.

Later, in the car, when the children had fallen asleep, Lennie said, "Maybe he saw a child in a restaurant playing with a blue horse."

"I thought he meant a decoration," said Susan.

"So did I, but maybe not. I love the way they think."

"That's good," Susan said. "I was afraid you were deciding you shouldn't have come."

"Oh, no. I knew what I was getting into."

Lennie sounded so certain—almost offended—that Susan said, "I didn't mean anything. You just seemed quiet there for a while."

"Well, I was thinking about something," Lennie said, after a pause. They were driving straight up I-91 and were almost in Massachusetts. Susan had been keeping an eye out for the sign at the state line, so she'd feel as if she'd accomplished something.

"What were you thinking about?" she asked.

"Susan, I have to tell you something," said Lennie. "I don't know how you're going to feel. You might even like this."

Susan knew what Lennie was going to say before she continued, and that in itself surprised her the most.

"Susan, do you remember that I met Dan Tobin when Claudie was in the hospital?"

"Yes."

"A few months ago, I ran into him at a conference. It was terribly sad, it was about child abuse, and we were both a wreck, and—well, we found each other. I've been seeing him ever since."

"Why didn't you tell me?"

"I didn't know if anything more would happen," said Lennie. "I didn't know how it would make you feel. I know you're not still in love with him, but I thought it might be hard anyway. But I also thought you might be pleased."

"I *am* pleased," said Susan. "I'm very pleased." But a knot had formed in her chest, a hard knot that she needed to rub and knead with her fingers—but couldn't, because she had to drive to Vermont and she was only in Massachusetts.

"I think you're not," said Lennie. "You know, you once told me you thought it would be good if he married Claudie, so you could have him in the family. I've been remembering that."

"I know," said Susan. But she was angry. "Why didn't you tell me?" That was it—the secret—why had there had to be a secret? "Did you talk about me? Have you been working up to telling me, and figuring out how you'd deal with my hysteria?" She did sound a little hysterical to herself.

"No."

"Then why didn't you tell me right away?"

"It's been only a couple of months," she said. "At first I thought it wasn't real, and I was embarrassed. There have been so many guys—I didn't want you to hear about one more who wasn't going to work out, especially this one. Also, I didn't want to—well, right at the beginning, I knew that if it bothered you, I'd tell him not to call me again. But I wanted to wait and see."

"So it's important?" She was hoping Lennie would say no, and blaming herself for that.

"Yes, it's pretty important."

They had passed Springfield. She couldn't remember how long the trip took. She wanted to stop for coffee, so she could sit still and think, and let the coffee warm the place in her chest that had clenched, but it was a mercy that all the children were asleep; if she stopped, somebody would wake up.

"You're angry," Lennie said.

"No, I'm just surprised." But she wasn't surprised. "Talk to me about it," she said. "Tell me what happened."

"I've met his parents," Lennie said. "They live in New Jersey.

We drove down to see them last Saturday, and we all went out to dinner. His father looks just like him."

"*How* did you meet him?" Susan didn't want to think about Dan's parents. She had never thought of him as having parents, though she had always known about his grandmother, and because he and Judith were cousins, somewhere in the background had been family. "No, I don't mean that. How did it turn into something?"

"Oh," said Lennie. "Well, we went out for coffee. This was at the conference. And we were so upset we just kept talking about cases we'd had, abused kids. It was horrible. We kept topping each other. And then he said, 'We can't deal with this. Let's duck out of the afternoon session and go for a walk.' The conference was at Columbia and we walked down Broadway—it wasn't far from where I lived when I first came to the city, so I took him into my favorite hardware store and he bought a salad spinner. He said he couldn't find one like it in his neighborhood."

"By then you were friends," said Susan. She thought she remembered that store.

"Yes."

"Did you talk about me?"

"A little. I think he thought I might not like him because of you—that I might think he had, well, been careless about you."

"I don't want him to think that. It was my doing as much as his, God knows."

"He doesn't think *you* think that," said Lennie. "He thought I might. Being protective of you. And it *was* a hard thing for you, Susan, it did give you lots of pain."

"It was worth it." Susan glanced over her shoulder into the backseat. Eliza would not be interested in this conversation, but Amy would sense feeling and have something to say. She thought both girls were asleep, but Susan didn't say anything more, anyway, and then James woke up, and it was necessary to talk about where they were and how far they had to travel.

The lake had not changed, but Susan could not take it in quite as she had before. In the past, the first glimpse had made her peaceful, but now it was as if she were looking through a dulled window at the pond glinting beyond the trees. She was still excited to be at the cabin. She drew the car into the open space next to it. The lake was below her, with its tiny beach, and two tree stumps, like markers.

Together she and Lennie carried in the luggage. The children had slept and awakened and slept again. They'd be up late. Now they woke up and Susan reached into the backseat to help Eliza out of her car seat and then went around to the other side to help Amy. James scrambled out himself.

In the cabin, the children wanted to figure out sleeping arrangements. Susan wanted only to sit down, but she couldn't resist them. There was a folding cot in a corner, and they got her to move it into the second bedroom, where all three children would sleep. They decided which bed would be whose, and supervised Susan as she put sheets on the beds, with waterproof mattress covers on Amy and Eliza's. Susan would sleep in the other bedroom, and Lennie on the sofa bed in the main room. "You don't have to put on *my* sheet yet," she said to Susan. "I can wait."

"That's very grown up of you."

"Thank you. Do you want me to drive into town and buy food for supper?"

They figured out a shopping list and Lennie took the car keys. When the sound of the car died away it was deeply quiet, and Susan realized how tired she was. She sat down at the table in the main room. The children were pretending to go to sleep, lying in their clothes on top of their beds.

"Eliza, now you say good night to Amy," came James's voice.

"G'night, Amy," said Eliza, laughing. "G'night, Amy Bamy."

James made the sound of snoring and they all laughed.

The knot in her chest didn't go away. She rubbed at the spot with her fingers. She was not sorry this had happened. For years, she had hoped Lennie would find someone, and Dan was the best person she knew. This way, she would know him again. That would be awkward, but only briefly. She'd never see much of him, because of

Tony—but she thought that after a while, they could all be friends. Still, the knot in her chest would not loosen.

She wanted order, though she was so tired. She unpacked her clothes. There was an extra dresser in the bedroom, and she dragged it into the main room for Lennie. Then she went into the children's room to put away their clothes. They wanted to go swimming, and were undressing. James had put on his bathing suit, and Susan helped Amy and Eliza with theirs. It was cool for swimming here, but it would be pleasant to sit at the lake. They'd brought pails and shovels and a big plastic dump truck, and they carried them all down to the water. James started organizing the digging, and then Amy said she was going to dig a house for fishes, and they all followed her. Susan was glad she'd brought James. She didn't have to talk. She took off her shoes and socks, and dug her feet into the damp sand. Then she turned onto her stomach and folded her arms around her head, lying on the sand, to hide her face.

She could hear the voices of the children, James's low and a little growly, Amy's a bit awkward—she had been slower to talk— and Eliza's confident and faster. None of them ever seemed to stop talking. Susan smiled while she lay there—though she had also begun to cry a little—because it was so efficient of her to be able to care for three children and do her crying privately at the same time.

After supper, Susan put the children to bed. When she finally returned to the main room, Lennie was clearing the table. They'd cooked spaghetti. Susan sank onto one of the unmatched kitchen chairs. Lennie had brought home a bottle of red wine, and Susan's glass, half full, was across the table. She reached for it and spilled it, and she put her head down next to the puddle and cried again.

Lennie took some paper towels and wiped up the spill, and then she came over to Susan and kneaded her shoulders with both hands. "It's not Dan," said Susan. "I'm crying because I drove you and the children all the way to Vermont. I was good all day."

"It can be Dan," said Lennie.

"I want to be happy about it," said Susan, "but my chest hurts."

"I thought you'd be pleased," Lennie said, and she sounded a little tense. "If I marry him, I'll be your cousin-in-law or something. I'll almost be Jewish."

"Let's see," said Susan, smiling with tears on her face. "He's Judith's cousin, so he's Frank's cousin-in-law, which makes him Tony's cousin-in-law-in-law, and my cousin-in-law-in-law-in-law. That will make *you* my cousin-in-law to the fourth power."

"*Family*," said Lennie, attempting a Yiddish accent.

"Are you going to marry him?"

Lennie got up again and washed a couple of plates. "You know me," she said. "It never works out for long. But I figure, sometime it's got to, right? Maybe this is the time."

"I could imagine you marrying him."

"Did *you* want to?"

"No," Susan said quickly, but that was what she had told herself at the time of their affair, to make sure it couldn't change her life too much. If she had met Dan when she didn't know Tony, or if Tony had found out and divorced her. . . . She thought, as she drank the wine, that she wouldn't have married him anyway—she wanted to be married to Tony—but she wasn't sure.

She tried to picture Lennie and Dan married to each other. She and Tony might be here with the children, and they might drive up for a weekend. She wondered whether Tony would ever let that happen. She pictured the four of them around this table, their chairs pulled back, a bottle of wine empty. They were in shorts. Dan said, "Lennie and I . . ."

Lennie took long swims every day, even when it was cold. She swam to a point that jutted out into the lake, then across the cove to an outcropping rock on the other side, and then back to their beach. She offered to watch the children while Susan swam, but Susan took only short swims. She had never known how well Lennie could swim. Lennie said she'd worked as a water safety instructor at a camp, summers, while she was in college, and she still had that confident look, striding into cold water without hesitation, the sun catching the ends of her short dark red hair.

Susan was sure that Lennie was angry with her. Watching her competent crawl, she felt awkward, out of step, unable to forget about something she didn't want, unable to give it gracefully to her friend. She was sure that while swimming Lennie thought about how difficult Susan was being. The tension in her chest persisted. She wanted Dan to show up and tell her he had always loved her better and would have spent his life with her if he could. That was foolish.

Then she and Lennie had a needless argument. Lennie had taken the children down to the beach while Susan swept out the cabin and wrote some postcards. When she glanced through the porch screen, she saw only two children, playing in the sand. She didn't see Lennie. Susan put down her pen and hurried to the shore. James and Eliza were playing there, and as she reached the beach Lennie and Amy came along the narrow trail that ran through the shrubbery at the edge of the lake.

"Where were you?" said Susan.

"Amy wanted to see that boat." It was an abandoned rowboat on the property next door. There was a boarded-up summer house there.

"But you left the other kids."

"I could see them," said Lennie calmly. "And I told them not to go into the water."

"But what if they had?" said Susan.

"They listen."

"If something had happened, you would have been too far away to help them."

"It's just a few steps, Susan," said Lennie tensely.

"When kids are near water, you have to be right there."

"I *was* right there."

Susan turned away. "All right." She didn't want to fight, and she didn't know whether she was being sensible or not.

"I know you've made up your mind that I'm an irresponsible, selfish person," Lennie said to her back. "I've been accusing myself of that all week—but I'm not like that. I'm not."

"I know," said Susan, turning. "I know you're not."

She went up to the cabin, and when Lennie and the children came, a little while later, neither she nor Lennie talked about what had happened. The children had played in the water for too long, until a wind came up, and they were chilled. Susan dried them and dressed them while Lennie took a long swim on her own. Then she headed straight into the shower. Susan made peanut butter and jelly sandwiches for lunch.

In the afternoon, they drove into town, where there was a fair with a carnival. Amy and Eliza loved the animals, especially the sheep and lambs, but they didn't want to go on the kiddie rides, and demanded cotton candy but then didn't like it. They became fretful and tired. James, though, wanted to take every ride, and to stay for the tractor-pulling and the calf-judging. Finally Lennie offered to stay at the fair with him while Susan took the girls home. "Do you mind driving back for us in the evening?" she said. "James and I can eat supper here. Big date."

Relieved, Susan packed her cranky, sticky daughters into the car and drove to the cabin. Both girls fell asleep, and when she arrived, she decided to leave them where they were. If she tried to carry them to their beds, they'd wake up and be even grouchier.

There was a car parked near the house, a small black car, not in great shape. Susan pulled in beside it and turned off the engine. It had to be Dan, she reasoned. She sat with her hands on the wheel. Lennie might have told him where they were going. No one in the family had a car like this one; no one else would come. The owners of the place were out of the country. She told herself it could be an intruder, a drifter who thought the cabin was not being used, even a burglar. Anyone could have slid a screen up and climbed in. But she was sure it was Dan.

She climbed out, leaving the car door open so the slam wouldn't wake the children. Opening the screen door carefully, Susan heard the radio playing a rock song she didn't know. On the sofa bed was Claudie, just waking up.

Her hair was short and it looked darker. She was thin, and wearing a lot of makeup, but she looked pale anyway. She still had that quick, rabbity look. Susan always glanced at Claudie's arms, which had old scars but no new ones. Her arms were thin, and Susan was reminded of Cat leaning on her elbow to speak to Eliza. "Sue, I lucked out—it's you," Claudie said.

"How did you know I was here?"

"I didn't know. I borrowed a friend's car and drove up from Boston. I thought it might be you and Tony, or somebody from the family, or nobody at all. If they'd rented it out, I'd just apologize and go for a swim at the public beach in town."

"You've been here before?"

"Sure, with Frank and Judith. Where's Tony?"

"Tony's in New Haven."

"You came alone? Where are the babies?"

"In the car," said Susan. "They're asleep. Lennie's here with me—remember her?"

"Sure."

"You lay down for a nap, not knowing who was staying here?" Susan said. "What if they *had* rented it out?"

"By then I knew. Your stuff—your blue bathrobe."

"Right." They went outside, so as to hear the children when they woke up.

"I really wanted to see those babies," said Claudie.

"They'll be happy to see you," Susan said. Then she said, "Cat hasn't heard from you in a while."

They walked down to the beach and sat on the sand. It was a still afternoon, and the lake was quiet and not glittery.

"I know," Claudie said at last. "I feel better, this way."

Susan didn't argue. "Where are you living?" she said.

"I'd rather not say."

"It's still a secret?"

"I don't want to be in touch with them. I don't want you to know and not be able to tell them."

"You're not getting along with them? Your parents?"

"No, it's not that. I just can't. Not right now."

"May I tell them I've seen you?" said Susan.

Claudie considered. "You will, whatever I say, won't you?"

"Of course."

"O.K., then. Sure, tell them."

She took her shoes off and pushed her jeans legs up so she could wade in the water. "That feels good," she said.

"Are you working, or going to school, or what?" Susan asked.

"I'm working. I'm starting school at night in the fall. I'm living with some other women. We're all vegetarians."

"I didn't know you were a vegetarian," Susan said.

"Oh, sure. I eat eggs and milk, though."

Susan began to plan meals, but Claudie said she'd stay only a few hours, certainly not overnight. Susan was able to talk her into staying for supper, but that was all. She stood before Susan, sounding eager to leave, but looking sad.

"Claudie," Susan said, "you miss us. You don't like being out of touch."

"No, that's not true."

"You need us."

"I know you think that, Suse, but it isn't true." She shook her head, but sat down, cross-legged, on the sand.

"Well, I need you, though," Susan said suddenly, surprised at herself. "I need you whether you need me or not. How about that?"

She was startled, hearing intensity in her own voice. She stood up and brushed the sand off her lap. Claudie was leaning back against one of the tree stumps, looking up at her, looking a little pleased, a little frightened.

"Do you remember Dan?" Susan said. She waited. She didn't know what Claudie would make of this. She had never mentioned Dan to her.

"I remember him. The doctor—Judith's cousin. He came to see me in the hospital."

"Lennie's going out with him," Susan said.

Claudie stood up and walked away from Susan, as if she had heard something important and strange. Her small, sharp face looked curious and cautious, now. She walked to the water's edge and threw a stick into the lake. Then she began to skip rocks. She threw three rocks, and the first two sank, but the third one skipped four times. Susan watched her, the feeling in her chest, which had receded, returning. She sat down on the sand, hugging her knees.

Then Claudie came back to her and knelt on the ground and put her hands on Susan's shoulders, just as Lennie had done the first night. She was behind Susan. "Oh, Sue, you were in love with him," she said.

"How do you know?" said Susan. "Did Judith tell you, too? Does everyone know?"

"No, I just knew," said Claudie. "Not at the time. I knew when Dan came to see me in the hospital, from the way he talked about you—and I remembered things. I had a crush on him myself, but that's not important. I sort of wanted to snare him so I could give him to you." She put her arms around Susan, and Susan turned and buried her face in Claudie's shoulder. Claudie leaned back against the tree stump to support them both, and held her. Susan was silent for a long time. It felt as if Claudie were willing to sit there forever. Susan didn't cry. She could hear the quiet sound of the lake touching land, and Claudie's breathing, and smell her sweat and the indoor, musty smell of her clothes.

She turned her head so her cheek rested on Claudie's shoulder, and closed her eyes. The sun was so bright her eyelids were rosy from behind. Susan felt sand under her body, and pine needles under her hands. She thought that she could stand up—maybe she would, pushing herself up with one hand—and leave this place, that maybe she ought to, except that she was so comfortable here in the sun, lying against Claudie's thin body. But she could. She could stand up, and stretch, and kiss Claudie good-bye and quickly take her clothes and Amy's and Eliza's and put them into suitcases and into the car. Then she could get into the car and drive away while the children were still sleeping.

Claudie would stay a little longer than she'd planned—she'd rescue Lennie and James, pick them up at the fairgrounds. They'd be all right. They could stay here, and then Frank would come and get them, horrified at what Susan had done.

For Susan would drive straight to New Haven on her way out of her life. She'd be driving most of the night, and she'd stop to look at the thickly clustered stars at times, pulling over to the side of the road to rest. She wouldn't go to the house, wouldn't face Tony. She'd drive straight to Bridgeport and wake up Cat, who'd be startled and confused, as if they'd come back for something they'd forgotten—but why—as if they'd stumbled into a dream of hers.

Susan would kiss Eliza and Amy all over—their hair and faces, their arms and legs and, picking them up, their stomachs and backs. Then she'd give them to Cat, with a note for Tony, a note full of sadness and apologies. Cat would stand in the doorway, trying to understand, taking the children from her arms without knowing what was happening. Then Susan would drive to Dan's office and wait for it to be late enough in the morning for him to come. "I'm here," she'd say. "I've always loved you. Don't you want me? Isn't that why you're going out with my best friend?"

Dan would take her in his arms and they'd go to his house and he'd make love to her—but she could not go further. In her imagination, Dan was saying, "I need to call Lennie," and she was in tears, stunned with the loss of her babies, while the thought of Tony was like a shadow cast over her and receding, a shadow she couldn't catch, as if he were being taken away from her.

She would leave Dan, keep driving, drive to someplace she had never been—Pittsburgh or Detroit or Chicago—and live in exile, wanting Tony and the children, but somehow unable to return. She would live in a dark rented apartment under a false name, having destroyed happiness behind her and also within herself. Yet there was a somber satisfaction in the thought: how, in a place she didn't know, she'd gradually find her way, leave her minimum-wage job in the evening and recognize the street corner where she had to turn, stop to buy food for one, go home and cook it. She wondered whether this was anything like the way Claudie lived. She pictured Cat trying to comfort Tony, caring for the girls, worn out by them, her hair tangled and wild, her glance distracted—over the children's shoulders, as if she were always looking for Susan. The children would never understand or forgive their mother.

Susan was almost asleep. She had never slept in a woman's arms before. She heard one of her daughters cry out.

Claudie played with Amy and Eliza in the afternoon, and went swimming, and then she and Susan made an omelet for supper and fixed hot dogs for the children, who wouldn't eat the omelet. Susan stacked the dishes in the sink and put the babies back into their car seats, and hugged Claudie. No, Claudie said, she really couldn't stay. They both drove down the dirt road, Susan first, and then Susan turned left and headed for the fairgrounds and Claudie turned right to take the road to Boston. "Where's Aunt Claudie going?" said Amy.

"She has to go home."

Lennie and James were waiting at the fairgrounds gate. "We saw everything," Lennie said. "We were the ultimate fairgoers. We saw pigs, machinery, prize cookies. I bought fudge for all of us."

"Can I eat some now?" said James.

"Maybe a little when we get back to the cabin," said Lennie.

"Aunt Claudie came," said Amy.

"Really? Claudie? No," Lennie said.

Susan explained. Lennie was sorry she'd missed Claudie. "Is she all right?"

"I guess so. She took care of me."

"Well, you've done it for her often enough. You *need* care," said Lennie.

Susan was pulling the car into the space near the cabin. She turned off the ignition and reached out awkwardly for Lennie's shoulder and put her arm around her. "I've regained my senses," she said.

Lennie looked at her. "What I want—it isn't going to be easy for you."

"But it's a good thing," said Susan.

"Yeah," said Lennie, running her hands through her hair and touching Susan's shoulder before she turned to get out of the car and help the children. "It really is. I really want it."

"What does Lennie want?" said Amy.

"Fudge," said James. "She wants fudge."

"No," said Amy. "Not fudge."

Susan reached in to lift her out of her car seat and set her on the ground. It was dark, and they all had to hold hands and walk carefully on the path to the cabin, for they had forgotten to bring a flashlight. "Look at the stars," said James, and they all stopped to look up at the country stars, rich sprays and aggregations and clusters of stars.

Amy and James and Eliza had been playing in the wet leaves all morning, and their overalls were damp. It had thundered and rained in the night—despite the starry evening—and Eliza had awakened, screaming. Susan had taken her into her bed and soothed her back to sleep. Now it was clear again but much colder, and the children were in sweaters. Lennie, in her flannel shirt, had gone down the road with a saucepan to gather blackberries.

Susan was reading, sitting on the beach, leaning against one of the stumps. The children ran past her. "Oh where, oh where is the queen?" James called, and the little girls echoed him. "Where is the queen? Where is the queen?"

Then she heard him stop and say, "Now, Amy, pretend you're the queen. I'm the truck driver, and this time we have to look for the lost girl."

They all sat down in a sunny place just above the beach, where there was a bare patch of dirt and some large rocks. "We could make a palace for trucks," she heard James say.

Susan liked the book she was reading, but now she closed it and laid it in her lap. The sky was a darker, more intense blue today than it had been before—fall was coming. The sky was large and clear and empty, bordered with the intricate outlines of pine trees.

The children ran toward her again. "Oh where, oh where?" Amy was saying. Eliza was puffing hard to keep up. They were on their way to the abandoned boat, and would probably play there for a long time.

"Pretend we're *all* lost," said James. "Pretend we're all truck drivers." Then they passed her, and he waved a hand in her direction as she watched the three of them run away, their sneakers covered with damp sand, their overalls damp at the hems. "Pretend she's your mother," James said.

A NOTE ABOUT THE AUTHOR

ALICE MATTISON runs the Anderson Street
Writing Workshops in New Haven, Connecticut,
where she lives with her husband and three sons. She
is also the author of a book of poems, *Animals*, and a
collection of stories, *Great Wits*.